Thinking for Writing

Thinking for Writing

Dorothy U. Seyler

M. Noel Sipple

Northern Virginia Community College

SCIENCE RESEARCH ASSOCIATES, INC.
Chicago, Palo Alto, Toronto, Henley-on-Thames, Sydney, Paris, Stuttgart
A Subsidiary of IBM

Acknowledgments

P. 76 "The Enticers, 1970; On TV, Who Do They Think You Are?" Copyright ©
1970 by The Condé Nast Publications Inc. Also used by permission of the author,
Stephanie Harrington.

P. 81 From *Language in Thought and Action*, third edition, by S. I. Hayakawa, ©
1972 by Harcourt Brace Jovanovich, Inc., and reprinted with their permission.

P. 91 Copyright 1967 by Newsweek, Inc. All rights reserved. Reprinted by permission.

P. 92 From "Censor Still Under Wraps" by UPI in *The Miami Herald*, 1969. ©
1969, United Press International. Used by permission.

P. 94 INSIDE REPORT by Rowland Evans and Robert Novak, Courtesy of Field
Newspaper Syndicate.

P. 98 From "The Computer and the Poet" by Norman Cousins, in *Saturday Review*, July 23, 1966. © 1966, Saturday Review/World, Inc. Used by permission.

P. 118 Copyright 1974 by Newsweek, Inc. All rights reserved. Reprinted by
permission.

(Acknowledgments continue on page 392.)

Compositor   Graphic Typesetting Service
Illustrator   Patricia Rogondino
Designer   Michael A. Rogondino
Acquisition Editor   Gerald Richardson
Project Editor   Sara H. Boyd

Library of Congress Cataloging in Publication Data

Seyler, Dorothy U
    Thinking for writing.

    Includes index.
    1. English language—Rhetoric.   2. College readers.
I. Sipple, M. Noel, joint author.   II. Title.
PE1408.S465   808'.042   77-22730
ISBN 0-574-22035-6

10 9 8 7 6 5 4 3 2 1

for
Anne and Ruth

Preface

Another composition text? Can it be justified? We believe that the answer to both questions is yes. We decided to write *Thinking for Writing* because the explanations and exercises we wanted our students to have were not available in a textbook, or were not available in the combination we consider most useful. *Thinking for Writing* brings together in one book discussion and practice of basic strategies for composition; instruction and exercises in critical reading, critical thinking, and persuasive writing; and a collection of readings (essays, newspaper and magazine articles and editorials, speeches) for study as models and for practice in critical reading. Thus *Thinking for Writing* is not only a composition text and a reader, but it is also a text with a special focus: critical thinking.

Several concepts about the writing process—and about college students—have shaped this text. Years of classroom teaching have convinced us that students have ideas, attitudes, and memories which can be the bricks and mortar of good essays. We believe that students should be taught to shape their ideas into communications rather than being asked to learn set structures to house their thoughts. *Thinking for Writing* encourages students to examine their ideas to see how they can express them best. This approach does not neglect form; it stresses, however, that when students write they should decide whether the bricks and mortar will become a house or a store and then what shape and color of bricks will make the best house or store.

A second idea behind *Thinking for Writing* is that instruction in critical reading should be given *after* students have mastered the basics of writing about their own experiences and perceptions. Only then are they ready to approach the more difficult tasks of understanding and writing about the ideas of others.

Finally, we believe that writing and reading skills are best developed through extensive practice in exercises and assignments which progress from the simple to the more complex. Thus the book begins with clear strategies for writing, moves to the simplest reading task—understanding content—turns to writing argument, and concludes with the most complex task of researching, evaluating, and synthesizing others' arguments. Numerous classroom exercises and writing assignments are included in each chapter to provide students with the practice necessary for skill development.

Acknowledgments

No text of any value is written alone. We are pleased to be able to thank, publicly, at least some of those who helped to shape this book. We wish to thank first our colleagues Carol Boltz, who read the manuscript in its earliest form, Joey Horobetz, who helped with proofreading, and Richard A. Wilan, who gave the second draft his thoughtful attention and helped with the proofreading. Further thanks should go to our colleagues Jenny N. Sullivan, Pamela E. Berger, Nancy W. Johnson, and Charles W. Scarborough, Jr., for allowing us to use some of their successful exercises and assignments. For her care in typing the final manuscript, a simple thanks to Mrs. Pauline B. Tooker seems insufficient. We are grateful as well for the support and encouragement, during "good times and bad," of David Seyler, Judy Riggin, and Brian Hansen, and for the patience and good faith of our editor, Gerald Richardson. Finally, we extend our thanks to all of the teachers, colleagues, and students who, by precept or example, have taught us how to write, to think, and to become what we are.

Dorothy U. Seyler
M. Noel Sipple

Contents

Section 1

THE WRITING
PROCESS

Writing well is not easy. We should establish this at the start so that, if writing turns out to be a difficult task, you will know you are in good company. The problem is compounded because most of us have difficulty judging the quality of our own work. We know what we meant and are puzzled when a reader says we have not expressed it very well. And, as if that were not enough, we often feel insulted when our work is criticized because writing is such an important extension of ourselves. Those words on the page express not just our ideas but also our styles and our personalities, and it is not pleasant to hear that a reader finds fault with them.

Recognizing that problems of ego make it hard to teach or take a writing course may help you overcome psychological barriers to learning to write. Remember that writing is a skill like playing bridge or dancing or driving. Some people will naturally be more talented at it than others, but almost everyone can become, at the very least, competent. As with any skill, you must develop yours.

In some courses, you must simply remember information; in

others, you will be successful if you follow a certain procedure. In writing, you may do both and still not write as well as you would like. The key is *practice*. We present information about writing throughout this book. We also include procedures which will help you. But, most important, we provide opportunities for practice.

Context

1

WHY ARE YOU WRITING?

Most people do their best writing (that is, writing that is convincing, interesting, moving, amusing) when their purpose is not just to write. They do not set out to write an essay, a book, an article; they set out to teach a consumer about the dangers of antibiotics, to divert an audience with a funny story, to convince the city council to put in a traffic light, or to encourage a nation to endure an energy crisis.

Unfortunately, if you are using this book, you are probably writing because your college requires a composition course for graduation or transfer and because your instructor has made an assignment. Too often in writing courses your only purpose is to write, and such a weak purpose can result in sloppy or self-conscious and stilted work. You might try assignments in which you draft suggestions to the local government for solving community problems, write essays or reviews to submit to a magazine or newspaper, or make consumer reports as the students did in the essay, "Ad-man, Business-man, Teacher-man," on pp. 254–59. If such assignments are impractical, create your own sense of purpose.

You have ideas, interests, opinions, hobbies. Write about them. Is there an article you have read and wanted to learn more about?

Have you recently expressed an opinion that you really could not support? Have you seen something beautiful or exciting? See if you can put that beauty or excitement into words. Whenever you can choose your own topic, write about something that interests you. Exercise intellectual curiosity and see where it will lead you. Above all, do not feel that you must choose a topic that is "supposed" to interest a college freshman. If you do not feel strongly about the legalization of marijuana, don't write about it. If the sexual revolution is not an issue for you, don't debate it. Use the opportunity to explore old or new interests. You might just stumble onto a field so intriguing it will become a profession or a lifelong hobby. Your purpose in writing can be to learn something and then to tell it to someone else.

In a class or at work an assigned writing topic may not interest you. In that case, involve yourself in the task of providing a full and vivid description, of presenting information clearly, or of convincing the reader that you have built a sound case for your argument. A strong interest in the intellectual process of writing can help you get through a dull assignment. Whenever you write, think carefully about your purpose.

WHO ARE YOU THIS TIME?

Kurt Vonnegut, Jr., has written a short story, "Who Am I This Time?," in which a character can lose his inhibitions only when he is acting roles in plays. New writers often have the opposite problem: when they write, they are anonymous. Before you write, decide what your role, or your *voice*, is to be. Just as in life you have different roles (son, brother, student, friend, worker), so you will have different voices for different writing purposes. When you write an essay for an exam, you are a knowledgeable, articulate, well-organized student. When you write an article for your newspaper criticizing a local company's disregard of environmental restrictions, you are an outraged but well-informed citizen. When you compose a report for a committee examining student lounge facilities on campus, you will be factual and noncommittal. When you write to ask for a job, you are a polite and confident applicant. When you write a fourth letter to the public utility company about an error in your bill, you are an irate and threatening consumer. *Voice* is created by the language you select. Even a simple greeting reflects a specific voice: "Hi. How are you?" "Hey, man. What's happening?" "Good morning, Ms. McGuire." These words convey the same message but have different voices— friendly, familiar, formal.

EXERCISES: Voice

A. How would you describe the voice in each of these statements of assent?

1. O.K.
2. Yes, sir.
3. Oh, absolutely. I'll get right to it.
4. Well, all right.
5. If you're sure that's what you want me to do.
6. Right on.
7. Yes.
8. Yeah.

B.   What would your voice be in each of these situations?

1. You are writing a letter to a former employer to tell him how you are doing in a course he recommended and to inquire if he will have any job openings for the summer.

2. You are drafting the minutes of the last student government meeting.

3. You are writing to your younger sister to convince her not to drop out of high school.

4. You are writing an article for the school newspaper on the misuse of student activity funds.

5. You are writing a letter to the editor deploring the messy school cafeteria.

6. You are writing a letter of apology to your closest friend.

7. You are writing to ask your congressman to investigate the cancellation of a government program which was to have provided the funds for your next year of college.

8. You are preparing a statement for your state tax department to justify not paying double taxes since you are a student in one state earning money and a resident in another state earning money in a summer job.

9. You are writing an article for the local newspaper promoting a student art show.

WHO ARE *THEY* THIS TIME?

Since most writing has readers, except perhaps a personal diary, it is essential to consider the *audience*. They, maybe even more than the writer himself, define the limits of the work—topic, length, word choice, sentence structure, complexity of information. Suppose you were writing two papers to explain the workings of a camera—first, to a group of fourth graders, and second, to an adult beginning photography class. The purpose is the same, but the two papers would be geared to very different audiences:

This camera is made so that you cannot accidentally take two pictures with the same piece of film. When you have taken a picture, the button cannot be pressed again until you have turned the film to the next position.

Once you have pressed the shutter button (Fig. 1), exposing the frame in position, the shutter button locks, preventing you from making double exposures. When you operate the cocking lever (Fig. 2), the shutter button is released, allowing you to expose the new frame.

Whenever you write, make sure you understand who your audience is. What is their level of understanding of your subject? Are they novices or experts? What is their general level of sophistication and education? Are they likely to be receptive or antagonistic to your subject?

Again, a writing course creates special problems since the instructor often seems too formidable an audience. Try to write your papers for someone other than your instructor—write a persuasive paper to your state legislator to pass a law against throwaway containers; write a refutation directly to the writer whom you are refuting; write an "open letter," such as a letter to the editor. If this is not possible, then consider as your audience the members of the writing class, *including* the instructor. Then you will not fall into the traps of writing dully as if in a vacuum or writing timidly and stiffly as if for a supercritic. How would you describe your class as an audience? Depending on the topic, this same audience might be biased or open-minded, knowledgeable or uninformed. One thing you can count on; as composition students, they will be alert to your style of writing, and you will have to write as well as you can in order to convince them.

EXERCISES: Purpose, Voice, Audience

Discuss with class members how you would write to the following people. Consider purpose, voice, and audience.

1. Your dean of students, who is preparing to decide a current campus issue.

2. Your mother, who ought to quit smoking.

3. Your congressman, who has voted against an issue that you favored.

4. Readers of "Letters to the Editor" in *Time* magazine who are interested in a previous article on the uses of sludge as fertilizer.

5. A reviewer in your newspaper who disliked a film that you liked.

6. A third grade class studying the origins of Easter customs.

7. Members of your writing class debating the value of a pass-fail grading system.

8. Members of your writing class interested in learning how to tune an engine.

WRITING ASSIGNMENT

A. Write a description of your classroom for someone who has never seen it.

B. Write an account of a success (or failure) in your life for an acquaintance who has never heard the story.

C. With a classmate, observe, but do not discuss, a small incident (two people eating lunch, a person trying to start a car, a dog overturning a garbage can), and write your observations to each other.

D. Explain to a parent your feelings when the two of you argue.

E. Write directions for a new student telling how to drive from your campus to a nearby gas station or drugstore.

Substance

2

WHAT ARE YOU GOING TO PROVE?

Perhaps the most important step in preparing an essay is formulating your *thesis*; that is, the assertion that you intend to support or prove for your audience. It could be called a one-sentence summary of the paper because every statement you make will relate directly to that thesis and convince your audience to accept your view. Every paper, even a very simple unargumentative paper such as the description of your classroom, needs a focus; the thesis provides that focus. *Room 204 of Chandler Hall is a suitable place in which to study composition.* This sentence tells the writer to emphasize the characteristics which make the room suitable for studying composition.

Remember that while you are always trying to persuade the reader to accept your thesis, there are different levels of intellectual demand and emotional involvement. To prove that a room is appropriate for study may require no more than description which emphasizes lighting, space, and furnishings. However, more abstract, analytical, moral, or controversial issues (women priests, capital punishment, the causes of inflation) will draw on all your powers of persuasion—skills which we shall discuss throughout this text. A carefully framed thesis begins the process of persuading by focusing the topic and also providing limitation and preliminary organization.

Limitation

In a writing course, an instructor will usually give you certain constraints (a suggested topic, a particular form or organization, a specified length), but *you* still have to formulate your ideas into a statement you can prove. Here are some suggestions for limiting your thesis:

1.   Make it specific. New writers often choose a broad topic, erroneously thinking that this will give them enough to talk about. But remember that you are going to have to *prove* your thesis, not just discuss it; if you have a broad thesis, you would have to write a very long paper (or even a book) to fulfill your obligation to your audience. Look at the following thesis:

> Many U.S. highways are bad.

This sentence needs to be narrowed. First, the subject, "many U.S. highways," is vague and leaves a writer without direction. Which of the thousands of U.S. highways should he discuss? And how many? To solve the problem, we choose a specific highway—the Hansen Beltway. Second, to define what we mean by "bad," let's say "dangerous."

> The Hansen Beltway is dangerous.

Now we have a specific thesis.

The next thesis has the opposite problem:

> Entrance ramp 41 of the Hansen Beltway is too short to allow cars to accelerate to merging speed.

This thesis is too narrow to be developed into a paper. Once a writer has given the figures to demonstrate that the ramp is too short, he will be finished.

Examine this thesis statement:

> The overpasses on the Hansen Beltway are structurally unsound.

This sentence is limited, and specific, but could be too technical. Unless the writer has some background in structural engineering, he should not attempt this topic. If you stay within your own areas of expertise and experience, it will be much easier to prove your thesis.

2.   Make it single. Be certain your thesis requires you to prove only one point. Look at this sentence:

> The Hansen Beltway is dangerous, and these dangers could have been avoided by careful engineering.

The two theses in this sentence could lead the writer into producing a very loosely organized paper. The same idea could have been stated:

> The dangers of the Hansen Beltway could have been avoided by careful engineering.

This restatement clarifies what the paper should emphasize. Stating your thesis as a single assertion with a single subject and attitude helps you to limit and thus sharpen the focus of your paper.

3.   Make it reveal an attitude. Your reader should know from your thesis how you feel toward your subject. In the examples above, it is obvious that the writer disapproves of the Hansen Beltway. What words reveal this attitude? Not every paper you write will contain a red-hot argument, but at least you should select a thesis worth proving. If no one in your audience needs to be convinced, why write?

It may be argued that some papers simply present information ("Automobiles cause pollution"; "Smoking causes cancer"), but they too have an implied attitude. If a writer demonstrates that automobiles cause pollution or smoking causes cancer, it is unlikely that he feels neutral about his subject. Even a process as factual as a recipe suggests that it is the *best* (quickest, tastiest, cheapest) way to prepare the dish.

If your thesis seems to lack an attitude, think back to your purpose. *Why* are you writing this paper? *Why* do you want to inform your audience? To alert them to a danger? To help them save money? To increase their enjoyment of Mozart? Knowing your attitude toward your subject, even if it remains implied, will help you to further limit your discussion and will help you to select relevant evidence later to develop the thesis. Another plus is that your voice will become more pronounced, making the paper more interesting.

EXERCISES: Thesis Statements: Effectiveness

Discuss the effectiveness of the following thesis statements for short essays (three or four pages) directed to your writing class:

1.   I thought I would never make it through my first day as a shoe salesman.

2.   Box lacrosse is the most exciting sport.

3.   Shakespeare was a great dramatist.

4.   Our country should continue to seek detente with Communist countries.

5.   Everyone has a right to smoke, and all "No Smoking" rules should be eliminated.

6.   All citizens should pay income taxes.

7. Last year was the most exciting year of my life.

8. This paper will discuss television violence.

9. This paper will prove that television violence should be limited.

10. The Heckman Candy Company manufactures fifty tons of candy each year.

Preliminary Organization

When you formulate a limited thesis suitable to your assignment, you are well on the way to organizing your paper. First, and most obviously, your thesis tells you what to exclude. If you are writing about the dangers to drivers on the Beltway, you will not need to be concerned with the cost of construction, the effect of pollution on the surrounding countryside, or anything else not connected directly to the thesis.

Second, you can add a "because (or and-the-proof-is) clause" to your thesis stating the reasons which led you to believe your assertion to be true:

> The Hansen Beltway is dangerous because
>> there are too few lanes to accommodate the volume of traffic,
>> most entrance ramps are too short to allow drivers to accelerate to an adequate merging speed,
>> bridge abutments, guard rails, and signposts are rigid,
>> the roadway is in poor condition,
>> current construction creates hazards,
>> the lighting is inadequate,
>> signs are confusing,
>> some curves are improperly banked.

At this point, check to see that all of your reasons carry just about equal weight and do not overlap or repeat. In this example, the reasons are not of equal weight and should be placed in groups.

> The Hansen Beltway is dangerous because
>> it is outdated
>>> too few lanes for current traffic volume
>>> roadway in poor condition (potholes, faded lines)
>> it is poorly designed
>>> entrance ramps too short
>>> rigid bridge abutments, guard rails, signposts

> inadequate lighting
>
> confusing signs
>
> improperly banked curves
>
> it is currently under construction
>
> sharp drop off shoulder
>
> temporary barriers blocking roadway

You now have a skeleton outline in which each reason represents a division of the argument, ready to be developed. When your thesis statement appears in the paper, you will probably not include the "because clause" since it is long and cumbersome, and the reasons will emerge as you develop your thesis.

A question often asked about a thesis statement is, where does it occur in the paper? Usually, it is placed near, but not at, the beginning of the discussion. In a three- or four-page essay, it might be the last sentence in the first paragraph. In a 10-page chapter, it might be in the third or fourth paragraph. This position (near, but not at, the beginning) gives the writer time to engage his reader before he asserts his thesis, yet the reader knows the thesis before he reaches the body of the paper. However, the placement of the thesis will depend on what works best in each essay. Sometimes you may want to place it last, carefully building up to it so that your reader will be ready to agree with you when he sees your thesis. Placing it near the end of the essay can also be advantageous when you have an unsympathetic or skeptical audience. You can thus persuade the reader with strong evidence before you present a thesis that might otherwise have alienated him. It is also possible that you may not state your thesis at all, but this implied thesis requires that your evidence must be so strong and your argument so thorough that the reader will be able (and willing) to state it himself at the conclusion of the essay. By far the safest placement of the thesis is near the beginning.

EXERCISES: Purpose and Thesis Statements

When you are given writing assignments in your courses, sometimes the topics will be specific and sometimes general. You will have to decide what the purpose of the assignment is. What is the assignment designed to teach you? Are you asked to present a focused argument? Or a broad study of a particular field? Before plunging in, read the directions carefully. If you are still unsure of the purpose, ask your instructor.

What do you think is the purpose of these assignments? Decide how you would proceed, and write effective thesis statements, including a "because clause."

1. Compare and contrast the merits of two products (cars, soaps, spaghetti sauces). Paper due in two days.

2. Social science final exam: "The American Dream has always been based on a combination of idealism and materialism." Agree or disagree. Time limit: 2 hours.

3. Write a letter to the editor of the school paper discussing a current campus issue. Limit: 350 words.

4. Report due in five weeks, 10–15 pages on a health problem.

5. Term paper (20–30 pages). Analyze and suggest a solution for a problem in your community.

6. Essay due in one week, 500 words. Describe an experience that changed you.

7. Report on women in the business world. Consider jobs available, education necessary, pay, opportunities for promotion, and so on.

Save these thesis statements to be used in Exercise B: Organization, p. 27.

HOW ARE YOU GOING TO PROVE IT?

When you assert your thesis, your reader expects that the rest of the paper will develop that thesis. After all, your thesis is only an opinion; until you have backed it up, a reader has little reason to accept it. An unsupported opinion may interest, but it will not persuade, the perceptive reader. His opinion may be different, and he may feel he has good reasons for it. Your job then is to back up your thesis (a generalization) with specific evidence. Think back to that dangerous Hansen Beltway. One of the dangers was that the entrance ramps were too short to allow cars to accelerate to merging speed. That is a generalization about all the entrance ramps. A specific example would be Entrance 41, which is only 45 feet long and does not allow a car to reach 55 mph before merging. Here is another specific example: of forty-six entrances, thirty-seven are less than fifty feet long. These specific examples are known as *detail*. Detail is essential to proving your thesis.

As you present your evidence, be as specific as possible. In description, use appropriate *sense impressions* (sounds, colors, sizes, shapes, textures, tastes, smells). Such descriptions not only help to prove your thesis but also add life and interest and precision to your essay. When they are relevant, include *facts*, such as statistics, dates, names, titles. It is more convincing to say that four out of ten cars turned left after the light had changed than to say that many cars made such a turn. Some assignments, such as those involving personal experience, may call for recounting *anecdotes* or *events*. If you were describing your younger brother as precocious, you would need to tell a story or two about his precocious behavior. In other cases, you may need to list *examples*, such as the names of basketball players who went into the NBA under the hardship rule.

Where do you find the details to prove the thesis? Depending on your thesis, the evidence may be drawn from your own experience and observation. If you have any expertise in your area of study, you should offer your credentials (five years' experience as an assistant to a professional photographer, a certificate in first aid, two summers as a lifeguard). Your experience will lend greater credibility to your evidence. However, some topics will require you to go to sources other than your own experience. In these cases, you should mention your source—first, to give credit to those who did the research or study, and second, to add the weight of an acknowledged authority to your own argument. In a paper which uses only one or two sources, such acknowledgment can be made in the text of the essay, rather than in a footnote. This is called *internal documentation* and can be quickly worked into a paper. For example, "In *Newsweek* (May 12, 1975), Shana Alexander noted that . . ." or "In his 1962 study, *Mark Twain: The Development of a Writer* (p. 23), Henry Nash Smith asserts . . . ." Your concern will be to give the reader enough information so that he can evaluate or locate your source if he wishes.

EXERCISES: Evidence

A. Here are exercises to help you practice generating accurate and descriptive detail.

   1. Write a paragraph describing, without telling the name or function, an object in the classroom. Read your paragraph to the class to see if they can tell what you described. If anyone else described the same object, compare the paragraphs.

   2. Find an object which seems to have a personality (a special coffee mug, a child's old teddy bear, a worn-out tennis shoe) and describe it so that the *details* convey the personality.

   3. Look at a pencil (or some other very simple object) and list *thirty* characteristics. Then rearrange your details in appropriate groupings.

   4. Examine closely the photographs on the following pages. Each projects a particular effect (an abstraction), which is created by concrete details in the photograph.

Fig. 2-1. The Kanawha River, West Virginia (Courtesy of
EPA-DOCUMERICA)

For example, the photograph of the Kanawha River (Fig. 2-1)
projects an effect of crowding. These are some of the details
which help to create this effect:

a. Most of the land onshore is covered with buildings, storage
    tanks, and furnaces.

b. In the top of the photo, the land beyond the road appears to
    be at the foot of a mountain, crowding the industry onto the
    river's edge.

c. The industry on the right side has spilled off the land and
    onto the island.

d. The island itself is completely covered with buildings, tanks,
    and furnaces which crowd out most of the vegetation.

Look at the other photographs in this chapter. Choose one, name an appropriate effect, and list the details which create it.

B. What sort of detail would be appropriate in the following papers? Assign an audience to each, and decide on purpose and voice.

1. An argument to show a need for more cashiers in a local supermarket.

2. A discussion of Dylan Thomas' use of color imagery in "Fern Hill."

3. An examination of the merits of deficit spending in your county.

4. An analysis of why you are always late for appointments.

5. An account of the opening of a new art gallery.

C. Read the following paragraph:

I had to complete a missed assignment for my Physical Education class in tennis. I had to accurately serve five balls in a row. I dragged down to the tennis court on a gloomy day to get it over with. I thought I had learned the correct service movements, but I couldn't seem to translate that knowledge into a successful serve. I tossed up the first ball, brought back my racquet, swung up on the ball—clunk—I hit the wood. I threw up the second ball, brought back my racquet, swung up on the ball—ping—it hit the strings and dropped down on my side of the net. I trudged around, collecting the tennis balls; I had only two of them.

How does the writer feel about her activity? Notice that she never *says* how she felt. Instead she *shows* how she felt through her choice of details and descriptive words.

Write a paragraph describing an activity which you liked or disliked. From your details and word choice, be sure your reader knows what you were doing and how you felt about it.

D. Which of the following topics do you know well enough to be able to write about in a *detailed* paper of three–four pages without doing outside reading?

1. Women in professional tennis

2. Proper care of a dog (horse, cat, fish, bird)

3. Payola in the record industry

4. Your own reaction to success or failure

5. Health food

6. Gasoline prices

7. The supersonic transport

8. The volunteer army

9. Honor codes in colleges

10. Values of "open classroom" high schools

Choose a topic from the list and formulate a thesis statement appropriate to a three–four page paper. List all the relevant details you can think of. Are there enough to develop and prove your thesis?

E. List topics in your areas of experience and expertise about which you could write a detailed paper. Consider your current and past jobs, hobbies, sports, travels, family experiences, and current and past studies.

F. List topics which you could develop in detail if you used outside sources.

Fig. 2-2. The New River (Courtesy of Gerald S. Ratliff, Department of Commerce, State of West Virginia)

Fig. 2-3.   A Young Girl (Courtesy of Images by Kamen)

Fig. 2-4. Saint-Gaudens' *Grief*. This statue by Saint-Gaudens was commissioned by Henry Adams as a memorial to his wife.

Fig. 2-5. Close-up of Saint-Gaudens' *Grief*

Fig. 2-6. Detlefson Painting of Old Mill Stream (Courtesy of Paul Detlefson)

Fig. 2-7. The Old Barn (Courtesy of Connie Treadway)

Shape

3

HOW WILL YOU ARRANGE THE EVIDENCE?

Once you have decided on the details that you want to use, you must arrange them to most effectively prove your thesis. Clear *organization* is as important to proving the point as convincing evidence, because it is this sensible arrangement of details which shows your reader the relationship of the details, both to one another and to the thesis.

The Whole Paper

When you formulated your thesis, including the because-clause, you began the organization by making certain divisions and groupings of the evidence. Now arrange the evidence to present the details in the clearest and strongest positions. First, check to see if your thesis suggests an obvious order such as a *time sequence* (the steps in a process or events in order of occurrence). An article discussing the image of adolescents in American films might begin with the movies of the 1930s, move to the 1940s, and continue to the present. Directions for assembling a bicycle would obviously move in order of execution. Perhaps your thesis will indicate a *spatial arrangement* (top to bottom, inside to outside). For example, a description of the Houston Astrodome might begin with the dome, proceed to the seats and scoreboard, and finally to the playing field. *Comparison-contrast* is still another order which your thesis might dictate. An argument which asserts that a Sony portable color set is superior to a Zenith could examine such items as clarity of image, trueness of color, and ease of tuning for each set. A discussion of the writer's experiences in a French lycée and in an American high school might tell first about similarities in the two schools and then turn to differences. Some theses may call for a *cause-and-effect* order. An examination of how a skiing accident has affected the writer might briefly describe the accident and then document its psychological, financial, and physical effects. Examples and discussion of these and other patterns of organization appear in the essay anthology, pp. 231–390.

If your thesis does not indicate such an order, arrange the material so that each reason or division is fully discussed and so that your evidence is presented in the best possible light—perhaps using the strongest evidence first and last. For example, in a paper discussing the merits of an Audi automobile, you might decide that your audience would be most interested in performance and economy. Thus, you might begin your presentation of evidence with a section on impressive performance and end with a section on money-saving possibilities; other merits, such as easy maintenance and attractive design, might come in between. Or in a paper examining the bias in a specific news article, you might begin with obvious errors of fact and follow up with stylistic techniques which reinforce the erroneous view. The point is that each essay must be structured so that individual details make a convincing overall case for your audience. After finishing your essay, the reader should feel that he has received an orderly and complete discussion of your thesis.

EXERCISES: Organization

A. Solve these organizational problems.

1. Given the following thesis statement, arrange the sections in an order which seems appropriate. Assume the paper is to be written to the city council.

    Thesis: The intersection of Sullivan Highway and Joseph Street needs a traffic light.

    Sections: Average amount of time and fuel wasted trying to drive across Sullivan Highway.

                     Number and type of accidents occurring there in 1977.

                     Number and type of pedestrians crossing both streets.

Amount of traffic using both streets at rush hour.
Discuss your arrangement with class members.

2. Given the following thesis statement and audience, group the reasons and arrange the sections in an appropriate order. Try several types of organization. Which seems most effective to you? Why?

Thesis: For short trips, air travel is no longer more convenient than bus or train.

Audience: Readers of a student newspaper on a large campus. Most readers are from towns between 100 and 200 miles from campus.

Reasons: Most airports are located outside of the city, requiring taxi or limousine service at both ends of the trip.

In most large cities, satellite bus and train stations are located in the suburbs.

Briefcases, purses, and carry-on luggage must be searched at the airport.

Trains and buses are seldom subject to weather delays.

Bus and train tickets are already printed and do not have to be filled out.

Large luggage may not be carried onto most planes.

Most bus depots and train stations are located inside the city, near local bus lines.

Passengers must be at the airport 30 minutes ahead of time.

Any luggage may be carried onto a train or bus.

There is an average 30-minute wait for checked luggage on planes.

3. This exercise summarizes the arrangement of material in a student essay. How can the organization be improved? Consider arrangement, relevance, and development.

Thesis: Instead of striking a balance, television programmers sate the public's taste for certain types of shows.

Audience: Members of a writing class.

¶ 1: The networks blindly follow the Nielsen ratings.

¶ 2: The current schedule is overloaded with "cop" shows.

Six private detective shows per week in prime time.

Thirteen police detective shows per week in prime time.

Five uniformed police shows per week in prime time.

Four syndicated police show reruns playing five days per week in non-prime time.

¶ 3:   My favorite "cop" show is "Streets of San Francisco."

The show judged most accurate by policemen is "Police Story."

¶ 4:   In the late 1950s the prime time schedule was overloaded with cowboy shows.

Now there are no cowboy shows.

¶ 5:   In the mid-1950s and early 1970s, prime time schedule was overloaded with medical shows.

Now only four medical shows in prime time.

¶ 6:   Currently only two singer-variety shows in prime time.

¶ 7:   Currently only nine family sitcom shows in prime time.

4. Read the following student essay, written in response to this assignment.

Assignment: Think of a time when you failed and later succeeded at an activity. Analyze what had happened in the interim to cause this change.

Audience: Class members, including instructor.

Evaluate the use of evidence and the organization.

Success

1   As I slowly opened my eyes and began to move, I felt the pain growing. I crawled to safety behind the tall metal fence and waited for my breath to return. Soon afterward, my fellow bull riders gathered around me asking if I was hurt. All I could do was groan. My body went numb as the pain grew. I now had my reason—revenge—to master the one-ton bull that had just bruised my body. Physical, mental, and emotional training were ahead if I was ever going to return to master the huge Brahman bull properly named "Captain Jack."

2   I began physical training the next day by trying to stand. For several days the pain was almost unbearable. I started running three miles a day in order to regain the strength and coordination in my legs and arms. Next to the rodeo arena was a "bucking barrel." It consisted of four poles sunk deep into the ground with long ropes holding a barrel about three feet from the ground. Pulling the ropes created a simulated bucking action. I spent many hours on the barrel trying to gain the rhythm needed to make the eight-second qualifying ride. I could feel myself growing stronger every day as my next chance approached.

3   Mentally I had to prepare myself to be able to see and hear what was happening during the ride. On my first attempt my thoughts were incoherent. Now I thought of what I would do if the bull started to spin, twist, or

buck back and fall. If any of this should happen, I had to be ready to react quickly and avoid another disaster like the first time.

4   At first my emotional outlook was poor. I was obsessed with fear and hatred for the animal. I would sit on the fence and watch, learning little personality traits about the massive creature. As time passed, the fear changed to respect. I respected him for what he was. Black in color with great muscles in his neck and legs, he had horns which were beautiful to look at until I thought of the ugly things they could do to me. Watching him changed my emotions from hate and fear to love and respect. Still I knew I was going to try again and this time succeed.

5   My chance came on a bright, sunny day. As I sat in the chute and pulled down my hat, I said a prayer. I nodded to the gate men and instantly the gate opened. The bull turned out and made its first powerful buck. The next seven seconds seemed like hours. I heard the buzzer ring and I knew it was over. I had won! As I hit the ground, my feet were already moving toward the safety of the fence. I turned and looked at the face of the bull. A great feeling of success came over me. I had set out to win and I had won.

5. For a sociology class, you are investigating different kinds of business firms in your city. Which organization best supports the thesis? Why?

    Thesis: The grocery business in this city is dominated by chain stores.

    a. List and discuss individual stores
        Fast Service
        Charlie's Market
        Super Clean Supermarket
        USA Foods
        One Stop Shop
        Mrs. Jordan's Groceries

    b. Classify by types
        Independent owner: Charlie's Market
                            Mrs. Jordan's Groceries
        Franchise: Fast Service
                    One Stop Shop
        Chain stores: Super Clean Supermarket
                       USA Foods

    c. Discuss only chain stores
        Super Clean Supermarket
        USA Foods

6. Suppose that you must write a paper for a course in the modern novel. You decide to examine a number of Utopian novels and formulate your thesis.

    Thesis: Whether they have a futuristic or fantasy setting, and whether they are optimistic or pessimistic, the purpose of modern Utopian novels is to satirize present society.

Audience: The instructor

Which organization will most effectively prove your thesis? Why?

a.   Classify the novels according to whether they have a futuristic or fantasy setting and discuss each.

Future	**Fantasy**
Walden Two	*Animal Farm*
1984	*The Hobbit*
Brave New World	
Cat's Cradle	
Stranger in a Strange Land	

b.   Classify the novels as positive or negative and discuss each.

Optimistic	**Pessimistic**
Walden Two	*Brave New World*
Looking Backward	*Animal Farm*
	1984
	Cat's Cradle

c.   Classify the novels according to aspects of the society satirized.

Government-political structure

Time Machine
Animal Farm
Walden Two
1984

Social class structure

Time Machine
Animal Farm
Walden Two
Brave New World

Human relationships, human values

Time Machine
Animal Farm
Walden Two
Cat's Cradle

7.   Essay examinations present organization problems which you must solve quickly. Take the time to solve those problems before you start to answer the question. The five or ten minutes you spend planning your answer for an hour exam will help you to write a clear and coherent essay.

   Pretend that you are taking an hour examination and, in five or ten minutes, plan an answer for one of these possibilities.

a.   Describe and evaluate a course which you have taken recently. Consider teaching methods, materials, testing or other evaluation, class atmosphere, and any other relevant aspects.

    b.   Make up an hour exam question for a course you are taking.

    c.   Use a question from an exam you have taken.

B.   Choose several of the thesis statements which you wrote for Exercise B, p. 13, and select and organize evidence to prove them. Discuss your evidence and organization with classmates.

The Formal Outline

You have been examining various ways of organizing material to develop effective essays. For a short essay, an informal outline—a list of the main points in the order you have selected them—will usually be a sufficient guide for a complete and ordered paper. But for a longer paper you may need a more detailed, formal outline. Preparing a formal outline before you write encourages you to think through the whole structure of the paper from beginning to end and see the relationship of parts. Because a formal outline requires you to make choices about the exact arrangement of the parts of your paper, an outline can help to produce a logically structured essay.

    The more completely you analyze your topic, the fuller the outline will be, and the more useful in guiding you to a structured and orderly paper. But do not expect more of an outline than it can provide. A logical and clear organization for your paper does not result from a detailed outline; rather, a detailed outline results from logical and clear thinking about your topic.

The Format of an Outline   The formal outline uses a combination of numbers and letters to show headings and subheadings. Remember these two points about formal outlines: 1) the parts of the paper indicated by the same *types* of numbers or letters should be of equal importance, and 2) one cannot subdivide into only one subsection, for to divide means to create at least two parts. Thus "A" and "B" under "I" should represent a logical division of "I"; and, if there is a "1" under "A," there has to be a "2."

Examples of Outlining   What follows is an outline of a short research paper. Notice that the student has included her thesis statement rather than beginning the outline with the first section labeled "Introduction," a label not helpful to either writer or reader.

SPACE COLONIZATION

Thesis: With the advent of space colonies comes the possible solution to earth's problems of energy, overcrowding, pollution, and natural resource depletion.

I.   The Space Colony Model

A.   Construction of main cylinder

B.   Construction and use of pods

C.   Source of energy

D.   Intercolony travel

II.   The Satellite Solar Power System

A.   Construction of the SSPS

B.   Use of SSPS to provide energy to earth

III.   Space Colony Size

A.   Number of inhabitants for each of the four proposed space colony models

B.   Impact of space colonization on earth's population

IV.   Resources for Space Colony Construction and Economic Viability

A.   Use of moon resources to construct first colony

B.   Use of Mars-Jupiter asteroid to construct other colonies

C.   Impact of colony industries on earth's pollution and natural resource depletion

How detailed, balanced, and complete does this outline seem? Can it be improved in any way? Can you justify the student's beginning with a description of a proposed space colony? Here is another outline; how detailed, balanced, and complete is it? How can it be improved?

LEARNING TO PLAY TENNIS

Thesis: Learning to play good tennis requires good equipment, lessons, and practice.

I.   Purchasing Good Equipment

A.   Purchase comfortable, appropriate tennis clothes

B.   Purchase a racquet that suits you

1.   Get the right grip size

2.   Wood or metal?

C.   Keep old balls for practice

II.   Obtaining Lessons

A.   Find a good pro to teach you

III.   Practicing

A. Practice often and on a regular basis

    1. Practice with someone who plays at your level or a little better

The Paragraph

We have been discussing the overall organization of the paper. Now we turn to a smaller unit: the paragraph. Indenting on a new line of an article or essay tells a reader that you have finished discussing one aspect of your topic and are turning to another. Paragraphing helps the reader keep up with you by providing him with a visual signal.

Developmental Paragraphs: Unity   The paragraphs which make up the body of a paper (*developmental* paragraphs) contain your evidence. Everything that applies to the ordering of a whole paper applies to each developmental paragraph. Instead of a thesis, you have a *topic sentence* (usually the first sentence) which tells your reader what the paragraph will discuss. Instead of sections developing reasons, you have sentences, filled with detail, which make clear, develop, prove, spell out the topic sentence. Each of these sentences must help to develop the topic sentence.

This grouping results in *unity* of a paragraph. In a unified paragraph, all the details directly relate to the idea set forth in the topic sentence. If the topic sentence states that learning proper breathing is necessary for becoming a good swimmer, then the rest of the paragraph must develop that particular topic and not skip to coordination of arm and leg movements. Double-check with the topic sentence to see that all the material you have placed in a paragraph belongs there. Just as the thesis limits the sections of a paper, the topic sentence controls the details that should appear in a paragraph.

How long should a paragraph be? When is it fully developed? Some people say four to five sentences. The only answer to that question is the same infuriating one as for the length of a paper—long enough to prove the topic sentence. You have to judge for yourself when you have enough detail so that your audience will be convinced of the validity of your topic sentence. You began to learn how to develop a generalization (your topic sentence) in Chapter 2, where we discussed details. Further practice will help.

EXERCISES: Paragraph Unity

A. Here are some paragraphs written by students. Does each have a clearly stated topic sentence? Is each paragraph unified? Is each fully developed?

1. Leatherstocking's morals about indiscriminate killing of passenger pigeons were highly civilized. Though there were millions, he quietly voiced his opinion that only what was needed should be shot. Although even Cooper couldn't possibly have foreseen the extinction of the passenger pigeon, since the last one died in our century, he skillfully used the hunter to be the prophetic voice. And finally, Leatherstocking displayed the never satisfied pioneer spirit by shunning man's normal habitations and institutions, thus imparting to the reader a desire to do so too.

2. The best way to improve one's skill is to practice, and my pool shooting ability was no exception. I lived down the street from Mark, who had a pool table in his garage. We weren't best friends, but we were good friends. Mark left the side door to the garage open so that I could slip in whenever I had a free moment to shoot. I had to walk past Mark's house on the way home from my bus stop. If the gang was already at Mark's house, then I would go home for a snack and then return, but if Mark or Bill were the only ones around, I'd stop and play pool while the table was clear and the distractions were few. I played five nights a week, all day Saturday, and sometimes Sunday afternoon.

3. Improperly adjusted headlights are not a major cause of highway deaths. The 1974 figures from the Division of Motor Vehicles show that improper equipment is rated sixth among the causes of fatalities on the highways, and that improper headlights rate far behind the leaders in this category. Improper brakes, faulty steering, illegal tires, faulty acceleration pedals, and even defective muffler and tailpipe systems make up 83% of this category, leaving a mere 17% to be distributed among improper headlights, faulty horns, and other mechanical problems. The Highway Statistics Division figures show that only 10% of all cars ever have headlight problems.

4. The first rule was that a doctor should do the ear-piercing to reduce the chances of infection. I questioned several doctors and found out that those I did ask use a method known as the "gun" to pierce ears. This method involves the use of an instrument which works like a stapler. It makes the hole with the post of the earring and automatically places the back of the earring on the post. Now this is the most modern technique used for ear-piercing. The chances of infection have been reduced drastically, but the fact is that this method is also used by well known department stores, gift shops, and jewelry stores. The chances of infection and the treatment would be the same in a store as in a doctor's office, except pricewise; a store charges less than a doctor.

5. The desert supports an animal population of considerable size. Animals adapt to desert life in many different ways. Many birds

and animals get the water they need from the food they eat. The coyote is one of a large portion of animals that are nocturnal. Many lizards escape predators by lying motionless and assuming the pale hues of the sand. Some desert animals estivate, that is, sleep through the hottest part of the summer. The desert snail builds a wall of mucous across the opening of its shell to help prevent evaporation. The desert tortoise is one of the animals that escape the heat by burrowing into the sand. The desert wasp assures an ample food supply for the next generation by killing a tarantula and laying her eggs on the body. The kangaroo rat often eludes a rattlesnake by kicking sand in its eyes. The chuckwalla, or puff-lizard, protects itself by lodging between two rocks and puffing itself up so that it cannot be pulled out. Rattlers, centipedes, and scorpions use poison against their enemies. These are some examples of the variety of life that exists in the desert.

6. Whenever I lost in a horse show, which was most of the time, I asked the judge what I had done wrong. I worked on correcting my faults at home before the next horse show. Therefore, instead of quitting just because I lost, I gained knowledge and put it into use.

B. Rewrite several of the paragraphs in Exercise A to improve them. Compare yours with those written by other class members.

Introductions and Conclusions   Besides developmental paragraphs, there are *introductions* and *conclusions*. An introduction must interest your reader and lead him into your thesis statement. With your purpose and audience in mind, think of material which is closely related to your thesis and which will engage the reader's attention. For example, you might open with an interesting anecdote, noteworthy statistics, or a startling generalization. The student who wrote the following introductory paragraph began with questions which would appeal to her audience (recent high school graduates), stated a hypothetical situation, and, as her thesis, disagreed with a long-accepted classroom taboo. She is now ready to prove her thesis.

> Remember when you were just a kid in grade school? What happened if one of the other kids brought a radio to school? The teacher would immediately confiscate the offending radio, not to return it until after class. In most schools this approach to music in the classroom has not changed—silence is still golden. I disagree. I believe that grade school children should be allowed to listen to music in their classrooms.

In the following introductory paragraphs, what devices have the students used to attract the attention of their audience, which in each case was their writing class?

1. About a month ago I filled out an application for admission to Prince Michael's Community College. After requesting my Social Security number, age, and sex, the form then asked for my name, as if it were an afterthought. I was mildly offended by this kind of format. I felt as if I had been depersonalized, and I wondered whether the readers of this application would take these few facts and use them to categorize me. Our society has the nasty habit of labeling certain groups of people. Construction workers are labeled as being bigoted and dumb. Housewives are categorized as homebodies, who can only be fulfilled by raising kids. Teenagers are pegged as being irresponsible, and backwoods folk are called hillbillies who must like fatback and chitlins.

2. *He:*   So tell me about yourself. What's it like moving all the time?

   Me: Nothing to tell. You get there, unpack, then pack up and move again.

   He: Man. You know, you sure are cynical.

      The preceding was part of a conversation I had with Steve recently. Like many people, Steve has spent most of his life in his hometown, so to him a life of travel appears exciting. To a military dependent like me, however, constant travel loses its novelty. Because traveling is no longer fun for me and because I do not miss old friends, Steve sees me as callous and insensitive, whereas I see myself as tired of moving and unable to make close friends.

3. Many words have similar meanings, but no two words convey exactly the same connotation. Synonyms can be distinguished by definitions as fingers can be distinguished by fingerprints. Through careful selection of words a person can express vividly how he visualizes or feels and wants his reader to visualize or feel about a subject. Through his choice of words in "The Modern High School," Friedenberg suggests that Milgrim High is like a prison.

4. Have you ever gone to a store and seen something really fantastic that you always wanted and knew you could not afford? Did you ever think of taking it? If you did take it, chances are you would not get caught. For every one person caught shoplifting, thirty-five got away. These people are not professionals with pseudonyms like "Stickyfingers"; most of them are shoplifting for the first time. Department stores make it too easy for people to shoplift.

In short essays, concluding paragraphs are often unnecessary. A restatement of the thesis at the end of the final developmental paragraph may suffice. Certainly, the readers of a four- or five-paragraph essay do not need a mechanical summary of major points. If you need a longer conclusion, sketch out a proposed solution for the problem you have documented, predict the outcome of a situation you have described, or end with an anecdote which drives home the point you have been making.

Paragraph Coherence   A unified paragraph does not necessarily sound unified. Therefore, a writer must make certain that his reader sees the unity of the paragraph by pointing it out to him. The process of pointing to a paragraph's unity results in *coherence*. Here are several methods you might try:

1. Arrange the sentences in an order that reflects clearly their relationship to one another. Just as you need to consider carefully the organization of a whole paper, so you must decide on a pattern for each paragraph. First, check the topic sentence for clues of time, space, comparison-contrast, or cause-and-effect. If none of these patterns applies, set up your details with the strongest (that is, most convincing) material first and last.

2. Use transition words which specify the relationships between sentences. Your arrangement should guide you here. If you use a time sequence, you might need words such as "first," "second," "then," "next," "finally." Indicate spatial order with such words as "above," "below," "beyond," "inside." For comparison-contrast, use "like," "unlike," "by contrast," "on the other hand," "however." Suggest cause-and-effect with "therefore," "thus," "consequently," "as a result." Introduce evidence with "for example," "for instance," "to illustrate." Remember to let the organization of the paragraph direct your use of transition words. Just throwing in a transition word or two does not make a poorly organized paragraph coherent, and indeed may distort meaning if it is the wrong transition word.

3. Repeat key words and sentence patterns. The sparing repetition of important words will help your reader to link sentences and thus ideas. In addition, parallel sentence constructions can set up the information so that the reader will see the connection.

4. Use pronouns with obvious antecedents in previous sentences. Your reader will automatically link the ideas when you give him a clear pronoun reference.

The following student paragraph uses most of these transition devices. Notice that the writer has chosen a time-sequence pattern.

An English course helped me learn to drive a standard shift car. I had tried and tried to learn, but nothing worked. Then I remembered the English class I had taken called Rhythm. And I remembered from that class the story of a test made on two golfers. Each man spent the same amount of time on the greens. But, in addition, one man mentally went over the rhythm of his golfing techniques for three minutes a day as he bathed or shaved. As a result of his practice, that man became a much better golfer than the other man. This rhythm method sounded like a long shot, but I was ready to try anything. During

repetition (learn)
transition (then)
parallel (I remembered)
reference (*that* class)
transition (but, in addition)
transition (as a result)
reference (*that* man)
reference (this)
transition (During the

the day, whenever my friend Alice drove, I studied her day, then at night)
technique and memorized the rhythm. Then at night be- repetition (rhythm)
fore I fell asleep I went through the rhythm in my mind.
For a month I drove mentally. Then one night when every- transition (then)
one was asleep, I sneaked the car out and started it up.
The actions came automatically; the car didn't jerk about,
and it didn't stall once. At last I knew that I wasn't un- transition (at last)
coordinated, and that I too could drive a standard shift.

In the next paragraph, the student uses a cause-and-effect order. The cause is "marching in a school band"; the effect is "poise and confidence." After asserting the cause-and-effect relationship in the topic sentence, the writer explains military marching style and shows its effect on the marcher's body and on his personality. Along the way, she uses transition words *(soon, because, in turn)*, repetition of key words *(band, military, marching)*, pronoun reference *(this, that, his)*.

> A child gains poise and confidence by learning to *march* in a school *band*. Many *bands march* in *military* style. *Military marching* takes a great deal of concentration. Backs must be straight, knees brought up high, faces turned forward and toes pointed. *This* posture becomes automatic after one *marches that* way for a while. *Soon* the child will unconsciously walk with back straight and face pointed forward. *Because* his proud posture suggests to others that he is confident, others will treat him with respect. *This* treatment, *in turn*, will increase the child's confidence.

In the following paragraph, the repetition of key words and sentence patterns ("*If* . . . , the *salesman should/ must* . . .") demonstrates that the writer is giving advice to those who would be successful shoe salesmen. In addition to gaining coherence through pronoun reference, the student avoids possible confusion by referring to the salesman as "he" and the customer as "she."

> *If* a shoe salesman is to be successful, *he must* follow some basic rules. *If*, after bringing out one pair of shoes, a salesman finds that the customer does not like them or that they do not fit, *he should* immediately bring out another pair. *If* a lady sits down to try on a pair of shoes, but her size is not in stock, *the salesman should not* say "sorry" and send her away. Instead, he *should* bring out a similar pair, or a couple of pairs, just as long as the customer's attention is captured. Remember, the chances of selling shoes are much higher if the customer sees a lot of shoes, and *if* the salesman is interested in selling the shoes. The thought that he may not have the shoes for a customer should never enter a successful salesman's mind. *He must* always keep showing the customer different styles until she buys the shoes she likes.

The following paragraph presents several details to support the topic sentence, beginning with government (U.S. Maritime Administration) and ending with industry (Ford, General Motors). Other devices include repetition *(metrics)*, pronoun reference *(its, their, they)*, and transition words *(recently, soon, also)*.

The conversion from English to the *metric* system of measure is proceeding steadily in the U.S. *Recently* the U.S. Maritime Administration announced their goal for complete conversion to the *metric* system by 1980. *Its* program consisted of dual dimensioning of all ships, equipment and cargo *(metrics and the English equivalent listed on each item)*. *Soon they* will phase gradually into the *metric* system by designing all new equipment in totally *metric* dimensions. Many U.S. industries are *also* introducing *metrically* designed machinery and products. Ford Motor Company recently introduced the first mass produced *metric* system automobile engine in this country. Ford started from scratch in designing their new 2.3 liter power plant for use in their Pinto and Mustang II models. General Motors, the largest manufacturer of automobiles in the U.S., is adopting a policy of producing all new parts in *metrics*. Like many other U.S. companies, G.M. wanted to change in order to standardize its U.S. operation with their other plants around the world.

EXERCISES: Paragraph Coherence

A. Analyze the effectiveness of the coherence in the following student paragraphs. What order is the writer using? What devices reinforce that order? What other methods of coherence are used? Are there any problems of unity or development?

1. I have a great deal of determination. When I have a goal to reach, I keep trying until I reach it. About two years ago, I was selected to participate in an audition for a role in a movie that was to be broadcast on an educational network. When I arrived at the studio, I found that there were about two hundred other students who were trying for a role. My first impulse was to turn around and go back home, but then I decided that I had as much of a chance as they did, and so I sat down and waited my turn. After a frustrating two-hour wait, my turn finally came, and a few days later I was informed that the part was mine. It was a small part, but nevertheless I had achieved my goal.

2. Another interesting characteristic of Franklin was his interest in the welfare of people. For example, after he opened the library, he seemed to like the fact that "these libraries . . . made the common tradesmen and farmers as intelligent as most gentlemen from other countries, and perhaps have contributed in some degree to the stand so generally made throughout the colonies in defense of their privileges." His interest in the welfare of people also shows in his concern about the education of youth. Later, after the academy was opened, Franklin "had the very great pleasure of seeing a number of the youth who have received their education in it distinguished by their improved abilities."

3. One of the assumed advantages of the busway was to provide maximum feeder service to the subway system, thus reducing the cost of the subway because of the higher passenger usage. The commission cannot justify this statement when the cost of such a busway is 186 million dollars, and the cost of purchasing 300 new American Motors buses, priced at 65 thousand dollars each, adds another 13.5 million dollars to the expense. With a charge of fifty cents per rider, it would take two decades just to pay off the 205.5 million dollar debt. The figure does not even represent normal maintenance and operating costs, which would be an extra added charge against any future savings. This does not appear to be such a good financial statement after all, once we examine it.

4. Van Gogh's masterpiece "The Garden of Doctor Gachet" has a menacing theme that often appeared in his works completed late in life. Initially, the observer would probably notice the plant on the right of the painting. It appears to be threatening the viewer with its long, sharply pointed leaves. Similarly, the grass or underbrush seems to be growing out of control and is choking off everything around it, including the footpaths. The tree on the left is interesting in that it gives a doomful hint of impending death. Except for a few green leaves, the long and seemingly lifeless trunk suggests a dead plant. The dominant figure in the painting is the large tree in the background that seems to overshadow the village with its dark and somber hue. Indeed, the village appears in danger of being swallowed up by foliage. Finally, ominous coloring and downward, pressing brushstrokes give the sky a foreboding appearance that seems to be crushing everything beneath it.

5. Both the articles deal with the financial aid that Sadat came for, but there are still some differences in the figures. They both discuss the 750 million dollar economic package that Ford put in front of Congress this week. There is also some discussion in the article about the five billion dollars in arms that Sadat hoped to purchase from the United States. However, one article states that Sadat wants the aid over a period of five years, while the other states he will take a period of ten years.

Rewrite one or two of these paragraphs, improving the coherence. Compare your rewritten paragraph with that of a class member.

B. Are the paragraphs you rewrote in Exercise B, p. 31, coherent? If not, what do they need?

C. Look up some of your previous writing and examine the paragraphs for unity and coherence.

Here is a theme written by a student in response to this assignment:

Subject: Choose a painting and, from close observation, decide how the artist feels toward his subject. What effect does he project? You must prove your conclusions with details drawn from the painting.

Audience: Members of writing class, including instructor.

Criteria: Clearly stated thesis
Relevant detail as proof
Clear and appropriate organization
Consideration of audience and purpose
Minimum of grammatical and mechanical error

Wheat Fields and Crows

1   Vincent Van Gogh lived the greater part of his adult life a sad, lonely, and distraught man. His artistic career spanned a mere ten years during which time he produced over seventeen hundred paintings and drawings. While he was able to create art which continues to bring pleasure to millions of people throughout the world, he found his own existence so intolerable that he took his life. *The feelings that drove him to such an extreme are strongly reflected in the colors and lines of "Wheat Fields and Crows," where the warmth he attempted to project toward the wheat fields is over-ridden by the feeling of anxiety in the overall painting.*

Introduction
(interesting, relevant)

Thesis statement
(clear, specific, single)

2   The artist clearly has a *warm* feeling for the autumn-ripened *wheat field* he creates in the painting. The yellow, amber, and gold tones are warm and full and encompass the major portion of the canvas. The fields are much brighter than the other parts of the painting and *may have represented the beautiful things Van Gogh found in the world.*

Words which link ¶ to thesis and introduce topic of paragraph

An unsupportable generalization

3   Surrounding the field, *however,* are the stark blues, blacks, and browns so characteristic of Van Gogh's periods of depression. Above the field is a dark, threatening sky in shades of blue and black with just a hint of bluish-green where the sun has not yet been completely consumed by the heavy, black, swirling clouds. At the bottom of the painting is a dark brown road or path which appears to engulf the field. There is a large flock of crows descending on the field. They are *also* dark, foreboding, and devoid of any detail.

Transition word (links ¶s, also shows shift of topic)

¶ unified
¶ coherent (uses spatial words, repetition)

4   *The effect the painting has on the viewer is to create a feeling of loneliness and depression coupled with anxiety and fear.* The wheat field is totally isolated by the other elements, which appear ready to devour the secluded prey. The short, deliberate strokes the artist uses to create the field project movement and hostility. It is almost as if the wheat field is striking back, attempting to protect itself from the

Awkward transition (to what does "also" refer?)
Topic sentence refers to thesis, but does not introduce topic of this ¶. Thus, the writer breaks unity of ¶ with sentence 2 of this ¶.

onslaught of the elements. The artist uses a wider brush with the same deliberate, short strokes and swirls to depict the turmoil in the sky. It appears as though the grain is being engulfed by the power and ravishing force of the clouds. The concave strokes used to produce the road or path seem to be slowly closing and tightening to strangle the amber field. At the same time, a flock of crows is descending on the field, threatening it. The crows lack individuality and are painted in the characteristic "V" shape of a bird of prey in attack.

5   "Wheat Fields and Crows" is one of Vincent Van Gogh's last three paintings. He shot himself a few days later. This painting depicts his extreme sadness, loneliness, and anxiety. Like his amber fields of wheat, he must have believed there was no hope of escape.

Conclusion (interesting, related to thesis and introduction)

The student has written an essay which is appropriate for her purpose (to convey her perceptions of a painting) and her audience (college level, but not well-versed in art).

Her thesis is especially well formulated, since its double nature (warmth and anxiety) could have caused problems. Instead, she has stated it so that these two aspects are clearly part of one unified statement. The organization grows out of the thesis, dividing the subject into two elements of painting (color and line) and showing how each element projects warmth overcome by anxiety.

The writer needs to pay closer attention to paragraph development, since this is where her problems lie in this essay. Paragraph 2 is sketchy, sometimes using vague words ("full," "encompass the major portion") instead of specific details. Her feeling that the paragraph was sketchy probably led her to speculate in the last sentence on what the fields "mean" instead of sticking to observable detail. Paragraph 3 is full, unified, and coherent. Paragraph 4 is full and coherent, but there are problems in the first and second sentences, as annotated above.

The writer of this essay had studied the material contained in Chapters 1, 2, and 3. She had not yet studied Style (Chapter 4), and that may explain why she sounds a little stiff and has difficulties with word choice and sentence length and structure. When you have studied Chapter 4, turn back to this essay and see if you can recognize and remedy the stylistic problems.

Style

4

HOW DOES IT SOUND?

Whether or not you prove your thesis and accomplish your purpose may depend on how your writing sounds to the audience. Your writing may sound lively, ponderous, clear, or confusing. This "sound" is called your *style*, and it is created by your selection and arrangement of words. An awkward, flat, or pretentious style could cost you your reader. An effective style is appropriate to your voice, audience, purpose, and subject. You may have heard certain "rules" about style: never use first person; never use contractions; never use slang. Few such rules apply all the time. For example, an account of an amusing experience written for a group of friends or classmates could, and probably should, break all these so-called rules. On the other hand, in a term paper researching the effects of noise on factory workers, contractions, first-person pronouns, and slang are inappropriate. Instead, you would use clear, direct, and technical language. Always consider the combination of voice, audience, purpose, and subject when you are deciding if the style should be simple or sophisticated, general or technical, colloquial or formal.

In each of the following examples, how does the style fit the context and subject?

In the first two examples, the students were recreating for

classmates an experience involving harassed workers. One writes as a worker, the other as an observer.

1.   It was around 8:00 P.M. when hordes of hungry people filled the spacious dining room. Suddenly I was swamped with every kind of imaginable work. Although the customers were loud, I could still hear the waiters' and waitresses' commands: "Brian, hurry up and get those damn salad plates off table B 14." B 14! I didn't even know where A 1 was! Not only did I get orders from them, but also from the customers. Some gray-haired lady sitting by herself repeatedly accused *me* of over-cooking her filet! Another customer, a man, shouted halfway across the room and exclaimed "Come on, boy! You're too slow to be a busboy. When I was your age . . ."

      I was really feeling like quitting, when things slowed down a bit. I was exhausted, hungry, and angry. As I was cleaning up a dirty table, my boss came up to me and said "Gee, Brian, you're lucky you started tonight. You should see us when we're busy."

2.   The club is packed as usual and our waitress, whom we call Lita, is working the back section. A hefty fellow who loves beer keeps calling after her for another. She hears him, but is unable to get it right now because she is waiting on another table. Very annoying.

      She finishes waiting on the table who just spilled their rum and coke all over the carpet and runs to the bar to get the fellow with the obesity problem a beer. She brings it back, smiling with contempt. As she turns, she feels a tight pinch on her behind. Degrading.

      Table three motions for her by waving an empty glass. She moves over, ready to take their order.

      "Three rum and co—no, two rum and—no, make that three rum and cokes."

      "How much are they? Oh, that's okay; it doesn't matter; he's paying. Ha-ha-ha . . ." She brings the drinks to them, ignoring the catcalls from the hefty fellow who now wants a pitcher.

      Another waitress calls her over and tells her she has to take her section for awhile. The more the merrier?

      "Bourbon and coke."

      "Schlitz!"

      "Three rum and cokes!"

      "Tom Collins and you, baby, heh-heh!"

      "I want some pretzels with my Schlitz."

      "This isn't bourbon."

      "Hey, baby, let's dance. Your place or mine?" Only two hours until closing.

The next example was written by a group of students trying to effect a change in their community.

3.   As students of Northern Virginia Community College and concerned citizens of Fairfax County, we wish to compliment the county on its introduction of recycling units to handle newspapers at the intermediate schools. However, in an effort to further combat the current shortages of our nation's resources and energy, we believe it is necessary to expand this program to include

glass, aluminum, and tin. Although individual effort is required for the success of such a program, county support is essential.

The following paragraphs were part of a term paper written to demonstrate an understanding of the power of politics on legislation.

4.   The legislation, commonly referred to as the "common situs" picketing bill, consisted of two sections. The more important section, Title II, recommended a program for partial restructuring of traditional union relationships and encountered little political resistance. Its intent was to concentrate more power in national labor leaders and, thus, reduce the competition for better agreements at the local level. In this sense, it would have had a stabilizing influence on wage levels and the economy. This Title was advantageous to management, at least in the short run, because the effect would be to hold wage levels down.

   The other section, Title I or the "common situs" section, was the *quid pro quo* for organized labor's support of the restructuring set forth in Title II. It would have allowed labor during an economic strike to close down the entire construction project even though the strike was not against the general contractor. According to A. S. Raskin of *The New York Times* (4 January 1976, Sec. 3, p. 9), this was union's way to get around a 1951 Supreme Court decision declaring such picketing illegal. It was this section of the bill that encountered massive political resistance.

One word of caution: Do not become preoccupied with your style. As you work with ideas which interest you and become more experienced, and therefore comfortable at writing, your style will develop naturally. Concern with style *instead of* substance results in an empty and artificial discussion. There are, however, some aspects of style which you can profitably examine—sentence structure and word choice.

SENTENCES

The sentence is the unit of writing which is perhaps most important for clearly expressing ideas. The most sensible organization and the most precise word choice will be useless if the sentences are mangled. For communication to be both clear and interesting, use a variety of sentence patterns—first, because variety adds interest; second, because clarity is enhanced when sentence patterns show relationships between ideas. To gain clarity and variety, you need to make choices among options. You usually vary sentence patterns unconsciously to express different ideas; in other words, you already know more about sentence structure than you may think. The following discussion of sentence patterns and sentence problems will help you become more aware of your options in shaping effective sentences.

The Simple Sentence

The simple sentence is the simplest grouping of related words to express a complete, independent thought; that is, the simple sentence contains a subject (which may be one word or a group of words) and a predicate (which may be one or more verbs or a verb with a complement). Grammarians usually describe the simple sentence as containing one *subject-verb-complement* pattern.

	Subject	*Verb*	*Complement*
1.	Birds	fly.	
2.	The carnation	is [linking verb *to be*]	beautiful. [predicate adjective]
3.	Ruth	threw	me the ball. [indirect [direct object] object]
4.	[*You*—understood subject]	Shut	the door. [direct object]

Even this most basic form of the English sentence can be varied. The imperative or command statement *(Shut the door.)* omits the subject; the question form *(Do you like to dance?)* varies the usual word order. Adding a few *modifiers* (words which expand or qualify the meaning of another word or words in the sentence) to these basic structures will clarify, enrich, and vary these simple statements.

1. Birds fly *south in the winter.*
              [adverb   [prepositional phrase
              describing   describing when]
              where]

2. Ruth threw me the *old, red* ball.
                        [adjectives describing appearance]

3. The *white* carnation is beautiful *and fragile.*
        [descriptive   [second adjective
        adjective]   added to predicate]

4. Shut the door *quietly.*
                  [adverb describing how]

Notice that these are still short, uncomplicated sentence patterns moving from subject to verb to complement.

Position in the Simple Sentence: Emphasis and Variety   Regardless of the length of a sentence, the beginning and the end are the positions of importance. Since what is said first and last is what a reader usually remembers, do not waste important, idea-carrying words by burying them in the middle. Rearrange the following sentences to emphasize the important words. If necessary, add or delete words. Try several versions of each sentence and choose the best. Why do you think your choices are best?

John received a severe bite from the dog.

Into the classroom crawled a spider, fat and brown.

In my opinion, the chairman is a fine speaker.

We were told by the President not to use fuel carelessly.

One way to achieve variety with simple sentences containing few modifiers is to alter the usual subject-verb-complement pattern. Instead of automatically writing "The girl clutched three nickels in her hand," consider reordering the sentence to read: "In her hand, the girl clutched three nickels." Notice that, in the second version of the sentence, the amount of money—three nickels—is emphasized because it now comes at the end of the sentence. If the amount of money is the most important point to be made, then your reordering has achieved two goals: variety and appropriate emphasis. Revise the following description by changing the subject-verb-complement pattern, when appropriate, for variety and emphasis:

> The red geraniums sat on the window sill. They sagged over the edges of the green pot. The green pot, with several cracks in it, seemed old and tired. The sun shone through the window. It could not seem to warm the geraniums or the pot, however. The flowers and the pot need to be retired.

Using Simple Sentences   Short simple sentences can be effective forms for presenting simple actions, especially if the writer wishes to convey a sense of activity, movement, or haste. Consider, for example, the following paragraph:

> My mother is a worrier. One morning she will worry herself to death. She jumps out of bed each morning at 6:00. She dashes to the kitchen. She feeds the cats and starts the coffee simultaneously. She removes milk, eggs, and butter from the refrigerator. Quickly she starts to scramble eggs and make toast. Then she dashes upstairs and bangs on my door. She repeats her warnings of lateness. These warnings are reinforced by a continuous banging on my door. I finally give in and get up. It is now 7:00. My bus leaves at 8:00. An hour to eat scrambled eggs and toast!

An entire essay composed of short simple sentences, however, will begin to sound like the "See Spot run" sentences found in the first-grade readers. Such a style, often described as "primer English," should be avoided because excessive repetition of any pattern is boring and a variety of sentence patterns is necessary to express sophisticated ideas.

The Compound Sentence

A compound sentence is a combination of two (or more) simple sentences joined together by a coordinate conjunction *(and, or, but, for, nor, yet, so)*, by a pair of conjunctions *(both/and, either/or, neither/nor, not only/but also)*, or by a semicolon. Compound sentences linked by a semicolon often contain transition words *(also, then, however, thus, moreover)*. These transition connectors are adverbs, not coordinate conjunctions; if they are used, the required punctuation is a semicolon, not a comma. The following are compound sentences; note that a comma precedes each coordinate conjunction, and a semicolon precedes each transition connector.

1. It is raining, and the temperature is 60°.
2. I would go with you, but I am too tired.
3. Drunk drivers are a menace to others, so they should have their licenses revoked, and they should be fined as well.
4. Jill's parents are wealthy; however, she buys only what she needs.
5. Either Ruth Cook will be elected, or Tim Brooks will be elected, for the Independent Party candidate does not stand a chance of winning.
6. Not only is tennis fun to play, but it is also good exercise.
7. I have apologized for breaking your vase; in fact, I have apologized twice.

For the writer seeking variety in sentence structure, the compound sentence appears to offer a relief from a long string of simple sentences. However, if a writer uses only compound sentences joined by *and*, the variety he seeks is then only a slight visual change, not a significant change in sentence structure. Compare, for instance, these brief passages; are they really different?

1. It is raining. The temperature is 60°. There is only a slight breeze. Winter seems far away.
2. It is raining, and the temperature is 60°. There is only a slight breeze, and winter seems far away.

To use compound sentences effectively for variety *and* emphasis, consider the other coordinate conjunctions: *but, or, nor, for, yet, so*. Or consider using a semicolon and one of the transitional connectors—*also, however, thus,* to mention only a few. They not only link together two simple sentences, but also show a relationship between the ideas expressed in each subject-verb-complement pattern. Observe the variety and emphasis possible in the passage we have been examining:

3. It is raining, but the temperature is 60°, and only a slight breeze is blowing. Winter seems far away.

The warm temperature and slight breeze are joined together *(and)* in contrast to the rain *(but)*, and the three statements about the weather are placed in one compound sentence. The statement about winter, separated from the weather information, is emphasized, as a conclusion drawn from the weather facts.

Problems with Coordinate Conjunctions   Just as you avoid the excessive use of *and* in compound sentences, be careful to select an appropriate connecting word which will show the correct relationship between the two statements in your sentence. *And* and *but* are not interchangeable; neither are *so* and *yet*. First, understand what relationship you want to show between ideas; then select the coordinate conjunction which shows that relationship.

Examine the following compound sentences. Do they say what you think that the writer meant? Do they make good sense as they are written:

1. It was sprinkling, so I went to the swimming pool.

The speaker went swimming *because of* the sprinkles, or *in spite of* the sprinkles? *But* shows the more logical relationship.

2. Either young people are getting smarter, but they are learning more in school.

But destroys the *either/or* pattern which the writer initiates, and fails to make the connection logical. *Or* is the appropriate connecting word.

3. Logan Field was shrouded in fog, yet the plane was forced to fly to LaGuardia.

The plane is forced to go to LaGuardia *even though* Logan is fogged in? That isn't consistent with our experience at airports. Probably the writer wanted to say that the plane flew to LaGuardia *because* Logan was fogged in.

EXERCISES: Coordinate Conjunctions

Revise the following sentences by selecting a more appropriate coordinate conjunction or transition connector.

1. Mark is handsome, but I love him.

2. Susie does not like peaches, or does she like apples.

3. Spaghetti is sometimes messy to eat, and I like to eat it anyway.

4. I am not interested in music; however, it bores me.

5. We are driving to New York City, yet we want to see the Statue of Liberty.

6. Fido and Rhett are the names of our two dogs, so I like Rhett the best.

7. John studied hard for the test; on the contrary, he passed it.

8. Will we learn to use solar energy, and will we continue to rely on fossil fuels?

Expanding Simple Sentences by Adding Modifiers

The goals are variety, emphasis, and clarity; what are your options, in addition to simple and compound sentences? One is the complex sentence, which we will examine later. Another is the simple sentence expanded, enriched, and varied by the addition of modifiers. Although the basic structure of the sentence remains simple (one subject-verb-complement), the addition of modifying words and phrases expands the basic structure so that the result is neither short nor simplistic. We can organize our study of the expanded sentence by the placement of modifiers: in the middle, at the beginning, and at the end. Then we will consider some of the problems of modifier placement.

Expanding by Insertion   Perhaps the most obvious way to break the monotony and ineffectiveness of a series of short sentences is to regroup the information into one expanded sentence by inserting modifying words and phrases. Consider the following passage:

> His name was Butterball. He was a beautiful orange and white cat. He curled up in a ball on the couch. He purred contentedly.

This four-sentence description can be reorganized into one expanded sentence by highlighting one part of the description as the core sentence and inserting the rest of the information in the form of modifiers. If we highlight the information in sentence 3, sentence 1 can be deleted by changing the *He* in sentence 3 to *Butterball*.

> Butterball curled up in a ball on the couch.

Sentences 2 and 4 add details about Butterball; they can be inserted between the subject and verb:

> Butterball, a beautiful orange and white cat, purring contentedly, curled up in a ball on the couch.

The shape and rhythm of the original passage has been altered without losing any of the details.

How might these three sentences be combined by inserting modifiers into one subject-verb-complement pattern?

> Rose Tramore looked bright but vague. She turned three or four things over in her mind. She seemed on the spot.

Try several possibilities. Which do you like best? Henry James, in his short story "The Chaperone," organized the sentence like this:

> Rose Tramore, on the spot, looking bright but vague, turned three or four things over in her mind.

When you expand by insertion you are separating subject and verb. Do not break up the basic sentence elements to the point of confusion;

make sure that the added modifiers are related to the basic elements of the sentence and add to or emphasize details. Also, punctuate the sentence correctly to avoid confusion. Examine the following sentences to see which contain helpful and which contain intrusive interruptions.

1. The second aim, and more important to me, is to win.
2. Hurricane Agnes, in the middle of the night, had arrived.
3. This, I believe, is an untrue statement.
4. The council will have enough money, I hope, to support an arts program in the schools.
5. We are therefore misdirecting our concern toward nuclear reactors.

Expanding by Adding Introductory Modifiers   Another way to expand and vary the simple sentence pattern is to place modifying words and phrases at the beginning of the sentence before the subject. You already employ this pattern with transition words and phrases to show relationships between ideas. *The 3:15 bus leaves before classes are dismissed.* Consequently, *we will have to take the 4:15 bus.* Introductory words and phrases not only vary the expected subject-verb-complement pattern; they vary emphasis as well. Short introductory modifiers, especially when set off by punctuation, usually acquire a special emphasis. For example: *Inside, the church was dimly lit.* The modifier *inside* not only adds information; it also emphasizes a contrast between the exterior and interior of the church.

Remember, though, that the other important position is the end of the sentence. Longer introductory modifiers can help build up to the key point of the sentence. *According to the latest polls, Elaine Caldwell will be elected.* Because of the placement of the modifier, the emphasis is not given to the polls but rather to the prediction of election. Examine the following brief passage:

The soldiers saw the advancing cavalry. The captain waved them into battle. They rallied to the charge.

These three simple sentences can be reorganized into a single expanded sentence by insertion or by using introductory modifiers. If you want to add suspense as you build to the captain's decision, the second choice is better:

Seeing the advancing cavalry and being waved into battle by the captain, the soldiers rallied to the charge.

Regroup the following sentences into one sentence, using introductory modifiers. Decide first which idea should be emphasized and place it in the basic part of the sentence pattern.

Dorothy wins the final point. She pounds her forehand deep into the corner. She then angles the volley across court.

Expanding by Ending with Modifiers: The Cumulative Sentence Many experts on sentence style believe that an effective way to expand the simple sentence is to add modifying phrases after the subject-verb-complement pattern. The cumulative sentence, as this pattern is called, opens up like the petals of a flower. The basic unit is presented first, then grows richer through modification at the end of the sentence. Each variation of the simple sentence has special uses and merits; the cumulative sentence provides another option. Here is an example: *The young colts galloped across the meadow, manes and tails flying, heads raised, delighting in the fresh smell of springtime.* As modifiers are added to the basic structure—*colts galloped*—the scene unfolds before the reader's eyes. Examine the following passage:

> There are many consequences of civil war. Anarchy and confusion often result. Another consequence is poverty. Still other results are desolation and ruin.

The key idea is stated in sentence 1 and the other sentences list consequences, but the structure of this passage lacks both variety and emphasis. If the writer's goal is to pile up results to confirm the devastation of civil war, his short sentences fail. But the passage can be revised into one cumulative sentence which *will* provide the desired objective:

> The consequences of civil war are many: anarchy and confusion, poverty, desolation and ruin.

In any expanded sentence, first decide what should be placed in the basic sentence unit and what should function as modifiers. In a cumulative sentence, choose an order for the modifiers which follow the basic sentence. How might the following passage be revised to form one cumulative sentence?

> He offered hope for the future. He commanded the affection and respect of those who worked for him. He was one of the best leaders of our time. He was intelligent and witty.

If we agree that in this passage sentence 3 contains the general assertion and the other sentences list supporting qualities, the cumulative sentence will begin to take shape:

No. 3 He was one of the best leaders of our time,	No. 1 offered hope for the future
	No. 2 commanded the affection and respect of those who worked for him
	No. 4 intelligent and witty.

Once we change the first two statements on the right into modifying phrases by changing the verb form, we will have a cumulative sentence. Or will we? Look again at the order of the modifiers, and remember that what is last has the greatest emphasis. An effective cumulative sentence is not just a random list of attached modifiers. Perhaps the most effective order would be to move from personal qualities to effect on staff to effect on a larger group. Working with this concept of order and emphasis, we could revise the sentence to read:

> He was one of the best leaders of our time, intelligent and witty, commanding the affection and respect of those who worked for him, offering hope for the future.

A cumulative sentence contains a single subject-verb-complement pattern followed by modifiers; an effective cumulative sentence results from careful planning to emphasize the central idea and the most significant modifier.

Modifier Placement: Some Problems   Expanding simple sentences by modification can result in awkwardness, lack of appropriate emphasis, even lack of clarity. As we have noted throughout this discussion, you need to plan the structure of a detailed sentence. Make sure that the central idea is in the basic sentence unit; choose the placement of modifiers —beginning, middle, end—to produce the desired emphasis. Pay attention to punctuation, visual signals that guide a reader through a lengthy sentence.

Two further points need to be considered. Some modifiers can be moved around to produce variety and create a particular emphasis, but other modifiers are *bound;* they cannot be shifted without changing the meaning of the sentence. For example, look at several pairs of sentences. What happens when the modifying phrases shift position?

> The student hurried down the aisle, *dropping his books.*

> *Dropping his books,* the student hurried down the aisle.

Did the student drop his books *as* he hurried down the aisle, which is what the first sentence says? Or did he drop his books and *then* hurry down the aisle, which is what the second sentence says?

> *Thrilled with victory,* Woody Hayes dashed across the field to shake hands with his opponent.

> Woody Hayes dashed across the field to shake hands with his opponent, *thrilled with victory.*

Who is thrilled with victory—Woody Hayes or his opponent? The first sentence gives the victory to Hayes; the second, to his opponent.

> *With tears in his eyes,* Billy watched George lick his ice cream cone.

> Billy watched George lick his ice cream cone *with tears in his eyes.*

Who has tears in his eyes, Billy or George? In the first, Billy is ready to cry; in the second, George is ready to cry while licking his ice cream. In each example the modifying phrase is bound; it needs to stand next to what it modifies. By shifting its position, we change the meaning of the sentence.

A second placement problem is what handbooks call the *dangling modifier*. They occur most often in sentences containing introductory verbal phrases. Here is an example: *Climbing in the dorm window, the Dean of Women caught her.* Who is climbing in the dorm window? This verbal phrase requires an actor to complete its meaning and will "attach itself" to the nearest noun in the main part of the sentence. If the nearest noun cannot logically be the actor, then the modifier dangles or is logically incomplete. Since experience tells us that the student, not the Dean, must have been climbing in the window, the sample sentence contains a dangling modifier. Here are several more examples. Why do the modifiers dangle?

Swimming at the pool, the sun shone brightly.

Thinking over the problems of drunk driving, fines should be increased.

Rowing rapidly, shore was soon reached.

Throwing out the entire sentence or crossing through the modifier is not the way to correct dangling modifiers. Knowing why some modifiers dangle will help you to revise sentences to correct the problem. Sometimes the change is simple: make the actor of the modifying phrase the subject of the basic sentence: *Rowing rapidly, we soon reached the shore.* Other sentences need complete overhauls: *As we swam at the pool, the sun shone brightly.*

Complex Sentences: Subordination

We said earlier that a compound sentence contained two complete subject-verb-complement patterns; thus each part can stand alone as a grammatically correct simple sentence. A *complex sentence* contains one complete subject-verb-complement pattern or independent clause and one or more dependent or subordinate clauses, sentence elements which cannot stand alone as a grammatically correct sentence. In a sense, the term *complex sentence* is an inappropriate label, for we have seen that many expanded simple sentences are "complex" in that they are detailed, sophisticated statements. However, grammarians use the term *complex sentence* to refer to a particular sentence pattern. The label is not important; your ability to use this particular sentence pattern in your writing is important. Why? Complex sentences provide variety and a means of showing complex relationships between ideas. The complex sentence provides a grammatical structure for showing a logical connection between two ideas while emphasizing one idea and deemphasizing or subordinating the other. We will look at the two most common subordinate clauses, those introduced by *relative pronouns* and then those introduced by *subordinate conjunctions*.

Subordination with Relative Pronouns   The complex sentence, *The biology class that I am failing meets at 9:00 A.M.*, combines two sentences into one, connected by the relative pronoun *that*. The information could be presented in two simple sentences: *My biology class meets at 9:00 A.M. I am failing my biology class*. If there were no relative pronouns in our language, the ideas would have to be expressed in separate sentences. But there are relative pronouns—*who, whose, whom, that, which, where, when, why* are the most common—that enable a writer to avoid overworking simple sentences by combining two related ideas. A relative clause adds a related idea to a basic sentence pattern; it helps to define or qualify a noun in the basic sentence. It also allows a writer to emphasize one idea over another; if both ideas were expressed in separate sentences, they would be given equal emphasis. You must decide which ideas to emphasize and which to subordinate, and then structure the sentence to reveal that relative emphasis. Consider the following two sentences:

The Turners live next door.

The Turners are good neighbors.

These sentences can be restructured into two different complex sentences, depending upon which idea you want to subordinate:

The Turners, who live next door, are good neighbors.

The Turners, who are good neighbors, live next door.

Here is another example:

The boy is my brother.

The boy is wearing a red shirt.

Again, there are two possible complex sentences:

The boy who is wearing a red shirt is my brother.

The boy who is my brother is wearing a red shirt.

Subordination with Subordinate Conjunctions   Writing effective complex sentences using subordinate conjunctions requires two judgments: which idea will be emphasized, and what is the appropriate conjunction to convey the relationship of the two ideas. Let us first examine the problem of emphasis. In the following statements, which should go in the subordinate position?

I love her.

She is not beautiful.

Probably the first statement is the more important. A reader might question the meaning of *Although I love her, she is not beautiful.* Didn't the writer really mean *Although she is not beautiful, I love her*?

The problem of emphasis is difficult to illustrate with sentences taken out of context. It is not always obvious that one idea should be subordinate. How would you form a complex sentence from these statements?

Mother called on Mrs. Jones.

Then she visited Mrs. Peters.

You could write *Mother called on Mrs. Jones before she visited Mrs. Peters.* But, in a particular context, a writer might want to say *After she called on Mrs. Jones, Mother visited Mrs. Peters.* To decide which visit to emphasize, the writer must examine the context in which the sentence will be used.

Selecting the appropriate subordinate conjunction can be a problem because only certain connections between two ideas in a sentence are logically possible. We would not write *Because I answered the phone, it rang.* Experience assures us that the cause/effect relationship expressed in this sentence is illogical; indeed, it is backwards. Here is another example:

Mary did not finish her homework although she was ill.

Although introduces a condition: *Although I am able to dance, I do not like to.* Experience tells us that illness is not a condition that will allow, or should allow for, the completion of homework. We are willing to believe, however, that illness could be a *cause* for not completing homework. Thus, we would accept the logic in this revised version: *Mary did not finish her homework because she was ill.*

Sometimes an inappropriate subordinate conjunction is selected because the writer is not thinking carefully about the relationship of the ideas he wishes to express. The more complex the ideas, the more careful you must be in selecting appropriate connecting words. Sometimes writers show illogical relationships in complex sentences because they are not sure of the meanings of the connectors. The chart on the facing page should alleviate that problem. It includes common coordinate conjunctions and transitional connectives used to form compound sentences, and common relative pronouns and subordinate conjunctions used in complex sentences. Notice that some words can be used to express more than one type of relationship.

EXERCISES: Subordination

Practice selecting appropriate subordinate conjunctions by making the following pairs of sentences into complex sentences. Subordinate the starred sentence in each pair.

COMMON COORDINATE CONJUNCTIONS AND TRANSITIONAL CONNECTIVES

Type of relationship shown	Coordinate conjunctions	Transitional connectives	Relative pronouns	Subordinate conjunctions
TIME		then, later, earlier		after, before, as soon as, when, while, since, until, whenever
ADDITIONAL RELATED IDEA	and, both/and, not only/but also	moreover, furthermore, likewise, also	who, whose whom, that, which	
CAUSE/EFFECT	so, for	in fact, therefore, thus, consequently, for this reason		because, since
CONTRAST	or, nor, either/or, neither/nor, but, yet	however, otherwise, on the other hand, nevertheless, on the contrary		whereas
ALTERNATE OR CONTRARY CONDITION	but, yet	however		even though, in spite of the fact, although
PURPOSE				so that, in order that
CONDITIONAL				if, whether, provided that

1. I had almost given up hope.
    I finally started the car.*

2. George ordered pie for dessert.
    He is supposed to be on a diet.*

3. I will help you with your math homework.
    Will you help me study for a history test?*

4. Joe did not realize the value of that old coin.*
    He sold it to a dealer for five dollars.

5. I want to earn some extra money.
    I want to buy a new bicycle.*

Sentence Economy; Sentence Sense

We have explored a variety of alternatives to the short simple sentence. Long sentences do not always mean effective sentences, however. If they are the result of *wordiness*—using more words than necessary to express an idea—the result will be ponderous, boring, or obscure. Check your work to see if you have used several words where one will do, or if you can rearrange a sentence to shorten it. Here are some sentences which have been improved:

> The majority of students felt the required time was necessary in order to finish their projects.
> Most students need the whole five weeks to finish their projects.

> Patience on the part of applicants is strained.
> Applicants' patience is strained.

> Due to the fact that the team lost four games, they will not take part in the championship tournament.
> Because the team lost four games, they will not play in the championship tournament.

Words, phrases, and sentences which add nothing to the meaning are called *deadwood*. Deadwood, like wordiness, interferes with an effective style. The revision is simple: strike out unnecessary words. Some deadwood results from a mechanical attempt to direct the reader. Don't confuse deadwood with necessary transitions; ask yourself if you're being heavyhanded. *I will examine two short stories and look at their similarities and differences.* An informative title and clear thesis statement make such a sentence unnecessary. *To sum up, it is only reasonable to conclude . . .* If the writer has not made his case, this prodding will not convince the reader; if he has made his case, the statement is unnecessary.

Sometimes deadwood is a writing equivalent of "uh" and "y'know." Remove the deadwood in the following sentences.

Billy Budd is Melville's attempt, as it were, to deal with the inequity of Fate.

In turning now, if you will, to the second part of the article, we read the senator's criticism of his opponent.

Everyone, of course, needs to be loved.

In *awkward sentences*, the problem is primarily construction, although wordiness may also result. The construction sounds unnatural and clumsy, almost as if the sentence had been translated from another language. Do not be too discouraged if awkwardness is your problem, because it often results from a writer's attempt to express his ideas in more complex sentence structures than usual. Just keep practicing the various expanded sentence patterns and examine your writing to find awkward sentences which will need revision. If you are tangled in an awkward sentence, ask yourself, "What am I trying to say?" Say the idea aloud, write it down, and polish the sentence. Here are some examples, with suggested revisions. Notice how often awkwardness results from not placing the main idea in the basic sentence pattern.

The use of dialog helps us to learn much quickly about Charles.
The dialog quickly reveals Charles's character.

I planned a time that held for me no appointments or commitments.
I found some free time in my schedule.

The surroundings of the new house indicate serenity.
The new house is in a quiet neighborhood.

The practicality of the first floor arrangement is a customer will go through at least two sales areas before he leaves.
The first floor arrangement is practical because a customer must go through at least two sales areas on his way out.

EXERCISES: Sentence Economy; Sentence Sense

Rewrite the following sentences to eliminate wordiness, awkwardness, and deadwood.

1. When we started to skate together, my partner needed to change the manner in which he skated very much.

2. It is true that food was not thought of for several days, but this was because the women were in so much pain that all they could do was to weep bitter tears.

3. On another occasion there was a severe disturbance within our area.

4. The coach expressed his choice of the NBA's Rookie of the Year. He picked Mitch Kupchak as his choice for Rookie of the Year.

5. Ten days is too short a time to develop any lasting situation which would help a person to keep a healthy eating habit.

6. These statements were completely false.

EXERCISES: Sentence Structure

A. Combine each group of sentences into one expanded simple sentence. Experiment with placement for emphasis.

1. The street vendor was a flower dealer.
    He tapped his feet impatiently.
    He stood behind a display of mums and carnations.
    His flowers glistened with raindrops.

2. Jenny emerged from the restaurant.
    She crossed the street to the bus stop.

3. The young mothers lounge about in the laundromat.
    They scream at their children.
    They smoke cigarettes and drink cola.
    Their hair is in curlers.

4. The swimmers' sleek bodies skim through the water.
    The swimmers drive for the pool edge and the hope of victory.
    The swimmers' arms and legs are fully extended.

5. Mrs. Sullivan concentrated on the ball.
    Mrs. Sullivan bent her head over the ball.
    Mrs. Sullivan slowly slid the putter back and then forward to stroke the ball.

6. The sleigh flew across the frozen lake.
    The sleigh was drawn by a team of horses.
    They were a beautifully matched team of horses.

7. Grandmother was a bent old woman.
    Grandmother was an angry woman.
    She cared more about her geraniums than people.

8. He learned to draw by study and practice.
    First he learned to draw a still life of fruits and flowers.
    Then he learned to draw a landscape with depth.
    Finally he learned to draw a perfectly proportioned human body.

B. Combine each group of sentences into either a compound sentence or a complex sentence (using either a relative pronoun or a subordinate conjunction). Pay attention to proper punctuation.

1. Bob is a good student.
   Bob was not elected to the Honor Society.

2. Joan likes to play golf.
   Joan is my sister.

3. It is going to rain soon.
   My back aches.

4. Do you want to borrow my car?
   You will have to buy some gas for it.

5. The Declaration of Independence was written by some Americans.
   These Americans believed that governments should provide safety and happiness for the governed.

6. Professor MacDonald is an expert in American Literature.
   Professor MacDonald is also an expert in linguistics.

7. I know when Clark Gable died.
   I am not going to tell you when Clark Gable died.

8. Roger and Elizabeth had been friends since childhood.
   Roger and Elizabeth reflected how little they knew each other.

9. Shakespeare was a great dramatist.
   Some readers think that Shakespeare is our greatest dramatist.

10. Macy's does not want to spend too much money on personnel.
    Macy's puts not more than six clerks in each department.

C. Rewrite the following paragraphs for variety and emphasis.

1. My eating habits were also formed while I lived on a farm. There was fresh cured bacon, ham, homemade sausage, fresh beef and pork. For fresh eggs, I had only to walk to the hen house. Each summer brought an array of fresh vegetables. Milk with thick, rich, yellow cream was available just for the milking of a cow. There was creamy fresh butter for piling high on home baked bread which had been sliced for toasting. Clabbered milk became cottage cheese with little effort. Water was pumped from a deep underground spring. In the woods, fresh mushrooms grew in abundance.

2. Recently the high scorer expressed his opinion about the dunk shot ruling. He stated that he would like to see the dunk shot be legalized in high school and college basketball. He feels that, since it is not legal, it takes something away from the ballplayer

and the game. He thinks that if the shot were allowed it would give the players a reason for driving to the basket. He states that since it is not allowed, the players don't go to the basket because all they can do is shoot a lay-up, and this has a greater chance of being blocked and is not so exciting to the player or to the crowd.

3. Lies actually do not help matters. Eventually the truth shows through. This is when friends are lost. When one lie is told, many more seem to develop. Once I told my parents I was going to babysit, when I was really going to a party. The party was being held at a boy's house and his parents were out of town. Later in the evening the party got out of hand, and the police raided it. They took me to the police station and called my parents. When I was confronted by my parents, I told them I had gone to my babysitting job, but the people had changed their minds and were not going out. I continued to tell them my friend had driven by and asked me to come with him to a party. I also added that I had absolutely no idea that the parents were not home at the party. My first lie led to at least four more. My parents found out about my first major lie. Their trust in me had been abused, and it took quite a long time to regain what had been lost. I should have told my parents about the party and saved myself a lot of tears and sitting at home. I learned a lesson from that little incident.

WORD CHOICE

One of the main ways in which a writer considers his audience is in word choice. By studying audience and voice you have already begun to think about the appropriateness of your word choice. Sometimes you use words that are slangy, sometimes formal, sometimes technical. Now we turn to choosing words that are not only appropriate but also precise, vivid, and interesting.

Variety

Strive for varied word choice to avoid boring your reader by overusing certain words or phrases.

Synonyms   When you have to keep mentioning an idea or object, it helps to use synonyms. For instance, in this book we have discussed your writing, your work, your essays, papers, articles, editorials, explanations, discussions—anything to vary the necessary reference to the subject. But don't overdo it; some careful repetition is useful for coherence or emphasis. You do not need to avoid all repetition, just that which sounds intrusive, as in the following examples.

Each reason represents a division of *the paper,* ready to be developed. When your thesis statement appears *in the paper,* you will probably not include the "because clause" as part of it, since it is long and cumbersome, and the reasons will quickly be spelled out *in the paper.*

Each reason represents a division of *the argument,* ready to be developed. When your thesis statement appears *in the paper,* you will probably not include the "because clause" as part of it, since it is long and cumbersome, and the reasons will quickly be spelled out *as you develop your thesis.*

Pronoun reference   When you are certain that the antecedent is clear, use pronouns to vary word choice.

> Many plumbers will not work on weekends. The plumbers who will often charge double-time.
> Many plumbers will not work on weekends. Those who will often charge double-time.

Verbs   When you think about synonyms and pronouns for the nouns in your work, remember also to vary the verbs. When it suits your style, use the verb which is most descriptive of the action (*strolled* instead of *walked slowly*), especially if it allows you to eliminate an adverb at the same time.

You could not dispense with the forms of the verb "to be," but since you must use them so often, try to substitute a more descriptive verb when you can.

> He is in the choir.
> He sings in the choir.

In English, the present tense can be expressed with or without a form of "to be." When you can, eliminate it.

> I can't hear if the phone is ringing when the water is running.
> I can't hear the phone ring when the water runs.

Another way to avoid overusing forms of "to be" is to use the passive voice as little as possible.

> Two polls were taken to assess student reaction.
> The S.G.A. took two polls to assess student reaction.

The passive voice is indirect (the subject is acted upon), while the active voice is direct (the subject acts) and therefore stronger. Often, using the passive voice can cause you to omit the subject, as in the example given above. Even when the actor appears in the sentence (*This paper was written by me.*), the passive voice subordinates, and thus deemphasizes, his role. *I wrote this paper* sounds more direct and, in English, more natural.

Problems in Word Choice

Vagueness   In Chapter 2, we talked about the need for detail in proving a thesis. Sharpen that detail by making it informative and concrete. *Concrete language* names items which can be seen or touched (dog, book, chair, sky). If your words are already concrete, see if they could be more *specific:* a dog/a red dachshund, a book/*Tristram Shandy.*

Smoking caused Bob to have a throat problem.
Smoking gave Bob a sore throat.

The bulletin board held different types of information.
Lost and Found notices, For Sale lists, advertisements for magazines, and an announcement of the Band Concert covered the bulletin board.

The boy ate his food.
The student ate his lunch.
The college student ate his hamburger and fries.

When you can use description, make it vivid. Remember that in addition to giving the reader information that he needs, you also add interest by providing him with a word picture.

She wore a bright colored dress.
She wore a bright yellow evening gown.

When numbers are called for, be specific.

Several of us share an apartment.
Three of us share an apartment.

Such words as *interesting, nice, useful, bad, unusual, very, amazing* don't tell a reader much. Try to pin down your meaning.

Finishing the cleaning made me feel good.
Finishing the cleaning made me feel efficient.

A different sort of vagueness results from a failure to remember who the audience is. An inattentive writer lapses into using "you" when he really means *anyone, someone, a person,* or even *I.* "You" is appropriate only when the writer is actually speaking directly to the reader. When we say "you" in this book, we mean *you.*

To be a good swimmer, you must be well coordinated.
Good swimmers must be well coordinated.

I found that you do your best studying at a well lighted desk.
I found that I do my best studying at a well lighted desk.

When you look at one of Mr. McDonald's tests, you are intimidated.
When a student looks at one of Mr. McDonald's tests, he is intimidated.

Stilted language   Stilted language results from substituting "big words" for ordinary ones, usually in a writer's attempt to sound sophisticated. Remember that as you study and read and write about complex ideas, you will naturally begin to use a more sophisticated vocabulary. And when these words are appropriate, you will use them automatically. To add big words here and there, instead of improving your writing, makes it sound artificial and sometimes obscures the meaning. Often the strongest expression is simple and direct.

The need for a party dress and a lack of money was not an isolated incident but a continuing factor in my life.

Often I needed, but could not afford, a new party dress.

His garage became the nocturnal gathering place for every male teenager within two blocks.

At nightfall the teenage boys in the neighborhood would gather in his garage.

Recycling paper allows better utilization of our resources.

Recycling paper allows better use of our resources.

Redundancy   Avoid phrases which say the same thing twice.

I *failed* the course *with an F.*

Currently in this *modern day and age,* people live longer.

We are *unique individuals.*

Have you fulfilled the *necessary requirements?*

Each of these sentences repeats itself. Should you find redundancy in your own work, choose the part of the phrase or sentence which makes clear your meaning and eliminate the rest.

Triteness   Certain expressions, especially those which create a vivid image, become so familiar through overuse that they lose their impact. Because you hear them so often, these trite expressions may come easily to mind as you write. However, triteness can make your writing sound flat and unoriginal. As soon as you recognize one of these expressions, substitute a more direct word or phrase.

Some trite phrases are old expressions and sayings.

Mother Nature has been good to our backyard.

Our backyard is filled with healthy trees and plants.

The snows of age had fallen on his head.

His hair had turned white.

Other trite phrases are current, but no less worn out.

Time has a different frame of reference from *Psychology Today*.
Time and *Psychology Today* have different audiences and purposes.

We had a breakdown in communications.
We didn't understand each other.

EXERCISES: Word Choice

A. For each of the following concrete nouns, list three more specific words. List either a noun or a noun with modifiers (glasses/steel-rimmed spectacles).

> cat
> person
> car
> house
> chair
> book
> flower

For each of the following vague modifiers, list three more precise words.

> *good* book
> *bad* road
> *interesting* speech
> *exciting* game
> *beautiful* room
> *wonderful* person
> *awful* essay

For each of the verbs in the following sentences, list three more precise verbs that could be substituted.

> Kim *went* over to the swings.
> Melissa *looked* around the room.
> Elliott *moved* down the hall.
> Scott and Carey *lifted* the heavy chest.
> Lisa *laughed* at the clown.

B. Examine the following sentences for problems in word choice. Rewrite each and compare yours with those of other class members.

1. Perhaps this product might be potentially hazardous.

2. Brian's behavior has been very unusual recently.

3. I decided to take all the time that I needed or that was required.

4. At this point in time, we do not know how much fuel will be needed during the winter months.

5. Two annoying and dangerous situations will be eliminated by the application of this solution.

6. After our family had bought the new house, we found that the grass is always greener on the other side.

7. I am familiar with three mystery writers. These mystery writers are Agatha Christie, Margery Allingham, and Dick Francis.

8. The past was very different from the way it is now.

EXERCISES: Stylistic Problems

A. Rewrite the following sentences to eliminate the stylistic problems.

1. In this writer's opinion, it seems as if the city council is making a mistake.

2. The pressure of too little time is almost always an unnecessary factor to any situation.

3. Walking down the highway, the car sped past him.

4. The difference in length is due to the type of magazine each article represents.

5. A quick phone call to the office would find that her statistics are wrong.

6. Various parts of this ad have certain functions to perform such as to attract potential customers, to induce a desire for the product, and eventually to sell the product.

7. The Simon Building is a fairly large building when you look at it from the highway.

8. *Gone with the Wind* is an exciting novel about the Civil War in our library.

9. This is not to say that I never do things which I don't plan, because the fact is that I do many things on the spur of the moment.

10. The main cause of friction between my mother and me deals with my stubbornness.

11. Locking the classroom door, the teacher's gradebook was left on her desk.

12. Marie's brother and she have always been very distant in communications.

13. After receiving her diploma, Susan shook hands smilingly with the principal.

14. In reference to learners' permits being issued for new drivers, the visual and written tests along with age limit are given to the applicant.

15. With the lowering of the pollution level, there has been an elimination of the physiological problems that could have taken place.

16. Most young people today drive their own cars, and most young people listen to loud music, frequently at the same time.

17. Michael had not been able to see any of the controls or instruments in the dark of night.

18. And lastly, the article said that the new film costs less per picture than the old film.

19. For the most part, Bob tries to consider the feelings of other people.

B. Examine the stylistic problems in the following student essay:

The Public Library

1   At the corner of Oak Avenue and Meadow Street sits the public library. The 319,900-dollar project is located on a one and one-half acre lot. Scattered oak and maple trees cast their shade over the lot. The large brick building is built with old fashioned "Williamsburg" style in mind. Because of its construction and services, the public library makes a useful contribution to this community.

2   The outside of the library is beautiful in its "Williamsburg" style. Covered sidewalks and large archways help convey this style. On sunny days the open courtyards and patios with benches make outdoor reading a real treat. On rainy days, however, the covered sidewalks and convenient outside book drop are truly handy. Rain or shine, there is always adequate parking available for both the bicyclist and the automobile driver.

3   The inside of the library is not in the colonial "Williamsburg" style as you might expect, but it is typical of modern twentieth century architecture. The library is divided into five convenient sections—the meeting room, the circulation desk, the back room, the children's section, and the adult section. The children's section is where the children's books are, and the adult section is where all the periodicals, encyclopedias, and adult books are located. The circulation desk is the place where books are to be checked out. The back room is for the employees to do the necessary paperwork, mend book spines, tape pages, and repair covers of books. Paperback books, periodicals, pamphlets, films, and records—along with the many rows of hardback books—are available to be checked out. A copying machine is quite convenient for copying newspaper articles, since newspapers cannot be circulated.

4   Any taxpayer or student in the county is eligible to obtain a library card. Some of the services that the holder of this card has at his disposal are a vast selection of books and periodicals and the special use of films and records. If

the library does not have the desired book or film available, it can be ordered from one of the other library branches in the county. If the book cannot be located somewhere in the county, then it may be ordered from another library anywhere in the United States for a charge of twenty-five cents. Also, the library has a meeting room that is available to any group that desires the use of it, except sales groups, and it is in use almost every night.

5   Although the library does not occupy a vast amount of space, it provides an exceptional group of services and contributes to the beauty of the community. This feature helps to attract people to use these services and tends to uplift the general culture of the community. Although it cost nearly a third of a million dollars, to the people who use it, the public library is well worth it.

C.   Look at the essay on pp. 37–38. Diagnose and remedy the stylistic problems.

D.   Examine your previous writing closely for stylistic problems and revise the style so it is appropriate to voice, audience, subject, and purpose.

Revision

5

In the writing process, it is rare to write a paper only once. When you have written your first draft, put it aside for at least a day and then see where it might need work. Whenever possible, go over the draft again with someone familiar with your audience. Consider his suggestions and use those which seem appropriate. Remember that the best writing is often rewriting, and always leave yourself plenty of time to revise. The following questions summarize the basics we have been discussing:

CHECK SHEET

A. Context

   1. Purpose
      Have you clearly defined for yourself why you are writing?

   2. Voice
      What is your role this time?

   3. Audience

      a. Who is your audience?
      b. How knowledgeable are they about your subject?
      c. What is their attitude toward your subject and toward you?

  d. How sophisticated are they?

4. Do your topic choice, paper length, and type of evidence reflect your purpose, voice, and audience?

B. Substance

  1. Thesis

    a. Is there one sentence which clearly expresses the thesis?
    b. Is it appropriately placed in the essay?
    c. Is it limited and specific?
    d. Is it single?
    e. Does it reveal your attitude toward the subject?

  2. Evidence

    a. Is each paragraph constructed mostly of details?
    b. Are there any unsupported generalizations?
    c. Are there any points that need further details to make them either clearer or more interesting?
    d. Do all the details help prove the thesis?

  3. Organization

    a. Does everything in each paragraph deal with the same part of the thesis?
    b. Is each paragraph relevant to the thesis?
    c. Are there any paragraphs that should be combined?
    d. Are the paragraphs in an order which clearly reflects their relationship to one another?
    e. Are the paragraphs unified and coherent?

C. Style

  1. Word choice

    a. Have you eliminated unnecessary repetition in word choice?
    b. Is the language specific and descriptive?
    c. Have you avoided trite expressions?

  2. Sentence structure

    a. Have you written emphatic sentences?
    b. Have you varied sentence length and structure?
    c. Have you eliminated wordiness, deadwood, and awkwardness?

  3. Is your style appropriate for your purpose, voice, and audience?

EXERCISES: The Whole Essay

Using the check sheet, evaluate the following student essay, written in response to this assignment.

Subject: Think of a time when someone saw you as different from the way you saw yourself. Discuss these differences in perception and examine possible reasons for them.

Audience: Members of the class, including instructor.

Criteria:
1. Well-stated thesis.
2. Development with relevant detail.
3. Clear and appropriate organization.
4. Consideration of audience.
5. Freedom from mechanical error.
6. Appropriate style.

Problems with My Supervisor

1 A tall, lanky, gray-haired woman, perhaps in her late fifties or early sixties, sitting at her desk at the head of a large office, diligently working on some pressing matter, suddenly laid down her pen, and stared pensively across the room. She slowly shook her head from side to side, with a pained expression on her face indicating some disquieting thought, and finally, with an exaggerated sigh, rose from her chair. All this I observed from my own smaller desk situated to the left and diagonally about twenty feet in front of hers. As she headed toward me, I had a definite foreboding.

2 She reached my desk, looked down at me, and, speaking in a quiet tone, said, "David, would you please come over to my desk? I have to speak with you." Feigning engrossment in my work, I nodded, and casually answered, "O.K., Mrs. Monday, as soon as I finish this last card." Then in her typical gauche manner, she replied, "That's all right, it won't be necessary." "This is it," I thought, "it was nice while it lasted." I followed her back to her desk, pulled up a chair, and prepared myself for the worst.

3 Mrs. Monday, my supervisor, did not waste any time getting down to business. "Listen," she said, "I can't do anything more for you. I'm going to have to terminate you." As she spoke, she looked searchingly into my eyes to see what my reaction would be. I knew she would have loved to have seen me grovel before her, and promise her anything in order to keep my job, so I just smiled and said "All right. Can I leave now?" But, no, she just could not resist this last opportunity to bend my ears with her old familiar harangue about all of my shortcomings. The substance of what followed was her assertion that I would never amount to anything because I lacked initiative, was irresponsible and immature, and because I was too easily influenced by my friends. That is what she saw. However, in actuality, I was being criticized because of my refusal to make the company for which we both worked the center of my life. While she saw the company as the most tremendous company in the world, worthy of complete devotion and unquestioning loyalty, I just looked at it as a good place to work.

4 From the very beginning of my employment in that office, about seven months prior to my termination, Mrs. Monday and I clashed on matters which I considered to be very petty. One specific area in which our attitudes toward the company differed was in our feelings toward the stratified structure of the people in the building. These distinctions between levels of employees were important to her, and her behavior was modified accordingly. I, however, could never convince myself that this was an important matter, and consequently my behavior must have seemed to her to be in contemptuous defiance of all she stood for. For instance, I had a friend who worked for the cleaning service in the building, and, as far as she was concerned, I should not even talk to him. She first brought this to my attention one day after he came into the office to talk to me. She was incredulous with me for allowing such a person in her office. "You know," she said, "the company frowns on its employees fraternizing with the cleaning people." "Yes, but he's my friend. I've known him for years." "Well, it looks bad for you to be seen with him, and it looks bad for the company."

5   I naturally resented this intrusion upon my personal life, so I made it a point to let her know I did not particularly care about appearances. When she saw that I took my morning breaks in the cafeteria with him, she tried to get me to stop, saying that it was for my own good and that I should grow up and realize this, but I just smiled and said, "Sure, sure." So, I did something which in her eyes was taboo, and this was incomprehensible to her. This had a lot to do with her opinion of me.

6   Another basis for her perception of me was her fear that my presence in the office was going to stir up discontent and rebellion among the other workers. There was another unwritten code of behavior which she chose to require for her department, which was that everyone should eat lunch together in the cafeteria. This was something which just did not agree with me. I wanted to spend my lunch hour away from any reminder of my work, preferably on a bar stool with an icy mug of draught in my hand. After a while, other people in the office began going out for lunch also. I was breaking up her cozy little arrangement, and I believe she resented me for this. However, she did not believe that I was going out to lunch because I wanted to. Why would anyone not want to eat lunch with her? Thus, she rationalized that it was my friend who was persuading me to go out, and I was just too weak to assert myself, but this was just not true. I was doing exactly what I wanted to.

7   Then, she noticed that I came back with beer on my breath, and she made a big stink about this. She told me that this was just a bad image for her department. What if some VIP should walk into her office and smell my breath? It did not matter that my work suffered none from the few beers I had; what concerned her was the image. So when I told her that I intended to have my beer with my lunch, she called me immature. I just, in her opinion, did not know how to behave.

8   I think perhaps the chief reason for her low opinion of me, though, was the fact that I was constantly requesting her to transfer me out of her department. I wanted to get into a training program for computer operators, and I knew that I would be eligible for the class after my first six months with the company, but I think she thought I wanted to get out of her department because I disliked her. "You're just not happy here, are you?" she would answer me. Try as I might, I could not make her believe that it was nothing personal. She felt put down, and so she reacted by putting me down.

9   In conclusion, then, I feel it was a combination of all these reasons that gave her the wrong impression of me. The very fact that our relationship was

a supervisor-worker one made this misunderstanding possible. She and I had a communication gap; she wanted me to honor her, her department, and her attitudes, and she would not allow any deviation, while I insisted on maintaining my own personal liberty.

WRITING ASSIGNMENT

A. Using one of the following topics (or one developed by you or your instructor), draft your essay.

1. Personal Experience

    a. (1) Narrate a crisis in your life. Discuss it in such a way that your reader will understand how you felt about it.

        (2) Write a second theme in which you analyze how you have been affected by that crisis.

    b. (1) We all play many roles in our lives (daughter, student, friend, salesperson). Discuss a time when playing a role was good for you. Why was it good?

        or

        (2) Discuss a time when playing a role was bad for you. Why was it bad?

        or

        (3) Discuss a time when two of your roles conflicted.

    c. Choose a person not related to you who made you play a role that changed you. Discuss the situation and its effect on you.

    d. Think of a person to whom you react in a way that makes you like (or dislike) yourself. Describe this relationship and analyze why it happens.

    e. Think of a rule you had to obey or a condition under which you lived as a small child. Discuss how it has permanently affected you.

    f. Think of a time when you failed, and later succeeded (or vice versa), at an activity. Analyze what had happened in the interim to cause this change.

2. Problem-solving (Address these to the person who has the power to make the change.)

    a. Suggest and justify a physical change on campus.
    b. Suggest and justify a policy change at your school.
    c. Suggest a method for correcting a traffic problem.
    d. Make a consumer complaint.
    e. Suggest a method for correcting an environmental problem in your community.

3. Perceptions

    a. Observe closely a painting, print, or photograph (and hand in a copy). What effect does the artist project? Prove your conclusions with details drawn from the picture.

    b. Observe a public building from the outside, and then from the interior. How is it designed to be appropriate (or inappropriate) to its function?

    c. Without being noticed, observe a person whom you do not know. (Spend about twenty minutes just watching, ten minutes making notes.) From your observation, what is that person like?

    d. Without being noticed, observe two people together whom you do not know. (Again, observe and then make notes.) What is the nature of their relationship?

B. Put your draft aside for at least 24 hours; then evaluate it, using the check sheet.

C. Go over your draft with a member of your class. Consider his or her suggestions.

D. Rewrite your essay.

Section 2

READING AND REASONING: CRITICAL ANALYSIS

Critical Reading

6

In Section I, you practiced forming your ideas into clear communication, usually writing from your experience and perceptions. But often writing requires that you respond to the work of other writers. Thus you must become a critical reader. The first step in formulating arguments for or against another writer's ideas is to make sure you understand his message. Until you have an accurate perception of what an author has said and a grasp of the techniques he has used to emphasize it, you are not ready to express effectively your own ideas about his subject. The sections on understanding content, attitude, style, context, and logic that follow are designed to help you gain skill in reading accurately and critically. We will first examine some material to see *what* it says. Then we will analyze other material to see *how* it makes its points.

UNDERSTANDING CONTENT

Read the following essay, "The Enticers, 1970; On TV, Who Do They Think You Are?," by Stephanie Harrington. Read carefully and try to understand what she says, but do not take notes.

A free-lance writer, Stephanie Harrington (b. 1937) publishes frequently in popular magazines. This essay appeared in Vogue *in January 1970.*

The Enticers, 1970;
On TV, Who Do They Think You Are?
Stephanie Harrington

1   Television commercials may be many things to many people, but two things are obvious—they're an index to our anxieties and a boon to anthropology. What better crash course in the values, mores, fantasies—and particularly the fears—of Americans?

2   How do Americans feel about sex? Consult your network television commercial. Consider the teaser about "Lovestick," a lipstick "men can look at but they can't taste." Are we overly concerned with surface appearances? Just try adding up the amount of television time spent on pushing make-up, hair spray, perfume, hair tonic, hair rinses, fashions, foundations, and the other products under which we seem determined to bury any part of us that's more than skin deep—not to mention the skin itself. Are we obsessed with cleanliness? If you have any doubts, they'll be quickly drowned in the flood of suds spilling out of the commercials for detergents, floor cleaners, soap flakes, shampoos, bath soaps, facial soaps, baby soaps, scented soaps, unscented soaps, hypoallergenic soaps, deodorant soaps.

3   What's the state of our collective nerves? Evidently, bad enough to support the headache remedies, tension relievers, and sleeping pills that are a staple of television advertising. In fact, we seem positively to enjoy our headaches. After all, two of the funniest commercials ever broadcast have been for Alka–Seltzer and Excedrin.

4   On the other hand, the absence of commercials for certain items offers some indication of what does not particularly concern the mass of Americans. For instance, have you ever stopped to think why one of the few things not advertised on television is books?

5   But getting back to the question about sex. Just how do we see our attitude as it is bounced back to us through the television tube? Well, in addition to the look-but-don't-touch message, there is the gamesmanship pitch: "A woman can taunt you, tease you . . . should you give her another tactic? Should you give her Ambush [perfume] by Dana?" And, of course, the big television tease of all time was the Noxzema Shave Cream commercial with a sultry blond Swede whispering over her bare shoulder, "Take it off, take it all off." It's all in the double entendre.

6   On the other hand, there's the sadomasochism of the misogynous message from Silva Thins (cigarettes) in which beautiful women get pushed out of

cars or into descending elevators by a slick-looking stud in shades. And then there's the straightforward conquest by virile male of passive female implied in the Black Belt After Shave and Cologne [ad]. In that one, a fine figure of a karate expert brings his hand down on a pile of boards or bricks or something equally resistant and, as filmed in slow motion, gracefully, effortlessly—lovingly?—slices right through it.

7   Sex, then, as projected by the American mind for the American mind (to persuade it to keep the American dollar in motion) is a game, a tease, a test of wiles versus brawn, of ego against ego. Or just plain conquest and submission.

8   If we can believe what our commercials tell us (and can all those psychologists, sociologists, market researchers, and pollsters be wrong?), the basic attraction that sets this *mano a mano* in motion is not the attraction of one human being for another, but of one product for another. It's really a case of Aqua Velva After Shave falling madly in love with Wind Song Perfume. "I can't seem to forget you," whispers the lithe, luscious man in the Wind Song (by Prince Matchabelli) commercial. "Your Wind Song stays on my mind." "There's something about an Aqua Velva man," croons the kittenish female in a pitch for "the after-shave girls can't forget." Love at first sniff. Indeed, Aqua Velva is presented not merely as the key ingredient of a man's surface charm, but as the definition of the man himself. Use it, advises the commercial, "to bring out the Aqua Velva man in you." Or, the essence is the essence. Essence of Aqua Velva, that is.

9   Of course, commercials indicate not only that there is a growing male market for cosmetics, but also that there is still considerable resistance among men to using sissy stuff like cologne and hair spray, for fear of calling their masculinity into question. The angst of this particular American dilemma is reflected in reassuring he-man commercials showing one rocky-looking male after another doing a real *man's* work—like running a pile driver or driving a truck—and telling you that he uses hair spray. And if hair spray is manly enough for a two-hundred-pound truck driver, it's manly enough, isn't it? This transsexual operation on the image of formerly women-only cosmetics involves christening the products with strong, virile names like Black Belt or Command. Command hair spray and Command Tahitian Lime antiperspirant are "for men only," an aggressive male voice informs us, adding almost threateningly, *"And I mean for men only."*

10   The American romance with superficiality as documented in our commercials does, however, have occasional moments of deeper meaning. As in the ad for Alton Ames men's clothes, in which another of those Swedish sex kittens practically blows in our ears on the subject of her man's (their relationship is naughtily but safely ambiguous) Alton Ames suits, fondling them as she purrs. It's clear that it's the suit she loves, not the man. Indeed, she would probably love any man who put it on (even you, Mr. Average Television Viewer). But at least in this case the relationship is not between two products but between a person and a product.

11   Flesh-and-blood people lead very precarious lives on television commercials. They are in constant danger of being rubbed, scrubbed, slimmed,

trimmed and deodorized out of existence, leaving no traces. There are certainly no clues remaining in our clothes, which can be purified with detergents like Dash, which not only gets out easily removable "outside dirt," but tough "ground-in body dirt" as well.

12   Body dirt! Under the influence of the staggering number of soap commercials on television, we were so busy using detergents, pre-soaks, bleaches, and enzyme-active stain removers to get out soil, grease, paint, blood, grass stains, food stains, and goodness knows what else, that we might have forgotten all about body dirt, if Dash hadn't come along with its anti-body dirt ingredient. (And if your husband cleans a lot of fish, you might like to know that, according to another commercial, a fisherman's wife washed his apron in Procter and Gamble's Gain and lo! the "set-in, dried-in blood stains were virtually gone, gone!" Which is the next best thing to bloodless fish.)

To Keep Our Dark, Physical Secrets

13   Of course, if we would only be provident enough to use a good antiperspirant in the first place, we wouldn't have to worry so much about something like body dirt. There are certainly enough preventive products to choose from. Like Dial Soap "with AT7" (it always helps to throw in some scientific-sounding ingredient like AT7). Or "ice-blue Secret." The name itself promises to keep our dark, physical secrets.

14   The amount of television time taken up by commercials for products that clean, deodorize, disguise, and sometimes almost threaten to dissolve our bodies and whatever touches them seems to indicate that there is something about bodies that makes us nervous. True descendants of our Puritan forebears, we spend an impressive amount of time and energy—and pass a lot of money over the counter—trying to deny the animal in us. It scares us. And the American mind, both fashioner and product of the consumer society par excellence, has developed the notion that our fears and insecurities, like everything else, can be bought off. After all, as long as we have them, we might as well make a profit.

15   Scared of sex? Buy Ambush and turn it into a game. Do you worry about being drab, uninteresting? Afraid that beneath your surface there's just more surface? Terrified that your body odor will make you a wallflower at the PTA or get you read out of the Rotary?

16   Afraid of being rejected by the opposite sex? Write to good ole Fran, paradigm of advice-to-the-wretched columnists. Sympathetic, motherly, solid. Fran knows best and Fran will tell you to buy Lavoris. Or, if you're a go-go type who hasn't the time to stop and gargle, chew Dentyne and, like the girl in the commercial, have "the freshest mouth in town." And, so the implication goes, like the girl in the commercial, look smashing in a bikini and get kissed by the dreamiest guy on the beach. So what if you have a mouth full of gum?

17   We seem to have convinced ourselves that there's no end to the relief that can be bought. Even political relief. When the kids complain about the System trying to co-opt the revolution, they know what they're talking about.

When it became clear that youth was in revolt, that the black ghettos were organizing their own resistance, retaliation came with the Dodge Rebellion. If you can't lick 'em, join 'em. Join the Dodge Rebellion. Buy a Dodge. Feel like Che Guevara just driving to the country club.

18   Feel stranded on the far side of the generation gap? Relax. Buy a beer. A Ballantine. According to the commercial, the three-ring sign is "a happy sign" because "both the generations go for Ballantine." And to prove it, a neatly dressed young man, with hair just long enough to qualify as an under-thirty growth but not long enough to make anyone really nervous, is shown clinking glasses with someone definitely over thirty.

19   The ad men are even trying to buy off women's liberation by selling the resurgent female militants a cigarette: Virginia Slims. "You've come a long way, baby," says the commercial, as it traces the emancipation of the woman smoker who starts out sneaking a puff in the basement and ends up in a smashing sexy mod outfit, dangling a cigarette designed just for her.

20   The cigarette commercials in general have been rather subtle in their way. They seem to be selling fantasies. Smoke a Marlboro and be what you always wanted to be when you grew up—a cowboy. Or smoke a Salem and feel like you're in the country even when you're in the city. Smoke a Winston and find contentment by yourself in some secluded spot.

In Selling Fantasies, They, Too, Are Buying Off a Fear

21   Fear of contaminated lungs. Of cancer. Of heart disease. For, you notice, almost all these fantasies take place in the great outdoors where the air is fresh and clean. Smoking, they seem to be saying—turning the threat into an asset—is good for you, as well as a way to find fun, romance, and *machismo*.

22   But two can play at the commercial game; and, ironically, some of the cleverest and most effective television advertisements now running are the anti-smoking commercials. And when it comes to working on a fear, they have the most obvious target. So until the cigarette commercials are finally off the air, the anti-commercials may provide a reasonably potent antidote.

23   There will always be other commercials to fill the breach. We start them young, after all. Probably the loudest, shrillest, densest concentration of commercials is to be found on children's programs, which hustle whole families of dolls and wardrobes of clothes to buy for them. There are miniature race tracks and garages and dozens of miniature cars to fill them with. There are miniature appliances, miniature pots, pans, dishes, plastic food to cook, dolls that crawl, walk, dance, clap, drink, grow teeth. Anything to make a little girl feel that the doll she has is passé and simply has to be replaced.

24   But with all this emphasis on spending money to buy a sense of security, one of the things we seem most insecure about is spending money. For one thing, we're afraid we'll be taken advantage of. Like the poor schnook in the Volvo commercial who can't even trade in his old car at the place where he bought it. After some quick calculations, the very salesman who sold him the car tells him its trade-in value is zero. Now he tells him. Taken again. (The point is, of course, that this doesn't happen with Volvos. They last.)

25   The fear of being conned, however, is secondary. The soothing commercials that comfort us with the assurance that we'll find a friend at Chase Manhattan or Irving at Irving Trust suggest that what we are really terrified about is that one day we may run out of money. And then how could we buy, buy, buy our anxieties away?

26   With worries like that, no wonder we get Excedrin headaches.

Accurate reading demands that you understand any words, terms, or references used by the writer, that you find or state the thesis, and that you see what evidence the writer offers to prove that thesis. Looking back at "Enticers," perform the following exercises.

EXERCISES: Understanding Content (Harrington)

A. Define or explain the following words.

anthropology 1	par excellence 14
double entendre 5	paradigm 16
sadomasochism 6	co-opt 17
misogynous 6	resurgent 19
wiles 7	machismo 21
mano a mano 8	breach 23
angst 9	passé 23
precarious 11	

Are there other words, terms, or references in the essay that you should look up? Find their definitions or explanations.

B. Locate in the essay or state in your own words a sentence which expresses Harrington's thesis.

C. List the evidence and/or subtopics which Harrington uses to prove her thesis.

D. In performing Exercises A through C, you have picked out the kind of information (thesis, evidence, key terms) necessary for writing a *summary* of an essay. (A summary is a short, nonevaluative restatement of the main points of the essay.) Write a brief paragraph summarizing "Enticers." Do not include every example, but describe the types of evidence used.

    When you have finished, compare your summary with those of other class members. Look for accuracy and completeness.

E. Consider the following questions:

1. Does Harrington prove her thesis to you? Did you agree or disagree with her thesis before you read the rest of the essay?

2. This essay appeared in 1970. Has advertising changed since then? If so, in what ways? What current commercials might Harrington include?

Read the essay that follows, entitled "Contexts," by S. I. Hayakawa. Read carefully and try to understand what he says as you go along, but do not take notes.

S. I. Hayakawa (b. 1906) is well-known for his many books and articles on language. He was a Professor of English at San Francisco State and currently serves as a member of the United States Senate. "Contexts" is a chapter from his book Language in Thought and Action, *first published in 1939 and revised in 1963.*

Contexts
S. I. Hayakawa

How Dictionaries Are Made

1   It is widely believed that every word has a correct meaning, that we learn these meanings principally from teachers and grammarians (except that most of the time we don't bother to, so that we ordinarily speak "sloppy English"), and that dictionaries and grammars are the supreme authority in matters of meaning and usage. Few people ask by what authority the writers of dictionaries and grammars say what they say. I once got into a dispute with an Englishwoman over the pronunciation of a word and offered to look it up in the dictionary. The Englishwoman said firmly, "What for? I am English. I was born and brought up in England. The way I speak *is* English." Such self-assurance about one's own language is not uncommon among the English. In the United States, however, anyone who is willing to quarrel with the dictionary is regarded as either eccentric or mad.

2   Let us see how dictionaries are made and how the editors arrive at definitions. What follows applies, incidentally, only to those dictionary offices where first-hand, original research goes on—not those in which editors simply copy existing dictionaries. The task of writing a dictionary begins with reading vast amounts of the literature of the period or subject that the dictionary is to cover. As the editors read, they copy on cards every interesting or rare word, every unusual or peculiar occurrence of a common word, a large number of common words in their ordinary uses, and also the sentences in which each of these words appears, thus:

> pail
> The dairy *pails* bring home increase of milk
>
> Keats, *Endymion*
> I, 44–45

3   That is to say, the context of each word is collected, along with the word itself. For a really big job of dictionary-writing, such as the *Oxford English Dictionary* (usually bound in about twenty-five volumes), millions of such cards are collected, and the task of editing occupies decades. As the cards are collected, they are alphabetized and sorted. When the sorting is completed, there will be for each word anywhere from two or three to several hundred illustrative quotations, each on its card.

4   To define a word, then, the dictionary-editor places before him the stack of cards illustrating that word; each of the cards represents an actual use of the word by a writer of some literary or historical importance. He reads the cards carefully, discards some, rereads the rest, and divides up the stack according to what he thinks are the several senses of the word. Finally, he writes his definitions, following the hard-and-fast rule that each definition *must* be based on what the quotations in front of him reveal about the meaning of the word. The editor cannot be influenced by what *he* thinks a given word *ought* to mean. He must work according to the cards or not at all.

5   The writing of a dictionary, therefore, is not a task of setting up authoritative statements about the "true meanings" of words, but a task of *recording,* to the best of one's ability, what various words *have meant* to authors in the distant or immediate past. *The writer of a dictionary is a historian, not a lawgiver.* If, for example, we had been writing a dictionary in 1890, or even as late as 1919, we could have said that the word "broadcast" means "to scatter" (seed, for example), but we could not have decreed that from 1921 on, the most common meaning of the word should become "to disseminate audible messages, etc., by radio transmission." To regard the dictionary as an "authority," therefore, is to credit the dictionary-writer with gifts of prophecy which neither he nor anyone else possesses. In choosing our words when we speak or write, we can be *guided* by the historical record afforded us by the dictionary, but we cannot be *bound* by it, because new situations, new experiences, new inventions, new feelings are always compelling us to give new uses to old words. Looking under a "hood," we should ordinarily have found, five hundred years ago, a monk; today, we find a motorcar engine.[1]

---

[1] *Webster's Third New International Dictionary* lists the word "hood" also as a shortened form of "hoodlum."
  The time that elapsed between *Webster's Second Edition* (1934) and the *Third* (1961) indicates the enormous amount of reading and labor entailed in the preparation of a really thorough dictionary of a language as rapidly changing and as rich in vocabulary as English.

Verbal and Physical Contexts

6   The way in which the dictionary-writer arrives at his definitions merely systematizes the way in which we all learn the meanings of words, beginning at infancy and continuing for the rest of our lives. Let us say that we have never heard the word "oboe" before, and we overhear a conversation in which the following sentences occur:

> He used to be the best *oboe*-player in town. . . . Whenever they came to that *oboe* part in the third movement, he used to get very excited. . . . I saw him one day at the music shop, buying a new reed for his *oboe*. . . . He never liked to play the clarinet after he started playing the *oboe*. . . . He said it wasn't much fun, because it was too easy.

7   Although the word may be unfamiliar, its meaning becomes clear to us as we listen. After hearing the first sentence, we know that an "oboe" is "played," so that it must be either a game or a musical instrument. With the second sentence the possibility of its being a game is eliminated. With each succeeding sentence the possibilities as to what an "oboe" may be are narrowed down until we get a fairly clear idea of what is meant. This is how we learn by *verbal context*.

8   But even independently of this, we learn by physical and social context. Let us say that we are playing golf and that we have hit the ball in a certain way with certain unfortunate results, so that our companion says, "That's a bad *slice*." He repeats this remark every time our ball fails to go straight. If we are reasonably bright, we learn in a very short time to say, when it happens again, "That's a bad slice." On one occasion, however, our friend says, "That's not a *slice* this time; that's a *hook*." In this case we consider what has happened, and we wonder what is different about the last stroke from those previous. As soon as we make the distinction, we have added still another word to our vocabulary. The result is that after nine holes of golf, we can use both these words accurately—and perhaps several others as well, such as "divot," "number-five iron," "approach shot," *without ever having been told what they mean*. Indeed, we may play golf for years without ever being able to give a dictionary definition of "to slice": "To strike (the ball) so that the face of the club draws inward across the face of the ball, causing it to curve toward the right in flight (with a right-handed player)" *(Webster's New International Dictionary, Second Edition)*. But even without being able to give such a definition, we should still be able to use the word accurately whenever the occasion demands.

9   We learn the meanings of practically all our words (which are, it will be remembered, merely complicated noises), not from dictionaries, not from definitions, but from hearing these noises as they accompany actual situations in life and then learning to associate certain noises with certain situations. Even as dogs learn to recognize "words," as for example by hearing "biscuit" at the same time as an actual biscuit is held before their noses, so do we all learn to interpret language by being aware of the happenings that accompany the noises people make at us—by being aware, in short, of contexts.

10   The definitions given by little children in school show clearly how they associate words with situations; they almost always define in terms of physical and social contexts: "Punishment is when you have been bad and they put you in a closet and don't let you have any supper." "Newspapers are what the paper boy brings and you wrap up the garbage with it." These are good definitions. They cannot be used in dictionaries mainly because they are too specific; it would be impossible to list the myriads of situations in which every word has been used. For this reason, dictionaries give definitions on a high level of abstraction, that is, with particular references left out for the sake of conciseness. (The term "high level of abstraction" is more fully explained in Chapter 10.) This is another reason why it is a great mistake to regard a dictionary definition as telling us all about a word.

Extensional and Intensional Meaning

11   Dictionaries deal with the world of intensional meanings, but there is another world which a dictionary by its very nature ignores: the world of extensional meanings. *The extensional meaning of an utterance is that which it points to in the extensional (physical) world,* referred to in Chapter 2. That is to say, the extensional meaning cannot be expressed in words because it is that which words stand for. An easy way to remember this is *to put your hand over your mouth and point* whenever you are asked to give an extensional meaning.

12   Of course, we cannot always point to the extensional meanings of the words we use. Therefore, so long as we are *discussing* meanings, we shall refer to that which is being talked about as the *denotation* of an utterance. For example, the denotation of the word "Winnipeg" is the prairie city of that name in southern Manitoba; the denotation of the word "dog" is a class of animals which includes dog_1 (Fido), dog_2 (Rex), dog_3 (Rover) . . . dog_n.

13   The *intensional meaning* of a word or expression, on the other hand, is that which is *suggested* (connoted) inside one's head. Roughly speaking, whenever we express the meanings of words by uttering more words, we are giving intensional meanings or connotations. To remember this, put your hand over your eyes and let the words spin around in your head.

14   Utterances may have, of course, both extensional and intensional meaning. If they have no intensional meaning at all—that is, if they start no notions whatever spinning about in our heads—they are meaningless noises, like foreign languages that we do not understand. On the other hand, it is possible for utterances to have no extensional meaning at all, in spite of the fact that they may start many notions spinning about in our heads. The statement, "Angels watch over my bed at night," is one that has intensional but no extensional meaning. This does not mean that there are no angels watching over my bed at night. When we say that the statement has no extensional meaning, we are merely saying that it is not operational, that we cannot see, touch, photograph, or in any scientific manner detect the presence of angels. The result is that, if an argument begins on the subject of whether or not angels watch over my bed, *there is no way of ending the argument to the satisfaction* *of all disputants,* the Christians and the non-Christians, the pious and the agnostic, the mystical and the scientific. Therefore, whether we believe in angels or not, knowing in advance that any argument on the subject will be both endless and futile, we can avoid getting into fights about it.

15   When, on the other hand, statements have extensional content, as when we say, "This room is fifteen feet long," arguments can come to a close. No matter how many guesses there are about the length of the room, all discussion ceases when someone produces a tape measure. This, then, is the important difference between extensional and intensional meanings: namely, when utterances have extensional meanings, discussion can be ended and agreement reached; when utterances have intensional meanings only and no extensional meanings, arguments may, and often do, go on indefinitely. Such arguments can result only in conflict. Among individuals, they may break up friendships; in society, they often split organizations into bitterly opposed groups; among nations, they may aggravate existing tensions so seriously as to become real obstacles to the peaceful settling of disputes.

16   Arguments of this kind may be termed "non-sense arguments," because they are based on utterances about which no sense data can be collected. Needless to say, there are occasions when the hyphen may be omitted—that depends on one's feelings toward the particular argument under consideration. The reader is requested to provide his own examples of "non-sense arguments." Even the foregoing example of the angels may give offense to some people, despite the fact that no attempt is made to deny or affirm the existence of angels. Imagine, then, the uproar that might result from giving a number of examples from theology, politics, law, economics, literary criticism, and other fields in which it is not customary to distinguish clearly sense from non-sense.

The "One Word, One Meaning" Fallacy

17   Everyone, of course, who has ever given any thought to the meanings of words has noticed that they are always shifting and changing in meaning. Usually, people regard this as a misfortune, because it "leads to sloppy thinking" and "mental confusion." To remedy this condition, they are likely to suggest that we should all agree on "one meaning" for each word and use it only with that meaning. Thereupon it will occur to them that we simply cannot make people agree in this way, even if we could set up an ironclad dictatorship under a committee of lexicographers who would place censors in every newspaper office and microphones in every home. The situation, therefore, appears hopeless.

18   Such an impasse is avoided when we start with a new premise altogether—one of the premises upon which modern linguistic thought is based: namely, that *no word ever has exactly the same meaning twice.*[2] The extent to which this premise fits the facts can be demonstrated in a number of

---

[2] In the same vein, the Greek philosopher Heraclitus argued that one cannot step into the same river twice.

ways. First, if we accept the proposition that the contexts of an utterance determine its meaning, it becomes apparent that since no two contexts are ever *exactly* the same, no two meanings can ever be exactly the same. How can we "fix the meaning" even for so common an expression as "to believe in" when it can be used in such sentences as the following:

> I believe in you (I have confidence in you).
> I believe in democracy (I accept the principles implied by the term democracy).
> I believe in Santa Claus (It is my opinion that Santa Claus exists).

19   Second, we can take a word of "simple" meaning, like "kettle," for example. But when John says "kettle," its intensional meanings to him are the common characteristics of all the kettles John remembers. When Peter says "kettle," however, its intensional meanings to him are the common characteristics of all the kettles he remembers. *No matter how small or how negligible the differences may be between John's "kettle" and Peter's "kettle," there is some difference.*

20   Finally, let us examine utterances in terms of extensional meanings. If John, Peter, Harold, and George each say "my typewriter," we would have to point to four different typewriters to get the extensional meaning in each case: John's new Olivetti, Peter's old Remington, Harold's portable Smith-Corona, and the undenotable intended "typewriter" that George plans to buy someday: "My typewriter, when I buy it, will be an electric." Also, if John says "my typewriter" today, and again "my typewriter" tomorrow, the extensional meaning is different in the two cases, because the typewriter is not exactly the same from one day to the next (nor from one minute to the next): slow processes of wear, change, and decay are going on constantly. Although we can say, then, that the differences in the meanings of a word on one occasion, on another occasion a minute later, and on still another occasion another minute later are negligible, we cannot say that the meanings are *exactly* the same.

21   To insist dogmatically that we know what a word means *in advance of its utterance* is nonsense. All we can know in advance is *approximately* what it will mean. After the utterance, we interpret what has been said in the light of both verbal and physical contexts and act according to our interpretation. An examination of the verbal context of an utterance, as well as the examination of the utterance itself, directs us to the intensional meanings; an examination of the physical context directs us to the extensional meanings. When John says to James, "Bring me that book, will you?" James looks in the direction of John's pointed finger (physical context) and sees a desk with several books on it (physical context); he thinks back over their previous conversation (verbal context) and knows which of those books is being referred to.

22   Interpretation *must* be based, therefore, on the totality of contexts. If it were otherwise, we should not be able to account for the fact that even if we fail to use the right (customary) words in some situations, people can very frequently understand us. For example:

> A: Gosh, look at that second baseman go!
> B: (looking): You mean the shortstop?
> A: Yes, that's what I mean.

A: There must be something wrong with the oil line; the engine has started to balk.

B: Don't you mean "gas line"?

A: Yes—didn't I say "gas line"?

Contexts often indicate our meaning so clearly that we do not even have to say what we mean in order to be understood.

Ignoring Contexts

23   It is clear, then, that the ignoring of contexts in any act of interpretation is at best a stupid practice. At its worst, it can be a vicious practice. A common example is the sensationalistic newspaper story in which a few words by a public personage are torn out of their context and made the basis of a completely misleading account. There is the incident of a Veterans Day speaker, a university teacher, who declared before a high school assembly that the Gettysburg Address was "a powerful piece of propaganda." The context clearly revealed that "propaganda" was being used, not according to its popular meaning, but rather, as the speaker himself stated, to mean "explaining the moral purposes of a war." The context also revealed that the speaker was a very great admirer of Lincoln. However, the local newspaper, ignoring the context, presented the account in such a way as to suggest that the speaker had called Lincoln a liar. On this basis, the newspaper began a campaign against the instructor. The speaker remonstrated with the editor of the newspaper, who replied, in effect, "I don't care what else you said. You said the Gettysburg Address was propaganda, didn't you?" This appeared to the editor complete proof that Lincoln had been maligned and that the speaker deserved to be discharged from his position at the university. Similar practices may be found in advertisements. A reviewer may be quoted on the jacket of a book as having said "A brilliant work," while reading of the context may reveal that what he really said was, "It just falls short of being a brilliant work." There are some people who will always be able to find a defense for such a practice in saying, "But he did use the words 'a brilliant work,' didn't he?"

24   People in the course of argument very frequently complain about words meaning different things to different people. Instead of complaining, they should accept such differences as a matter of course. It would be startling indeed if the word "justice," for example, were to have the same meaning to each of the nine justices of the United States Supreme Court; we should get nothing but unanimous decisions. It would be even more startling if "justice" meant the same thing in the United States as it does in Russia. If we can get deeply into our consciousness the principle that no word ever has the same meaning twice, we will develop the habit of automatically examining contexts, and this will enable us to understand better what others are saying. As it is, however, we are all too likely, when a word sounds familiar, to assume that we understand it, even when we don't. In this way we read into people's remarks meanings that were never intended. Then we waste energy in angrily accusing people of "intellectual dishonesty" or "abuse of words," when their only sin is that they use words in ways unlike our own, as they can hardly help doing, especially if their background has been widely different from

ours. There are cases of intellectual dishonesty and abuse of words, of course, but they do not always occur in the places where people think they do.

25   In the study of history or of cultures other than our own, contexts take on special importance. To say, "There was no running water or electricity in the house," does not condemn an English house in 1570 but says a great deal against a house in Chicago in 1970. Again, if we wish to understand the Constitution of the United States, it is not enough, as our historians now tell us, merely to look up all the words in the dictionary and to read the interpretations written by Supreme Court justices. We must see the Constitution in its historical context: the conditions of life, the state of the arts and industries and transportation, the climate of opinion of the time—all of which helped to determine what words went into the Constitution and what those words meant to those who wrote them. After all, the words "United States of America" stood for quite a different-sized nation and a different culture in 1790 from what they stand for today. When it comes to very big subjects, the range of contexts to be examined—verbal, social, and historical—may become very large indeed.

26   In personal relations, furthermore, those who ignore psychological contexts often make the mistake of interpreting as insults remarks that are only intended in jest.

The Interaction of Words

27   All this is not to say, however, that the reader might just as well throw away his dictionary simply because contexts are so important. Any word in a sentence—any sentence in a paragraph, any paragraph in a larger unit—whose meaning is revealed by its context is itself part of the context of the rest of the text. To look up a word in a dictionary, therefore, frequently explains not only the word itself but the rest of the sentence, paragraph, conversation, or essay in which it is found. All words within a given context interact with one another.

28   Realizing, then, that a dictionary is a historical work, we should understand the dictionary thus: "The word *mother* has most frequently been used in the past among English-speaking people to indicate a female parent." From this we can safely infer, "If that is how it has been used, that is what it *probably* means in the sentence I am trying to understand." This is what we normally do, of course; after we look up a word in the dictionary, we reexamine the context to see if the definition fits. If the context reads, "Mother began to form in the bottle," one may have to look at the dictionary more carefully.

29   A dictionary definition, therefore, is an invaluable guide to interpretation. Words do not have a single "correct meaning"; they apply to *groups* of similar situations, which might be called *areas of meaning*. It is for defining these areas of meaning that a dictionary is useful. In each use of any word, we examine the particular context and the extensional events denoted (if possible) to discover the *point* intended within the area of meaning.

Now that you have finished reading the essay, write a summary of

Hayakawa's ideas. Assume that the summary should remind you two weeks from now what the essay said and also should inform someone who has not read the essay. After you have written your summary, put it aside while you complete the following exercises about "Contexts."

EXERCISES: Understanding Content (Hayakawa)

A. Define or explain the following words.
    1. context   3
    2. intensional meaning   11
    3. extensional meaning   11
    4. denotation   12
    5. connotation   13

    Are there other words, terms, or references in the essay that you should look up? Find their definitions or explanations.

B. Locate in the essay or state in your own words a sentence which expresses Hayakawa's thesis.

C. List the evidence which Hayakawa uses in "Contexts" to prove his thesis.

D. Analyze your summary. Is it hampered by your lack of understanding of any of Hayakawa's key words? Does it include his thesis? Does it briefly remind you of the evidence which he used? Have you been inaccurate in any way? If necessary, revise your summary to make it complete and accurate.

E. Here are summaries written by students who have read "Contexts." Which is the best? How does it compare with yours? What problems do you see in the others?
    1. This write-up is a selection from S. I. Hayakawa, a professor in language arts. He talks about words and their different functions throughout the years. He writes about how words have many different contexts and meanings. He stresses that there is no one complete definition for a word, and we should not depend on a dictionary for word definitions. Hayakawa believes a dictionary is useful for defining "areas of meaning."
    2. We learn the meaning of practically all our words not from dictionaries, not from definitions, but from hearing these noises as they accompany actual situations in life. The extensional meaning of an utterance is that which points to something in the extensional world (physical). Extensional meaning cannot be expressed

in words. When we express the meaning of a word by uttering more words, we are expressing intensional meaning. The importance or meaning of a word depends more on how it is used than the denotation of the word.

3. "It is widely believed that every word has a correct meaning, that we learn these meanings principally from teachers and grammarians, and that dictionaries and grammars are the supreme authority in matters of meaning and usages." S. I. Hayakawa shows examples of different types of usage in this essay, language types such as verbal, physical, extensional, and intensional. He explains the "one word, one meaning" fallacy, ignoring the context and interaction of words. He also shows how a dictionary is formulated and put together through research of many people, not just one.

4. In his essay "Contexts," S. I. Hayakawa discusses the ways in which we learn the meanings of words. He believes that the dictionary can only give a historical record of what a word has meant in the past, but does not really inform the reader of the entire meaning of the word right at this moment. He goes on to explain that people can only know the true meanings of words when they experience them in verbal, physical, and social contexts. Yet, even then words can be used in so many different ways it is impossible to ever know all the meanings of any one word. It is then useful to examine the contexts that words are used in to help in determining as nearly as possible their intended meaning.

5. S. I. Hayakawa's selection called "Contexts" is talking about the changes in words and word forms. He breaks his selection up into categories: How Dictionaries Are Made, Verbal and Physical Contexts, Extensional and Intensional Meaning, The "One Word, One Meaning" Fallacy, Ignoring Contexts, and The Interaction of Words. He makes it clear a context of a word or sentence can have different meanings and you cannot depend on a dictionary.

F. Here are some questions which you may wish to discuss with classmates who have also read "Contexts":

1. Where does Hayakawa state his thesis?

2. What does the writer accomplish by opening his essay with the material on writing a dictionary? Why does he describe the process instead of giving us his opinion that dictionaries should not be cited as final authorities? Was this a new idea for you? What do you think of it?

3. Why do you think Hayakawa uses many examples drawn from everyday life (for example, ¶s 8 and 10)?

4. What is the purpose of ¶ 23?

5. What is the purpose of ¶ 29?

6. What is the effect of the subheadings?

G. Read "What It Would Be Like if Women Win" by Gloria Steinem, pp. 287–92 in the collection, and summarize it accurately.

UNDERSTANDING ATTITUDE

In order to understand fully a writer's work, you need to be aware of his attitude toward his subject as well as to comprehend the content of his subject. Does he have positive or negative feelings? Does he approve or disapprove? What reaction to the subject does his writing cause in you? How can you tell his feelings?

Read the following excerpt from a weekly newsmagazine. The writer is discussing President Johnson's explanation of his policies in Vietnam.

> All week he pushed the point, parading State's Dean Rusk and the Pentagon's Robert McNamara through a public defense of his course in the White House lobby and a series of private briefings for Congressional leaders. The briefings followed a set scenario. McNamara opened with a computerized rundown on the military arithmetic, followed invariably by a Rusk exhortation to back the boys at the front—and a pledge: "We shall win!" The performance brought standing ovations for Rusk—and left dovish congressmen sitting in bemused silence.

How does this writer feel about his subject? Does he approve of what he describes? How do you know? Word choice.

Denotative and Connotative Meanings

Certain words in the selection above are often used to discuss a performance: "parading," "scenario," "exhortation," "performance," "standing ovations." These words seem to suggest that the briefings and public statements were part of an act, not the honest behavior that most people want from their government leaders. Adding to this idea are the words that suggest this "performance" was always the same: "all week," "set," "invariably." The writer also uses phrases which suggest a robotlike quality ("computerized rundown," "military arithmetic"), as if Mr. McNamara were interested only in statistics. On the other hand, Mr. Rusk's speech is summarized with a cliché, "back the boys at the front," suggesting that his responses were also hackneyed, and the only quotation ("We shall win!") is hardly a memorable phrase. The importance of the two men is also minimized by saying they were *paraded* and by using possessive nouns instead of titles before their names. In light of this evidence, would you agree that the writer has a negative attitude toward his subject?

Here is the paragraph as it has been rewritten by students who wanted to give it a positive attitude:

> For the past week President Johnson, with the help of Secretary of State Dean Rusk and Defense Secretary Robert McNamara, has been defending the administration's policy concerning the war in Indochina through a series of press conferences and private briefings for congressional leaders. Mr. McNamara gave a precise account of the military status while Secretary Rusk expressed confidence in meeting the objectives set forth by the present administration. Rusk encouraged those present to support the military effort overseas. Many congressmen expressed approval of the policy illustrated by McNamara and Rusk.

The student writers have not changed the information, yet they have greatly altered the outlook on the subject. This version suggests that the briefings were open and informative and that the speakers were dignified and responsible. What is the difference? Only the word choice.

Often words may have almost the same meaning, but are certainly not interchangeable. That is, their *denotation* (dictionary meaning) is the same, but their *connotation* (suggestion, association) is different. List words that mean "a human female" or "a human male"; then categorize them. You will find that some terms are positive, some are negative; some are formal, some informal. Some are cold; others are endearing. The differences occur in the connotations. Just as you avoid using words with the wrong dictionary meanings (denotation), you must be equally careful not to use words with inappropriate associations (connotation). For example, you would probably be very careful not to call some "gentleman" a "dude" or a "hunk."

The following newspaper article disapproves of one part of its subject and approves of another part. See if you can pick out the connotative language that reveals these attitudes.

Censor Still Under Wraps

WASHINGTON—(UPI) President Nixon has been asked to identify the standby director of censorship who would be empowered to screen news for the government in the event of a national emergency.

Samuel J. Archibald of the Washington office of the Freedom of Information Center at the University of Missouri made the request. He said he learned unofficially that the standby censor was "a lobbyist for one of the giant corporations."

The official was appointed by former President Lyndon B. Johnson, but his identity carried a "security classification." Archibald said the public has a right to know who its censors are if a democratic society has to submit to censorship in an emergency.

It is likely that the highly connotative words you have chosen work together to give the article a *bias* or *slant* toward Mr. Archibald and against the censor and those who shield him. Biased or slanted language is not necessarily bad (in fact, it is to some degree unavoidable), but you should be aware that it is being used. For example, both of the items we have studied were drawn not from editorial or opinion sections but from the "straight news" sections of the magazine and newspaper. It can be very risky to accept a writer's information without paying attention to his attitude.

Another device which strengthens the writer's impact in this last article is his use of *loaded words*. Loaded words are those which almost automatically draw a strong response from most members of a particular society. Examples here are "censor," "freedom," and "democratic." Other examples of loaded words are "mother," "home," "cancer," "death." Note others as you think of them or find them in your reading.

Tone

Closely related to a writer's attitude is his *tone*. As we have seen, the attitude will be positive, negative, or (infrequently) neutral, but this attitude can be reinforced and refined by using any of a variety of tones. A negative attitude might be shown through an angry, ironic, somber, pessimistic, sad, or sarcastic tone. A positive attitude could be revealed in an amusing, enthusiastic, serious, admiring, or light tone. The tone is created by the writer's style—his word choice and sentence structure. How would you describe the tone in each of the following paragraphs concerning the same event?

> It is tragically inexcusable that this young athlete was not examined fully before he was allowed to join the varsity team. The physical examinations given were unbelievably sloppy. What were the coach and the trainer thinking of not to insist that each young man be examined while undergoing physical stress? Do we dare to trust our sons and daughters to a system so bent on victory that it ignores the health of our children?

> It was learned last night that none of the players was given a stress test as part of his physical examination. The oversight was attributed to laxness by the coach and trainer, who are described today as being "distraught." It is the judgment of many that the entire physical education program must be rigorously reexamined with an eye to the safety and health of all students.

> How can I express the loss I feel over the death of my son? I want to blame someone, but who is to blame? The coaches, for not administering more rigorous physical check-ups? Why should they have done more than other coaches have done in the past or than other coaches are doing at other schools? My son, for not telling me or the coaches that he "felt funny" after practice? His teammates, for not telling the coaches that he casually mentioned to them how he felt? Myself, for not knowing somehow that something was wrong with my only child? Who is to blame? All of us and none of us. Blaming won't help us now anyway.

EXERCISES: Understanding Attitude

A. Read the following newspaper column, taking care to look up any words or references which you do not understand.

Kennedy and Strauss: Clearing Up a Misunderstanding

1   Democratic National Chairman Robert S. Strauss paid a secret emergency visit to Sen. Edward Kennedy on Capitol Hill at noon Tuesday to patch up a serious misunderstanding that exposed a caldron of dangerous problems seething beneath the flimsy lid of party unity.

2   The misunderstanding concerned a televised interview in Dallas. Saying more than a party chairman should, Strauss was drawn into speculation about problems to be considered by Kennedy in deciding whether to run for president. This was grossly distorted in inaccurate press accounts as blunt criticism of Kennedy by Strauss. Once Kennedy was shown the transcript of the interview, his relationship with Strauss—if not quite what it was a week earlier—at least returned to surface amiability.

3   But left-wing partisans in the Democratic Party have seized on the incident as their first opening to attack Strauss in his more than a year as chairman, revealing how fragile is the fabric of unity Strauss has labored to weave. Moreover, the political combustibility of Ted Kennedy—the party's most popular, powerful and controversial figure—has been underscored.

4   On Friday, Jan. 18, in Strauss's home town, he went to TV station WFAA to tape "Face to Face" to be shown the next evening. Interviewer Murphy Morton pondered out loud whether the Chappaquiddick tragedy made it "problematical for Sen. Kennedy to run in the wake of Watergate" and then asked Strauss: "Would you care to comment on it?"

5   Savvy party pro Strauss should have ducked instinctively. Instead, he gave this reply (quoted here in full): "I think that's a concern and I think it's going to be written and talked about more and more. I primarily think that Sen. Kennedy has a number of personal problems with which he's beset. He's responsible as the only member of a very large family with a lot of children. He has a son who is ill and who had very serious surgery. And I talk to Ted Kennedy regularly and he doesn't know what he's going to do and he hasn't made up his mind, so it's silly for me to try to speculate about him."

6   But the account distributed nationally by the Associated Press gave a far different impression. Strauss was quoted as calling Kennedy "questionable as a candidate" for president and contending there is a "valid concern" about his candidacy. Contrary to the transcript, the AP story said Strauss "listed" Kennedy's "problems as including Chappaquiddick."

7   When this story appeared in morning newspapers last Monday (under the headline "Strauss Hits Kennedy as '76 Candidate" in *The Washington Post*), Democratic politicians were stunned—none more than Ted Kennedy and Bob Strauss.

8   Strauss telephoned Kennedy's Washington office Monday morning and found that Paul Kirk, Kennedy's quietly tough aide, was not happy. Strauss read the transcript to him, but several telephone calls to Kennedy's office convinced the chairman that the attitude there remained frigid. Consequently, Strauss traveled to Capitol Hill Tuesday noon, calling Kennedy off the Senate floor for a private conversation.

9   Shown the transcript, Kennedy was convinced Strauss meant him no ill will and was trying to be fair (though, the senator added, the chairman's answer to the interviewer might have been a little more positive about Kennedy's accomplishments). In good humor, he introduced Strauss to a passerby as "my new campaign manager." Kennedy later told us Strauss "has always been fair and even-handed toward me."

10   One diehard Kennedyite in New York was stunned reading the story in Monday's *New York Daily News,* figuring Strauss had begun a conservative drive to discredit Kennedy and push Sen. Henry M. Jackson. But after reading the actual transcript, he agreed "a job has been done on Strauss."

11   Others are not so fair-minded; one close-in Kennedy advisor insists in the face of facts he can see "no big difference" between the news story and the transcript. Moreover, liberal activists who originally opposed Strauss for chairman now ignore his fastidiousness in preserving factional and ideological neutrality. Seizing on this first opening, they now assault him as a Kennedy-hating Neanderthal.

12   Their attitude confirms warnings from Strauss's allies who feel Strauss has been too optimistic about Texas soft soap and compromises as a cure for the great Democratic schism of 1972. Indeed, the left's Pavlovian fury at the sight of Strauss's blood indicates it remains very much unappeased by him.

13   Strauss tells friends his wounds may be "incurable." One key advisor hopes the chairman has learned a valuable lesson: "Hold thy tongue." But, in truth, top-level Democrats talk in private every day about Kennedy's political debits, including Chappaquiddick. It is now clearer than ever that these debits cannot be alluded to in public, even indirectly, by a party leader.

Rowland Evans and Robert Novak
The Washington Post, Jan. 26, 1974

1.   How do the writers feel toward Strauss? List the words and phrases which reveal this attitude.

2.   How do the writers feel toward Kennedy? List the words and phrases which reveal this attitude.

3.   How do the writers feel toward Democratic liberals? List the words and phrases which reveal this attitude.

4.   How would you describe the writers' tone?

B.   Now that you have finished your analysis of the writers' attitudes, evaluate these essays written by students on the attitudes expressed by Evans and Novak in the column. Does each have a clear thesis? Is the evidence relevant and sufficient? Does each have an accurate view of the column?

Evans and Novak: Clearing Up a Misunderstanding?

1   The language of the Evans-Novak article is slanted pro-Strauss and anti-liberal, while remaining basically neutral toward Kennedy.

2   Kennedy is shown as an affable, good-natured fellow, a "popular" figure "in good humor" after the misunderstanding has supposedly been cleared up (Kennedy's aides, not Kennedy, are described as "frigid"). The writers admit he has his political "debits" and is a "controversial" and "combustible" figure; however, this seems less a description of Kennedy than a recognition of problems faced by the Democratic party and acknowledgment of a popular viewpoint.

3   The writers take quite a different view of the "left-wing partisans," the liberals who are referred to as "activists," who are not seen as being "fair-minded." They are shown as being less sophisticated than Strauss, even to the point of being considered primitive. Strauss's remark is their "first opening to attack" Strauss; they are also depicted as "seizing on this first opening." The writers manage to create an image of Strauss as vulnerable prey to the predatory and animalistic liberals. Their "Pavlovian fury at the sight of Strauss's blood" indicates a violent, base response to a simple human error. Strauss's "wounds" are liberal-inflicted, yet the liberals remain "unappeased"—surely an illogical (at best) attitude, condemned by the authors.

The Great Misquote

1   With modern means of instant communication, great effort must be taken to report the news accurately. People can easily be misquoted and as a consequence their remarks may be taken out of context. This news column, written by Rowland Evans and Robert Novak for *The Washington Post*, concerns a problem which can arise from misunderstanding. The attitudes of Novak and Evans are favorable toward Strauss, hostile toward the liberals, and neutral and factual toward Kennedy.

2   Besides favoring Strauss, the writers scold him at the same time, "saying more than a party chairman should," and saying he "should have ducked instinctively" when referring to his interview with Murphy Morton of television station WFAA. They appear to scold him because they call him "savvy party pro," which means they have a great deal of respect for him as a knowledgeable professional in politics and therefore Strauss should not have left himself open for criticism. By saying Strauss was "drawn into speculation," Evans and Novak give the impression of an unsuspecting man being forced to comment on a particular aspect of Kennedy's life. Readers are inclined to side with Strauss because he was obviously misquoted. The misquote forced Strauss to call "Kennedy off the Senate floor for a private conversation" in order to prove there was "no ill will." The fact that Evans and Novak mentioned the efforts of Strauss to set the record straight gives us a favorable impression of Strauss.

3   Novak and Evans were hostile toward the liberals in their choice of words when referring to their actions. Words such as "seized," "assault," and "attack" suggest violence. When speaking of the liberals, the writers make it clear that the liberals are against Strauss and refer to them as "left-wing partisans." This means they are radical in nature and biased in

thought. The writers claim the liberals "assault him [Strauss] as a Kennedy-hating Neanderthal." This is hardly a friendly gesture. The word "assault" implies that the liberals are violent and hostile people.

4   When speaking of Kennedy, the writers never really take a stand for him or against him. They seem to take a neutral position. Meaningful words such as "popular," "powerful," and "controversial" are used when speaking of Kennedy. These remarks are only factual. It was known that Kennedy was the "party's most popular." These good points mentioned when speaking of Kennedy were neutralized by his "political debits," such as Chappaquiddick.

5   This column was primarily based on the writers' attempt to support Strauss and his effort to maintain "the fabric of unity" that he had "labored to weave." Despite the emphasis given to the liberal activists' attempt to "assault" Strauss, Evans and Novak point out a lesson well worth learning, that is, what to say when and where. Many issues may be continually discussed in private and behind closed doors but should be left unsaid in public by party leaders or officials.

WRITING ASSIGNMENT

Read "The Tarnished Age," found on pp. 308–11 in the collection of essays. When you are certain that you have fully understood what the writer is saying, write a theme showing how he reveals his attitude toward his subject by the language which he uses. Assume that your audience has read and understood the essay.

Other Devices

In addition to connotative language and tone, writers may reinforce their attitudes in other ways. It would be impossible to list every method, but we can discuss some of the most common. A writer may place a phrase in quotation marks and thus question its validity, as in the censorship article (p. 92) when the writer mentions "security classification." The phrase "so-called" can create the same effect. Italics or underlining can emphasize a particular word and thus its connotation. Sentence structure can reveal a writer's attitude. A series of questions could suggest doubts about the subject. An overly simple sentence structure is sometimes used to show that the writer thinks his subject is silly or childish or insulting.

> See the nice moviestar. See the nice moviestar come into the room and smile. See the public applaud and pay money.

Organization can emphasize or play down a point. Is the idea discussed at the beginning or end of an essay or paragraph, or is it buried in the middle? The amount of development tells something about how a writer feels toward his subject. He can examine an idea thoroughly, or he can dismiss it briefly. As you read and analyze attitudes, you can add other methods to this list.

In this section on understanding attitude, we have used writing about politics and government as examples not because it is the only slanted writing, but because the slanting is often so obvious that the techniques are easy to spot. However, almost any material written on any subject will be biased by the writer's attitude. Possible exceptions include purely technical writing such as recipes, mechanical processes, and directions, but even these imply that their way is best.

Should writers slant, either blatantly or subtly, their writing? First, since words are inseparable from their connotations, and the writer must choose some words and not others, he cannot help slanting his work. Second, because the best writers have a strong sense of purpose, they will slant their work in order to convince you, the reader. Therefore, the question changes. Should readers know how to perceive a writer's bias? Of course. To practice discerning a more subtly expressed attitude, read "The Computer and the Poet" by Norman Cousins, noting the devices he uses to express his feelings toward his subjects.

Norman Cousins (b. 1912), a much-honored author, has been the editor of Saturday Review *since 1940. He has long been an advocate of educational television and radio. "The Computer and the Poet" appeared in* Saturday Review, *July 23, 1966.*

The Computer and the Poet
Norman Cousins

1   The essential problem of man in a computerized age remains the same as it has always been. That problem is not solely how to be more productive, more comfortable, more content, but how to be more sensitive, more sensible, more proportionate, more alive. The computer makes possible a phenomenal leap in human proficiency; it demolishes the fences around the practical and even the theoretical intelligence. But the question persists and indeed grows whether the computer will make it easier or harder for human beings to know who they really are, to identify their real problems, to respond more fully to beauty, to place adequate value on life, and to make their world safer than it now is.

2   Electronic brains can reduce the profusion of dead ends involved in vital research. But they can't eliminate the foolishness and decay that come from the unexamined life. Nor do they connect a man to the things he has to be connected to—the reality of pain in others; the possibilities of creative growth in himself; the memory of the race; and the rights of the next generation.

3   The reason these matters are important in a computerized age is that there may be a tendency to mistake data for wisdom, just as there has always been a tendency to confuse logic with values, and intelligence with insight. Unobstructed access to facts can produce unlimited good only if it is matched by the desire and ability to find out what they mean and where they would lead.

4   Facts are terrible things if left sprawling and unattended. They are too easily regarded as evaluated certainties rather than as the rawest of raw materials crying to be processed into the texture of logic. It requires a very unusual mind, Whitehead said, to undertake the analysis of a fact. The computer can provide a correct number, but it may be an irrelevant number until judgment is pronounced.

5   To the extent, then, that man fails to make the distinction between the intermediate operations of electronic intelligence and the ultimate responsibilities of human decision and conscience, the computer could prove a digression. It could obscure man's awareness of the need to come to terms with himself. It may foster the illusion that he is asking fundamental questions when actually he is asking only functional ones. It may be regarded as a substitute for intelligence instead of an extension of it. It may promote undue confidence in concrete answers. "If we begin with certainties," Bacon said, "we shall end in doubts but if we begin with doubts, and we are patient with them, we shall end in certainties."

6   The computer knows how to vanquish error, but before we lose ourselves in celebration of the victory, we might reflect on the great advances in the human situation that have come about because men were challenged by error and would not stop thinking and probing until they found better approaches for dealing with it. "Give me a good fruitful error, full of seeds, bursting with its own corrections," Ferris Greenslet wrote. "You can keep your sterile truth for yourself."

7   The biggest single need in computer technology is not for improved circuitry, or enlarged capacity, or prolonged memory, or miniaturized containers, but for better questions and better use of the answers. Without taking anything away from the technicians, we think it might be fruitful to effect some sort of junction between the computer technologist and the poet. A genuine purpose may be served by turning loose the wonders of the creative imagination on the kinds of problems being put to electronic tubes and transistors. The company of poets may enable the men who tend the machines to see a larger panorama of possibilities than technology alone may inspire.

8   A poet, said Aristotle, has the advantage of expressing the universal; the specialist expresses only the particular. The poet, moreover, can remind us that man's greatest energy comes not from his dynamos but from his dreams. The notion of where a man ought to be instead of where he is; the liberation from cramped prospects; the intimations of immortality through art—all these proceed naturally out of dreams. But the quality of a man's dreams can only be a reflection of his subconscious. What he puts into his subconscious, therefore, is quite literally the most important nourishment in the world.

9   Nothing really happens to a man except as it is registered in the subconscious. This is where event and feeling become memory and where the proof of life is stored. The poet—and we use the term to include all those who have respect for and speak to the human spirit—can help to supply the subconscious with material to enhance its sensitivity, thus safeguarding it. The poet, too, can help to keep man from making himself over in the image of his electronic marvels. For the danger is not so much that man will be controlled by the computer as that he may imitate it.

10   The poet reminds men of their uniqueness. It is not necessary to possess the ultimate definition of this uniqueness. Even to speculate on it is a gain.

EXERCISES: Content and Attitude

Cousins uses several devices to reinforce the reader's understanding of his attitude.

1.   How does Cousins feel toward computers? What connotative language helps you to know his feelings? What words show you his attitude toward poets? How does the language in the quotation from Greenslet (¶6) contribute to Cousins' argument?

2.   Look at ¶2. What do the transition words ("but," "nor") suggest? Notice that Cousins frequently uses this pattern of stating an assertion and then making an exception. Where else do you find it?

3.   This essay contrasts the uses and values of the computer and the poet. Cousins uses a "whole by whole" organization, first discussing the computer and then turning to the poet. How does such an order reinforce Cousins' attitude?

CHARACTERIZING STYLE

In Chapter 4, we defined style as a writer's choice and arrangement of words, and we examined some of the problems which often bother new writers. Now we shall discuss how to describe and evaluate any writer's style, including your own. An awareness of a writer's style may help you to analyze his attitude and understand his meaning.

In examining style, we will be looking at the kinds of words a writer uses and at the way he has arranged those words. Here are some questions to ask as you begin to look at style.

A. Elements of style

1. *Word choice*
   What is the level of the language (slang, conversation, everyday, technical, scholarly, sophisticated, educated)? Is the language highly connotative?

2. *Sentence patterns*

 What are the lengths? Is there a variety of lengths? Is the structure simple, compound, complex? Does one type dominate or is there an even mixture?

3. *Volume*

 Does the writer use many words to make his point (expansiveness) or has he been brief and concise (economy)?

4. *Concreteness*

 How extensive and vivid is the use of sense impression, fact, description, and other details?

5. *Transitions*

 Are transitions between sentences, paragraphs, and sections smooth or choppy?

6. *Sound*

 Has the writer used parallelism, repetition, interruption, or alliteration?

B. **Tone**

 1. What is the tone?

 2. How is it created?

C. **Appropriateness**

 Now that you have described each of the six elements of style and the tone, do you think they are appropriate to the writer's audience, purpose, and subject?

 Turn back to the Evans and Novak column on pages 94–95, and examine their style. You might characterize and evaluate their style in the following way.

A. **Elements of style**

 1. The language level is casual and everyday, bordering occasionally on slang ("patch up," "savvy"). The language (as we have seen) is highly connotative.

 2. The sentences are almost all the same length, neither very short nor very long.
 The dominating sentence pattern is complex. Approximately one-third of the sentences are simple. With the exception of Strauss's quote, few sentences are compound.

 3. The work leans toward brevity and conciseness rather than expansiveness.

 4. Sense impressions are used extensively; the language is concrete.

 5. The writers use pronoun reference, transition words, and repeti-

tion of key words to create smooth, but sometimes mechanical (¶s 3 and 6 begin with "But"), transitions.

6. The writers frequently use interruption.

B. Tone

The tone is gossipy and light in spite of the seemingly serious intention.
The interruptions and colorful language help to create the tone.

C. Appropriateness

Because an audience of newspaper readers is very broad, the fairly simple level of language, medium sentence length, and concrete language are appropriate. The writers' colorful language and chatty interruptions seem designed to keep the interest of a hurried reader and to make him feel that he is learning about the secrets of politics. The style, while not especially distinguished, is appropriate.

Norman Cousins, also writing a column, has a different style in "The Computer and the Poet," pp. 98–100. His level of language is more difficult, and, although it is connotative, it is not so colorful as that of Evans and Novak. The sentences are usually of medium length, though Cousins sometimes punctuates his meaning with a short sentence. Complex and compound-complex sentences dominate, although about one-third of the sentences are simple. The column is neither especially concise nor especially expansive. The language is often abstract ("problem," "intelligence," "logic," "values," "sensitivity"), but Cousins also uses concrete images ("sprawling" facts, "fruitful" errors, "cramped" prospects).

Cousins signals transitions with pronoun reference, repetition of key words, and parallel sentence structure. He frequently uses the pattern of "*not* this, *but* that" to point up his contrast. Cousins emphasizes certain ideas by using repetition, parallelism, and interruption. His tone is calm and reasonable.

Cousins' style (balanced, intellectual, elegant) is appropriate to his audience of *Saturday Review* readers, who are likely to be educated and interested in his subject.

EXERCISES: Characterizing Style

A. Characterize and evaluate the style in each of the essays studied in this section (Harrington, Hayakawa, Steinem, and TRB).

B. Look at some of your own work. Characterize and evaluate your style. Do you sound like yourself? Or are you having trouble letting *your* voice come through? Do you always sound the same? Or do you have different voices? How could you improve your style?

EXAMINING THE CONTEXT

To continue your critical evaluation, remember what you learned from Hayakawa and consider the material in its context. Who is the author? Who is his audience? Why is he writing? These questions bring you to another step in your analysis.

1. *Who is the author?* Does he have a reputation for honesty, thoroughness, and objectivity? How is he regarded by his colleagues in his field of special knowledge and skill? Is the work on a subject in the author's field of specialization? Is he identified with a particular ideology?

Answering these questions will help you to judge the credibility of the author. If you do not recognize the name of a particular writer, or know anything about his reputation, some possible sources of information would be biographical dictionaries or indexes, and the *Book Review Digest* for reviews of the author's publications. These are available in the reference section of the library.

Another important consideration is whether or not the author is writing in his field of expertise. Advertisements often ask us to value a celebrity's opinion of a product about which he has no special knowledge. As consumers we need to become immune to the pleas of a famous actress to purchase a luxury automobile. As critical readers we need to remember that a reputable expert cannot transfer his expertise from his area of specialization to another. Thus, when a well-known football player speaks in favor of a political candidate, he speaks only as a private citizen, not as an expert.

Besides examining his work, how do you find out an author's beliefs? It might help if you know his occupation or can identify him as a participant in a particular institution or organization. For example, a member of a Republican administration might be expected to favor a Republican president's policies. A priest in the Catholic church might be expected to argue against abortion. But these clues give you only hints; do not decide what the writer's bias will be before you have examined his work. Be alert for anticipated biases, but do not stereotype the author.

2. *What kind of audience is being addressed?* Remember that you are not necessarily part of the intended audience. Does the writer anticipate a "popular" audience, a general but educated audience, or a specialized audience of experts in his particular field? Does the author expect an audience who will share his own cultural, political, or religious biases?

Often you can judge the audience by noting in what kind of publication the work appears. For example, a popular magazine such as *Reader's Digest* is written to appeal to a very broad and general reading public. Other popular magazines such as *Time*, *Harper's*, and *Psychology Today* aim toward a general but more knowledgeable reader. You can expect their articles to provide competent introductions or overviews (but not fully researched and thoroughly documented analyses) to a wide variety of subjects. On the other hand, articles appearing in specialized journals such as the Publication of the Modern Language Association (*PMLA*) are written by literature and language scholars for other scholars and will thus be addressed to an audience with highly specialized knowledge.

It is also helpful to consider whether or not an author's expected audience will alert you to a particular bias. Some newspapers and magazines are fairly consistently liberal (for example, *The New Republic* and *The Washington Post*), while others are usually politically conservative (for instance, *The Chicago Tribune* and *U.S. News and World Report*). The particular interests of magazines such as *Playboy* and *Ms.* should be taken into account if you are analyzing their articles. Since no writer is completely neutral, you need not distrust works with a bias; rather, you should be aware of a writer's biases and judge his credibility in the light of his special interests.

3. *What is the author's purpose in writing?* Is his primary intention to report information, or is it to persuade his reader to accept his thesis? The title of a book or article or the preface or table of contents of a book may clarify the writer's purpose (for example, "Let's Save Our Lakes!"), but you will probably have to read the article or the first chapter of a book before you know the author's intention. If the writer's purpose is to persuade, then you will have to pay particular attention to his handling of evidence. Remember that a writer intent on convincing you of the validity of his thesis may, either willfully or unintentionally, distort evidence.

4. *What are the writer's sources of information?* Has he documented his sources? Is his information still valid? Where did he get it? Be suspicious of writers who fail to mention where they obtained their evidence, or those who urge readers to believe that their unnamed "sources" are "reliable." Pay close attention to dates and try to judge whether or not the information is current. For example, an article urging the curtailing of county growth based solely on population statistics from the 1960s would no longer be reliable.

EXERCISES: Examining the Context

Considering audience, author, and purpose of evidence, what can you speculate about the reliability or bias of the following?

1. An article on the Republican administration written by a former campaign worker for a Democratic presidential candidate.

2. A discussion of the Baltimore Colts' hope for the next Super Bowl published in *The Baltimore Sun*.

3. A letter to the editor about conservation written by a member of the Sierra Club.

4. A column in *Newsweek* on economics.

5. A 1948 article in *Nutrition Today* on food additives.

6. A book published by Oxford University Press entitled *Metaphysical Poetry.*

7. A pamphlet by Jerry Lewis urging you to contribute to a fund to combat muscular dystrophy.

8. An article by a doctor in *Family Circle* about a special vegetarian diet.

9. A discussion in *Ms.* on the Equal Rights Amendment.

10. An editorial entitled "Stop the Highway Killing" in your local newspaper.

EXERCISES: Content, Attitude, Style, Context

A. Find an example of slanted writing and bring it to class for classmates to analyze. Prepare questions about content, attitude, style, and context.

B. Analyze an issue of your favorite magazine. Look first at the editorial pages and articles written by the staff, then at articles contributed by other writers. Answer these questions for both staff and other writers.

   1. Who is their audience?

   2. Describe their style and tone. How appropriate are style and tone?

   3. What is the purpose of the articles and of the entire magazine?

   4. What type of article dominates?

   5. Is the magazine an example of responsible or irresponsible journalism? Give reasons.

C. Group work (three to four students): Choose a public event which was expected or which required some planning, such as the Super Bowl, the Olympics, the presidential election, a local election or event, a total eclipse, the Academy Award presentations, the premiere of a new television series.

   Look up material that was written *before* and *after* the event occurred. First, examine the material written after the event. Do all accounts agree factually? If not, which appears to be accurate? Why? What are the various attitudes and purposes? Are the accounts responsibly written? Next, examine the earlier material. Which was most accurate in its speculations? Which was least accurate? Can you account for these differences?

Duplicate several of the most interesting items and present your analysis to the rest of the class.

WRITING ASSIGNMENT

Choose two articles, essays, or editorials dealing with the same product, person, performance, or event. Write an analysis in which you evaluate each source in terms of purpose, accuracy, attitude, and/or style.

Here is a student essay written in response to the same assignment. Class members were the audience. Evaluate it for practice.

A Slightly Different Point of View

1   The consumer frequently realizes that an advertisement is used to sell a product. However, many ads deliberately overlook faults in their products in order to obtain a greater profit. Comparing a Peugeot car ad with *Consumer Reports* write-ups (April 1975 and August 1975) about the Peugeot, one finds three major areas of disagreement in reporting the quality of the Peugeot. These areas of difference are the literary presentation of the two sources, the advantages and disadvantages of the car, and the actual cost of owning the car. Upon careful examination of the two sources, the ad and *Consumer Reports* write-ups, it is clear that this half-truth attitude is very prominent in the advertisement.

2   The difference in reporting accurately the advantages and disadvantages of the Peugeot is the biggest area of disagreement. The ad clearly cites several advantages of the Peugeot; for example, "it has more luggage space than the Lincoln Continental." The fuel conservationist will be satisfied because "it [the Peugeot diesel] goes farther on a dollar's worth of fuel than practically any car sold in America." Tall people should enjoy the car because "the Peugeot has more front headroom than a Cadillac deVille, and a mere eight-tenths of an inch less legroom than a Chrysler Imperial." Judging from the ad, the Peugeot is a great car to drive. Nevertheless, *Consumer Reports* adds several relevant but overlooked details. For example, the trunk is spacious; however, this is due to "the spare tire being strapped to the underside of the trunk floor, making it very inaccessible." (Aug. 1975, p. 492) The Peugeot diesel may also save on fuel cost, but "the diesel engine costs $1,000 more than the standard engine." (Aug. 1975, p. 494) Several other facts not mentioned are also worth knowing: "The lever on the right side of the steering column operates the turn signals—and the horn. The lever on the left side of the steering column operates the headlights." (Aug. 1975, p. 491) Both of these deviations from conventional car designs could cause accidents, "especially for those who don't drive the car regularly." (Aug. 1975, p. 491) Another safety hazard is the speedometer: "With both miles per hour and kilometers per hour gradations, plus wide spacing of numbers and reflective glare, it is difficult to know how fast one is going." (Aug. 1975, p. 491) In reply to Peugeot's stated roominess, *Consumer Reports* asserts that "tall drivers found the accelerator *too* close and *too* far to the left" for comfortable driving. (Aug. 1975, p. 491) Although the Peugeot ad does state partially true advantages, it does leave out some very important disadvantages.

3   The literary presentation is the second major disagreement to be observed. The Peugeot advertisement uses a great amount of connotative language such as "a luxuriously engineered car" and "Peugeot, a different kind of luxury car." *Consumer Reports* states basic facts: "The Peugeot is rated as a four-passenger sedan." (Aug. 1975, p. 491) No glamorous language or subtle inferences are suggested by *Consumer Reports*. The advertisement entices the consumer to buy the car; *Consumer Reports* is stating facts that have been obtained through testing the car. The ad is very biased toward the good points of the car as shown in paragraph two, while *Consumer Reports* states both good and bad points of the car without prejudice.

4   Finally, the last point of contrast is the cost of actually owning the car. The advertisement does not come out and say, "The Peugeot costs this much to run." Instead it beats around the bush, stating that "The Peugeot diesel uses fuel that, on the average, costs several cents a gallon less than regular gasoline; it is very frugal with every gallon it uses; and no more costly tune-ups." *Consumer Reports* bluntly says that "Peugeot's total cost per mile was 13¢ for one year and 27,000 miles." (April 1975, p. 224) That is a "total cost of ownership of $3,568." (April 1975, p. 224) This total includes "$475 for routine service, $187 for tires, $453 for fuel, $1115 operating cost and $2453 dollar depreciation." (April 1975, p. 224) The advertisement in this area is vague and ambiguous, whereas *Consumer Reports* is factual, clear, and understandable.

5   For a product to sell on today's market, its advertising has to be good. However, the consumer must become aware that not all the facts are given in an advertisement. The consumer should consult additional information on a product, realizing that ads conveniently ignore faults in their product while overglorifying virtues.

TESTING THE LOGIC

In our discussion of attitude we concluded that a writer cannot avoid slanting his work, and that the important point is not whether he should, but whether a reader knows how to detect his attitude. Before turning to an examination of logic, let us consider another matter: Should writers be fair and responsible in presenting their ideas? Unlike the question on attitude, this one can be answered firmly. *Yes, they should.* Unfortunately, many writers, either through carelessness or deceit, are not fair and responsible. Therefore the critical reader must know how to evaluate a writer's argument. This evaluation involves testing the logic.

Logical thinking and writing result primarily from using skills which you have already begun to develop. Whether you are examining your own ideas or someone else's, you are checking to see if the argument contains a thesis which is proven to the intended audience. Logical argument need not involve the study of complicated rules and procedures; nevertheless, an understanding of certain common errors in sound thinking (*logical fallacies*) can be helpful.

LOGICAL FALLACIES

For convenience let us divide these fallacies into three groups which denote similar problems in reasoning: errors in generalizing, oversimplification, and attempts to ignore the issue. After each definition is one example which is explained and one which is left for you to explain.

Generalization

As you learned when you first began to write essays, you cannot prove your thesis without adequate detail.

- To generalize, or draw a conclusion, without sufficient proof is *hasty generalization*.

  Green is Tom's favorite color; he wore a green shirt twice last week. (Did he wear it because he liked the color or because it was his only clean shirt? Is this the only color he wears frequently?)

  The government should force all cities to adopt the same clean air standards that improved Springdale's air quality.

- To exclude, consciously or unconsciously, part of the evidence or to generalize from erroneous evidence is *faulty generalization*.

  Bing Crosby couldn't act; he only played in musicals. (Your generalization wouldn't stand on the evidence; remember *The Country Girl?*)

  Good students are those who always follow orders.

- To assume that all members of a group are alike or to overlook certain group traits is *stereotyping*.

  Children love clowns. (Many children are afraid of clowns.)

  Women are too weak to excel in professional sports.

- To phrase an argument so that you admit no exceptions (using words such as *all, every, always, never, none*) may result in *overstatement*.

  Everybody thinks we need stronger drunk driving laws. (It only takes one person who disagrees to disprove this generalization.)

  Every front-line soldier has witnessed atrocities.

Simplification

Sometimes erroneous conclusions are drawn when a writer skips steps in his reasoning. Thus he may overlook a point which would convince him and his audience that his conclusion is unsound.

- To assume, because one incident happened after another, that the second was caused by the first is *post hoc, ergo propter hoc* (literally, after this, therefore because of it), usually shortened to *post hoc*.

   This meat is poisoned; my dog ate some and then he got sick. (What else did he eat? Is there a chance that he caught a disease?)

   We should throw out the whole city council. Since they were elected, the city has gone into deficit spending.

- To state, without making the necessary connections, that one circumstance indicates or predicts another may result in a *non sequitur* (literally, it does not follow).

   Connie loves horses; therefore she will be a wonderful rider. (Does she have the necessary athletic skill and determination?)

   If Mr. Thompson could accomplish all this as a private citizen, just think what he can do if he is elected.

- To suggest complete comparison between two objects or circumstances on the basis of a very limited similarity is *false analogy*.

   This is a great automobile. Like the finest watches in the world, it is made in Switzerland. (Does the similarity of origin prove anything about the quality of the car?)

   Like Abraham Lincoln, the nominee had humble beginnings. Let's vote honesty back into office!

- To assume that there are only two alternatives may create a *false dilemma*.

   A student must be either a good student or a good athlete. (He could be both or he may be neither.)

   If we cannot maintain peace in Southeast Asia through diplomatic talks, we shall have to send military aid.

Ignoring the Issue

Sometimes a writer may try to convince his audience by appealing to their emotions or prejudices instead of dealing with the real issue.

- To attack the supporter of a proposal instead of the proposal itself is *argumentum ad hominem* (literally, argument to the man).

   How can you trust his arguments on curing recession? His credit rating is terrible. (He may not practice what he preaches. His credit rating may be based on expenditures by his whole family.)

His book does not deserve a Pulitzer Prize. He has been married nine times.

- To use the audience's biases about the supporters of an object or idea in order to attack or praise the object or idea itself is *transfer*. Here are three common forms of transfer:

  Testimonial:

  The world's most skillful quarterbacks use this soap. (A good athlete may know nothing about the quality of soap.)

  President Eisenhower often relaxed by playing golf. We should take up golf, too.

  Poisoning the source:

  I wouldn't vote for him. Many of his programs are basically Marxist. (But would the programs themselves be bad for our society?)

  Taking an employee's fingerprints is a threat to freedom. The Nazis did that, too.

  Bandwagon:

  Ninety percent of the citizens of this county voted for Smith in the last election. Re-elect Smith. (Has Smith done a good job in office? The issues may be different this year; does Smith have the necessary qualifications for dealing with them?)

  Polls show that four out of five people favor this toothpaste.

Another form of ignoring the issue occurs when a writer tries to divert his audience's attention to a different issue while ignoring the real one.

- To assume that part of the argument is true without examining it is *begging the question*.

  Since lowering the standards would be bad for the students, a pass-fail system should not be adopted. (Would it be bad for the students? Maybe the standards are too high. Does a pass-fail system lower standards?)

  How can you ignore the opinion of the best movie critic in town?

- Similar to begging the question is *circular reasoning*, trying to prove an idea with a reworded version of the same idea.

  Basketball is exciting because it is such a stimulating sport. ("Exciting" and "stimulating" convey the same meaning.)

- To introduce a side issue that does not properly belong in the argument is a *red herring*.

  She supports a four-day work week, and, besides, she is a feminist.

Before we decide to hire a lawyer, we should remember that many lawyers have recently been found guilty of corruption. (If your own lawyer is honest, the recent convictions are irrelevant.)

- To attribute to an opponent a view which he does not hold (especially if it is obviously erroneous or ridiculous) so that his view can be easily refuted is to build a *straw man*.

The president is trying to conserve fuel by driving the price of gasoline up to $3 per gallon. (He may have advocated higher gas prices, but not that high.)

Those who favor gun control legislation just want to take all the guns away from responsible citizens and put them in the hands of criminals.

EXERCISES: Testing the Logic

A. Here in outline form is a list of the fallacies we have discussed. Make up or collect from your reading examples of each fallacy.

 I. Generalization
   A. Hasty generalization
   B. Faulty generalization
   C. Stereotype
   D. Overstatement

 II. Simplification
   A. Post hoc, ergo propter hoc
   B. Non sequitur
   C. False analogy
   D. False dilemma

 III. Ignoring the Issue
   A. Diversion by emotion or prejudice
     1. Argumentum ad hominem
     2. Transfer
       a. Testimonial
       b. Poisoning the source
       c. Bandwagon
   B. Diversion to another issue
     1. Begging the question
     2. Circular reasoning
     3. Red herring
     4. Straw man

B. No doubt you have noticed in examining the definition and examples of fallacies that a fallacious statement might fit in several categories of fallacy. Do not waste time in prolonged debate over what name to apply to an illogical statement; instead try to spot the errors in the argument itself. In the sentences that follow, explain what is wrong with the argument and *then* name the fallacy or fallacies that seem applicable.

Example: Anyone who makes good grades in English will be a wonderful English teacher. (This argument oversimplifies the issue by failing to note that it takes more to be a good teacher than an understanding of the subject. Non sequitur. Overstatement. Hasty generalization.)

1. A student will excel in either language or chemistry; no one can be good at both.

2. A young person today who doesn't smoke pot is rejected in much the same fashion as one who didn't attend church every Sunday in the nineteenth century.

3. In the Professional Basketball Association, the Virginia Patriots signed two new players for well over $100,000 each. Then the franchise went broke and eventually folded.

4. The upsurge in crime on Sundays is caused by the lower rate of church attendance in recent years.

5. Illegal drug use is a victimless crime, and any social or individual problem it creates is not solved by sending a person to jail.

6. Since a higher gas tax would cause people to use less gas, we should increase gas taxes at once.

7. Freeland's theories of economics can't be any good because he doesn't have a degree in economics.

8. The government must create jobs. A factory in Illinois has had to lay off half of its workers.

9. The writer suggests a law forbidding the sale of pornography to minors, but how can you have a policeman in every bookstore or movie house?

10. While there is legitimate cause for protest against genuine sexual discrimination, a woman cannot alter the fact that she was born female and should enjoy her status.

11. The university spent $10,000 studying the use of the yo-yo. How can they refuse money to study the effects of weightlessness on man's ability to solve problems?

12. How can she criticize the life of a tennis bum? She has never lived it.

13. The Democratic party must be responsible for inflation since they were involved in so many other crises.

14. It is understandable that Harry isn't as smart as Sam because Harry grew up in the South.

15. Either we put better lighting in the streets or we will fail to reduce crime.

C. Examine the logic in this argument. Be prepared to discuss your evaluation with other class members.

The Pass-Fail System

1   It's time to abolish letter grades and go to a pass-fail (p-f) system. Many progressive, forward-thinking students have been agitating for this. The fuddy-duddy instructors who oppose it are too stiff to change their thinking from five to two grades; they don't know how to have fun anyway. Did you hear about the instructor who hasn't smiled in ten years? Actually, what more avant-garde instructors want is the p-f system. What we want is what avant-garde instructors want. Let's adopt the p-f system.

2   Consider the Constitution angle. To stigmatize a student with a low grade is cruel and inhuman punishment; it causes neurotic behavior. It stereotypes the student. To label me a B student is the same as labeling all Scotchmen sourpusses or all Texans filthy rich. As for constitutional rights, value judgments are a necessary part of grades. Racism is a system of value judgments. Racism is thus a necessary part of grades. So either we admit we're racist or go with p-f.

3   I asked a group of really all-together students over at the pinball machines in the lounge what they thought. Their thoughtful opinion was that they would like to go with p-f. Besides that, I asked a guy who had a p-f course at Progresso U and he was for the idea. Furthermore, a survey commissioned by the *faculty* at Nonprogresso U on the use of the p-f system in gym classes there revealed that the idea worked well. And it could do just as well here. People like p-f.

4   A sound grading system is a p-f system. What we need is a sound grading system, right? What we need is the p-f system. I favor it. My buddy Felix favors it. My girl Samantha favors it. All us modern students favor it. Come on, let's go suggest it to the Campus Council. Grades are something we inherited from the Middle Ages. Inhuman torture is something we inherited from the Middle Ages too. Grades are inhuman torture.

D. Read "The Feminine Mistake" and "Confessions of a Female Chauvinist Sow" on pp. 275–87.

1. Examine each argument thoroughly, noting the context and testing the logic. Discuss these essays and your analyses with members of the class.

2. Select one essay and write a theme analyzing and evaluating the writer's logic.

Persuasive Writing

7

In Chapter 6 we tested logic in the arguments of others. Now you need to begin rigorously applying these same tests to your own writing. Perhaps one of the most difficult aspects of writing well is gaining the objectivity necessary to judge whether or not you are constructing logical arguments. Yet such objectivity is vital if you are to become a convincing writer.

Argumentation, or persuasive writing, is much like any other form of expository writing. Aren't you usually trying to persuade your audience that your thesis is true? Whether you are demonstrating that Evans and Novak had a negative attitude toward liberals in their January 26, 1974, column (analysis) or whether you are arguing that beer should be sold in the student union (argumentation), you are writing to convince your reader.

FORMING AN ARGUMENT

The process of forming an argument remains the same as the process you have used previously.

1. *Have a reason for writing.* As a student, you may support a change in grading policies; you might suggest that a new course be taught; you could promote a move to build better recreational facilities on campus. As a voter, you might urge your congressman

to vote against raising taxes. As a consumer, you could pressure local grocers to use a unit pricing system.

2. *Define your audience and your voice.* In persuasive writing you will be trying to convince your reader to take action or change his attitude, often about abstract and/or controversial issues. The fact that you need to persuade suggests that the reader is not already on your side. Therefore, it is doubly important that you know who he is and how he can be reached. Is he against you or just undecided? Will he respond to logic alone? Will he be moved by emotion? As we have seen in the study of fallacies, an argument which appeals *only* to emotion or prejudice will work only as long as your audience fails to examine your logic. A movingly stated opinion is not a substitute for facts. However, understanding your audience's biases and emotions provides you with a powerful and legitimate method of persuasion, and you should learn to use it properly. Emotion generated by accurate and thorough evidence *may* win your case.

3. *Formulate your thesis.* Be certain that your reader knows exactly where you stand. An analysis may show all sides of a question equally, but persuasion takes a side and supports it. In the course of your discussion, you may anticipate your opponents' arguments, but you will include them only to demonstrate their weaknesses before they are advanced by the other side.

4. *Gather and organize your proof.* If you are to convince your reader, you must demonstrate that you are honest and well-informed by constructing a logically reasoned and thoroughly documented proof—allowing him to examine your evidence for himself. Understanding the difference between fact, inference, and judgment and making scrupulous distinctions among them will help you to convince your reader that he can trust you as a reliable writer. Look at the following statements:

The sun rose today at 7:02 A.M. E.S.T.

The sun will rise tomorrow at 7:01 A.M. E.S.T.

Today's sunrise was beautiful.

A fact: *The sun rose today at 7:02 A.M. E.S.T.* This statement is a fact because it can be observed and/or measured and/or verified and thus agreed upon by other observers including the reader. I observed and measured the phenomenon when I looked east, saw the sun peep over the horizon, and checked my watch—set correctly and working properly. I verified the statement by checking with the U. S. Weather Bureau, which, most citizens agree, is a trustworthy source. *Facts* give the reader specific and observable information which is not open to dispute. In a dispute about "facts," one persons has facts and the other does not. Observation (checking the phenomenon itself or checking with reliable sources) will solve an argument.

An inference: *The sun will rise tomorrow at 7:01 A.M. E.S.T.* This statement could be a fact tomorrow, but until then it is an inference because it is an opinion based on fact. I infer that the sun will rise tomorrow because it has risen every day in recorded history. I infer that the time of rising will be 7:01 A.M. E.S.T. because one minute is the amount of difference predicted for this time of year (on the basis of experience) by the U.S. Weather Bureau, a reliable source. *Inferences* give the reader opinions based directly on facts but possibly open to different interpretations. The closer the inference to fact, the less likely a difference of opinion.

A judgment: *Today's sunrise was beautiful.* This statement is a judgment because it is my opinion, based on my preferences. I like sunrises which reflect pink and purple and yellow on the clouds and on the ice-covered branches and snow-covered ground. *Judgments* give the reader opinions based on preferences, beliefs, or values that are open to dispute. A writer may build a sound case for his judgment, and he may convince his reader, but he cannot shut out differences of opinion. Judgments may be aesthetic (Today's sunrise was beautiful), moral (It is wrong to take another person's life), ethical (Lawyers should not advertise), or functional (Johnny Unitas was the best quarterback the NFL has ever had); they deal in right and wrong, good and bad, best and worst. A writer persuades his reader by explaining his judgment with facts and carefully drawn inferences. Often the judgment will require the setting and defining of criteria to demonstrate to the reader why the subject does or does not measure up. These criteria are especially useful in aesthetic or functional judgments when the writer is ranking or setting values. For example, in asserting that Johnny Unitas is the best quarterback of NFL history, a writer would give criteria of a good quarterback and then show how Unitas has filled that function best. Try the following exercises to practice working with facts, inferences, and judgments.

EXERCISES: Facts, Inferences, and Judgments

A. Compile a list including several statements of fact, several inferences, and several judgments. Discuss these items with other class members.

B. Construct paragraphs of facts supporting the following inferences.

   1. This bread is nutritious.

   2. Carol caused the wreck I was in last week.

   3. The dogs must have gotten out under the fence during the night.

   4. The price of beef will go up next year.

C. Group work (three to four students): Establish criteria for selecting the following. Make the criteria as specific as possible.

   1. A textbook for a course you are taking.

2. The best male rock singer of the year.

3. The most annoying current television commercial.

4. A good design for a college library.

D. Choose a judgment from the list you compiled in Excercise A and list the facts and inferences which would help you to prove it. Would this judgment also require the statement of criteria?

REFUTATION

Argumentation naturally generates counterarguments. You read an editorial in the newspaper and decide to write a letter to the editor objecting to his ideas. You are asked on an exam to agree or disagree with a critic's statement about *The Scarlet Letter*. A friend says he thinks your favorite movie is just a waste of film and you want to convince him that, even if he didn't enjoy it, the movie has merit. In each case you will find yourself involved in *refutation*, disproving or correcting someone else's argument.

How do you write a strong refutation? It should not surprise you to find that you follow the same old rules; you prove your thesis with relevant evidence presented in a style that will appeal to your particular audience. However, given an argument which you wish to refute, there are certain steps which you can follow as you work out your refutation.

1. *Read accurately.* Make sure you have understood your opponent's argument. There is no need to waste your time writing a refutation only to discover that you have not interpreted the original argument correctly. Therefore, take the time to pick out the writer's thesis, to look up terms and references which you cannot define, and to examine his evidence. If you still disagree, then you have a topic for refutation.

2. *Pinpoint the weaknesses in the original argument.* Analyze the argument to see exactly where it is open to attack. Has the writer used enough evidence? Is his evidence reliable? Has he oversimplified the issue and failed to consider important aspects? Has he brought in irrelevant issues? Has he been responsible in his use of emotion?

3. *Formulate your thesis.* Now you will have to decide whether you disagree with your opponent's entire thesis or whether you disagree with only part of his argument or evidence. It may be that you agree with his thesis but feel that he has based it on a false assumption which you will state and disprove. Or, you may agree with his thesis but object to part of his evidence. Your own thesis must make clear the exact area of your disagreement.

4. *Gather evidence to correct the weaknesses.* In a refutation, it is not enough to point out the fallacies in your opponent's logic; you must do what he has not—supply full and reliable evidence which will prove your thesis and thus disprove his. For this reason, you will need to be careful to engage in refutation only when you can marshal evidence from either your experience or your reading.

5. *Write your refutation.* While every paper demands its own particular organization, you will find that most refutations follow the same general order: his argument, your thesis, your evidence.

(a) His argument. Do not, under most circumstances, assume that your reader has read, understood, and remembered your opponent's argument. Therefore, very early in the paper, state—briefly and accurately—his argument.

(b) Your argument. The organization of your evidence will depend on the issue itself. If there is only one major disagreement, it will be stated fully in your thesis, and you will then organize your own evidence in the way which seems most effective. If there are many small points of disagreement, you may want to state and refute them one by one. Be certain that you construct a logical argument, and that you make your organizational plan clear to your reader.

In the following article, which originally appeared in *Newsweek*, Vernon E. Jordan, Jr., executive director of the National Urban League, refutes what he feels is an erroneous view of the black middle class.

The Truth About the Black Middle Class

1   Recent reports of the existence of a vast black middle class remind me of daring explorers emerging from the hidden depths of a strange, newly discovered world bearing tales of an exotic new phenomenon. The media seem to have discovered, finally, black families that are intact, black men who are working, black housewives tending backyard gardens and black youngsters who aren't sniffing coke or mugging old ladies.

2   And out of this "discovery" a new black stereotype is beginning to emerge. Immaculately dressed, cocktail in hand, the new black stereotype comes off as a sleek, sophisticated professional light-years away from the ghetto experience. As I turn the pages of glossy photos of these idealized, fortunate few, I get the feeling that this new black image is all too comforting to Americans weary of the struggle against poverty and racism.

3   But this stereotype is no more real than was the old image of the angry, fire-breathing militant. And it may be just as damaging to black people, for whom equal opportunity is still a theory and for whom a national effort to bring about a more equitable distribution of the fruits of an affluent society is still a necessity. After all, who can argue the need for welfare reform, for guaranteed jobs, for integrated schools and better housing, when the supposed beneficiaries are looking out at us from the pages of national magazines, smiling at the camera between sips from their martinis?

4   The "new" black middle class has been seen recently in prime time on a CBS News documentary; it has adorned the cover of *The New York Times Magazine*, and it has been the subject of a *Time* cover story. But its much ballyhooed emergence is more representative of wishful thinking than of reality. And, important as it is for the dedication and hard work of countless black families finally to receive recognition, the image being pushed so hard may be counterproductive in the long run.

5   The fact is that the black middle class of 1974, like that of earlier years, is a minority within the black community. In 1974, as in 1964, 1954, and in

the decades stretching into the distant past, the social and economic reality of the majority of black people has been poverty and marginal status in the wings of our society.

6   The black middle class traditionally included a handful of professionals and a far larger number of working people who, had they been white, would be solidly "working class." The inclusion of Pullman porters, post-office clerks and other typical members of the old black middle class was due less to their incomes—which were well below those of whites—than to their relative immunity from the hazards of marginal employment that dogged most blacks. They were "middle class" relative to other black people, not to the society at large.

7   Despite all the publicity, despite all the photos of yacht-club cocktail parties, that is where the so-called black middle class stands today. The CBS broadcast included a handyman and a postal worker. Had they been white they would be considered working class, but since they were black and defied media-fostered stereotypes, they were given the middle-class label.

8   Well, is it true that the black community is edging into the middle class? Let's look at income, the handiest guide and certainly the most generally agreed-upon measurement. What income level amounts to middle-class status? Median family income is often used, since that places a family at the exact midpoint in our society. In 1972 the median family income of whites amounted to $11,549, but black median family income was a mere $6,864.

9   That won't work. Let's use another guide. The Bureau of Labor Statistics says it takes an urban family of four $12,600 to maintain an "intermediate" living standard. Using that measure, the average black family not only is *not* middle class, but it earns far less than the "lower, non-poverty" level of $8,200. Four out of five black families earn less than the "intermediate" standard.

10   What about collar color? Occupational status is often considered a guide to middle-class status, and this is an area in which blacks have made tremendous gains, breaking into occupations unheard of for non-whites only a decade ago. When you look at the official occupation charts, there is a double space to separate higher-status from lower-status jobs such as laborer, operative, and service worker. That gap is more than a typographical device. It is an indicator of racial separation as well, for the majority of working whites hold jobs above that line, while the majority of blacks are still confined to the low-pay, low-status jobs below it. At the top of the job pinnacle, in the elite categories of the professions and business, the disparity is most glaring, with one out of four whites in such middle-class jobs in contrast to every tenth black worker.

11   Yes, there are black doctors, dentists, and lawyers, but let no one be fooled into thinking they are typical—these professions include only 2 percent blacks. Yes, there are black families that are stable, who work, often at more than one job, and who own cars and homes. And yes, they are representative of the masses of black people who work the longest hours at the hardest jobs for the least pay in order to put some meat on the table and clothes on their backs. This should be emphasized in every way possible in order to remind this forgetting nation that there is a dimension of black reality that has never been given its due.

12   But this should not blind us to the realization that, even with such superhuman efforts, the vast majority of blacks are still far from middle-class status. Let us not forget that the gains won are tenuous ones, easily shaken from our grasp by an energy crisis, a recession, rampant inflation, or nonenforcement of hard-won civil-rights laws.

13   And never let us fall victim to the illusion that the limited gains so bitterly wrenched from an unwilling nation have materially changed the conditions of life for the overwhelming majority of black people—conditions still typified by discrimination, economic insecurity, and general living conditions inferior to those enjoyed by the majority of our white fellow citizens.

Notice that this refutation follows the conventional order. In the first two paragraphs, Jordan summarizes the original argument. In the third paragraph he asserts his disagreement and then gives specific evidence which supports his thesis. His evidence is convincing because it is observable and often based on facts and statistics.

EXERCISES: Refutation

A.   Here is a letter to the editor.

> As a mother who often finds herself reading comics to her children, I feel compelled to complain about the image of women on these pages. Women in the funny papers are almost always shown as dumb, dependent, or overbearing.
>
> Look at the wives and mothers. Nina ("Gasoline Alley"), Blondie, and Dennis' mother (Could it be coincidence they are all helpless blondes?) all spend most of their time worrying about or disciplining their husbands and children. Momma, Loweezy ("Snuffy Smith"), and Andy Capp's wife, Flo, get their way by manipulation and deceit, apparently because no one loves them enough to please them without being pushed into it.
>
> The career women are no better. June Gale ("Rex Morgan"), Poteet ("Steve Canyon"), Lizz ("Dick Tracy")—surely, you've noticed these strips are all named after their supermen heroes—are assigned by men to have adventures which are never quite as exciting as the adventures the heroes have. When they get in trouble—as they usually do—do I have to tell you who bails them out?
>
> I'm sure you're getting ready to tell me about Brenda Starr, Mary Worth, and Broomhilda. Ha. Brenda Starr really spends most of her time looking for her dream man; Mary Worth mooches off the people whose lives she's poking into; the less said about Broomhilda the better.
>
> You wouldn't dare publish comics that put down a particular race or religion. Why are you so hard on women?
>
> *Judith Gray*

1.   Using your own examples drawn from the comics, construct a refutation to this letter.

2. Here are three responses which also appeared as letters to the editor. Are they effective refutations? Why or why not?

a. As a devotee of the funny papers for over half a century I applaud the recent letter deploring sexism in the comics. But maybe that person does not realize how much they have changed over the years. I have been reading them long enough to know that Mary Worth occasionally does secure gainful employment.

In my childhood "Bringing Up Father" was one of the most popular strips. Here the *nouveau riche* Jiggs was in constant terror of Maggie, his social climbing wife, who would clout him with a rolling pin every time he was caught sneaking out to join his low-life friends at Dinty Moore's, a stag bar. Maggie was the prototype of the cartoon wife of that period, a spendthrift and a violence prone shrew.

My mother blames my lifelong bachelorhood on my addiction to those comics, which she says gave a distorted view of married life. I never had the nerve to tell her that what I read was sometimes corroborated.

One old favorite (still extant) was "The Katzenjammer Kids." Hans and Fritz have a talent for elaborate practical jokes, generally performed on "Der Captain." Their victim is to an extent *in loco parentis* since he makes his home with "Momma," who is unaware that "der liddle anchuls" are capable of so much mischief. This created another pattern, one of disrespect for elders, especially those of the masculine gender.

Another surviving old-timer is "Little Orphan Annie." Although both juvenile and female, Annie exhibits wisdom and self-reliance.

Now we have Andy Capp, who never works, as he lives off his wife, whom he frequently beats and threatens to desert. His outside activities consist of playing soccer and boozing in pubs, where he cavorts with girls young enough to be his daughters. This British import can hardly be called a stereotype, but Andy perhaps is what most married men secretly wish they could be.

Leon A. Doughty

b. Judith Gray's recent letter in which she attacks sexism in the comics is the best recent example of the ludicrous attitude that some feminists display toward the arts. Her contention that women in the comics are shown only as weak, stupid, and insipid demonstrates her self-induced blindness to what the comics really are. Many male characters in the comics possess undesirable traits. To parallel some of Ms. Gray's examples: Dagwood is lazy and not a little stupid; Li'l Abner is beef-witted while Pappy Yokum is spineless and securely under the thumb of Mammy Yokum; Andy Capp is a drunk and a bully, certainly a poor model for any young man. On the other hand, Mammy Yokum is portrayed as the strong-willed problem solver of the family; and self-reliant Orphan Annie has led a life of adventure for over 40 years. The point is that we laugh at and are entertained by these characters, but we do not emulate them.

Ms. Gray appears to share the view that artistic expression should be limited to "desirable" political and social attitudes. Were we to accept that view, our art, including our comics, would have all the appeal of Communist Chinese opera. The *Post*, as a responsible newspaper, should not be swayed by those who are so insecure as to be unable to tolerate the humorous depiction of all kinds of people.

Neil and Eileen Katz

c. May I contribute my oink to the growing furor over the rampant sexism in our comics?

As an ardent disciple of male chauvinism, I find refuge in the comics whenever women's liberation rears its frightening head. Without the comics I would surely have succumbed long ago to enlightenment. But instead I am a robust male chauvinist pig drawing daily sustenance from tales of exalted men and their dumb, docile women.

Now, don't get me wrong. I am not without a twinge of sympathy for the women's "movement." It is a grim plight indeed to be without a comic strip character to emulate. And I, for one, would be at a loss to deal with life's crises if each didn't have a precedent in the comics.

But, on the other hand, those who feel that a purge of our comics is direly needed if ever women's liberation is to be consummated are taking our funnies too seriously.

It's true that our funnies mirror our mores, ideals, ills, and woes, but isn't it a bit rash to assume that our society operates within the context of the comics?

In these troubled, er, changing times we male chauvinist pigs are a beleaguered lot, a vanishing breed, a species threatened with extinction. We've gone a long way, baby.

Take away our jobs, our roles, our prerogative, our supremacy. But please, ladies, leave us our comics. Is nothing sacred?

Howard G. Simkins

B. The following is an editorial which appeared in *The Washington Post*.

Sen. Gravel Wins One

1 The Senate did a seamy little thing in cutting Czechoslovakia out of the benefits of the Trade Reform Act last week. It ruled that the Czechs would not receive equal tariff treatment and access to government credits, and would not get back 18 tons of Czech gold held here since World War II, until Prague pays 100 cents on the dollar for some $50 million worth of American property nationalized in the wake of the war. Other East European countries have paid 40 cents on similar claims. The reason for this tawdry act of discrimination against Czechoslovakia seems to lie entirely in the deep sympathy felt for one claimant, Aris Gloves of California, by Sen. Mike Gravel (D-Alaska). It was his amendment that was first passed by the Senate and then sustained by the conference in the final bill.

2 Now, from the viewpoint of American realpolitik, Czechoslovakia

weighs very little. It's a small central European country which pops into consciousness only every 10 or 20 years, usually at moments of international pain or misfortune which underline the vulnerability of independence and liberty in small central European countries. But that is just the point. Once again, in a fashion no less mean for being modest and beyond the concern of most people, Czechoslovakia is being victimized through no fault of its own. One claimant with access to one senator has cleverly seen a way to squeeze some extra bucks out of an antique claim that had long been all but forgotten. Congratulations, Sen. Gravel, on joining the long line of those who have stuck it to the Czechs.

1. Group work: Working in groups of three or four, plan how to refute the editorial.

2. Here is Senator Gravel's answer as it was published in the *Post*. Is it an effective refutation?

Sen. Gravel on Czech Obligations

1   Your thirty-line editorial of December 30 opposing my position on the repayment of Czech obligations to U.S. citizens was so loaded with vitriolic adjectives and phrases—"seamy little things," "tawdry act," "victimize," "squeeze some extra bucks," "stuck it to the Czechs"—that it left little room for presentation of the facts.

2   The Communist take-over of Czechoslovakia resulted in the expropriation without compensation of $364 million worth of property from 2,650 American citizens.

3   President Truman reacted by holding 18 tons of gold and certain steel mill equipment on the condition that the Czech government arrange for adequate compensation.

4   Upon recommendation of President Eisenhower, the Congress fully adjudicated and reduced the Czech-American awards to $113 million. The Kennedy administration paid $8.5 million on the claims out of the liquidated steel mill property, leaving the current balance of $105 million.

5   Recently the State Department asked Congress to reduce the U.S. awards to $20.5 million, payable in 12 annual installments without interest. Thus the 1948 Czech obligations would be paid off at 19¢ on the dollar by 1987. In return, the U.S. would release the 18 tons of gold (currently worth approximately $130 million) and make the Czech government immediately eligible for most favored nation (MFN) tariff status, grants, and loans. The latter benefits would total hundreds of millions of dollars.

6   In rejecting the State Department's proposal and adopting my amendment, the Congress plainly decided that the time has finally arrived when some fair measure of justice should be provided to the thousands of U.S. citizens who hold expropriation awards against Czechoslovakia before the Communist government of that nation receives the return of its gold and the other vast benefits described above.

7   The provision in the Trade Reform Act does no more than reaffirm and reinforce a 26-year-old U.S. policy. It does not, as your editorial claims, force Prague to pay 100 cents on the dollar. It directs the State Department to reopen negotiations which I am hopeful will bring a minimum payment of at least the principal amount ($64 million) that Czechoslovakia owes on the $105 million award.

8   All Czechoslovakia has to do is negotiate a just and fair amount. It could be taken from the $130 million in gold currently held in the United States. The balance would be returned to Czechoslovakia along with eligibility for all benefits our government has withheld from it for years.

9   The facts of the matter are very simple: civilized nations pay for the expropriated property of foreign nationals. Czechoslovakia's neighbor Yugoslavia paid 100 percent, Germany over 70 percent, and recently Chile and Venezuela paid 100 percent to American citizens and companies. In none of these cases did the U.S. hold gold or other properties as a bargaining point.

10   Nations shouldn't enter into commercial relationships with partners who have a track record of not meeting their financial obligations, particularly when it perpetuates an injustice on its own citizens. A *quid pro quo* to better relationships based on overlooking past injustices begins, at best, on shaky ground.

11   Unlike most other nations, the Czechoslovakian government has up to this point delayed payment to U.S. citizens in the apparent hope that the government of that Eastern European nation would be able to avoid fair repayment, as well as obtain Most Favored Nation status.

12   Expropriation is in one nation's best interest. Nonpayment of claims is solely in that nation's best interest. MFN status is far more advantageous to the Czech government than to us. The road to detente is not a one way street; it is a multilane superhighway with traffic laws in force for the benefit of all who wish to travel.

Mike Gravel,
U.S. Senator (D-Alaska)

C.   Here are several refutations written by students. Their assignment was to refute a specific article, essay, or editorial in such a way as to convince a general audience, consisting of classmates and teacher, who had not read the original article. Evaluate each refutation.

1.   Innovations

1   In his letter in "Voice of the Fan" (*The Sporting News*, January 18, 1975), Gregory Knapp complains about the use of "backward and naive" reasoning by the advocates of the designated-hitter rule (in major league baseball) to argue their position. He is worried that the designated-hitter rule signals an impending "maze of innovations" that will destroy the game as it is. Mr. Knapp overlooks the fact that the designated-hitter rule is but one of many innovations adopted by major league baseball to increase the action and excitement of the game. And, according to the statistics obtained from the *1975 Baseball Almanac*, the designated-hitter rule has done just that.

2   The designated-hitter (D.H.) rule, as it exists in the American League (A. L.), simply states that the manager has the option of replacing the pitcher in his batting line-up with a "designated" hitter who, in the course of a game, never plays a position in the field with the rest of his teammates.

Now, assuming that fans go to the games to see action, one need only compare the 1974 American and National League (N. L.) season statistics to see that A. L. fans got more of what they went to see than did their N. L. counterparts.

3   The N. L. pitchers, collectively, batted only .165 with only 18 home runs. They drove in only 298 runs. By contrast, the designated hitters in the A. L. batted .256 as a whole with 167 home runs and 888 runs batted in. The pitchers of the N. L. struck out 1,549 times in 4,712 official trips to the plate, a ratio of 1 for every 3.0 official at-bats. They drew 242 walks. The designated hitters in the other league struck out 1,098 times in 7,431 official trips, a ratio of 1 for 6.8. They reached base on passes 740 times. The designated hitters of the A. L. not only struck out less often, but they reached base by way of walks three times more often than the pitchers of the N. L. The N. L. pitchers' trips to the plate did not provide the type of action that fans go to the games to see—unless they go to see strikeouts and overall poor hitting.

4   It's a fact that good hitting, big-name players draw big crowds. The D. H. rule makes it possible for those big-name players to continue helping their club, on the field and in the box office, long after that dreaded time for retirement that would have resulted from a loss of defensive ability. For example, as a designated hitter in 1974, Frank Robinson hit more home runs by himself (20) than all the N. L. pitchers put together.

5   With the designated hitters, the A. L. managers were inclined to let their starting pitchers stick around longer in close games. This brought about more exciting pitchers' duels and resulted in 650 complete games by the A. L. pitchers against only 439 by N. L. pitchers. In addition, the A. L. had nine 20-game winners to only two in the N. L.

6   In previous decades, baseball men with similar "backward and naive" reasoning gave us such innovations as a more lively ball, better gloves, abolition of the rule concerning hitting base runners with the ball, averaging walks in with base hits, and so on. Without these innovations, baseball would not be the game it is now.

7   Mr. Knapp is concerned about innovations like the D. H. rule destroying the game as it is, but, in fact, innovations such as the D. H. have *made* the game what it is.

2. Horse Identification

1   In the February issue of *Horse and Rider* magazine the article "Horse Identification" by Tex Rogers was presented. The American Horse Council, the United States Department of Agriculture, and the U. S. Animal Health Association are proposing a passport system as a sure-fire way of protecting horses against disease and identifying them. The system will also serve as a much-needed nationwide horse census. The associations leave the distinction of regulations and the cost per horse up to the individual states.

2   The idea of a horse passport system is too complicated an ordeal to jump into without consideration of all the facts. The associations have expressed all the good points of the system and completely ignored the weak points. I am against the plan because there are too many if's and not enough facts. In the following paragraphs I'll point out the weak points and why the plan won't work.

3   The associations are adopting the horse identification system on a state level. In this way each state probably won't have the same regulations. As in the case of the disease Equine Infectious Anemia (EIA), all states had different rules. Virginia was one of the first states to be hit hard, losing a lot of horses' lives. Neighboring states adopted rules while other states didn't, thus letting the deadly disease spread even more. Also under state guidance was the control of Venezuelan Equine Encephalitis (VEE). Some horses were given shots while others weren't. The states didn't enforce the shots, and consequently, in Arizona alone, 1000 equines (horses) and eight humans died. These examples show that there isn't enough enforcement on the state level. The federal government should make nationwide laws and enforce them.

4   A main idea of the proposal is to get a much-needed horse census. In 1974, funds for a census were almost appropriated but were withdrawn after former President Nixon vetoed the entire appropriations bill before leaving office. If the passport system is passed, it would be a means for states to get funds and get nationwide census information at the horseowner's expense; this shows a census is a good idea at someone else's expense besides the government's.

5   The officials are overlooking the important point that the wrong people are going to be affected by having this system. The resolution indicates it will enforce the system by first regulating the Registries, then the breeders, boarding stables, trainers, and then the showmen. These are the people who already care and protect their horses against disease. It's already required to have tests and shots before owners' horses can be registered, bred, boarded, sent to a trainer, or entered in a show. The resolution ends with the statement, "Other means of identification can be developed for grade (unregistered) horses if needed." This statement defeats the whole idea of getting a horse census and protection—if means aren't established for the backyard horse also. The reason the diseases spread so quickly before was because the backyard (unregistered family horse kept at home) horse's owner didn't want the expense of protecting his horse or didn't realize the danger that was there. The statement "if needed" makes one feel the idea of a census was to appropriate funds for the state only; also, a count wouldn't be accurate if the backyard horse wasn't included.

6   The last downfall of the passport system is its failure to protect the horse from disease. The passport has the owner's name and address, the horse's name, age, sex, height, color, brands, markings, and whorls (cowlicks). All of these items will help distinguish and protect against theft. There is no place on the passport to write in dates of shots or results of tests. For this reason the passport only proves identification and ownership. It does nothing to protect the horse against the threat of disease.

7   For these reasons I feel the passport system is just another way for states to get funds. The system is not going to benefit the horse owner, but is going to be another hassle and expense.

3.   Why a Travel Agent?

1   In an article from the magazine *Travel & Leisure* entitled "Why a Travel Agent?", the author stated that, when planning a trip, the traveller is as-

sured of a cheaper and better trip if planned through a travel agent. A travel agent "can assure you a hotel within walking distance of the heart of the city . . ." "Your expenditures are added up before you go," and one "is guided to avoid arriving at the wrong season or just after a big event." I take issue with the author's claims. Based on experiences I have had travelling, I think a traveller is at an advantage planning his or her own trip.

2   On our first trip to Europe all our travel arrangements were made through a travel agent.

3   Despite the fact that we had requested hotels in the heart of the cities with public transportation easily accessible, one hotel was located outside the city limits. The name of the street the hotel was on was not even listed on the city map we had purchased. The closest bus stop was a 15-minute walk from the hotel. No one in the hotel was able to give us any information on the time schedules and the routing the buses followed except that the last bus stopped running at 10 P.M. Consequently we wound up riding cabs, which not only increased our expenses but strained our nerves.

4   We arrived at the next city and the hotel seemed to be centrally located. As we talked to some of the local people, we were warned about walking after dark in the area of the hotel. After we pursued the remark, the people told us the hotel was located in a seedy section. Checking our map, we also found that everything we wanted to see was on the other side of town. There was a metro stop a few blocks from the hotel but after having been warned about the neighborhood we were scared to use it.

5   In both of these incidents not only were the hotels not centrally located but they were not easily accessible to public transportation we could use, and the outcome was added expenditures to cover all the cab fares. Although the travel agent had told us all our fares and taxes were included in our cost, during one flight an extra landing tax was required before we could enter the country. The travel agent had promised economy but what we found was false economy.

6   We arrived in London on a Friday for a four-day stay, only to find the Bank Holiday was that weekend. The Bank Holiday meant that all banks, shopping districts, and many restaurants would be closed Saturday, Sunday, and Monday. Before we could get our bearings we had to rush to the bank and estimate how much money we would be spending during our stay so we could exchange our money before the bank closed. There was an exchange bank at the railroad station but the rate of exchange was not as high and we needed all the money we could get. On Friday we also had to try to do all our shopping, which turned out to be impossible.

7   While in London we had planned a trip to Canterbury via the railroad. The agent had told us we did not need to purchase train tickets in advance, so we got to the train station in what we thought was plenty of time to get our tickets. It was then we discovered why the city had seemed so empty. All the Londoners were at the train station leaving the city. We couldn't get on the train we had planned because it was sold out, so we had to waste several hours waiting for the next scheduled train. As it was, we were barely able to board that train and, when we finally got on, we had to stand most of the time.

8   We had a list of restaurants we wanted to try when we got to Paris. But to our disappointment we found out that a large number of Parisians leave

their city for the month of August and don't return until the middle of September. As a result many of the good restaurants, including all the ones we wanted to try, closed for the holiday. The agent had not mentioned August being a holiday for most of France.

9   The travel agent had advised us to take only a light jacket or raincoat since the weather would still be warm. The temperature range in all the countries we visited, except one, was in the 60s. Aside from all the problems and disappointments we encountered on our trip, we had the added discomfort of being cold for three weeks.

10   We planned our next trip ourselves with the help of guide books, maps, and airline folders.

11   The guide books recommended various hotels and pensions (which are boarding homes owned by local families). Beside each hotel listed was the address, the rates charged, a description of the facility, and the section of town in which it was located.

12   In another section of the books, all the important sights were listed with addresses or general directions. Since these books are printed yearly, most of the information given is correct and up-to-date.

13   With the help of the maps we purchased we were able to locate the hotels we wanted at the price we wanted, and located just where we wanted to be.

14   The books also contained admission charges to museums and galleries as well as typical cab fares and bus fares. This information enabled us to make up a budget on how much we were likely to spend in each city on public transportation and admissions.

15   After reading various airline folders, we found the most inexpensive way to get to our cities and made reservations.

16   The guide books had a temperature range listing for each city we were planning to visit and recommended to the traveller what to wear and what to pack.

17   The planning of this trip took more time than the one planned by the travel agent; but the accommodations and arrangements were better, our expenses were less, and we enjoyed the spirit of adventure.

WRITING ASSIGNMENT: REFUTATIONS

1. Choose an article or essay which does not advance a judgment, and refute it using only fact and inference.

2. Choose an article, essay, or editorial which does advance a judgment, and support the opposite (or a different) judgment.

PERSUASION

Read the following argument, "One Small Step for Genkind," by Casey Miller and Kate Swift. The questions which follow the essay will help you to evaluate its effectiveness as persuasive writing.

Casey Miller (b. 1919) and Kate Swift (b. 1923), authors of Words and Women, *have a writing and editing partnership. "One Small Step for Genkind" was published in the April 16, 1972,* New York Times Magazine, *a Sunday supplement to the newspaper.*

One Small Step for Genkind
Casey Miller and Kate Swift

1   A riddle is making the rounds that goes like this: A man and his young son were in an automobile accident. The father was killed and the son, who was critically injured, was rushed to the hospital. As attendants wheeled the unconscious boy into the emergency room, the doctor on duty looked down at him and said, "My God, it's my son!" What was the relationship of the doctor to the injured boy?

2   If the answer doesn't jump to your mind, another riddle that has been around a lot longer might help: The blind beggar had a brother. The blind beggar's brother died. The brother who died had no brother. What relation was the blind beggar to the blind beggar's brother?

3   As with all riddles, the answers are obvious once you see them: The doctor was the boy's mother and the beggar was her brother's sister. Then why doesn't everyone solve them immediately? Mainly because our language, like the culture it reflects, is male-oriented. To say that a woman in medicine is an exception is simply to confirm that statement. Thousands of doctors are women, but in order to be seen in the mind's eye, they must be called women doctors.

4   Except for words that refer to females by definition (mother, actress, congresswoman), and words for occupations traditionally held by females (nurse, secretary, prostitute), the English language defines everyone as male. The hypothetical person ("If a man can walk 10 miles in two hours . . ."), the average person ("the man in the street") and the active person ("the man on the move") are male. The assumption is that unless otherwise identified, people in general—including doctors and beggars—are men. It is a semantic mechanism that operates to keep women invisible: *man* and *mankind* represent everyone; *he* in generalized use refers to either sex; the "land where our fathers died" is also the land of our mothers—although they go unsung. As the beetle-browed and mustachioed man in a Steig cartoon says to his two male drinking companions, "When I speak of mankind, one thing I *don't* mean is womankind."

5   *Semantically speaking, woman is not one with the species of man, but a distinct subspecies.* "Man," says the 1971 edition of the Britannica Junior Encyclopedia, "is the highest form of life on earth. His superior intelligence, combined with certain physical characteristics, have enabled man to achieve things that are impossible for other animals." (The prose style has something in common with the report of a research team describing its studies on "the development of the uterus in rats, guinea pigs and men.") As though quoting the Steig character, still speaking to his friends in McSorley's, the Junior Encyclopedia continues: "Man must invent most of his behavior, because he lacks the instincts of lower animals. . . . Most of the things he learns have been handed down from his ancestors by language and symbols rather than by biological inheritance."

Thesis

6   Considering that for the last 5,000 years society has been patriarchal, that statement explains a lot. It explains why Eve was made from Adam's rib instead of the other way around, and who invented all those Adam-rib words like *fe*male and *wo*man in the first place. It also explains why, when it is necessary to mention woman, the language makes her a lower caste, a class separate from the rest of man; why it works to "keep her in her place."

7   This inheritance through language and other symbols begins in the home (also called a man's castle) where man and wife (not husband and wife, or man and woman) live for a while with their children. It is reinforced by religious training, the educational system, the press, government, commerce and the law. As Andrew Greeley wrote not long ago, . . . "man is a symbol-creating animal. He orders and interprets his reality by his symbols, and he uses the symbols to reconstruct that reality."

8   Consider some of the reconstructed realities of American history. When school children learn from their textbooks that the early colonists gained valuable experience in governing themselves, they are not told that the early colonists who were women were denied the privilege of self-government; when they learn that in the 18th century the average man had to manufacture many of the things he and his family needed, they are not told that this "average man" was often a woman who manufactured much of what she and her family needed. Young people learn that intrepid pioneers crossed the country in covered wagons with their wives, children and cattle; they do not learn that women themselves were intrepid pioneers rather than part of the baggage.

*End of introduction
Paragraphs 8-9:
textbook examples*

9   In a paper published this year in Los Angeles as a guide for authors and editors of social-studies textbooks, Elizabeth Burr, Susan Dunn and Norma Farquhar document unintentional skewings of this kind that occur either because women are not specifically mentioned as affecting or being affected by historical events, or because they are discussed in terms of outdated assumptions. "One never sees a picture of women captioned simply 'farmers' or 'pioneers,' " they point out. The subspecies nomenclature that requires a caption to read "women farmers" or "women pioneers" is extended to impose certain jobs on women by definition. The textbook guide gives as an example the word *housewife*, which it says not only "suggests that domestic chores are the exclusive burden of females," but gives "female students the idea that they were born to keep house and teaches male students that they are automatically entitled to laundry, cooking and housecleaning services from the women in their families."

10 *Sexist language is any language that expresses such stereotyped attitudes and expectations, or that assumes the inherent superiority of one sex over the other.* When a woman says of her husband, who has drawn up plans for a new bedroom wing and left out closets, "Just like a man," her language is as sexist as the man's who says, after his wife has changed her mind about needing the new wing after all, "Just like a woman."

                            Definition

11 Male and female are not sexist words, but masculine and feminine almost always are. Male and female can be applied objectively to individual people and animals and, by extension, to things. When electricians and plumbers talk about male and female couplings, everyone knows or can figure out what they mean. The terms are graphic and culture free.

12 Masculine and feminine, however, are as sexist as any words can be, since it is almost impossible to use them without invoking cultural stereotypes. When people construct lists of "masculine" and "feminine" traits they almost always end up making assumptions that have nothing to do with innate differences between the sexes. We have a friend who happens to be going through the process of pinning down this very phenomenon. He is 7 years old and his question concerns why his coats and shirts button left over right while his sister's button the other way. He assumes it must have something to do with the differences between boys and girls, but he can't see how.

13 What our friend has yet to grasp is that the way you button your coat, like most sex-differentiated customs, has nothing to do with real differences but much to do with what society wants you to feel about yourself as a male or female person. Society decrees that it is appropriate for girls to dress differently from boys, to act differently, and to think differently. Boys must be masculine, whatever that means, and girls must be feminine.

14 Unabridged dictionaries are a good source for finding out what society decrees to be appropriate, though less by definition than by their choice of associations and illustra-

                            Paragraphs 14-19:
                            dictionary examples

tions. Words associated with males—*manly*, *virile* and *masculine*, for example—are defined through a broad range of positive attributes like strength, courage, directness and independence, and they are illustrated through such examples of contemporary usage as "a manly determination to face what comes," "a virile literary style," "a masculine love of sports." Corresponding words associated with females are defined with fewer attributes (though weakness is often one of them) and the examples given are generally negative if not clearly pejorative: "feminine wiles," "womanish tears," "a womanlike lack of promptness," "convinced that drawing was a waste of time, if not downright womanly."

15 Male-associated words are frequently applied to females to describe something that is either incongruous ("a mannish voice") or presumably commendable ("a masculine mind," "she took it like a man"), but female-associated words are unreservedly derogatory when applied to males; and are sometimes abusive to females as well. The opposite of "masculine" is "effeminate," although the opposite of "feminine" is simply "unfeminine."

16 One dictionary, after defining the word *womanish* as "suitable to or resembling a woman," further defines it as "unsuitable to a man or to a strong character of either sex." Words derived from "sister" and "brother" provide another apt example, for whereas "sissy," applied either to a male or female, conveys the message that sisters are expected to be timid and cowardly, "buddy" makes clear that brothers are friends.

17 The subtle disparagement of females and corresponding approbation of males wrapped up in many English words is painfully illustrated by "tomboy." Here is an instance where a girl who likes sports and the out-of-doors, who is curious about how things work, who is adventurous and bold instead of passive, is defined in terms of something she is not—a boy. By denying that she can be the person she is and still be a girl, the word surreptitiously undermines her sense of identity; it says she is unnatural. A "tomboy," as defined by one dictionary, is a "girl, especially a young girl, who behaves like a spirited boy." But who makes the judgment that she is acting like a spirited boy, not a spirited girl? Can it be a coincidence that in the case of the dictionary just quoted the editor, executive editor, managing editor, general manager, all six members of the Board of Linguists, the usage editor, science editor, all six general editors of definitions, and 94 out of the 104 distinguished experts consulted on usage—are men?

18 It isn't enough to say that any invidious comparisons and stereotypes lexicographers perpetuate are already present in the culture. There are ways to define words like

Anticipation of argument

womanly and tomboy that don't put women down, though the tradition has been otherwise. Samuel Johnson, the lexicographer, was the same Dr. Johnson who said, "A woman preaching is like a dog's walking on his hind legs. It is not done well; but you are surprised to find it done at all."

19 Possibly because of the negative images associated with womanish and womanlike, and with expressions like "woman driver" and "woman of the street," the word woman dropped out of fashion for a time. The women at the office and the women on the assembly line and the women one first knew in school all became ladies or girls or gals. Now a countermovement, supported by the very term women's liberation, is putting back into words like woman and sister and sisterhood the meaning they were losing by default. It is as though, in the nick of time, women had seen that the language itself could destroy them.

20 Some long-standing conventions of the news media add insult to injury. When a woman or girl makes news, her sex is identified at the beginning of a story, if possible in the headline or its equivalent. The assumption, apparently, is that whatever event or action is being reported, a woman's involvement is less common and therefore more newsworthy than a man's. If the story is about achievement, the implication is: "pretty good for a woman." And because people are assumed to be male unless otherwise identified, the media have developed a special and extensive vocabulary to avoid the constant repetition of "woman." The results, "Grandmother Wins Nobel Prize," "Blonde Hijacks Airliner," "Housewife to Run for Congress," convey the kind of information that would be ludicrous in comparable headlines if the subjects were men. Why, if "Unsalaried Husband to Run for Congress" is unacceptable to editors, do women have to keep explaining that to describe them through external or superficial concerns reflects a sexist view of women as decorative objects, breeding machines and extensions of men, not real people?

21 Members of the Chicago chapter of the National Organization for Women recently studied the newspapers in their area and drew up a set of guidelines for the press. These include cutting out descriptions of the "clothes, physical features, dating life and marital status of women where such references would be considered inappropriate if about men"; using language in such a way as to include women in copy that refers to homeowners, scientists and business people where "newspaper descriptions often convey the idea that all such persons are male"; and displaying the same discretion in printing generalizations about women as would be shown toward racial, religious

Paragraphs 20-23: news examples

and ethnic groups. "Our concern with what we are called may seem trivial to some people," the women said, "but we regard the old usages as symbolic of women's position within this society."

22   The assumption that an adult woman is flattered by being called a girl is matched by the notion that a woman in a menial or poorly paid job finds compensation in being called a lady. Ethel Strainchamps has pointed out that since lady is used as an adjective with nouns designating both high and low occupations (lady wrestler, lady barber, lady doctor, lady judge), some writers assume they can use the noun form without betraying value judgments. Not so, Strainchamps says, rolling the issue into a spitball: "You may write, 'He addressed the Republican ladies,' or 'The Democratic ladies convened' . . . but I have never seen 'the Communist ladies' or 'the Black Panther ladies' in print."

23   Thoughtful writers and editors have begun to repudiate some of the old usages. "Divorcée," "grand-mother" and "blonde," along with "vivacious," "pert," "dimpled" and "cute," were dumped by The Washington Post in the spring of 1970 by the executive editor, Benjamin Bradlee. In a memo to his staff, Bradlee wrote, "The meaningful equality and dignity of women is properly under scrutiny today . . . because this equality has been less than meaningful and the dignity not always free of stereotype and condescension."

24   What women have been called in the press—or at least the part that operates above ground—is only a fraction of the infinite variety of alternatives to "woman" used in the subcultures of the English-speaking world. Beyond "chicks," "dolls," "dames," "babes," "skirts" and "broads" are the words and phrases in which women are reduced to their sexuality and nothing more. It would be hard to think of another area of language in which the human mind has been so fertile in devising and borrowing abusive terms. In "The Female Eunuch," Germaine Greer devotes four pages to anatomical terms and words for animals, vegeta-bles, fruits, baked goods, implements and receptacles, all of which are used to dehumanize the female person. Jean Faust, in an article aptly called "Words That Oppress," suggests that the effort to diminish women through lan-guage is rooted in a male fear of sexual inadequacy. "Woman is made to feel guilty for and akin to natural disasters," she writes; "hurricanes and typhoons are named after her. Any negative or threatening force is given a feminine name. If a man runs into bad luck climbing up the ladder of success (a male-invented game), he refers to the 'bitch goddess' success."

25   The sexual overtones in the ancient and no doubt honorable custom of calling ships "she" have become more

Paragraphs 24-29:
sexuality examples

explicit and less honorable in an age of air travel: "I'm Karen. Fly me." Attitudes of ridicule, contempt and disgust toward female sexuality have spawned a rich glossary of insults and epithets not found in dictionaries. And the usage in which four-letter words meaning copulate are interchangeable with cheat, attack and destroy can scarcely be unrelated to the savagery of rape.

26 In her updating of Ibsen's "A Doll's House," Clare Booth Luce has Nora tell her husband she is pregnant—"in the way only men are supposed to get pregnant." "Men, pregnant?" he says, and she nods: "With ideas. Pregnancies there [*she taps his head*] are masculine. And a very superior form of labor. Pregnancies here [*taps her tummy*] are feminine—a very inferior form of labor."

27 Public outcry followed a revised translation of the New Testament describing Mary as "pregnant" instead of "great with child." The objections were made in part on aesthetic grounds: there is no attractive adjective in modern English for a woman who is about to give birth. A less obvious reason was that replacing the euphemism with a biological term undermined religious teaching. The initiative and generative power in the conception of Jesus are understood to be God's: Mary, the mother, was a vessel only.

28 Whether influenced by this teaching or not, the language of human reproduction lags several centuries behind scientific understanding. The male's contribution to procreation is still described as though it were the entire seed from which a new life grows: the initiative and generative power involved in the process are thought of as masculine, receptivity and nurturance as feminine. "Seminal" remains a synonym for "highly original," and there is no comparable word to describe the female's equivalent contribution.

29 An entire mythology has grown from this biological misunderstanding and its semantic legacy; its embodiment in laws that for centuries made women nonpersons was a key target of the 19th-century feminist movement. Today, more than 50 years after women finally won the basic democratic right to vote, the word "liberation" itself, when applied to women, means something less than when used of other groups of people. An advertisement for the NBC news department listed Women's Liberation along with crime in the streets and the Vietnam war as "bad news." Asked for his views on Women's Liberation, a highly placed politician was quoted as saying, "Let me make one thing perfectly clear. I wouldn't want to wake up next to a lady pipe-fitter."

30 One of the most surprising challenges to our male-dominated culture is coming from within organized religion, where the issues are being stated, in part, by con-

Paragraphs 30-35: religious examples

fronting the implications of traditional language. What a growing number of theologians and scholars are saying is that the myths of the Judeo-Christian tradition, being the products of patriarchy, must be reexamined, and that the concept of an exclusively male ministry and the image of a male god have become idolatrous.

31   Women are naturally in the forefront of this movement, both in their efforts to gain ordination and full equality and through their contributions to theological reform, although both these efforts are often subtly diminished. When the Rev. Barbara Anderson was ordained by the American Lutheran Church, one newspaper printed her picture over a caption headed "Happy Girl." *Newsweek*'s report of a protest staged last December by women divinity students at Harvard was jocular ("another tilt at the windmill") and sarcastic: "Every time anyone in the room lapsed into what [the students] regarded as male chauvinism—such as using the word 'mankind' to describe the human race in general—the outraged women . . . drowned out the offender with ear-piercing blasts from party-favor kazoos. . . . What annoyed the women most was the universal custom of referring to God as 'He.' "

32   The tone of the report was not merely unfunny; it missed the connection between increasingly outmoded theological language and the accelerating number of women (and men) who are dropping out of organized religion, both Jewish and Christian. For language, including pronouns, can be used to construct a reality that simply mirrors society's assumptions. To women who are committed to the reality of religious faith, the effect is doubly painful. Professor Harvey Cox, in whose classroom the protest took place, stated the issue directly: The women, he said, were raising the "basic theological question of whether God is more adequately thought of in personal or suprapersonal terms."

33   Toward the end of Don McLean's remarkable ballad "American Pie," a song filled with the imagery of abandonment and disillusion, there is a stanza that must strike many women to the quick. The church bells are broken, the music has died; then:

And the three men I admire most,
The Father, Son and the Holy Ghost,
They caught the last train for the Coast—
The day the music died.

34   Three men I admired most. There they go, briefcases in hand and topcoats buttoned left over right, walking down the long cold platform under the city, past the baggage wagons and the hissing steam onto the Pullman. Bye, bye God—all three of you—made in the image of male supremacy. Maybe out there in L.A. where the weather is warmer, someone can believe in you again.

35 The Roman Catholic theologian Elizabeth Farians says "the bad theology of an overmasculinized church continues to be one of the root causes of women's oppression." The definition of oppression is "to crush or burden by abuse of power or authority; burden spiritually or mentally as if by pressure."

36 When language oppresses, it does so by any means that disparage and belittle. Until well into the 20th-century, one of the ways English was manipulated to disparage women was through the addition of feminine endings to nonsexual words. Thus a woman who aspired to be a poet was excluded from the company of real poets by the label poetess, and a woman who piloted an airplane was denied full status as an aviator by being called an aviatrix. At about the time poetess, aviatrix, and similar Adam-ribbisms were dropping out of use, H. W. Fowler was urging that they be revived. "With the coming expansion of women's vocations," he wrote in the first edition (1926) of "Modern English Usage," "feminines for vocation-words are a special need of the future." There can be no doubt he subconsciously recognized the relative status implied in the -*ess* designations. His criticism of a woman who wished to be known as an author rather than an authoress was that she had no need "to raise herself to the level of the male author by asserting her right to his name."

37 Who has the prior right to a name? The question has an interesting bearing on words that were once applied to men alone, or to both men and women, but now, having acquired abusive associations, are assigned to women exclusively. Spinster is a gentle case in point. Prostitute and many of its synonyms illustrate the phenomenon better. If Fowler had chosen to record the changing usage of harlot from hired man (in Chaucer's time) through rascal and entertainer to its present definition, would he have maintained that the female harlot is trying to raise herself to the level of the male harlot by asserting her right to his name? Or would he have plugged for harlotress?

38 The demise of most -*ess* endings came about before the start of the new feminist movement. In the second edition of "Modern English Usage," published in 1965, Sir Ernest Gowers frankly admitted what his predecessors had been up to. "Feminine designations," he wrote, "seem now to be falling into disuse. Perhaps the explanation of this paradox is that it symbolizes the victory of women in their struggle for equal rights; it reflects the abandonment by men of those ideas about women in the professions that moved Dr. Johnson to his rude remark about women preachers."

39 If Sir Ernest's optimism can be justified, why is there a

Paragraphs 36-39: professional examples

movement back to feminine endings in such words as chairwoman, councilwoman and congresswoman? Betty Hudson, of Madison, Conn., is campaigning for the adoption of "selectwoman" as the legal title for a female member of that town's executive body. To have to address a woman as "Selectman," she maintains, "is not only bad grammar and bad biology, but it implies that politics is still, or should be, a man's business." A valid argument, and one that was, predictably, countered by ridicule, the sure-fire weapon for undercutting achievement. When the head of the Federal Maritime Commission, Helen D. Bentley, was named "Man of the Year" by an association of shipping interests, she wisely refused to be drawn into lighthearted debate with interviewers who wanted to make the award's name a humorous issue. Some women, of course, have yet to learn they are invisible. An 8-year-old who visited the American Museum of Natural History with her Brownie scout troop went through the impressive exhibit on pollution and overpopulation called "Can Man Survive?" Asked afterward, "Well, can he?" she answered, "I don't know about him, but we're working on it in Brownies."

40   Nowhere are women rendered more invisible by language than in politics. The United States Constitution, in describing the qualifications for Representative, Senator and President, refers to each as *he*. No wonder Shirley Chisholm, the first woman since 1888 to make a try for the presidential nomination of a major party, has found it difficult to be taken seriously.

Paragraphs 40-41: political examples

41   The observation by Andrew Greeley already quoted —that "man" uses "his symbols" to reconstruct "his reality"—was not made in reference to the symbols of language but to the symbolic impact the "nomination of a black man for the vice-presidency" would have on race relations in the United States. Did the author assume the generic term "man" would of course be construed to include "woman"? Or did he deliberately use a semantic device to exclude Shirley Chisholm without having to be explicit?

42   Either way, his words construct a reality in which women are ignored. As much as any other factor in our language, the ambiguous meaning of *man* serves to deny women recognition as people. In a recent magazine article, we discussed the similar effect on women of the generic pronoun *he*, which we proposed to replace by a new common gender pronoun *tey*. We were immediately told, by a number of authorities, that we were dabbling in the serious business of linguistics, and the message that reached us from these scholars was loud and clear: It — is — absolutely — impossible — for — anyone — to — introduce —

Paragraphs 42-45: solution

a — new — word — into — the — language — just — because — there — is — a — need — for — it, so — stop — wasting — your — time.

43 When words are suggested like "herstory" (for history), "sportsoneship" (for sportsmanship) and "mistresspiece" (for the work of a Virginia Woolf) one suspects a not-too-subtle attempt to make the whole language problem look silly. But unless Alexander Pope, when he wrote "The proper study of mankind is man," meant that women should be relegated to the footnotes (or, as George Orwell might have put it, "All men are equal, but men are more equal than women"), viable new words will surely someday supersede the old.

44 Without apologies to Freud, the great majority of women do not wish in their hearts that they were men. If having grown up with a language that tells them they are at the same time men and not men raises psychic doubts for women, the doubts are not of their sexual identity but of their human identity. Perhaps the present unrest surfacing in the Women's Movement is part of an evolutionary change in our particular form of life—the one form of all in the animal and plant kingdoms that orders and interprets its reality by symbols. The achievements of the species called man have brought us to the brink of self-destruction. If the species survives into the next century with the expectation of going on, it may only be because we have become part of what Harlow Shapley calls the psychozoic kingdom, where brain overshadows brawn and rationality has replaced superstition.

Anticipation of argument

45 Searching the roots of Western civilization for a word to call this new species of man and woman, someone might come up with *gen*, as in genesis and generic. With such a word, *man* could be used exclusively for males as *woman* is used for females, for gen would include both sexes. Like the words deer and bison, gen would be both plural and singular. Like progenitor, progeny, and generation, it would convey continuity. Gen would express the warmth and generalized sexuality of generous, gentle, and genuine; the specific sexuality of genital and genetic. In the new family of gen, girls and boys would grow to genhood, and to speak of genkind would be to include all the people of the earth.

EXERCISES: Miller and Swift

The following questions will help you to examine some techniques used in this argument.

1. What was your opinion about sexist language before you read this argument? Did Miller and Swift convince you? Why or why not?

2. How would you describe the intended audience? Are you in that group?

3. Why have the writers devoted forty-one paragraphs to explaining and documenting the problem and four paragraphs to their suggested solution? What does this tell you about their purpose and audience?

4. Why is the opening effective?

5. What is the writers' attitude? What is their tone in ¶s 8, 20, 33-34, 37, 39?

6. Why is the example in ¶10 effective?

7. How fair are the examples in ¶s 14 and 20? Find examples to support your judgment.

8. Read the last sentence in ¶17. Do the facts support this inference?

9. Why do the writers often ask questions, as in ¶s 17, 20, 37, 39, 41? Why are questions found only in the last half of the essay?

10. Are there any instances of overstatement in the argument?

11. In ¶36, the writers say, "There can be no doubt he subconsciously recognized the relative status implied in the *-ess* designations." Is this assertion supported by evidence?

12. Will the solution work? How is language changed? Has language changed already because of the women's movement?

13. Is this an effective argument? Have they proven their thesis?

14. Read "Textbooks as Brainwashers" in the anthology. Compare it with this argument.

EXERCISES: Persuasion

A. In the anthology in Section 4, three groups of arguments deal with a specific environmental issue, with the broader issue of television newscasters' responsibility, and with the abstract topic of a person's feelings about his country.

   1. The New River and the Blue Ridge Project, pp. 365–90.
   2. The Responsibility of Newscasters, pp. 317–42.
   3. My Country, Right or Wrong? pp. 302–16.

   Evaluate each argument and be prepared to discuss it in class.

B. Evaluate the following student arguments.

1.   Protecting the Public

1   Recently, the Federal Aviation Administration has been trying to impose restrictions on military jets using commercial air space for training. Two of their recommendations are to require the installation of transponders, devices which enable the air traffic controllers to identify aircraft with great speed and accuracy, and to restrict military planes flying in commercial airspace. As a civilian pilot with seven years of flying experience, I support these recommendations.

2   On June 6, 1971, a Hughes Air West plane was rammed by a U.S. Marine Corps jet fighter, near Duarte, California, killing fifty people, including the pilot of the Marine jet. On October 11, 1974, a New Jersey National Guard F-106, conducting an intercept exercise, struck a single-engine private aircraft, pulverizing it and its occupants. F.A.A. records show that, from January 1969 through June 1975, there were twenty-four near collisions between military and commercial aircraft. All of the commercial aircraft were at assigned altitudes on their proper headings. Each one was confronted by a military jet that was not following the rules. I still shudder to think of the far too many instances when I found myself about to be inhaled by a jet intake. A Cessna 150 is no match against several tons of fighter.

3   The proposed regulations would not hinder military training flights in any way. The military has training areas large enough to handle the type of training military pilots need. And the military has clearly designated climb corridors to these training areas. Military and F.A.A. reports show that the only time training is hindered is when military jets stray out of these areas.

4   Some people will argue that the installation of transponders is too expensive. The National Pilots Association in August 1975 reported, "The only cost would be in installing transponders in each military jet at $125.00 per plane. These funds would come out of the existing defense budget." It is clear that the military can obtain the proper equipment with no extra cost to the U.S. taxpayer. The transponders will enable the radar controllers to identify military jets on their radar screens, and alert them if the jets get too close to commercial aircraft.

5   On the basis of F.A.A. statistics, and from my own experiences, I support the restriction of military jets in commercial air space and the required installation of transponders. Unless the rules are changed, too many civilian aircraft may one day become fodder for hungry military jets.

2.   A Kind of Madness

1   Rachel Carson, marine biologist and author, warns that DDT, a pesticide, has infiltrated our life chain to such an extent that it has brought about genetic effects in mosquitoes, killed fish, poisoned birds, and is recognized as a carcinogen (cancer causing agent). The spray that was used to kill a bug has a continuing life cycle that infiltrates our soil, waterways, and animals to such a degree that most of us living in the U.S.A. ingest, daily, a portion of poison.

2   Consider an apple sprayed with DDT. Repeated washings will not remove this spray because of its clinging oil base and because it has been sprayed at various stages of its growth, so there is DDT in the apple's interior. There may be more apples on the market than there used to be, but their consumption doesn't mean better health. As with Lady Macbeth's bloody hands, no amount of rubbing will render them clean.

3   There is a joke going around that cannibals will no longer eat Americans because we contain too much DDT for their taste. This joke loses its humor when one considers that most nursing mothers are actually feeding their babies DDT in their milk. Also, a study by independent scientists prepared for EPA states, "Small amounts of pesticides absorbed by plankton and insects are transferred in increasing concentrations to fish, birds, animals, and eventually to man through food." ("Pesticide Registration," EPA, Feb. 1974, p. 3)

4   When Paul Revere rode through the streets calling, "The British are coming," it was an immediate and direct threat and we knew who our enemy was. It is less simple now, and the enemy is more deadly. There are 32,000 pesticide products made from one or more of the 900 chemical compounds currently registered at the EPA. The danger is compounded when these materials are combined because scientists do not yet know the effects of many of the combinations.

5   One of the saddest aspects of this pesticide spraying is that the main consumers, farmers, are the least educated about pesticides' adverse effects. A study by the EPA entitled "Farmers' Pesticide Use Decisions" (July 1974) showed that the primary source of information about whether and how much spray to use came from chemical salesmen. The same study details the resistance that weeds and pests develop to chemicals. The farmer, in his dilemma, increases the pesticides' intensity.

6   Bugs are developing a resistance to sprays, but still sprays are used. Both Rachel Carson and *Environmental Magazine,* which is the official publication of "Scientists Institute for Public Information," have alternate suggestions for pesticides which they claim do not pose a hazard to our environment.

7   It's like a grade–B Boris Karloff movie in which a loony scientist, who is nevertheless brilliant in the laboratory, sets out to even up the score against a mosquito. With a concoction of this and that, he destroys the world.

3. Vegetables Are Better

1   No truly compassionate person is proud of the fact that he eats the flesh of innocent animals. Many would-be vegetarians are skeptical about whether or not a vegetarian diet would provide them with their nutritional requirements. Until last December, when I chose to eat meat again because of my gluttony, I had not eaten meat for three years. During the time I was a vegetarian, I did not suffer from indigestion, heartburn, or a sluggish feeling after eating. Vegetarians are more aware of what they are putting into their mouths, and are usually thinner and healthier than many meat eaters. A vegetarian diet is better than a diet based on eating meat.

2   Obtaining a balanced vegetarian diet is not as impossible as it might seem to be. Grocery stores, health food stores, and fruit stands sell abundant supplies of protein-rich foods and fruits and vegetables. While much of the produce sold in grocery stores is chemically treated, produce found at fruit stands is not treated.

3   Produce is not the only food that contains chemicals. Meats are treated with chemicals for coloring. In addition, if the animal had eaten treated

grains before death, then the chemicals will be present in its flesh. Cancer researchers are investigating a possible link between cancer, the ink used in stamping meats, and the plastic wrap meats are sold in.

4   Many people believe that man is by nature a meat eater, needing meat to survive. Our ancient ancestors had teeth that resemble those of a cow. Sharp teeth are needed to tear the meat into small pieces for efficient digestion. Our canine teeth are too blunt to do this efficiently. A personal example of this is that I have found that I occasionally get a sore throat when swallowing meat that isn't torn into small pieces.

5   While our teeth are too blunt to chew meat efficiently, our digestive tract is too long to digest meat. Bacteria and fat from meat stay in our intestines for long periods of time. Other meat eaters have short intestines, while vegetarian animals have long ones. Since last December, I often get indigestion from beef and other fatty meats and cannot digest pork and shrimp without stomach pain. Apparently, we must train our systems to digest meats as it does not come naturally.

6   Meat is not necessarily the best source of protein and B vitamins. The most economical source of both can be found in bottles at almost any drugstore. While we need protein, the amount meat eaters are currently consuming far exceeds the amount needed. Too much protein will upset the pH balance of our blood and will lead to serious illness.

7   Does meat have a natural flavor of its own? Variety meats such as hot dogs, sausages, and luncheon meats have flavorings added to them. Recently I heard a representative from the American Vegetarian Union state that the flavor of meat comes from uric acid which enters the flesh after death. I had always thought blood gave meat flavor. Either way, when meat is properly cooked to kill bacteria, it loses its flavor. Gravies, vegetables, and sauces are then added for flavor.

8   Researchers are currently checking out the possibilities that meat eating might be contributing to heart disease and cancer. Vegetarians have lower rates of these illnesses than do meat eaters. I believe research will prove that a vegetarian diet is better for man. When this occurs, I hope that we will stop exploiting animals and at the same time become healthier. Personally I decided a few weeks ago to return to a vegetarian diet.

EXERCISES AND WRITING ASSIGNMENT

A. 1. With the class or by yourself, decide what would be necessary to create sound arguments on the following subjects.

> Grading systems
> Sale of alcoholic beverages on campus
> Changes in National Football League rules
> Use of dunk shot in college basketball
> Neutering of pets
> Four-day work week
> Use of aerosol sprays
> High school English courses

Right turn on red traffic light
Use of biodegradable packaging
Driver retraining instead of fines for violations

2. From your experience only, draft a convincing argument dealing with one of these subjects or a similar subject of your own choice. Construct your thesis so that you are arguing *in favor of* something.

3. Put your draft aside for at least 24 hours. Then examine it and evaluate your logic. (Don't change anything yet; just note your ideas for improvement.)

4. Group work: Working in groups of three people, devise a complete check list for the evaluation of a persuasive paper.

5. Group work: Continuing to work in your groups and using your check list, thoroughly examine each student's draft. Remember that it is your responsibility to help each person in the group write a good argument.

6. Using your own and the group's criticisms, rewrite your paper.

B. Rewrite your paper again, supporting your argument with two or three sources. Use internal documentation.

C. Construct a sound persuasive argument which makes an aesthetic or functional judgment, and make certain that your audience understands your criteria. Follow Steps 3–6 in Exercise A.

D. 1. Discuss the following topics' requirements with class members. Why might they be more difficult to argue than the topics in Assignment A?

Legalization of marijuana
Abortion on demand
Death with dignity
Rape laws
Mandatory death penalty for murder and kidnapping
Women priests
Public school integration

2. Choose one of these topics or another which makes a moral or ethical judgment, and construct a sound persuasive argument. Follow Steps 3–6 in Exercise A.

Section 3

THE RESEARCH
PROCESS

Getting Started

8

The purpose of this section is to help you acquire or sharpen skills in the research process and to provide you with a reference manual for use in writing documented papers for advanced courses. These same research skills will often be needed in your future professional and business report writing.

THE DOCUMENTED PAPER: DEFINITION AND OVERVIEW

Definition

The documented paper is organized and written by the student, but its development is dependent in part upon information gathered from appropriate source materials. Information, ideas, and opinions obtained from others are carefully documented in the form of footnotes, and a bibliography or list of materials used by the student accompanies the paper. When you write a research paper, much of your time and energy will have to be devoted to finding and reading source materials and to shaping your paper into the format which is expected of you, a format which has become standardized over many years of research by thousands of scholars.

As you concentrate on the mechanics of research, however, you need to remember that the success of your paper will depend primarily on the freshness of your approach to your topic and the critical judgment you exercise in the selection and arrangement of source materials. The secondary role of library source materials cannot be overemphasized. Whenever you write, you draw upon your "sources"—direct experience, informal reading, or detailed study of a specific subject—to fulfill your purpose in writing and to develop and support your thesis.

Report or Evaluation

Research papers can be roughly categorized as either reports or evaluations. Be sure to understand which type of research paper you want to write. A *report* is an *account* of your study of a specific topic; its purpose is to impart information. Your task in writing a report will be the careful selection and organization of what you consider to be the pertinent information on your topic. But keep in mind that a report is not a series of brief summaries lumped together. Your report reflects your critical judgment in the selection and arrangement of information. Rarely, as you know from newspaper reading, do two reports describe an event identically. Your report enables the reader to "see" your subject as you do.

An *evaluation* is the *result* of your study of a specific topic. Your purpose is not only to provide information but to utilize information from various sources to document, convincingly, a particular attitude toward your topic. If you excluded the formal pattern of documentation, your research paper would resemble the kinds of essays that you have been writing—analysis, refutation, argument/persuasion. For example, "Recent Changes in Sunday Closing Laws" is the title of a report; "Why Archaic Blue Laws Are Slowly Being Abolished" is the title of an evaluation paper. Notice that the first paper focuses on reporting *what* has happened; in the second paper the writer analyzes what has happened and explains *why* it has happened. A third possibility can be seen in the title "Archaic Blue Laws Should Be Abolished." In this case the evaluation would take the form of a documented argument.

The Research Process in Brief

The basic steps in the research process remain essentially the same, regardless of the specific class assignment.

Step 1:   Select and limit a topic in keeping with the guidelines of your assignment.

Step 2:   Decide on a tentative thesis, or the question that you will seek to answer, and the possible limits and focus of your paper.

Step 3:   Gather a list of relevant materials from the library or other appropriate sources in a systematic manner.

Step 4:   Locate source materials, read, and gather information on note cards.

Step 5:   Plan the structure of your paper, and, with note cards arranged accordingly, write the first draft.

Step 6:   Prepare the final draft with footnotes and bibliography.

HOW TO CHOOSE A TOPIC

Selecting a Topic

In many classes in which you are asked to write a documented paper, you will be given some guidelines to follow or constraints to work within. While following the guidelines of the assignment, try to write about what interests you. For example, in a modern history or political science course you might be asked to explore the impact of any federal law passed in the twentieth century. If you have an interest in the "Roaring Twenties," this might be the time to explore the impact of prohibition on that era. This research assignment could provide the push you need to become engrossed in an exciting period of American history. It would be wise, however, to avoid those topics which either demand greater technical knowledge than you have acquired or which provoke such a highly emotional response in you that you may find it difficult to examine all evidence fairly.

Limiting a Topic

At times students find it difficult to select a sufficiently narrowed topic for a research assignment. Limiting a subject requires consideration of certain guidelines, knowledge of the topic, and practice.

Guidelines   The required length of the paper, the time you have to complete the assignment, and the availability of source materials are three important constraints. Suppose your paper can be any length, but it must be about a modern American novelist. You enjoyed reading *The Sun Also Rises* and would like to do a paper "on Hemingway," but your paper is due in three weeks. Do you have time to read all—or even several—of Hemingway's other novels? Time alone should lead you to limit your paper to a topic on *The Sun Also Rises* or perhaps to a contrast between theme, character, or narrative point of view in this and one other Hemingway novel which you have time to read and think about in the time allowed.

Knowledge of the Subject Area   The more a student knows about a subject, the easier it will be for him to realize when potential topics are too broad for a particular assignment. Consider, for example, this list of topics:

> The Civil War
> Major Civil War Leaders
> Generals Lee and Grant as Civil War Leaders
> General Lee's Leadership Abilities
> General Lee's Battle Strategies
> General Lee's Strategy for the First Battle of Bull Run

The first three topics are clearly too broad for an undergraduate research paper, but one should recognize that topics four and five are also too broad. Remember that the more you limit your topic the more specific—and thus more informative—your paper can be.

Writing a Thesis or Statement of Purpose

Once you have selected and narrowed your topic, you will need to write a tentative thesis statement to guide your thoughts, organization, and selection of sources. Some instructors may ask you to submit a statement of purpose (rather than a thesis) for approval before you proceed with your research. Here is an example which illustrates the difference between a topic, a statement of purpose, and a thesis.

Topic:	General Lee's Strategy for the First Battle of Bull Run
Statement of Purpose:	To show Lee's skill as a military leader by examining his strategy for the First Battle of Bull Run.
Thesis:	General Lee's success at the First Battle of Bull Run was the result of his skill as a military leader.

Sometimes you may choose a topic because you have a tentative thesis or hypothesis which you want to test through further study. At other times you may want to explore a topic of interest about which you know very little. In that case you will need to begin with a more open-ended statement of purpose or a question instead of a thesis. The goal of your research will be to arrive at a thesis by answering the question you have posed. Using the topic above, here is an appropriate open-ended statement of purpose and a question which will lead you to a thesis:

Statement of Purpose:	To examine Lee's strategy for the First Battle of Bull Run to evaluate his skill as a military leader.
Question:	Does Lee's strategy for the First Battle of Bull Run demonstrate that he was a skillful military leader?

EXERCISES Choosing and Limiting Topics

A.   Choosing a Topic

Evaluate the following as possible topics for an undergraduate research paper of 1000–2000 words. Place each topic in one or more of the following categories: a) too broad, b) too narrow, c) too technical, d) too highly charged, e) insufficient data available, f) appropriate.

1.   energy problems

2.   an analysis of the subliminal messages in cigarette advertising

3.   the closing of Shimer College

4.   the Watergate affair

5.   Henry Kissinger's role in solving the Mid-East crisis

6.   Nick's effectiveness as narrator in *The Great Gatsby*

7.   the Sioux Indians

8.   the use of infrared sensing by the Ertz satellite for natural resources mapping

9.   the effectiveness of the Billy Graham crusades

10.   the novels of Herman Hesse

11.   recent interpretations of the constitutional guidelines for impeachment

12.   the pros and cons of gun legislation

13.   the effect of recent Federal Reserve Bank actions on the state of the economy

14.   the success of the Peace Corps

Go through the list again and decide which "appropriate" topics you would write about in a 1000–2000 word paper due in five weeks. Explain why, briefly; consider your interests, your knowledge, and the availability of source materials.

B.   Limiting a Topic

From the list of proposed topics in Exercise A, Part 1, select a topic which seemed too broad and develop two or three more limited topics from it which would be sufficiently narrowed for a research paper of 1000–2000 words.

C.   Limiting a Topic and Writing a Thesis

You have been asked to write a paper in one of the following broad subject areas. Select an area you know well, focus on an acceptable topic for a research paper of 1000–2000 words, and write a statement of purpose and a thesis statement. If none of the subject areas seems suitable, select your own and complete the exercise.

1. comic strips
2. science fiction novels
3. recent horror films
4. the Revolutionary War
5. TV advertising
6. ecology

The Working Bibliography

9

After you have chosen your topic and considered the focus and limits of your paper, your next task is to compile a working bibliography, that is, a list of source materials. The usual place to begin, the library, houses the various reference guides: major subject indexes, biographical indexes, periodical indexes, reference works, and the card catalog. Use your time wisely by recording *all* potentially helpful sources the first time around. It is annoying to have to search the library again for the listing of a book or article which seems necessary later.

Most students find 3 × 5 index cards a valuable tool in putting together a working bibliography. If you devote one card to each potential source (book, article, government pamphlet), then you can easily make additions while keeping the cards alphabetized, grouped according to source location, or organized in the sequence in which you plan to read them. Eventually, the unused cards can be thrown away, and the remaining ones can be alphabetized for your final bibliography. Index cards are most valuable because of their flexibility.

To develop your working bibliography efficiently, copy onto the cards the information needed to locate the source, to guide you in its use, and to complete your final bibliography. It is important to learn the accepted form for bibliographic citations *before* you start collecting your working bibliography; if you copy all of the needed information in the correct form initially, you will avoid a return trip to the library at the last minute when you are preparing your final bibliography.

BIBLIOGRAPHY FORM

Study the model entries below to develop a general understanding of the *kind of information*, the *order of information*, and the *pattern of punctuation* required in a bibliography, but do not try to memorize each model. Instead, when you are gathering your working bibliography, take this book to the library and use the models as guides. Through practice you will learn the accepted patterns of citation.

Basic Bibliography Form for Books and Articles*

The simplest bibliography form for a book would include the following information, in this order:

1. The author's full name, last name first;

2. The title (and subtitle) of the book, underlined;

3. The facts of publication: the place of publication, the publisher, and the date of publication.

Observe the pattern and the punctuation:

```
Nairn, Ian. The American Landscape: A Critical View. New York:
    Random House, 1965.
```

Other information (name of the editor, number of the edition, or number of volumes) is added in the appropriate places to this basic pattern for complete identification of the book. These variations appear in the samples below.

The simplest form for an article in a journal, weekly magazine, or newspaper would include the following information, in this order:

1. The author's full name, last name first;

2. The title of the article, in quotation marks;

3. The facts of publication: the title of the journal, underlined; the volume; the date; and inclusive page numbers.

---

*The following information and examples are based on guidelines for bibliography form in *The MLA Style Sheet,* 2nd ed. (New York: Modern Language Association, 1970) and in *A Manual for Writers of Term Papers, Theses, and Dissertations,* 3rd ed., by Kate L. Turabian (Chicago: University of Chicago Press, 1967).

In other words, the basic pattern is the same for books and articles, but articles require the title of the journal as well as the title of the article, and the other facts of publication are different from books.

Observe the pattern and punctuation:

> Warren, Austin. "Hawthorne's Reading." <u>New England Quarterly</u>, 8 (1935), 480–97.

As you will see in the samples of bibliography form for articles, the presentation of volume number and date varies, depending on the type of work in which the article appears; however, these are minor variations of the same basic format (author, title, facts of publication) for both books and articles. Other variations are illustrated and explained in the sample entries which follow.

SAMPLE BIBLIOGRAPHY ENTRIES

Books

A book by two or three authors:

> Beard, Charles A., and Mary R. Beard. <u>The American Spirit: A Study in the Idea of Civilization in the United States</u>. New York: Macmillan, 1942.

(Second and third authors' names appear in signature form. Subtitles may be omitted in footnotes but must be included in the bibliography; a colon separates title and subtitle.)

A book with more than three authors:

> Baugh, Albert C., and others. <u>A Literary History of England</u>. New York: Appleton–Century–Crofts, 1948.

(Use the name of the first author to appear on the title page. The Latin abbreviation "et al." may be used instead of "and others.")

An edited work (editor named in addition to author):

> Franklin, Benjamin. <u>The Autobiography of Benjamin Franklin</u>, ed. Max Farrand. Berkeley: University of California Press, 1949.

(A comma follows the title, and the abbreviation "ed." is used.)

> Lynn, Kenneth S., ed. <u>Huckleberry Finn: Text, Sources, and Criticism</u>. New York: Harcourt, Brace and World, 1961.

(If what is important to your paper is the author's work itself, then the author's name should come first, with the editor's name following the title, as in the first sample of an edition. If what is important is the editor's work, or if what has been edited is a collection of works by various writers, then the editor's name should come first, as in the second example.)

A translation:

Solzhenitsyn, Alexander. <u>August 1914</u>, trans. Michael Glenny. New York: Farrar, Straus and Giroux, 1972.

A book in two or more volumes:

Sewall, Richard B. <u>The Life of Emily Dickinson</u>. 2 vols. New York: Farrar, Straus and Giroux, 1974.

(A period follows the title, and the abbreviation "vols." is used.)

A book in its second or subsequent edition:

Curti, Merle. <u>The Growth of American Thought</u>. 3rd ed. New York: Harper and Row, 1964.

(Notice the location of the edition number, and the abbreviations used. Always include the number of the edition you have used, if it is not the first.)

A book in a series:

Waggoner, Hyatt H. <u>Nathaniel Hawthorne</u>. University of Minnesota Pamphlets on American Writers, No. 23. Minneapolis: University of Minnesota Press, 1962.

(The series name—and number, if there is one—follows the title but is not underlined.)

A book in a paperback series:

Kott, Jan. <u>Shakespeare, Our Contemporary</u>, trans. Boleslaw Taborski. Anchor Books. Garden City, N.Y.: Doubleday, 1966.

(Add the state or country to place of publication if necessary to avoid confusion, e.g., Cambridge, Mass. or Cambridge, England.)

A work in a collection:

Fogle, Richard H. "Ambiguity and Clarity in Hawthorne's 'Young Goodman Brown,' " <u>New England Quarterly</u>, 18 (Dec. 1943), rpt. in <u>A Casebook on the Hawthorne Question</u>, ed. Agnes McNeill Donohue. New York: Thomas Y. Crowell, 1963.

(The abbreviation for reprinted is "rpt." Notice that the original facts of publication are provided as well as the facts of publication for the collection. Single quotation marks are used for titles of works that are a part of the title of the article.)

A reprint of an earlier work:

> Marlowe, Christopher. The Works of Christopher Marlowe, ed. C.
> F. Tucker Brooke. 1910; rpt. Oxford: Clarendon Press, 1966.

(Since the date of a work is often important in evaluating it, cite the
original date of publication as well as the facts of publication for the
reprinted version.)

A corporate author:

> Brown University Library. Dictionary Catalogue of the Harris
> Collection of American Poetry and Plays. 12 vols. Boston: G.
> K. Hall, 1972.

> New York State Office of Planning Coordination. Local Planning
> and Zoning, 1969: A Manual of Powers and Procedures for
> Citizens and Governmental Officials. Albany, N.Y.: Office of
> Planning Coordination, 1969.

An encyclopedia article:

> K[enne]y, E[dward] J. "Ovid." Encyclopedia Britannica. 1972.

(When articles are signed or initialed, the author's name can be cited.
Material added for clarification should be placed in *square brackets*.
Articles are updated regularly; thus year rather than edition should
be provided.)

Articles

*An article in a journal that has continuous paging throughout the issues
published in a given year:*

> Armstrong, William A. "George Bernard Shaw: The Playwright as
> Producer." Modern Drama, 8 (Feb. 1966), 347–61.

(Quarterly journals would require season and year [Fall 1966]; yearly
journals would require simply the year [1966] in parentheses.)

An article in a monthly magazine that has separate paging in each issue:

> Chaneles, Sol. "A Job Program for Ex-convicts That Works."
> Psychology Today, March 1975, pp. 43–46.

(Although providing the volume number would not be incorrect, the
month and year are sufficient for locating such an article. Notice that
when the volume is not given, month and year are not in parentheses
and "p." or "pp." precedes the page numbers.)

An article from a weekly magazine:

> Barnes, Peter. "Bringing Back the WPA." The New Republic, 15
> March 1975, pp. 19–21.

(The exact date—month, day, and year—is necessary for locating an article in a weekly magazine; notice the order of day, month, and year.)

An anonymous article:

> "The Palestinian Tug of War." Newsweek, 4 Nov. 1974, pp. 36–38.

(The order is the same for any article. The missing name is sufficient indication that the article is anonymous. The citation would be alphabetized under "P.")

An article from a newspaper:

> Denlinger, Kenneth. "Johnny Miller: Shooting Par Is No
> Disgrace." The Washington Post, 14 March 1975, p. D5, col. 5.

(Notice that this form is the same as for an article in a weekly magazine except that a section letter precedes the page number, if the newspaper is sectioned, and column numbers are included. If the city is a part of the newspaper's title on the masthead, it is italicized; if not, it should be added but not underlined. Examples: *The New York Times,* but *The* [London] *Times* or the Cleveland *Plain Dealer*.)

An editorial:

> Editorial. "Rights and Remedies." The New York Times, 25
> January 1976, Sec. 4, p. 16, col. 2.

A letter to the editor:

> Boltz, Paul W. "In the Right Direction," in "Letters to the
> Editor." The Wall Street Journal, 12 January 1976, p. 9, col.
> 2.

A signed review:

> Thurman, Judith. "Unchanged by Suffering?" rev. of Anya, by
> Susan Fromberg Schaeffer. Ms. Magazine, March 1975, p. 46.

(Since titles of review articles often omit the subject of the article, cite the title of the work being reviewed and its author, preceded by "rev. of.")

An unsigned review:

> "Viewpoints," rev. of "The Autobiography of Miss Jane Pittman"
> (a TV film shown on CBS, 31 Jan. 1974). Time Magazine, 4 Feb.
> 1974, p. 65.

Other Sources

The materials in this section, though often useful for research projects, do not always lend themselves to documentation by the basic forms illustrated above. Good sense dictates that you follow the basic order—author, title, facts of publication—as much as possible and that you add whatever information is necessary to make the citation both clear and useful to your reader.

An unpublished thesis or dissertation:

> Upton, Dorothy Louise. "The Minor Characters in the Four Major Novels of Hawthorne." Unpublished Master's thesis, Columbia University, 1960.

A pamphlet:

> So You'd Like to Do Something About Water Pollution. Publication #344. Washington, D.C.: League of Women Voters of the United States, 1969.

A bulletin:

> Krasnowiecki, Jan, and others. Legal Aspects of Planned Unit Residential Development, with Suggested Legislation. Technical Bulletin No. 52. Washington, D.C.: Urban Land Institute, 1965.

Some public documents:

> U.S. Constitution, Art. I, Sec. 3.

(The Constitution is referred to by article and section.)

> Turner v. Arkansas, 407 U.S. 366 (1972).

(The citation of a court case lists the name of the case, volume number, number of law report[s], page number, and year.)

> Labor Management Relations Act (Taft–Hartley Act). Statutes at Large. Vol. 61 (1947). U.S. Code, Vol. 34 (1952).

(Bills which have become law are published annually in *Statutes at Large*. Later they are published in the *United States Code*. The citation should include the title of the bill, the source, preferably *U.S. Code* if the bill has been published there, the volume number, and year. References to both sources can be given as a convenience to your reader.)

> U.S. President. Public Papers of the Presidents of the United States. Washington, D.C.: Office of the Federal Register, 1961.

A lecture:

>   Fowler, William. "Henry VIII." Lecture delivered at the
>   College of William and Mary. 1956.

An interview:

>   Interview with Dr. T. Norman Hurd, Budget Director, State of
>   New York. 1967.

A letter:

>   Information in a letter to the author from Dr. Cecil M.
>   McCulley. 5 June 1968.

Mimeographed or dittoed material:

>   Burns, Gerald. "How to Say Some Interesting Things About
>   Poems." Garden City, N.Y., 1972. (Dittoed.)

A TV documentary:

>   "The Making of a Foreign Policy." A PBS telecast produced by
>   the National Public Affairs Center for Television. 26 March
>   1975.

SAMPLE BIBLIOGRAPHY CARDS

In addition to writing necessary information in the correct order on your
bibliography cards, you should include additional information to help in
locating and using the books and articles you have chosen. If you are
using both your school library and a public library, indicate on each bibliography card the location of the source. At the card catalog, copy on
your bibliography cards the full call number for each potential source.
Finally, note the contents of the work or how you expect to use it. Here
are sample bibliography cards.

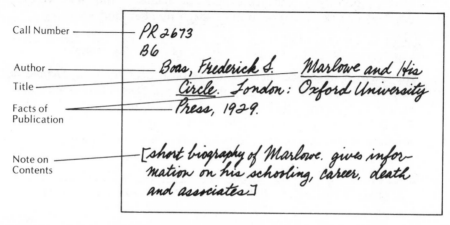

Fig. 9-1. Sample Bibliography Card for a Book

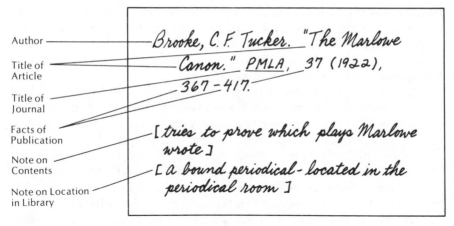

Author ——————————— *Brooke, C. F. Tucker.* "*The Marlowe*

Title of ———————————— *Canon.*" *PMLA*, 37 (1922),
Article

Title of ————————————— 367–417.
Journal

Facts of ——————————— [*tries to prove which plays Marlowe*
Publication   *wrote*]

Note on ———————————— [*a bound periodical– located in the*
Contents   *periodical room*]

Note on Location
in Library

Fig. 9-2. Sample Bibliography Card for an Article

PRIMARY AND SECONDARY SOURCES

Depending on the guidelines for your research paper and the nature of your topic, it may be important to distinguish between primary and secondary sources. *Primary sources* have the most immediate or direct relationship to the subject. For historical topics, they would include original documents such as state papers, speeches, legislation, letters, and autobiographies. For literary topics they would include the literary works themselves plus journals, diaries, early drafts of a work, and autobiographies. *Secondary sources* are the studies and interpretations of primary sources such as histories, biographies, and literary criticism. Depending on the course and the constraints of a particular research assignment, you may be asked to base your paper solely on primary sources; more typically, you will use a balance of primary and secondary source materials. In a freshman writing course, your instructor may not expect you to select topics requiring the use of primary sources. Instead, you might be asked to write a documented opinion paper rather than a completely original paper.

EVALUATING SOURCES

As you gather a working bibliography, keep in mind the distinction between primary and secondary sources. Judging the reliability and usefulness of potential source materials is perhaps more important to the research process. You get credit only for the *result* of your hours of purposeful reading, note-taking, and thinking—the completed paper. Consequently, *what* sources you select and *how* you use them determine the success of your project.

In Chapter 6, you learned that one step in evaluating a work is identifying the writer's audience. This is particularly helpful in compiling a bibliography for a research paper. Since you can often estimate the degree of specialized knowledge in a work from knowledge of the writer's anticipated audience, you can save time by eliminating potential sources from your working bibliography which are too general, too elementary, or too specialized to fit the particular project.

Remember that, to convince you, a writer *may* distort evidence. That is why primary sources in research projects are so valuable. Using primary sources relevant to your topic provides a check against inaccuracies or distortions of evidence. You should never, for example, attempt a critical evaluation of Shakespeare's *Romeo and Juliet* based entirely on critical studies, until you have read the play yourself. The careful researcher finds an important difference between the entire text of a President's speech, a news story about that speech (even "straight news" has a definite point of view), and an editorial on it. If the speech is a vital part of your research paper, you must know it thoroughly. Everything else you may choose to read about the speech is of secondary importance.

EXERCISES: Bibliography Form and Evaluating Sources

A.   Bibliography Form

To practice bibliography form, make each of the following detailed statements about a published work into a correct bibliographic citation. Pay attention to quotation marks, italics (underlining), and punctuation.

1.   George Vernadsky wrote the book A History of Russia. The 4th revised edition was published in 1954 at New Haven by Yale University Press.

2.   In 1921, for Prentice-Hall in New York, E. H. C. Oliphant edited, in two volumes, a book entitled Shakespeare and His Fellow Dramatists.

3.   A book called Who Runs Congress? was published in 1972 by Bantam Books, New York. The book, written by Mark J. Green, James M. Fallows and David R. Zwick, is part of the Ralph Nader Congress Project series.

4.   An article called The Tragedy of Marlowe's Doctor Faustus appeared in volume 5 of College English, on pages 70-75. The article, published in 1943, was written by Arthur Mizener.

5.   On January 19, 1976, an article entitled Humphrey: How to Succeed Without Really Trying appeared on pages 12 and 13 of Time Magazine.

6.   The Wall Street Journal printed an article by Eric Morgenthaler called How Many Beers Make a Steel Worker Lose His Decorum? The article, printed 12 January 1976, appeared on page 1, column 1 and page 22, column 6.

7. The book Power Shift, written by Kirkpatrick Sale, is reviewed in an article entitled South Against North. The article, written by James Fallows, appeared on pages 76, 80, and 82 of the February 1976 issue of Harper's Magazine.

B. Evaluating Sources

Evaluate the following works as potential sources for research papers. State briefly why the work would or would not be a useful source. Consider the author, the anticipated audience, and the research writer's purpose and audience.

1. "The Private Anguish of Judy Agnew" by Nick Thimmesch in *McCall's Magazine*. To be used for a paper on the significance of former Vice President Spiro Agnew's resignation.

2. An article on the brain in *Time Magazine*, for a paper on recent scientific investigations of the brain. To be used for a paper in a graduate course in biochemistry.

3. An article on the development and uses of the concept of executive privilege, from *The New Republic*, by special contributor Dr. Whilte, Chairman of the History Department at Harvard University. To be used for a paper which examines changes in the concepts of executive privilege.

4. An Art Buchwald column on the "Ripoff Oil Company." To be used for a paper examining causes for the increasing cost of gasoline.

5. The *Dictionary of American Biography*'s biographical essay on General Robert E. Lee. To be used as background reading for an undergraduate paper on Lee's military strategies in the First Battle of Bull Run.

6. An article in the *Proceedings of the National Academy of Sciences* titled "Lymphocyte Cytotoxicity to Autologous Liver Cells in Chronic Active Hepatitis." To be used for an undergraduate research paper analyzing possible social causes for the increase in cases of hepatitis.

7. The "Cliff's Notes" study of *The Scarlet Letter*. To be used for a paper on Hawthorne's symbolism for a seminar in the American novel.

Locating Sources in the Library

10

For most research assignments, your library will provide the best collection of source materials. Familiarize yourself with its layout, hours, regulations, and procedures for obtaining materials as soon and as thoroughly as possible. Librarians are willing to give assistance, but you will save time if you know your way around. Once you learn how to find materials in one library, you will be at home in most others.

THE CARD CATALOG

The card catalog, chief guide to your library's book collection, is comprised of: 1) author cards, considered main entry cards; 2) title cards, like author cards except that titles are typed in lower-case letters at the top of the cards; and 3) subject cards, like author cards except that subject headings are typed in capital letters at the top of the cards.

Interpreting a Catalog Card

Each catalog card contains a wealth of helpful information in addition to author, title, and call number. Here is an annotated card and

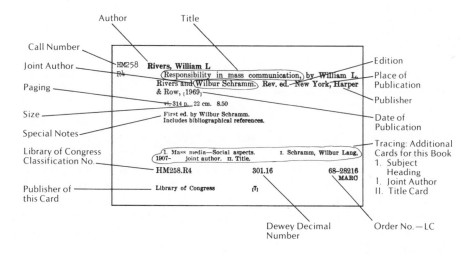

Fig. 10-1. Annotated Catalog Card

a list of the information you should copy onto your bibliography cards or at least note as an aid to gathering additional materials.

1. *Call number:* Necessary to locate the book in the library.

2. *Author, title, facts of publication:* Necessary for your final bibliography.

3. *Paging:* The length of the book will help you gauge the extent of coverage and plan your study time.

4. *Special notes:* Always check here to see if the book contains a bibliography, which would be another list of source materials to aid in your research.

5. *Tracing:* Note the subject headings under which you find a card for this book and check them in the catalog for additional books on the topic.

Using the Card Catalog

A few libraries file author, title, and subject cards together alphabetically in one large catalog; more often, the cards are separated into three catalogs. Many libraries are now placing their entire card catalogs on microfilm or microfiche to save space. Whichever method is used, certain conventions for filing are followed.

Author catalog This catalog contains cards filed alphabetically by the author's last name first, and includes cards for editors, translators, illustrators, and organizations which "author" publications. When several types of "authors" have the same name, the order of filing is 1) person (e.g., Raleigh, Sir Walter), 2) place or thing (e.g., Raleigh, Chamber of Commerce; Raleigh, North Carolina).

Title catalog   This catalog contains title cards filed alphabetically word by word, excluding *a, an,* and *the* at the beginning of titles. If you know the title of a book but not its author, use this catalog.

Subject catalog   This catalog contains subject cards filed alphabetically word by word according to the subject headings. These include people (WILLIAMS, TENNESSEE; ROOSEVELT, ELEANOR), topics (GOVERNMENT AND THE PRESS; POP ART), and place names (CANADA; SAN FRANCISCO). Thus, if you want a book *by* Hemingway (his novels or collected short stories), use the Author Catalog, but if you want a book *about* Hemingway (biographies, criticism), use the Subject Catalog and look under HEMINGWAY.

Cards for books listed under a specific subject heading are filed alphabetically by author's name. When many books exist on a particular subject (e.g., SHAKESPEARE), further subdivisions under that subject heading may be used to classify the books (e.g., SHAKESPEARE: BIOGRAPHIES, CRITICISM, BIBLIOGRAPHIES). The order of cards within each subdivision is alphabetical by author.

CLASSIFICATION OF BOOKS

Books are shelved in the library according to either the Library of Congress classification system or the Dewey decimal system; both are standardized codes combining numbers and letters which classify books by subject. You are probably familiar with the Dewey system used by many smaller, usually public, libraries. Since most college libraries now use the Library of Congress (LC) system, you will need to familiarize yourself with this system also.

Outline of the Library of Congress Classification

The initial letter indicates the major subject divisions:

A — General Works
B — Philosophy and Religion
C — History, Auxiliary Sciences
D — History and Topography, except America
E — American History and General U.S. History
F — U.S. History (local), Latin America, and Canada
G — Geography and Anthropology

H— Social Sciences
J — Political Science
K — Law
L — Education
M— Music
N— Fine Arts
P — Language and Literature
Q— Science
R — Medicine
S — Agriculture, Forestry, Hunting, and Fishing
T — Technology
U— Military Science
V — Naval Science
Z — Library Science and Bibliography

Major subdivisions within each general subject category are indicated by a second letter. For example, some subdivisions under "D" (History) are "DC" (French History) and "DK" (Russian History). Further subdivisions reflecting type, date, author, and specific work are indicated by Arabic numerals and the first initial of the author's last name. A specific British history text, for instance, George M. Trevelyan's *The English Revolution, 1688-1689,* would have the following number:

DA
452
.T7

Arrangement of Books on the Shelf

The classification number (or "call number") of each book is found in the upper left-hand corner of the catalog card and on the spine of the book, where it can be seen when the book is shelved. Be sure to copy the complete call number accurately before you look for a book. LC call numbers arrange books on the shelves in the following order:

1. alphabetical
2. numerical
3. decimal

Fig. 10-2. Model of Shelf Order for Books

THE REFERENCE COLLECTION

In most libraries you will find a separate area devoted exclusively to reference materials. A library's reference collection is shelved in the reference room, according to the classification system used by that library, with an "R" preceding the book's call number to indicate that the book is part of the reference collection and hence does not circulate.

The materials in the reference collection are an invaluable aid to the student researcher because they include information of a factual nature in a condensed format such as atlases, dictionaries, encyclopedias, general histories, critical studies, and biographies. In addition, various reference tools such as bibliographies and indexes will be found. Familiarize yourself with the general reference materials in your field(s) of study. Among the most important reference materials for all researchers are the biographical dictionaries and the general indexes to books and periodicals.

Biographical Dictionaries

Universal

Contemporary Authors. 1962 to date. A biographical and bibliographical guide to current fiction and non-fiction writers and their works.

Current Biography. 1940 to date. Provides articles on living persons of significance in a variety of fields throughout the world. Each volume contains a list of persons included, classified by profession.

International Who's Who. 1935 to date. Contains brief biographies of important persons from almost every country; each new edition updates existing biographies and adds new ones.

Webster's Biographical Dictionary. A one-volume biographical reference work, worldwide in scope, this dictionary has been enlarged with each new edition since its beginnings in 1943.

American

American Men and Women of Science. (Formerly *American Men of Science.*) 12th ed. 8 vols. 1973. Provides brief sketches for more than 150,000 scientists. Lists degrees held and fields of specialization.

Dictionary of American Biography. 20 vols. 1928–37. Supplementary volumes issued in 1944 and 1958. Reliable biographical and critical essays on important Americans no longer living.

Who Was Who in America. 6 vols. 1951–73. Contains brief biographical sketches of Americans no longer living.

Who's Who in America. 1899 to date. Brief biographical sketches on living Americans, continually updated.

Who's Who in American Women.   1958 to date. Contains brief articles on more than 24,000 women who have been selected for their "achievement or occupational position."

British

Dictionary of National Biography.   63 vols. 1885–1901. Reprinted in 22 vols., 1908–09. Supplements to 1960. Authoritative biographies of important English men and women no longer living.

Who's Who.   1849 to date. A source of biographical information on living English men and women.

Indexes to Periodicals

Periodicals (scholarly journals, popular magazines, and newspapers) provide good source materials for research projects. Some of the most important studies of specialized topics are found in journal articles, and recent issues of newspapers and magazines offer information and opinions on current events. Periodicals are usually located in a separate area of your library and are shelved alphabetically by title. Back issues of journals are bound in hard-cover volumes; current issues may be shelved with the bound volumes or on a separate rack. Current issues of newspapers are stored on rollers. Many libraries maintain back issues of magazines and newspapers on microfilm. Lists of a library's periodical collection (both alphabetically by title and also by subject heading) are usually located at the circulation desk, the reference desk, and in the periodical room.

The most efficient way to obtain source materials from periodicals is to use one or more of the periodical indexes. Three of the most-used indexes are described and interpreted below.

The Reader's Guide to Periodical Literature (1900 to date), probably the most-used periodical index, indexes popular magazines. It combines author and subject headings in alphabetical sequence. It is a cumulative index, issued twice monthly (except monthly in July and August) and bound in hard-cover volumes annually. Permanent volumes are cumulated for two years and are published in odd-numbered years. When a person is both author and subject, articles *by* the person are given first, followed by articles *about* him. When an author's name and a subject heading are the same, the order is: author, subject, subject with further subdivision (see sample entries on p. 170).

While the *Reader's Guide* is your best reference guide to popular magazines, the *Social Sciences and Humanities Index* (1916 to date; vols. I-XVIII are titled *International Index)* is one of the most useful guides to articles in scholarly journals for literature, history, political science, sociology, and related subjects. Like the *Reader's Guide*, this is a combined author-subject index. The order of information provided in each entry and the abbrevia-

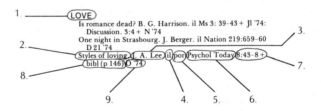

1. subject heading: Love.
2. title of article: "Styles of Loving." Only the first letter of the title is capitalized; no quotation marks are used.
3. author: J. A. Lee.
4. article contains illustrations.
5. por: article contains portrait(s).
6. title of magazine: *Psychology Today*. Magazine titles are often abbreviated.
7. volume and page numbers: vol. 8, pp. 43–48 and continued on additional pages in same issue.
8. bibliography on p. 146.
9. date of publication: Oct. 1974.

Fig. 10-3.   Interpretation of a *Reader's Guide* Entry

tions used are similar to those in *Reader's Guide;* a list of the abbreviations used for the periodicals indexed is included at the beginning of each volume.

Newspapers are a good source of information about a contemporary topic. Since it is one of the most thorough and respected newspapers, *The New York Times* is available in most libraries; back issues are on microfilm. Become familiar with *The New York Times Index* (1913 to date). It is a subject index, issued twice each month and cumulated annually, with articles arranged chronologically under each subject heading. The *Index* provides brief summaries of articles. Fig. 10-4 shows sample entries.

To index many sources, compilers must abbreviate extensively. Learn the code for volume, date, and paging information for magazine articles (plus other abbreviations used), and rearrange that information on your bibliography cards to be consistent with the standard form described in Chapter 9.

Most libraries own the following specialized indexes to periodicals and source books. The titles of most of the indexes reveal their special uses.

Applied Science and Technology Index.   1958 to date. For materials prior to 1958 see *Industrial Arts Index*, 1913–57. A subject index to periodicals including engineering, data processing, earth sciences, space science, and more.

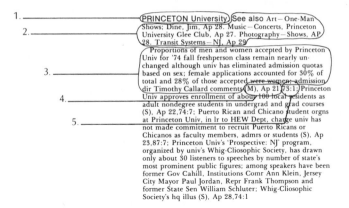

1. ————————
2. ————————
3. ————————
4. ————————
5. ————————

1. subject heading

2. references to other articles on subject under other subject headings

3. summary of article

4. date of publication: April 21

5. page and column number: p. 73, col. 1

Fig. 10-4.   Interpretation of a *New York Times Index* Entry

Art Index.   1929 to date. Both author and subject index to periodicals in fine arts, crafts, films, interior decoration, and photography.

Biography Index: A Cumulative Index to Biographical Material in Books and Magazines.   1946–47 to date. Indexes biographical materials for both living and deceased persons.

Biological and Agricultural Index.   1964 to date. Formerly *Agricultural Index,* 1919–64. A subject index including nutrition.

Book Review Digest.   1905 to date. Arranged by author of the book reviewed. Condenses several reviews of both fiction and non-fiction works.

Business Periodicals Index.   1958 to date. For materials prior to 1958 see *Industrial Arts Index.* A cumulative subject index.

Education Index.   1929 to date. Both author and subject index of books, pamphlets, and government reports, as well as periodicals on topics in education.

Engineering Index.   1884 to date.

Essay and General Literature Index.   1934 to date. (Covers material from

1900.) An author and subject index that includes references to both biographical and critical materials. Lists works *by* as well as *about* an author. Chief focus is literary criticism.

Public Affairs Information Service (PAIS) Bulletin.   1915 to date. An index to books, pamphlets, reports, and articles on economics, government, social issues, and public affairs.

Vertical File Index: A Subject and Title Index to Selected Pamphlet Material. 1932–35 to date. The best index to pamphlets; gives descriptions, prices, and means of obtaining the pamphlets.

Additional Reference Books of General Interest

This section lists other representative dictionaries, handbooks, encyclopedias, and histories available in most libraries. Most of these works are updated periodically. Your library also has workbooks and atlases, which have not been listed here. Take a moment to check the date (some information becomes outdated quickly), purpose, and organization of any library reference book you plan to use. Remember, too, that reference materials are best used for preliminary information gathering; most instructors will not accept a research paper based primarily on generalized reference works.

Guides to Reference Books

Gates, Jean Key. *Guide to the Use of Books and Libraries.* 2nd ed. 1965.

Murphy, Robert W. *How and Where to Look It Up.* 1958.

Shores, Louis. *Basic Reference Sources.* 1954.

Winchell, Constance M. *Guide to Reference Books.* 8th ed. 1967. Supplements.

General Encyclopedias

Encyclopedia Americana. 30 vols. Revised annually.

Encyclopaedia Britannica.   30 vols. Revised annually.
   The two best multi-volume encyclopedias for college use.

Yearbooks (Current Events and Statistics)

Congressional Record. 1873 to date. Detailed information about activities of Congress. Issued daily during sessions.

Facts on File. 1940 to date. Digest of important news events. Issued weekly.

Statesman's Year Book. 1964 to date. Political and economic information of international scope. Issued every two years.

Statistical Abstract of the United States. 1878 to date. Annual publication of Bureau of the Census providing information on American institutions.

Quotations

Bartlett, John. *Familiar Quotations.* 14th ed. 1968.

Stevenson, Burton. *The Home Book of Quotations.* 10th ed. 1967.

Mythology and Folklore

Frazer, Sir James G. *The Golden Bough.* 12 vols. 1907–15; Supplement, 1936; 1955. An exhaustive study of myths. A one-volume condensed version is available.

Funk and Wagnalls Standard Dictionary of Folklore, Mythology, and Legend. 2 vols. 1949.

Hamilton, Edith. *Mythology.* 1942. A brief guide to Greek, Roman, and Norse myths.

The Arts

Architecture Through the Ages. Rev. ed. 1953.

Bryan's Dictionary of Painters and Engravers. 5 vols. Rev. ed. 1964.

The Dance Encyclopedia. Rev. ed. 1967.

Encyclopedia of World Art. 15 vols. 1959–68.

Grove's Dictionary of Music and Musicians. 5th ed. 1954. 9 vols. and supplements.

Oxford Companion to Art. 1970.

Oxford Companion to Music. 10th ed. 1970.

Oxford Companion to the Theatre. 3rd ed. 1967.

Reference Books in the Mass Media: An Annotated, Selected Booklist Covering Book Publishing, Broadcasting, Films, Newspapers, Magazines, and Advertising. 1962.

Theatre and Allied Arts: A Guide to Books Dealing with the History, Criticism, and Technic of the Drama and Theatre, and Related Arts and Crafts. 1952.

Economics and Commerce

Accountant's Handbook. 4th ed. 1956.

Dictionary of Modern Economics. 1948.

Encyclopedia of Banking and Finance. 6th ed. 1962.

International Bibliography of Economics. 1952 to date.

The McGraw-Hill Dictionary of Modern Economics. 1965.

Education

Encyclopedia of Educational Research. 4th ed. 1969.

Dictionary of Education. 2nd ed. 1959. Defines educational and related terms.

World Survey of Education. 4 vols. 1955–66.

Health Technologies

Black's Medical Dictionary. 13th ed. 1974.

Handbook of Clinical Laboratory Data. 2nd ed. 1968.

The Macmillan Dictionary for Practical and Vocational Nurses. 1966. A handy dictionary of simpler medical terms.

History and Political Science

American Political Terms: An Historical Dictionary. 1962.

Cambridge Ancient History. 5 vols. Rev. ed. 1970.

Cambridge Medieval History. Rev. ed. 1967.

Cambridge Modern History. 14 vols. 1957. Superseded by the *New Cambridge Modern History.*

Dictionary of American History. 5 vols. and supplement. 2nd ed. 1961.

The Dictionary of Dates. 2 vols. 1934.

Dictionary of Political Science. 1964.

Harvard Guide to American History. 1954. Contains useful reading lists for each period.

Political Handbook of the World. 1927–.

Political Science: A Bibliographical Guide to the Literature. 1965.

Literature

Annual Bibliography of the English Language and Literature. 1921 to date.

Cambridge Bibliography of English Literature. 5 vols. 1941–57.

Cambridge History of English Literature. 1907–49.

A Literary History of England. 4 vols. 2nd ed. 1967.

Literary History of the United States. 3 vols. 1949–64. Contains an extensive bibliography.

MLA International Bibliography of Books and Articles on the Modern Languages and Literature. 1921 to date.

Oxford Companion to American Literature. 4th ed. 1965.

Oxford Companion to Classical Literature. 2nd ed. 1937.

Oxford Companion to English Literature. 4th ed. 1967.

Twentieth Century Authors. 1942. Supplement, 1955.

Philosophy and Religion

The Concise Encyclopedia of Western Philosophy and Philosophers. 1960.

The Encyclopedia of Philosophy. 8 vols. 1967.

Encyclopedia of Religion. 1945.

Encyclopedia of Religion and Ethics. 12 vols. 1908-27.

A History of Philosophy (Frederick Copleston). 8 vols. 1946–67.

History of Western Philosophy (Bertrand Russell). 1945.

Science and Technology

It is impossible to mention here even the most basic reference books in the many areas of specialization within the pure and applied science fields. The following list, although limited, suggests the kinds of books available in the reference collection.

Encyclopedia of the Biological Sciences. 1961. Contains a bibliography.

The Encyclopedia of Chemistry. 2nd ed. 1966.

Encyclopaedic Dictionary of Physics. 9 vols. 1962.

General Engineering Handbook. 2nd ed. 1940.

Guide to the Literature of Mathematics and Physics Including Related Works on Engineering Science. 2nd ed. 1958.

Harper Encyclopedia of Science. 2 vols. Rev. ed. 1967.

Larousse Encyclopedia of the Earth: Geology, Paleontology, and Prehistory. 1961.

McGraw-Hill Encyclopedia of Science and Technology. 15 vols. 1960. Supplements, 1962 to date.

Van Nostrand's Scientific Encyclopedia. 1968.

Social Sciences

Anthropology Today: An Encyclopedic Inventory. 1953.

Comprehensive Dictionary of Psychological and Psychoanalytic Terms. 1958.

A Dictionary of Psychology. Rev. ed. 1964.

A Dictionary of Sociology. 1968.

Encyclopedia of Human Behavior: Psychology, Psychiatry, and Mental Health. 2 vols. 1970.

Encyclopedia of the Social Sciences. 8 vols. 1937.

Encyclopedia of Social Work. 1965. (Formerly *Social Work Yearbook.* 1929–60.)

Discovering Specialized Reference Works
in Your Field(s) of Interest

Listing all of the important reference works in each field of study is a nearly impossible task and would probably be of little use to the beginning researcher. What we can suggest are strategies for finding the important works in your field. Since faculty members in each department usually recommend book orders and journal subscriptions to the library staff, the books and journals in your library should represent those most valued by your department. You can begin by browsing through the shelves in the reference area. Discover what reference works are available and how you can use them effectively. Check the appropriate subject cards in the card catalog or, if your library allows access to the general collection shelves, walk through the rows of books in your field to determine their scope.

Browse through the periodical collection as well. Does your field have an "official" journal, perhaps published by a national association of experts? If your library subscribes to a number of journals in your field (for example, *Chemical Society Proceedings; Chemical News; Journal of Chemical Education*), look through several issues of each to identify the kinds of articles (subjects, lengths, and levels of sophistication) each journal prints. Finally, keep in mind books, journals, and authors referred to by instructors and textbooks. A combination of these strategies of discovery and extensive reading should help you become a successful researcher in your chosen field.

SOURCES LOCATED OUTSIDE THE LIBRARY

Books and articles in school or public libraries are the source materials most used by students for research papers. Here are some other sources to consider, depending on the nature of your assignment and topic:

1. *Government publications:* PAIS, *The Vertical File*, and the periodical indexes will lead you to many studies and reports published by government agencies. Such materials can usually be obtained, free or at minimal cost, directly from the appropriate agency.

2. *Correspondence:* Business and government officials are usually willing to respond to brief, well-written requests for information.

3. *Interviews:* Some officials may also be available for personal interviews, but make the appointment well in advance and prepare specific questions.

4. *Questionnaires and surveys:* Consider the possibility of developing and circulating a survey, but remember that good questionnaires take careful preparation. Your instructor could help with this project.

5. *TV news programs and documentaries, films, filmstrips, records, tapes:* The written word is by no means the only medium to consider for infor-

mation and reliable opinions about a research project. Science shows, documentaries on current issues, and filmed or taped interviews with public officials are especially valuable.

EXERCISES: Using the Library

A. Library Skills Test

The following questions will test your ability to find and use materials in the library. If you are unsure about any answers, restudy the appropriate sections of Chapter 10.

I. Interpret the information on the catalog card to answer questions 1–5.

HM51
B45
    Berger, Peter L
        Invitation to sociology; a humanistic perspective.   ₁1st
    ed.₁   Garden City, N. Y., Doubleday, 1963.
        191 p.   18 cm.   (Anchor books)
        Includes bibliography.

        1. Sociology.   ɪ. Title.

    HM51.B45   301   63—8758 ↕

    Library of Congress   ₁69f2₁

---

1. What is the call number?
2. Who is the author?
3. Who is the publisher?
4. What will be the subject heading in the subject catalog?
5. What is the title?

II. On the following page are Library of Congress classification numbers. Arrange them into the proper shelf order by answering questions 6–9 with the correct letter.

(a)
```
PR
253
.N28
```

(b)
```
PN
635
.B1
```

(c)
```
PR
67
.T324
```

(d)
```
PR
253
.N216
```

6. First on the shelf?

7. Second on the shelf?

8. Third on the shelf?

9. Fourth on the shelf?

III. Interpret the following entry from *The Reader's Guide to Periodical Literature* by answering questions 10–15.

FEDERAL reserve banks
   Can 2 + 2 = 5? A look at what voluntary membership in the Federal reserve system means to the economy. P. D. Nigro. bibl Intellect 103:48–50 O '74

10. Who is the author?

11. What is the name of the periodical?

12. What is the subject heading?

13. What is the title of the article?

14. What is the volume number?

15. What is the date of the periodical?

IV. Interpret the following entry from *The New York Times Index* by answering questions 16–20.

PRESIDENTIAL Elections (US). See also Elections (US)—Finances, Ap 23
   Univ of Mich's Inst for Soc Research study dir John P Robinson says even though US public ranks TV as its major source of campaign news, newspaper endorsements carry more weight in outcome of Pres elections and are consistently related to Pres votes (S), Ap 30,23:7

16. What is the subject heading for the article?

17. What is the date that the article appeared?

18. Under what other subject heading is the article indexed?

19. What are the page and column numbers?

20. Is *The New York Times Index* an author, title, or subject index?

B. Using Reference Materials

The left-hand column below lists research problems: the right-hand column lists various indexes and reference materials that have been described in this chapter. Indicate the *best* source of information by placing the appropriate letter from the right-hand column after each problem in the left-hand column.

1. magazine articles on the 1964 World Series

2. Kurt Vonnegut's birth date

3. the author of "to err is human, to forgive divine"

4. condensed text of the President's State of the Union speech

5. the reliability of books by Erich Fromm

6. the number of years Ben Franklin served as the Colonies' representative in France

7. the birthplace of Coretta Scott King

8. the place and date of George VI's coronation as King of England

9. a list of articles on *The Scarlet Letter*

10. reports of government proposals to utilize the Colorado River as an energy source

11. the name of the Greek god of war

12. sources of pamphlets on drug abuse

a. *New York Times Index*

b. *Social Sciences and Humanities Index*

c. *Who's Who in American Women*

d. *Book Review Digest*

e. *Dictionary of National Biography*

f. *The Reader's Guide to Periodical Literature*

g. *Familiar Quotations*

h. *Current Biography*

i. *Bulletin of the Public Affairs Information Service*

j. *Dictionary of American Biography*

k. *Vertical File Index*

l. Hamilton, *Mythology*

C. Library Question Sheet

Take a library-sponsored tour, read your library's manual on its facilities and services, and make a careful investigation of the library, asking questions when necessary, to learn where to find and how to use your library's resources. Then answer these questions:

1. What is the loan period for books?

2. Do periodicals circulate? If so, what is the loan period?

3. Where is the card catalog?

4. Where are the periodical indexes?

5. Where are the *Book Review Digest* volumes?

6. Where are the encyclopedias?

7. Where is *The New York Times Index?*

8. Where will you find the lists of available periodicals?

9. Is there a record collection? Where is it kept?

10. Is your library open on Sunday? What are the hours?

11. Where are the microfilm readers located?

12. Where are reserve books located?

13. Are the stacks (the bookshelves) open to students?

14. What classification system is used for arranging books?

D. Working in the Library

1. Select one pair of biographical dictionaries listed immediately below, examine both dictionaries carefully, then write a brief report about them answering the four questions below.

   The Dictionary of American Biography
   Who Was Who in America

   The Dictionary of National Biography
   Webster's Biographical Dictionary

   American Men and Women of Science
   Current Biography

   a. What is the scope of each dictionary? How extensive is the coverage and on what basis are subjects selected?

   b. How is each dictionary organized?

   c. How is each entry structured? What type of information is included and how extensive is it?

   d. Under what circumstances would you use each dictionary? What use(s) would each best serve?

2. Select three journals in your field of interest (for example, *Science, Scientific American,* and the *Proceedings of the National Academy of Sciences*) or three journals that you could use in preparing your research paper. Examine the articles in at least one

issue of each journal for the same year. Then write a brief report comparing the journals on these points:

a. What kinds of topics are covered? How extensive is the range of topics?

b. How technical are the articles? How would you characterize the style of writing?

c. Who would you judge to be the anticipated audience for each journal?

d. Under what circumstances, for what purposes, would you be likely to turn to each journal?

3. Choose a subject that interests you, or one that relates to your research project, or one from the list immediately below and look it up in both a general, multivolume encyclopedia and a specialized reference work. Read both articles and write a brief report answering the four questions below.

Possible subjects: Zen, ESP, the Federal Reserve System, DNA, Aphrodite, plate tectonics, naturalism, the Third Reich, jazz, the planet Jupiter, surrealism

a. Which reference work contains the longer entry on your subject?

b. Which reference work contains a more technical or sophisticated discussion of the subject?

c. What format is used by each work? (formal essay? briefer sections with headings for each reference? lists?)

d. Under what circumstances would you be likely to use each reference work? What does each work seem best suited for?

Note-Taking

11

WHAT REALLY HAPPENS WHEN YOU READ AND TAKE NOTES

Purposeful reading and note-taking are critical steps in the research process. First, they constitute a considerable portion of the total time you devote to a research project. Second, and more important, the note-taking "step" is really *a series of interrelated intellectual activities which result in the construction of your paper.* While writing the paper and preparing the final bibliography are steps yet to be completed, at the reading and note-taking stage you will include, and in many cases repeat, some of the steps described in previous chapters.

In other words, the note-taking "step" actually consists of: (1) reading and rereading your sources; (2) perhaps gathering additional sources; (3) rethinking and possibly changing your tentative thesis or the focus and limits of your paper; (4) evaluating the reliability and usefulness of your sources (especially if you redirect the focus of your paper); (5) developing a preliminary organizational pattern—at least for the main sections of your paper.

As an example: Having read *Common Sense* with interest, you decide to write a paper on "Thomas Paine's role in the American Revolution" for your American history class. Knowing that your topic is too broad, you start to read books and articles on Paine and the Revolution. You find several references to the *Crisis* papers; you realize that Paine wrote other essays in support of the American cause, so you return to the library to get—and read—a good edition of them. You realize that what really interests you is the power of Paine's writing style. Thus you narrow the focus of your paper and formulate the thesis that "Paine's skill as a persuasive writer provided uncertain colonists with both good arguments and an emotional commitment to revolution." Now you can reread and take notes on *Common Sense* and the *Crisis* papers with a clear purpose in mind, and select a few relevant studies of Paine that will enlarge your understanding and support your views. This complex process we can appropriately describe as the *construction* of your paper.

GUIDELINES FOR NOTE-TAKING

With an understanding of the complexity of the reading and note-taking process, we can now turn to some general note-taking guidelines.

1. Do not start to take detailed notes until you are familiar with your chief sources and know how you will use the notes. Otherwise you will either take many unusable notes, or later try to fit into your paper notes which have become irrelevant.

2. If you do not have a clear focus for your paper when you begin reading, it is often helpful to summarize and evaluate the initial sources that you read. Once you have decided on a definite thesis, you will know which sources to reread for purposeful note-taking.

3. Although individual research projects offer special problems, you are wise to begin your reading and note-taking with primary sources before secondary sources and with general studies before specialized ones. For example, you should become thoroughly familiar with Paine's *Common Sense* before reading interpretive studies of his writings. Similarly, digest the biographical essay of Paine in the *Dictionary of American Biography* for the general facts of his life before tackling a more specialized study such as Davidson's *Propaganda and the American Revolution*.

4. Each note card should contain a single idea, piece of information, or group of related facts to be used together in your paper. The whole purpose of note-taking is destroyed if you do not adhere to this principle. Since you do not know at the outset exactly how you will organize your information, you need the flexibility provided by cards which can be shuffled and reshuffled as the structure of your paper becomes clearer.

5. Remember that part of the originality of your paper lies in the creativity of your approach to the topic, and in the insight reflected in your ordering of the information you have gathered. If you simply copy ideas and information from your sources in long lists, you run the risk of mechanically transferring the organization of the sources to your own paper. The result will be a series of "summaries" of your sources, not an original paper.

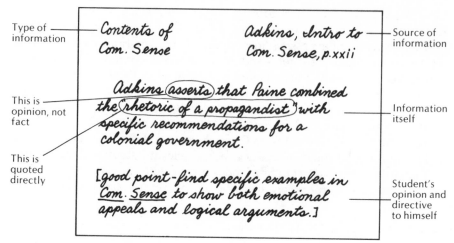

Fig. 11-1.   Sample Note Card

FORMAT FOR NOTE CARDS

Materials

Notes should be written in ink because penciled notes will blur with shuffling and rearranging. Usually 4 x 6 or 5 x 7 cards, or letter-size notebook or typing paper cut in half, are the best size because there is more space for writing and you will be able to distinguish easily between note cards and the 3 x 5 bibliography cards. A sample note is shown in Fig. 11-1.

Necessary Information

Each note card should contain three kinds of information:

1. A word or phrase placed at the top of each card to identify *the type of information* contained in the note. This facilitates arrangement of cards into major sections.

2. *The source of information,* which should include a shortened reference—the author's last name, a shortened form of the title, or both—and the *exact page(s)* from which the note was taken. Remember that *all borrowed information (facts, ideas, and opinions) must be footnoted in your paper with exact page references.*

3. *The information itself,* recorded either as summary, paraphrase, or direct quotation. A discussion and illustration of these three types of notes will be found below.

Additional Information

Note-taking should be mechanical only insofar as you develop the habit of recording all necessary information in a consistent pattern on each card. Notes are actually brief "letters" which must make sense to you weeks after you first write them. Consequently, you should make two important distinctions:

1. Distinguish carefully between fact and opinion. Notes may simply state facts, but notes that record opinion should be introduced with such statements as "Smith believes that," "Smith asserts that," or "Smith concludes that."

2. Distinguish clearly between ideas or opinions taken from sources and your own opinions. Record your thoughts about an idea, but be sure to enclose them in brackets at the bottom of the note card to avoid confusion later.

THREE BASIC KINDS OF NOTES: SUMMARY, DIRECT QUOTE, AND PARAPHRASE

Summary

The summary note should be used less often than either the direct quote or paraphrase because it is useful only in the preliminary, information-gathering stages of your reading since it does not contain specific information with precise page references. Remember the techniques of good summary that you practiced in Chapter 6.

Direct Quotation

Since most of your paper should be in your own words, most of your notes should be paraphrases rather than direct quotes. A paper which is a string of quotes glued together with a few transitional sentences is mere patchwork, not your own paper at all. The best way to resist using too many quotations is not to take notes which are direct quotes. Recording a direct quote rather than a paraphrase only postpones the task of saying that information in your own words.

Here are four legitimate uses of direct quotation in a research paper. If you cannot justify a direct quote based on these guidelines, take a paraphrased note instead.

1. *Statistical information:* Paraphrasing a series of statistics without distorting the evidence is difficult. Also, you may not be sure, at the note-taking stage, how much of the statistical information you will need to include in your paper.

2. *Examples of a writer's ideas or style of writing:* When your purpose is to examine a writer's ideas or stylistic techniques, you must give specific examples of his ideas or style in direct quotes and then analyze them. For example, the student writing on Thomas Paine's skill as a persuasive writer would take notes from *Common Sense,* in direct quotes, as samples of Paine's style.

3. *Authoritative opinion:* When the opinion of an authority is crucial evi-

dence in support of a controversial thesis, it may be important to
present his opinion in his exact words.

4. *Aptness of phrasing:* At times a writer's views will coalesce in a phrase
   or sentence that cannot be paraphrased without changing the meaning or losing the power of the statement. Be careful not to overuse
   this justification for quoting.

When it is appropriate to copy a direct quote on a note card, check
your note against the source for accurate spelling, punctuation, and com-
pleteness, and then enclose the entire quotation in quotation marks.

Paraphrase

The paraphrased note differs from the summary note because it is not a
condensed version of the source, and it differs from a quoted note because
it uses the student's own words. The paraphrased note is a restatement in
the student's language of a fact, idea, or opinion. Most of your notes will
be paraphrases. But since you must still acknowledge your source in a
footnote, paraphrased notes, like direct quotations, must include the precise page(s) on which the information was found.

SOME EXAMPLES OF NOTE-TAKING

Suppose that you have decided to write a research paper on space colonization, but you haven't yet decided on a specific thesis. Here is an excerpt
from a relevant article which appeared in the May 26, 1975, issue of *Time
Magazine*.

Colonizing Space

When Princeton Physicist Gerard K. O'Neill made the proposal that space
colonies be established to relieve the earth's overcrowding, increasing pollution, and energy shortages, many of his more skeptical colleagues dismissed
the scheme as one more exercise in scientific fantasy. But, unlike many other
far-out proposals, the idea has not faded into oblivion. . . .

As it was first spelled out (*Time*, June 3), O'Neill's scheme called for
assembling in space large aluminum cylinders that would house self-
contained communities. The cylinders would be built at the constantly moving "libration points," where the gravity of the earth and of the moon cancel
each other out. Permanently in orbit at those positions, each pair of huge
cylinders (1,100 yds. long and 220 yds. in diameter) would support 10,000
people; they would contain an atmosphere like earth's, water, farmland and
a variety of flora and fauna. The cylinders would rotate slowly, thus simulat-
ing gravity and holding people, buildings and soil "down" on the inner
surfaces. For power, the space colonizers would rely on ever-present sunlight, captured by large external mirrors that could be controlled to create the
effect of night and day and even of seasonal change. . . .

Future Shock. As an added incentive, says O'Neill, the early colonies could be devoted to space manufacturing—for example, the construction of large turbogenerators driven by sunlight. Much easier to build in the gravity-free environment around the colonies, these giant machines could be towed back to the vicinity of the earth, parked in fixed orbit and then used to relay the captured solar power down to earth as a beam of microwaves.

O'Neill concedes that such conceptions are "very rich in future shock" and larger than anything yet attempted in space or even planned on the drawing boards of space scientists. But he is firmly convinced that they could be achieved with technology that is either already available or almost perfected. In fact, says O'Neill, the first space habitat—he thinks the word colony connotes exploitation—could be functioning by the start of the next century. Its early inhabitants would probably be "hard-hat types," O'Neill says, but after the initial construction is finished almost anyone with a spirit of adventure could live at L5.

Since you have not decided on a thesis yet, you should take a summary note so that you will know whether or not to reread this article once you have narrowed the focus of your paper. (See Fig. 11-2.)

After sampling other available material and taking summary notes, you decide to base your thesis on the advantages outlined by O'Neill: "Space colonization offers one good solution to our problems of pollution, energy shortages, and overpopulation." You reread the *Time* article to take several detailed notes, such as those shown in Fig. 11-3 and 11-4.

Although initially you might record the sentence in Fig. 11-4 as a direct quote, you would probably incorporate it into your paper in your own words; there is no reason to quote from the article.

Summary Note   <u>Time</u>, "Colonizing Space,"
                                            p. 60.

According to physicist O'Neill, space colonies can be made out of large cylinders powered by the sun and with a form of gravity and an "earth-like" environment. Early colonies could manufacture solar power generators for earth's use. Article gives construction details and advantages of space colonization.

Fig. 11-2.   Sample Summary Note Card

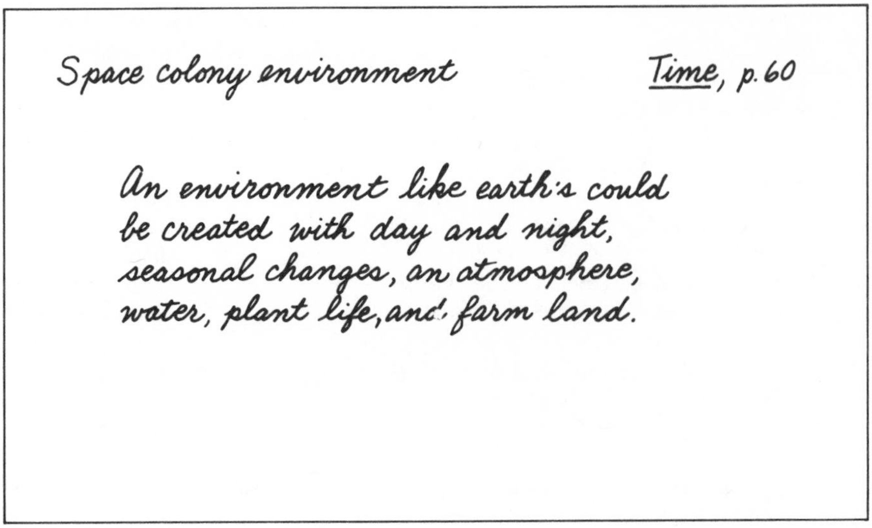

Space colony environment   *Time*, p. 60

An environment like earth's could
be created with day and night,
seasonal changes, an atmosphere,
water, plant life, and farm land.

Fig. 11-3. Sample Paraphrase Note Card

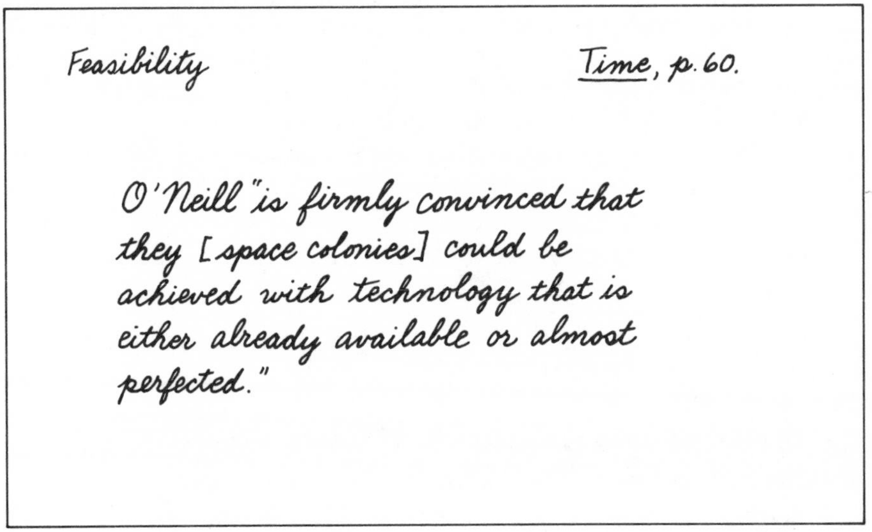

Feasibility   *Time*, p. 60.

O'Neill "is firmly convinced that
they [space colonies] could be
achieved with technology that is
either already available or almost
perfected."

Fig. 11-4. Sample Direct Quote Note Card

   This brief example of note-taking reveals the number of steps in the
process, the number of judgments you have to make. You need brief but
accurate summary notes in the early stages of your reading, but, once you
have established your thesis, return to the relevant early material (guided
by your summaries) to note specific information. When you are ready to
transform notes into a paper, you may decide that the information cannot
be incorporated into the paper in its original format on the note card.

Once you know what to look for, it is relatively easy to take useful notes from the brief essay "Colonizing Space." Often library materials are more difficult to work with because the style of writing is sophisticated or technical or the ideas are complex or unfamiliar. The test of your grasp of complicated materials is your ability to restate key ideas in your own words. Suppose you are writing a paper on the characteristics of conservative thought in America from 1865 to 1900. In Richard Hofstadter's well-known study of Social Darwinism you read the following paragraph:

> As a phase in the history of conservative thought, social Darwinism deserves remark. Insofar as it defended the status quo and gave strength to attacks on reformers and on almost all efforts at the conscious and directed change of society, social Darwinism was certainly one of the leading strains in American conservative thought for more than a generation. But it lacked many of the signal characteristics of conservatism as it is usually found. A conservatism that appealed more to the secularist than the pious mentality, it was a conservatism almost without religion. A body of belief whose chief conclusion was that the positive functions of the state should be kept to the barest minimum, it was almost anarchical, and it was devoid of that center of reverence and authority which the state provides in many conservative systems. Finally, and perhaps most important, it was a conservatism that tried to dispense with sentimental or emotional ties.

The sentences are complicated and some terms may be unfamiliar, but the paragraph does have a clear structure. It can be divided into the following sections and subsections that clarify Hofstadter's main points:

Sentences 1 and 2

Social Darwinism was an important form of American conservatism. Its conservative characteristics were:

1. favoring the status quo
2. opposing social change

(This could be one note with the heading "Types of conservative thought.")

BUT

Sentences 3, 4, 5, and 6

It was unlike most forms of conservatism because:

1. it was secularly, not religiously, oriented
2. it did not value governmental authority and wanted governmental functions to be limited
3. it lacked a sentimental or emotional basis

(This could be another note with the heading "Characteristics of social Darwinism.")

Two valuable note cards can be obtained by the patient student who takes the time to understand the paragraph and distill from it the key points. This distilling process has several advantages:

1. unnecessary direct quoting is avoided

2. excessive dependence on Hofstadter's language (and the danger of plagiarism) is avoided

3. the student actually learns about social Darwinism

Only when you have to restate ideas in your own language rather than copying them verbatim will you truly learn your subject.

EXERCISES: Note-Taking

Some of the following passages are more difficult in style or concepts than others, but all three warrant careful reading. After studying each passage in relation to the research subject, practice writing whatever note(s) you think appropriate. Then explain briefly why you selected the information you recorded and why you chose to quote or to paraphrase.

1. For a paper on the causes of the Detroit riot in the summer of 1967, you read the following passage from the *Report of the National Advisory Commission on Civil Disorders.* What note(s) would you take? Why?

> In virtually every case a single "triggering" or "precipitating" incident can be identified as having immediately preceded—within a few hours and in generally the same location—the outbreak of disorder. But this incident was usually relatively minor, even trivial, by itself substantially disproportionate to the scale of violence that followed. Often it was an incident of a type which had occurred frequently in the same community in the past without provoking violence.
>
> We found that violence was generated by an increasingly disturbed social atmosphere, in which typically not one, but a series of incidents occurred over a period of weeks or months prior to the outbreak of disorders. Most cities had three or more such incidents; Houston had 10 over a five-month period. These earlier or prior incidents were linked in the minds of many Negroes to the pre-existing reservoir of underlying grievances. With each such incident, frustration and tension grew until at some point a final incident, often similar to the incidents preceding it, occurred and was followed almost immediately by violence.
>
> As we see it, the prior incidents and the reservoir of underlying grievances contributed to a cumulative process of mounting tension that spilled over into violence when the final incident occurred. In this sense the entire chain—the grievances, the series of prior tension-heightening incidents, and the final incident—was the "precipitant" of disorder.

2. You are writing a paper examining the speech habits of four-year-olds. What note(s) would you take from this paragraph in Arnold Gesell's *The First Five Years of Life?*

> As compared with other stages of preschool development, the age of 4 years may be described as the flowering period of language. The 3-year-old,

though talkative enough, has not as yet discovered the transcendent power of words and the excitement of using them to control or to enrich all types of situations. The more mature 5-year-old—a young adult by the side of Three and Four—handles his language equipment with relative deliberation and self-control. But the 4-year-old talks—talks about everything, plays with words, questions persistently, elaborates simple responses into long narratives, comments with approval on his own behavior, and criticizes that of others, balances comparisons. The examination of a bright, active child of 4 years often resembles nothing so much as a headlong free-association experiment.

3. What note(s) would you take from this paragraph in Franz Boas' *Anthropology and Modern Life* for a paper exploring the nature of political "doublespeak" in the 1970s?

More important than this is the emotional tone of words. Particularly those words that are symbols of groups of ideas to which we automatically respond in definite ways have a fundamental value in shaping our behavior. They function as a release for habitual actions. In our modern civilizations the words patriotism, democracy or autocracy, liberty are of this class. The real content of many of these is not important; important is their emotional value. Liberty may be nonexistent; the word-symbol will survive in all its power, although the actual condition may be one of subjection. The name democracy will induce people to accept autocracy as long as the symbol is kept intact. The vague concepts expressed by these words are sufficient to excite the strongest reactions that stabilize the cultural behavior of people, even when the inner form of culture undergoes considerable changes that go unnoticed on account of the preservation of the symbol.

Problems in Writing

12

In this chapter we will examine some of the problems in presenting information in research papers. There are several models of what not to do, because sometimes it is easier to understand what to avoid by considering faulty writing rather than good writing. We will study only those writing problems which are special hazards of the research paper: careless acknowledgment of sources, misleading, inaccurate, or ungrammatical quoting, awkward or unclear combination of sources, and the disastrous "cut and paste" research paper.

ADEQUATE AND INADEQUATE ACKNOWLEDGEMENT OF SOURCES: PLAGIARISM

Until you give any cause for question, your instructor will assume that you are a sincere and conscientious student, that you have done your own reading, note-taking, and writing. If you are indeed a sincere student, then you do not want to be penalized for unintentional *plagiarism* that is the result of careless writing. Remember that plagiarism is a form of stealing; it is the presentation of someone else's information, ideas, or opinions as your own.

   Student plagiarism usually occurs in two ways: (1) a student will take notes carelessly, neglecting to put down precise page references, and will use the information without properly documenting his sources in a footnote; (2) a student will present borrowed material in such a way that even though he has footnotes, he misrepresents the nature of his indebtedness to the source. This second type of plagiarism is a writing problem, and we will examine it next.

The general guideline is to clarify the nature and degree of your indebtedness to your sources not just by placing footnote numbers appropriately, but also by the words you use to introduce or to comment on another writer's ideas. Here are three specific guidelines.

1. Be careful when you vary the standard introductions such as "Smith says" or "Smith states" that you do not select alternatives which are misleading. Substituting "Smith implies" for "Smith states" misrepresents Smith's attitude toward his material.

2. If you vary the pattern of acknowledgment by mentioning Smith after you have incorporated his ideas into your paragraph, be sure that your reader can tell precisely which ideas in the passage belong to Smith. If your entire paragraph is a paraphrase of Smith's views, it isn't fair to conclude with, "This idea is presented by Smith." Which of the several ideas in the paragraph is Smith's?

3. Be sure that your paraphrased notes are in your own words so that you do not incorporate Smith's ideas into your paper in his style of writing. To use Smith's words and/or sentence structure, even in a condensed version, is to steal Smith's work.

It is not sufficient to place a footnote at the end of a paragraph to indicate your source, if you have misrepresented your dependence on that source in the body of your paper.

Here is a paragraph from Robert E. Spiller's *The Cycle of American Literature* that serves as the basis for the following samples of adequate and inadequate acknowledgment of sources.

> Fiction and drama turned to classicism more slowly and reluctantly than did poetry and criticism; in some degree even avoiding its extremes completely. The generation of novelists who became prominent in the thirties, in addition to Wolfe and Hemingway, included James T. Farrell, John Steinbeck, Erskine Caldwell, and William Faulkner. Naturalists all in their primary inspiration, these men also developed in varying degrees the possibilities of symbolism and moved generally in the direction that Sherwood Anderson rather than Dreiser had indicated, toward fantasy and away from literal realism. At first unnoticed, the silvery laughter of the comic spirit began to be heard above the voices of tragedy, corruption, and death, with which their work was most concerned. As the theme of illusion which had so obsessed O'Neill came more and more to supplant that of reality, their art grew increasingly self-conscious and objective. From the most realistic of them all (Farrell) to the most symbolic and purely aesthetic (Faulkner) there is progress in technical virtuosity and philosophical depth. American fiction, like

American poetry and drama, reached its highest point of achievement in the equilibrium of conflicting forces that characterized the mid-thirties, rather than in either extreme.

Which of the following examples of student writing, based on Spiller's ideas, represent adequate acknowledgment of the writer's indebtedness, and which do not? In the examples of inadequate acknowledgment, exactly how has the student erred? Study the samples carefully to be sure that you can recognize various types of inadequate acknowledgment.

1.   What characterized American fiction in the 1930s?

First of all, who were the important novelists at this time? The most prominent were Wolfe, Hemingway, Farrell, Steinbeck, Caldwell, and Faulkner. Although they were all influenced by the naturalists, they all, some more than others, developed into symbolic writers. They followed Anderson rather than Dreiser in focusing more on fantasy than on realism with the result that they became more consciously interested in technical innovations and at the same time more philosophical. The best works were those which found a balance between reality and fantasy. This attitude is emphasized by Robert Spiller, a critic of American literature.[2]

2.   What characterized American fiction in the 1930s?

We can agree that the writers who became prominent in the thirties, besides Wolfe and Hemingway, were Farrell, Steinbeck, Caldwell, and Faulkner. Naturalists in their primary inspiration, these writers also examined the possibilities of symbolism and moved in the direction of Anderson rather than Dreiser, that is, toward fantasy and away from realism. The silvery laughter of the comic muse was heard in their novels, and their art grew more self-conscious and objective and more philosophically deep. We may agree with Robert Spiller that their fiction reached its highest achievement in the balance of conflicting forces that characterized the mid-thirties, rather than in either extreme.[4]

3.   What characterized American fiction in the 1930s?

According to Robert Spiller, "American fiction . . . reached its highest point of achievement in the equilibrium of conflicting forces that characterized the mid-thirties." He observes that the most important writers (Wolfe, Hemingway, Farrell, Steinbeck, Caldwell, and Faulkner) were "naturalists all in their primary inspiration," but they moved "toward fantasy and away from literal realism" and "developed . . . the possibilities of symbolism." The result, Spiller asserts, was progress in technical virtuosity and philosophical depth.[5]

PROBLEMS IN QUOTING

Although only No. 3 above demonstrates adequate acknowledgment of the writer's indebtedness to Spiller, if most of the student's paper resembled that paragraph, we would have to label it a "cut and paste" job. The student relies too heavily on direct quote (although direct quotes are always preferable to plagiarism!) and is in general too dependent on his source. On the other hand, he has made the extent of his indebtedness to Spiller clear to his reader, he has quoted accurately, and he has woven quotes smoothly into his sentences. Thus, when you consider the possibility of quoting directly, you have three judgments to make:

1. You have to decide what constitutes an appropriate balance between your own words and ideas and what you borrow from your sources.

2. You have to consider the form in which the quoted material is presented.

3. You have to consider the style of the sentence or paragraph in which you present direct quotes.

We have considered the first problem in Chapter 11, when we suggested that you say borrowed information in your own words whenever you cannot justify a direct quote according to the four guidelines outlined on pp. 185–86. Keep in mind that long quotes from your sources are not what a reader wants to find in your paper. If he wants to read Robert Spiller's ideas on American literature, he can turn to *The Cycle of American Literature;* when he reads your paper, he wants to hear what you have to say. When you do quote, consider problems of form and style. Here are some guidelines and examples.

Guidelines for Presenting Direct Quotations: Form

1. Quote accurately. Check and recheck the note card on which you have copied quoted material against the source of the quote.

2. Enclose all quoted material in quotation marks, and do not change words or punctuation which are part of a direct quote. Any words which you need to add within a quote to make the meaning clear should be placed in square brackets, not parentheses.

Original: "The most important common feature of American fiction today is that it has all been produced in the interval between two world wars. . . ." From Joseph Warren Beach, *American Fiction 1920–1940* (New York, 1941), p. 11.

Incorrect: Joseph Warren Beach says that "the most important common feature of American fiction between 1920 and 1940 is that it has all been produced in the interval between two world wars." [4]

Correct: Joseph Warren Beach says that "the most important common feature of American fiction today [between 1920 and 1940] is that it has all been produced in the interval between two world wars." [4]

3. If quoted material runs to more than three lines, present it in *display form:* center the quotation on the page and, when typing, single-space. Then quotation marks are not used, but a footnote is still needed. For example:

> Dr. David M. Barnes, the top federal official on smoking and health, asserts:
>
> > There is ample evidence that involuntary smoking causes annoyance and minor eye and throat irritations to a substantial percentage of the population. It may cause major and, occasionally, life-threatening problems to people with heart and lung disease.[3]
>
> This and other disclosures by health authorities . . .

More than two lines of poetry should be presented in display form; for example:

> In the opening speech of the chorus, the image of Faustus as the overreacher is established with the analogy to the Greek myth of Icarus:
>
> > Till, swollen with cunning, of a self-conceit,
> > His waxen wings did mount above his reach
> > And melting, heavens conspired his overthrow.[3]
>
> In his study of Christopher Marlowe, Harry Levin sees . . .

4. Place the footnote number at the end of the quoted material, after the final quotation mark, or at the end of the display form quote, as in the examples given above.

5. When quoted material forms only a part of a sentence, the first quoted word is not capitalized even if it was capitalized in the original source, unless it follows a formal introduction which ends in a colon.

Incorrect: In his essay on self-reliance, Emerson asserts that "Whoso would be a man, must be a nonconformist."

Correct: In his essay on self-reliance, Emerson asserts that "whoso would be a man, must be a nonconformist."

Also
Correct: Emerson sums up his concept of self-reliance in the following assertion: "Whoso would be a man, must be a nonconformist."

In addition, when quoted material comes at the end of a sentence, use only the punctuation that is appropriate to complete the sentence.

Incorrect: One of Emerson's famous phrases is "trust thyself:."

Correct: One of Emerson's famous phrases is "trust thyself."

6. Use single quotation marks (the apostrophe key on your typewriter) to identify quoted material within quoted material; thus:

In *The Social Contract*, Rousseau argues that "the words 'slavery' and 'right' are contradictory; they cancel each other out."

7. To reduce the length of your direct quotes, omit irrelevant portions. Indicate omitted sections by the use of the *ellipsis* mark (three spaced periods: . . .). If the omitted material comes at the end of a sentence, use four periods, one to indicate the completed sentence.

Edgar Allan Poe observes that Hawthorne's tales "belong to the highest region of Art. . . ."

Guidelines for Presenting Direct Quotations: Style

1. The correct form for presenting a quoted passage with unimportant parts omitted is the use of the ellipsis mark; however, be careful not to omit portions of a quoted passage if the omissions distort the meaning or tone of the original.

Original: Strauss tells his friends his wounds may be "incurable."

Misleading: Strauss is said to have "incurable" "wounds."

Better: Strauss said that his wounds "may be 'incurable.' "

(The use of the passive "is said" in the misleading version leaves the speaker's identity unknown; in addition, the misleading version does not make clear that "incurable" is Strauss's term and that it is qualified with "may be.")

2. Do not distort or confuse meaning by quoting out of context or giving so little information in direct quote that it is impossible to evaluate its significance.

Some words and phrases Evans and Novak use to denote the liberals are "left-wing," "seized on the incident," "first opening to attack," and "assault."

(The student is trying to present evidence to show that the language used by Evans and Novak to describe liberals is slanted or pejorative. But only the first quote, "left-wing," which is clearly a label, can be understood out of context. The other three quotes all reveal some aggressive action, but, since the reader is not given enough of the description of the action, it is impossible to tell that Evans and Novak are indeed describing the action in a pejorative way.)

3. Do not distort the meaning of a quoted passage by your introduction to the quote.

Spiller asserts that because the writers of the 1930s were naturalists they "moved toward fantasy."

(Misleading, because Spiller states that they were "naturalists" and that they "moved toward fantasy," but he does not say that one caused the other.)

4.   Quotes woven into the writer's sentence must not distort the grammar, syntax, or logic of that sentence. Words, phrases, or clauses quoted in a series must maintain parallel structure, and quoting is not an excuse for incomplete or illogical thoughts. Here are several examples:

Sentence
fragment: Just below the picture a title to the article, "Watergate Notoriety Pays Off for Some."

Revised: Just below the picture is the title of the article which says: "Watergate Notoriety Pays Off for Some."

Illogical: *Time*'s description is ". . . prose style is a cross between 'Dear Abby' and early Chinese fortune cookie."

Revised: *Time* describes the prose style as "a cross between 'Dear Abby' and early Chinese fortune cookie."

Not
parallel: *Time* states that legalized abortion may help to solve such problems as "overpopulation," "the number of unwanted babies," and "probably lower the suicide rate of pregnant women."

Revised: *Time* states that legalized abortion may help to solve such problems as "overpopulation," "the number of unwanted babies," and the high "suicide rate of pregnant women."

SYNTHESIZING SOURCES

Adequate acknowledgment and appropriate form and style for quotes require correct word choice and sentence structure. Difficulties in synthesizing material from different sources also stem from methods of paragraph structure and the total organization of your paper.

Presented here are four paragraphs from a paper on the constitutional rights of students. The writer's thesis is that, because students are citizens, they are entitled to the same constitutional rights as adults, although ensuring those rights guaranteed under the First, Fourth, and Fourteenth Amendments causes some problems in the public schools. The writer presents and examines recent court rulings relevant to these three amendments. The following paragraphs discuss the Fourth Amendment, and the three raised numbers refer to footnotes citing rulings of three separate court cases.

1   The Fourth Amendment, which protects against unreasonable search and seizures, has not been exploited nearly as much as the First and Fourteenth Amendments, but nevertheless is still an important constitutional

right of all students. What is "reasonable" is left to definition by school administrators. A few more Supreme Court decisions show that students have very little Fourth Amendment protection, but are entitled to it.

2   A principal may search a bank of lockers to determine the origin of bad odor in the general area.[7] A police officer may use evidence taken from a student's locker, but first he must have the consent of the student and principal prior to the search.[8]

3   An administrator may call a student to his office and require him to empty his pockets, based on a tip given to the principal by another student.[9]

4   The court's rulings on these issues are in the best interest of the school administrator and of the students who are in school for the purpose of getting an education. Their ruling is not in the best interest of students who use the school to sell drugs, store weapons, or engage in other illegal activities.

The passage reflects several problems in organizing the information and making its significance clear to the reader. What does the writer mean by "exploited"? "A few more" implies that other decisions have been presented, when they haven't. Is there any clear rationale for presenting the first two rulings in one paragraph and the third by itself in another paragraph? What is a better way of organizing the summaries of the three decisions? Do all three rulings show that students have little protection but are entitled to it, or is support for the first and second assertions divided? Are all three rulings evidence for the conclusions drawn in paragraph four? Now reread the four paragraphs and decide on a way to synthesize the information into a more purposeful organization.

THE CUT AND PASTE PAPER

The writer on the constitutional rights of students had a clearly stated thesis, and had read widely on recent court rulings. His problems lay in finding an organization that would make the significance of the evidence clear to his reader. Smoother synthesizing and careful revision could result in a competent freshman research paper. By contrast, the paper which follows is practically hopeless; it is nothing but borrowed information. To facilitate your understanding of the weaknesses illustrated by this paper, evaluations and suggestions for revisions appear in the margin.

The British Coal Strike

1   Prime Minister Edward Heath has declared a state of emergency, his fifth in the past three years. He has ordered industry and business to cut power by 35%, which put the country on a 3-day work week.[1]

The two statements in ¶1 are not an adequate introduction. What is the thesis? How will the paper be organized?

2   With all power cut by 35%, coal production is off by 30%, automotive output is off by 40%, and the steel production is down by 50%.

¶2
Are these statistics relevant? If so, how?

According to industrial sources, this is only the beginning.[2]

3   The coal strike means a 40% pay cut for 15 million workers. At the present time, 809,000 Britons, about 6% of the industrial force, are unemployed. The British Steel Corporation has laid off nearly half of its 235,000 men. They claim that for every week of the 3-day work week, it will take a full month to catch up to their full production schedule.[3]

4   New Year's Day was declared a holiday for the very first time. All TV stations have been ordered to sign off at 10:30 p.m.

5   The 1973 trade loss is more than $5.2 billion, the largest in British history, and prices on imported oil will add about $4.5 billion to the 1974 trade deficit. Welfare benefits will cost the government $170 million a week and Social Security will cost $92 million a week. The British Confederation of Industry is predicting a wave of bankruptcies.

6   The social status of the coal miners is far from good. The country blames them for the dimmed lights and the 3-day work week. They have been placed in the position of social outcasts, and, as one magazine put it, are beginning to "consider themselves another country."[4] Some businesses and shops have even gone so far as to refuse service to coal miners.

7   The coal miner feels that the work is degrading and that the pay should make up for it. The coal miner must work in an area 2'9" tall and is continually on his knees. There are 40,000 miners in Britain who have black lung disease. Miners' jobs are both dangerous and necessary, yet a miner earns less than a London secretary.

8   At present, pay for journeymen-miners is $92 a week. They are asking for a 33% increase which would amount to $112.50 a week.[5] 270,000 miners have refused to work overtime until they get a settlement giving them a basic increase of $18 to $22 on weekly wages, which are $57 to $83.[6] Heath made a gesture at buying off miners who currently earn between $57 and $83 a week. The miners refused and caused the reduction of coal production by 40%.

¶s 2, 3, 4, and 5
Apparently this information is presented to indicate the seriousness of Britain's problem. It should be reorganized into one ¶ with a clear topic sentence.

¶5
Because the cost information is not common knowledge, the source should be acknowledged in a footnote.

¶s 6, 7, and 8
The paper shifts at ¶6 to a discussion of the miner's work, his pay, and so on, but, again, the organizational pattern is not clarified for the reader by introductory statements, and ¶ structure is not used to reinforce organization. The first two sentences of ¶8 belong with the last sentence of ¶7.

9   Heath then offered an increase of $5 to $6 a week; any more he says, would exceed the 11% limit of his Phase III counter-inflationary plan.[7] Heath states that the problem would be solved if only the coal miner would accept the government's $101 million wage-increase package. It would mean a 16.5% wage increase for miners.[8] Heath is determined to preserve his anti-inflationary guidelines against the miners' demand for a 33% increase. The miners call Heath's attempt to settle "pantomime."[9]

10   Edward Heath's conservative government is greatly disliked by the miners. A miner's wife was quoted as saying, "Heath has love and a kiss on the cheek for the oil sheiks, but he has a slap in the face for the British miner."[10]

11   Some critics believe that there is enough coal in Britain to maintain enough power to keep industry at a near-normal level for 35 weeks. Heath, on the other hand, has placed the country's usable coal supply at 15.5 million tons. He states that this would have fallen to a critical 7 million tons within a month if he had not declared a 3-day work week.[11]

12   Richard Mills, a Birmingham plant inspector, said, "When this crisis passes, we'll have a boom, and then there'll be strikes and overtime bans. Then another crisis reaction."[12] This current dispute began in November 1973. But this is not the first British coal strike.

13   Britain, January 1972.

Prime Minister Edward Heath declares that he will not give in to a 25% wage hike demanded by British coal miners because it is far beyond his 8% national wage guidelines. The miners strike for seven weeks, causing power blackouts, layoffs of tens of thousands of other workers, and widespread industrial chaos. Finally, Heath appoints a special commission to arbitrate the miners' demands. The commission recommends a 21% wage increase. Both sides accept. The crisis is settled.[13]

14   "It's getting to be part of the British way of life."[14]

¶s 9, 10 and 11 Again the focus of the paper shifts, now to Heath's response to the miners, his justification for his position, and some criticism of his actions, but ¶ structure and transitional statements are not used to make the structure clear. The shift to Heath actually begins in ¶8, sentence 3. Also, no evaluation is offered of either Heath's position or the attitudes of his critics. Information is pasted together without any meaningful order imposed or any judgments made.

¶11 is a good example of random information being presented. How much coal did exist? Whose figures were right? And what purpose do these figures serve in the development of the paper?

Because the student has no thesis, he has just pasted information together haphazardly. He therefore has no real conclusions to draw, so he "concludes" by stringing three quotes together suggesting that coal strikes occur frequently in Britain. Is the student saying that because strikes happen often they aren't serious or important?

What can we learn from the two previous models demonstrating inadequate synthesis of source materials? Here are suggestions for avoiding the pitfalls of the "cut and paste" paper:

1. Know what you want to say. If you do not have a clear thesis, you have no basis for selecting information and no guidelines for determining a purposeful structure. The worst examples of "cut and paste" papers stem from this fundamental writing problem.

2. Have an organization in mind. While a detailed, formal outline may not be necessary for a short research assignment, you will need, for any essay, an organization that is planned both to serve the purpose of your paper and to be clear to your reader. Until you have a reason consistent with the purpose of your paper for organizing information in a certain way, you cannot impose a sensible order on your note cards.

3. Let your note cards reflect new knowledge which you have contemplated and understood. Avoid transferring undigested information from sources to note cards, and then from note cards to your paper.

The following paragraph from a student paper titled "A Solution to the Gun Problem" demonstrates a successful synthesis. The student has combined information from two sources with his own ideas to produce a unified opening paragraph. The paragraph simultaneously presents his thesis and stresses the seriousness of the issue he is examining.

> Our present laws concerning the possession and use of guns, particularly handguns, are badly in need of revision. Handguns have their legitimate uses, but they were also used in 10,340 murders in the United States in 1973 and in most of that year's 279,169 other gun-related reported crimes.[1] While many parrot the slogan, "Guns don't kill people, people kill people," guns surely make it easier. We should remember that handguns were developed expressly for the purpose of killing people at close range.[2] It is not surprising that they were the cause of 53% of all murders in 1973, while shotguns and rifles were responsible for only 8% and 6%, respectively.[3] As an alternative to the unlikely passage of a comprehensive law totally forbidding the use and possession of handguns, the need for registering all handguns to licensed citizens is imperative. Public acceptance and support of meaningful gun legislation is equally vital.

EXERCISES: Problems in Writing

A. Showing Indebtedness

Assuming that you are writing a paper on American attitudes toward money in the 1920s, write a paragraph that incorporates some of the ideas and opinions presented in the following excerpt from Frederick Lewis Allen's *Only Yesterday*. Show clearly the extent of your indebtedness to Allen.

At home, one of the most conspicuous results of prosperity was the conquest of the whole country by urban tastes and urban dress and the urban way of living. The rube disappeared. Girls in the villages of New Hampshire and Wyoming wore the same brief skirts and used the same lipsticks as their sisters in New York. The proletariat—or what the radicals of the Big Red Scare days had called the proletariat—gradually lost its class consciousness; the American Federation of Labor dwindled in membership and influence; the time had come when workingmen owned second-hand Buicks and applauded Jimmy Walker, not objecting in the least, it seemed, to his exquisite clothes, his valet, and his frequent visits to the millionaire-haunted sands of Palm Beach. It was no accident that men like Mellon and Hoover and Morrow found their wealth an asset rather than a liability in public office, or that there was a widespread popular movement to make Henry Ford president in 1924. The possession of millions was a sign of success, and success was worshiped the country over.

B.   Quoting

You have read the following paragraph from Constance Rourke's *American Humor* for a paper on humor in *Huck Finn*. Use it to practice the various forms and styles that borrowed material can take.

Born in the precise era when the American comic sense was coming to its first full expression, in 1835, Mark Twain had grown up in a small town on the Mississippi, in a region where the Crockett myth had taken shape and the tall tale had grown in stature. As a young printer he must have read newspapers of St. Louis and New Orleans that overflowed with the familiar comic narratives; he must have caught the full impact of that spirit of burlesque flourishing so broadly up and down the Great Valley. He could remember—as his tales of the Mississippi show—a crowd of wayward figures given to comedy, troupers, minstrels, itinerant preachers, wandering adventurers from the other side of the world: the variegated lot of migrants who could be seen anywhere in that period moving along the river or toward the plains.

1.   Select some material to present in a direct quote and explain why you chose that passage.
2.   Select a somewhat longer passage to quote directly and use the ellipsis to exclude unimportant material. Explain your choice of quoted and excluded material.
3.   Weave a short direct quote into a sentence you wrote and explain your choice.
4.   Select a passage to paraphrase; explain your decision to paraphrase rather than to quote.

C.   Class Practice in Synthesizing

Prepare yourself for a 20-minute class discussion on a topic agreed upon by the class or recommended by your instructor several days in advance. Be ready to participate and take notes during the discussion. After the discussion, write a brief essay on the topic, representing fairly what classmates have said and developing your own views. Pay attention to organization; you may wish to introduce the issue, summarize the main arguments, and conclude by stating your opinions compared with others'. Keep balance in your writing; do not devote the entire essay to one minor point.

Documentation

13

If you developed a complete, accurate set of bibliography cards and your notes include all necessary information, then the formal documentation needed to complete your project will not be difficult. This chapter provides guidelines for documentation and models of form. Your goal should be to make all documentation *accurate*, *consistent* with the accepted format, and *concise*.

TYPES OF DOCUMENTATION

1. *Reference footnote:* Most documentation will be reference footnotes that credit sources and provide information needed by the reader to check sources. While many of your important sources may be referred to in the body of your paper by author and perhaps title, the complete facts of publication and precise page references in your footnote will enable your reader to verify a quotation or study the passage in more detail.

2. *Internal documentation:* In formal research papers, the first use of a chief source should be documented fully in a reference footnote, but subsequent references to the same source should be given in the body of your paper whenever possible. Internal documentation (see p. 14 for examples) should be used to identify fre-

quent quotations from a work which is the subject of your paper. Let your reader know in the first full reference footnote that subsequent references in the body of your paper are from the same edition. For example:

[1]F. Scott Fitzgerald, The Great Gatsby (New York: Scribner's, 1925), p. 1. All subsequent references in the text are to this edition.

3. *Additional information footnote:* Occasionally you may need to provide additional useful information, explanation, or commentary that is not central to the development of your paper. These additions belong in content footnotes, but use them sparingly and never as a way of proving your thesis. Many instructors object to content footnotes, and prefer only reference footnotes in student papers.

4. *The "See also" footnote:* More acceptable to most readers is the footnote that refers to other sources of evidence for or against the point being established in the paper. Such footnotes are usually introduced with "See also" or "Compare," followed by the reference information. For example:

Chekhov's debt to Ibsen is indeed obvious and should be recognized, as should his debt to Maeterlinck and other playwrights of the 1890s who were concerned with the inner life of their characters.[3]

[3]See Eric Bentley, In Search of Theatre (New York: Vintage Books, 1959), p. 330; Walter Bruford, Anton Chekhov (New Haven: Yale Univ. Press, 1957), p. 45; and Raymond Williams, Drama from Ibsen to Eliot (New York: Oxford Univ. Press, 1953), pp. 126–29.

WHEN TO DOCUMENT

If you achieve a balance between your ideas and material borrowed from sources, your paper will not be dotted with footnotes as if it had the measles! On the other hand, the honest researcher gives full credit to the sources he has used. What might be considered an excessive dependence on sources is far less serious an offense than a failure to acknowledge indebtedness to the work of others.

Not only should you footnote all direct quotations, but also paraphrased information, ideas, and opinions. Do not footnote common knowledge even if your sources give references to well-known facts or ideas you want to use. Examples of common knowledge include undisputed dates, the fact that Napoleon was defeated at Waterloo, or that Benjamin Franklin experimented with electricity. But you should credit a historian who analyzes the causes for Napoleon's defeat, or a scientist who evaluates Franklin's contribution to the study of electricity. The more you read on your subject, the easier it will be to decide what is considered common knowledge. If, after careful reading and using common sense, you are still uncertain about footnoting, defend your integrity by documenting the information.

Be sparing in the use of footnotes by consolidating references whenever possible. For example, three separate quotations in one paragraph from the same source can be documented with one footnote. Be wary, however, of attaching a "catch-all" footnote at the end of a paragraph; never sacrifice clarity for the sake of economy.

GUIDELINES FOR ARRANGING FOOTNOTES IN YOUR PAPER

Footnote Numbers

1. Footnotes should be numbered consecutively throughout your paper, beginning with 1.

2. Footnote numbers are "superior" (raised) numbers; type or write them slightly above the line of type.

3. Footnote numerals are always Arabic, and are never followed by a period.

4. Footnote numbers should be placed at the end of borrowed material, after final punctuation, or after a quotation mark; they never precede borrowed material.

Location and Presentation of Footnotes: Two Patterns

If you plan to use the pattern of placing footnotes at the bottom of the page on which the borrowed material is located, follow these guidelines:

1. Footnote references must appear on the *same* page as the borrowed material. You need to calculate—before you begin to type—the amount of space needed to complete all of the footnote references that occur on that page. If you miscalculate, retype the page.

2. The first footnote reference begins three spaces below the last line of text.

3. The first line of each footnote is indented as if you were paragraphing. Begin with the footnote number, again slightly raised, which corresponds with the number in the text, skip one space, and then begin the reference.

4. If the footnote reference runs to more than one line, single-space between lines and begin the second line flush with the margin.

5. If more than one footnote appears on the page, double-space between footnotes. Here is an example:

[7] S. S. Koteliansky and Leonard Woolf, trans., <u>Note-book of Anton Chekhov</u> (New York: B. W. Huebsch, 1921), p. 100.

[8] Vladimir Nemirovich-Danchenko, <u>My Life in the Russian Theatre</u>, trans. John Curnos (Boston: Little, Brown, 1936), p. 119.

Instructors often prefer that all footnotes be placed on separate pages. Because footnotes at the back of a paper are easier to prepare and also easier for your instructor to read, we recommend this pattern. Follow these guidelines:

1. Footnote references are given in consecutive order corresponding to the footnote numbers in the text.
2. The first line of each footnote reference is indented as if you were paragraphing. Begin with the footnote number, slightly raised, skip one space, and then begin the reference.
3. If the footnote runs to more than one line, double-space between lines, beginning the second line flush with the margin.
4. Triple-space between footnotes.
5. Title your page(s) of footnotes "Notes." Place your page(s) of Notes after the last page of text and before the Bibliography. Examine the page of Notes in the sample research paper presented in Chapter 14 for a model of this pattern.

FOOTNOTE FORM: FIRST REFERENCE

The simplest form of the first complete footnote reference for a book would include the following information in this order:

1. The author's full name, in regular order;
2. The title of the book, underlined (subtitles may be omitted in footnotes but not in the bibliography);
3. The facts of publication: place, publisher, and date of publication;
4. The precise page reference for the documented material. Note the chief differences between footnote and bibliography form by contrasting them for the same book.

Bibliography form:

> Nairn, Ian. <u>The American Landscape: A Critical View</u>. New York: Random House, 1965.

Footnote form:

> [1] Ian Nairn, <u>The American Landscape</u> (New York: Random House, 1965), p. 25.

There are three basic differences in these two forms of citation. In a foot-note, the author's name is in regular order because you are not al-phabetizing, the page reference is included because you are documenting specific borrowed material, and the punctuation differs. In a footnote, the author and title are separated by a comma, the facts of publication are enclosed in parentheses, and a comma separates the facts of publication from the page number. As with the bibliography, other information is added to this basic pattern to identify a particular book. To help make the distinction, the examples below demonstrate footnote form for the same books used as examples of bibliography form in Chapter 9.

The simplest form for the first full footnote reference to an article in a journal, weekly magazine, or newspaper includes the following informa-tion, in the order shown below.

1. The author's full name in regular order

2. The title of the article in quotation marks

3. The facts of publication: title of the journal, underlined; volume; date; and precise page reference

Observe the differences between bibliography and footnote form for articles.

Bibliography form:

    Warren, Austin. "Hawthorne's Reading." New England Quarterly,
        8 (1935), 480-97.

Footnote form:

    ² Austin Warren, "Hawthorne's Reading," New England
    Quarterly, 8 (1935), 483-84.

In footnote form, the author's name is in regular order, the precise page reference is given, and the three main types of information (author, title, facts of publication) are separated by commas rather than periods.

As the sample footnotes below indicate, the presentation of volume and date varies (as it does for bibliographic citations), depending on the type of work in which the article appears. Sources other than books and articles, for which bibliography form is illustrated in Chapter 9, are not included in the sample footnotes. Once you have a model of bibliography form and know how it differs from footnote form, knowledge and good sense can guide you in footnoting more unusual sources.

The pattern of documentation illustrated here is based, like the bib-liography form illustrated in Chapter 9, on the Modern Language Associa-tion *Style Sheet.* This pattern is accepted in humanities courses, some so-cial science courses, and technical fields. Patterns of documentation in science fields differ from the *MLA Style Sheet* and from one field to another. If you write documented papers for science courses, ask your instructor which manual of style to follow, obtain that manual, and then follow the models of form shown in the manual.

SAMPLE FOOTNOTES

Books

A book whose author's name has been given in the text:

[3] The American Landscape (New York: Random House, 1965), p. 25.

(If the author's full name has been given in the paper, do not repeat it in the first footnote, but give the title even if it has already been presented in the text.)

A book by two or three authors:

[4] Charles A. Beard and Mary R. Beard, The American Spirit (New York: Macmillan, 1942), p. 63.

(The subtitle has been omitted, but must be included in the bibliography.)

A book by more than three authors:

[5] Albert C. Baugh and others, A Literary History of England (New York: Appleton–Century–Crofts, 1948), p. 6.

An edited work (editor named in addition to author):

[6] Benjamin Franklin, The Autobiography of Benjamin Franklin, ed. Max Farrand (Berkeley: University of California Press, 1949), pp. 6–8.

[7] Kenneth S. Lynn, ed., Huckleberry Finn: Text, Sources, and Criticism (New York: Harcourt Brace and World, 1961), pp. 21–23.

(Notice that no comma is used after the editor's name when it follows the title and precedes the facts of publication, but a comma does separate the abbreviation "ed." and the title.)

A translation

[8] Alexander Solzhenitsyn, August 1914, trans. Michael Glenny (New York: Farrar, Straus and Giroux, 1972), p. 251.

A book in two or more volumes:

[9] Richard B. Sewall, The Life of Emily Dickinson (New York: Farrar, Straus and Giroux, 1974), II, 52.

(The total number of volumes is given in the bibliography citation; in the footnote, the volume referred to is given in Roman numerals followed by a comma and the page reference, without the abbreviations for "volume" or "page.")

A book in its second or subsequent edition:

> [10] Merle Curti, <u>The Growth of American Thought</u>, 3rd ed. (New York: Harper and Row, 1964), pp. 15–16.

(Always include the number of the edition you have used, if it is not the first, in both footnotes and bibliography.)

A book in a series:

> [11] Hyatt H. Waggoner, <u>Nathaniel Hawthorne</u>, University of Minnesota Pamphlets on American Writers, No. 23 (Minneapolis: University of Minnesota Press, 1962), p. 4.

(The series name and number follow the title, separated by a comma, but are not underlined.)

A book in a paperback series:

> [12] Jan Kott, <u>Shakespeare Our Contemporary</u>, trans. Boleslaw Taborski, Anchor Books (Garden City, N. Y.: Doubleday, 1966), pp. 63–65.

(Notice that all pieces of information added after the title are separated by commas, but a comma does not immediately precede the parenthesis; however, a comma always comes after the last parenthesis, before the volume or page numbers.)

A work in a collection:

> [13] Richard H. Fogle, "Ambiguity and Clarity in Hawthorne's 'Young Goodman Brown,'" <u>New England Quarterly</u>, 18 (Dec. 1943), rpt. in <u>A Casebook on the Hawthorne Question</u>, ed. Agnes McNeill Donahue (New York: Thomas Y. Crowell, 1963), p. 208.

A reprint of an earlier work:

> [14] Christopher Marlowe, <u>The Works of Christopher Marlowe</u>, ed. C. F. Tucker Brooke (1910; rpt. Oxford: Clarendon Press, 1966), p. 240.

(Both the original date of publication and the facts of publication for the reprint are enclosed in parentheses.)

A corporate author:

> [15] Brown University Library, <u>Dictionary Catalogue of the Harris Collection of American Poetry and Plays</u> (Boston: G. K. Hall, 1972), VI, 3. Hereafter referred to as <u>Harris Collection</u>.

(Shorten titles whenever possible in subsequent footnotes, but tell your reader what the shortened title is.)

An encyclopedia article:

> [16]E[dward] J. K[enne]y, "Ovid," <u>Encyclopaedia</u> <u>Britannica</u> (Chicago: University of Chicago Press, 1972).

(Articles in reference works arranged alphabetically do not need to be identified by volume and page number. An even simpler form for well-known reference works is the title, followed by a comma, and the year, not in parentheses.)

Articles

An article in a journal with continuous paging throughout the issues published in a given year:

> [17] William A. Armstrong, "George Bernard Shaw: The Playwright as Producer," <u>Modern</u> <u>Drama</u>, 8 (Feb. 1966), 360–61.

(Notice that the three main types of information are separated by commas.)

An article in a monthly magazine with separate paging in each issue:

> [18] Sol Chaneles, "A Job Program for Ex-Convicts That Works," <u>Psychology</u> <u>Today</u>, March 1975, p. 44.

(The volume number is not needed to locate this article. When the volume number is not given, month and year are not in parentheses, and "p." or "pp." precedes the page numbers.)

An article from a weekly magazine:

> [19] Peter Barnes, "Bringing Back the WPA," <u>The</u> <u>New</u> <u>Republic</u>, 15 March 1975, p. 19.

An anonymous article:

> [20] "The Palestinian Tug of War," <u>Newsweek</u>, 4 Nov. 1974, pp. 36–37.

An article from a newspaper:

> [21] Kenneth Denlinger, "Johnny Miller: Shooting Par Is No Disgrace," <u>The</u> <u>Washington</u> <u>Post</u>, 14 March 1975, p. C5, col. 5.

An editorial:

> [22] Editorial, "Rights and Remedies," <u>The</u> <u>New</u> <u>York</u> <u>Times</u>, 25 Jan. 1976, Sec. 4, p. 16, col. 2.

A letter to the editor:

> [23] Paul W. Boltz, "In the Right Direction," in "Letters to the Editor," <u>The</u> <u>Wall</u> <u>Street</u> <u>Journal</u>, 12 Jan. 1976, p. 9, col. 2.

A signed review:

²⁴ Judith Thurman, "Unchanged by Suffering?" rev. of <u>Anya</u>, by Susan Fromberg Schaeffer, <u>Ms</u>. <u>Magazine</u>, March 1975, p. 46.

An unsigned review:

²⁵ "Viewpoints," rev. of "The Autobiography of Miss Jane Pittman" (a TV film shown on CBS, 31 Jan. 1974), <u>Time</u> <u>Magazine</u>, 4 Feb. 1974, p. 65.

FOOTNOTE FORM: SUBSEQUENT REFERENCES

All documentation following the first full footnote reference should be as brief as possible without sacrificing clarity. Here are more specific guidelines:

1. The simplest footnote form for all references after the first citation is the author's last name (never abbreviated) and the precise page number(s). For example: Curti, p. 56, or Sewall, I, 25.

2. If more than one work by the same author is used, cite the author's last name followed by a clear short title. Never use subtitles, and shorten long titles whenever possible. For example: Matthiessen, *James*, p. 12, and Matthiessen, *The James Family*, pp. 22-25.

3. If more than one writer with the same last name is used, add the first name to the footnote. For example: James E. Miller, Jr., *Reader's Guide to Melville*, p. 56, and Perry Miller, *The Raven and the Whale*, p. 235, if short titles are needed, or, more simply, James E. Miller, Jr., p. 56, and Perry Miller, p. 235.

4. When the reference is to an article and the title is needed, always use the article title (shortened if possible), not the journal title.

5. When the reference is to an anonymous article, use the title of the article followed by the page number(s).

Observe the form for second and subsequent references to previously cited works in the following series of footnotes:

¹ Kenneth S. Lynn, <u>Mark Twain and Southwestern Humor</u> (Boston: Little, Brown, 1960), p. 6.
² C. S. Lewis, "Psycho–Analysis and Literary Criticism," <u>Essays and Studies</u>, 27 (1941), 15–16.
³ Kenneth S. Lynn, "Huck and Jim," <u>Yale Review</u>, 47 (April 1955), 424.
⁴ Lynn, <u>Twain</u>, pp. 42–43.

(A short title is necessary because two works by Lynn are cited.)

⁵ Sinclair Lewis, "Fools, Liars, and Mr. DeVoto," <u>Saturday Review of Literature</u>, 27 (15 April 1944), 10.

[6] Bernard DeVoto, <u>Mark Twain's America</u> (Boston: Little, Brown, 1932), p. 82.
    [7] Sinclair Lewis, p. 12.

(The first name is needed because two writers with the same last name have been cited.)

[8] DeVoto, pp. 51–53.

(The simplest form to use when there is no possibility of confusion.)

THE USE OF LATIN ABBREVIATIONS

Of all the Latin abbreviations formerly used in footnoting, only "ibid." (no longer underlined because it is considered an Americanism) still appears with any regularity, and even its use is now being discouraged by the Modern Language Association. Since "ibid." means "in this place," it is correct only when one footnote immediately follows another for the same reference. When footnotes to the same reference are *not* consecutive, the author's last name must be given. It is more consistent to always give the author's last name for every footnote that comes after the first full citation. Also, "ibid." only tells your reader to consult the previous footnote, whereas the author's last name is more informative. Thus both consistency and clarity are served by discarding Latin abbreviations.

LIST OF COMMON ABBREVIATIONS

The following abbreviations are often used in footnoting. Note that "ibid.," "op. cit.," and "loc. cit." have been eliminated. Of the Latin abbreviations, only *"passim"* and *"v."* *(vide)* are still considered foreign words that require italics (underlining).

anon.	anonymous
ca. (or c.)	*circa* (about); used with approximate dates, e.g., ca. 1850
cf.	*confer* (compare); do not use cf. when "see" is meant
ch., chs. (or chap., chaps.)	chapter(s)
col., cols.	column(s)
d.	died
ed., edn.	edition
ed., eds.	editor(s)
e.g.	*exempli gratia* (for example)
esp.	especially
et al.	*et alii* (and others)
f., ff.	and the following page(s); exact references are better, e.g., pp. 24-26 rather than pp. 24ff.

i.e.	*id est* (that is)
illus.	illustrated
introd.	introduction
l., ll.	line(s)
MS, MSS	manuscripts(s)
N.B.	*nota bene* (take notice, mark well)
n.d.	no date (of publication) given
n.p.	no place (of publication) given
numb.	numbered
p., pp.	page(s)
passim	throughout the work, here and there
rev.	revised
ser.	series
st., sts.	stanza(s)
trans.	translator, translation, translated ("by" understood in context)
TS	typescript (by contrast to MS)
v.	*vide* (see)
v., vv. (or vs., vss.)	verse(s)
vol., vols.	volume(s)

The Complete Paper

14

Although fairly precise guidelines can be established for completing the steps in the research process, no simple formula exists for merging all the parts into a unified and coherent paper. At this point you need to review the more general guides to good writing established in Section I.

As you have read and taken notes with your thesis clearly in mind, ideas for organizing the information have probably occurred to you. The heading (indicating the *type* of information) you place on each note card will divide the topic into major subtopics and also help order the material. When you have finished note-taking, arrange the cards according to topic headings and read them through again. You will probably discover that some cards are not relevant, and that additional reading and note-taking may be necessary on other topics.

DRAFTING THE PAPER

Good writing takes time, patience, and a commitment to the value of revision. Writing a good research paper requires the additional concern for accurate presentation of others' ideas and proper footnote and bibliography form. As we stressed in Chapter 12, you should exercise care in choosing words which introduce and explain your source material. Work closely from your note cards, checking and rechecking the accuracy of direct quotes, the appropriateness of word choice, and the correctness of footnote placement.

These suggestions may help you avoid some of the problems involved in research papers:

1. As you prepare your first draft, leave wide margins and extra lines so revisions can be easily read when you are ready to type the final draft.

2. Put in footnote numbers as you draft your paper; waiting until the draft is completed can result in failure to footnote accurately.

3. Whenever you place a footnote number in the draft, write out the complete footnote on a separate sheet of paper. When you finish the draft, the footnote numbers will be correctly placed in the text, and corresponding footnotes will be in order.

4. Remember that, while a research paper is more formal than a personal essay, it is still *your* own writing, and thus it should sound like your writing. Try to avoid colloquial expressions and other informal speech patterns, but do not reach for unfamiliar five-dollar words just to make your paper sound better. Your paper will sound best when you use language with exactness and sensitivity.

5. Avoid lengthy, formal introductions and conclusions. The best introduction, regardless of the length or complexity of the paper, is an opening paragraph which briefly and interestingly introduces the subject, presents your thesis, and gives the reader an indication of the scope and limits of the paper. Similarly, the best conclusion briefly summarizes the key points or restates the thesis.

6. Finally, *revise*. Work through the paper several times, focusing on different issues each time. Check first for logic and clarity of organization. (Remember that rearranging the draft probably means rearranging the footnotes.) After you are satisfied with the total structure of your paper, examine it for purposefully organized paragraphs, precise and appropriate words, and correct grammar and punctuation. Full and accurately documented information is not enough; a good research paper is the result of clear thinking and precise, forceful writing.

THE FINAL DRAFT

When your research project is submitted to your instructor, it will be in this order:

1. title page

2. thesis statement, statement of purpose, and/or outline if required (if the outline is more than one page, number the second and subsequent pages with small Roman numerals)

3. body or text of the paper (which may contain footnotes at the bottom of the pages)

4. footnotes placed on separate page(s) after the text, if the format recommended in this book is followed

5. bibliography, or list of works cited

SAMPLE RESEARCH PAPER

The sample research paper which follows represents the successful completion of a research assignment for a class in English composition. The student was asked to select a current topic of interest and to develop and support an opinion based on pertinent information from current newspapers, magazines, and journals. Our comments about her paper appear in the margin of each page.

This title page is a good
example of one
appropriate format.

LET THE SUNSHINE IN

by
Ruth Johnson

English 112
Dr. Hornor
17 March 1975

LET THE SUNSHINE IN

OUTLINE

Thesis: Solar energy seems to hold the most
         promise as an energy source for the
         future.

  I. The need for solar energy

 II. A brief history of solar-energy research

III. Advantages of solar energy
     A. Unlimited supply
     B. Non-pollutant
     C. Not dangerous
     D. Not controlled by any country
     E. Inflation-proof
     F. Technology not as complex
        as nuclear technology

 IV. Explanation of solar energy
     A. A solar-heated, solar-cooled home
     B. A solar-powered home

  V. Costs of solar energy
     A. Costs for private homes
     B. Costs for public buildings
     C. Costs relative to climate

 VI. Attitudes about using solar energy
     A. Plans for future use in various
        cities and states
     B. Advantages expressed by scientists
     C. Support of solar energy by Congress

The formal outline,
when required, follows
the title page. Notice
that the thesis has been
included and labeled
simply "thesis."

Note that the title is repeated at the top of page one and that no page number appears, although it is counted as the first page of text.

LET THE SUNSHINE IN

1   Almost every American is aware that the country is faced with a serious energy crisis. America's energy problems are serious, despite popular belief that difficulties vanished with the end of the Arab oil embargo in 1974. Our problems remain because the world's supply of fossil fuel is not endless. With increased technology, more nations are becoming more dependent on oil and its by-products. Also, with the cost of fossil fuel increasing and the supply becoming more limited, the search is on for a new form of energy as abundant as fossil fuel, and a source that can be economically processed. One of the energy sources that is being scrutinized very closely is solar energy. With demand and cost for fossil fuel increasing not only in the United States but all over the world, solar energy seems to hold the most promise for the future.

2   The idea of utilizing the sun's energy for man's needs is not new. However, research in solar energy has been stagnating primarily because in past years fossil fuel was cheaper and more plentiful. Dr. Aden Meinel, Director of the Optical Sciences Center of the University of Arizona, affirms that ". . . as recently as 1969, solar energy was dismissed as holding little promise for contributing to the future energy needs of the United States."[1] However, when it became obvious that the energy problem was real, several scientists started exploring the idea of the sun as an alternative source of energy. One of the pioneers of solar energy is Dr. Joseph W. Kayne, Department of Physics and Astronomy, Hasbrouck Laboratory at the University of Massachusetts [1971], whose studies reveal that considerable research had

The student interests her readers by reminding them that an energy problem exists and then noting three specific causes. She heads directly to her topic —solar energy—and concludes her first ¶ with a clearly stated thesis: ". . . solar energy seems to hold the most promise for the future."

Notice that the student's first borrowed material does not appear until ¶2; the introduction represents her own thinking and language. ¶2 provides a brief history of solar energy research; the experts' credentials accompany their views.

gone into developing solar cookers, solar heating for individual dwellings, and solar furnaces for various "high-tempered applications."[2] Currently research seems to be focused on using the sun's energy to provide both heating and cooling for homes and one-story public facilities and to generate electricity.

3   Solar energy has many impressive features, including its unlimited supply. Allen L. Hammond in Science states that the abundance of the sun's energy is adequate for a country as industrialized as the United States. Further, he affirms that "the energy arriving on 0.5 percent of the land area of the United States is more than the total energy needs of the country to the year 2000."[3] A writer for The New Republic also lists many pluses for solar energy. Among them: solar energy, unlike fossil fuel, does not pollute the air; it does not create any dangerous waste products as nuclear power does; it is not controlled by any nation and, therefore, cannot be embargoed; it is almost inflation-proof; and, finally, its technology is not as complex as nuclear technology.[4] With all these good things going for solar energy, there is promise for its widespread use in the not too distant future.

4   Many homeowners and building contractors have been attracted to harnessing the sun's energy for heating and cooling primarily because of the eventual low cost and the simplicity of the system. Omer Henry, an engineer, explains that the basic principle of solar heating is not complex. If one wishes to convert an old house or build a new house to include the solar system, the first step is to install specially treated glass roof panels facing southward. For heating purposes, water is pumped up to the specially treated solar

¶3 summarizes the advantages of solar energy. The student has successfully combined material from two sources into one ¶, and has put almost all of the borrowed information into her own words. She has quoted statistical information directly.

Showing an awareness of her audience, the student describes in detail a solar energy heating and cooling system to demonstrate its advantageous simplicity.

2

panels on the roof. The water becomes hot, "sometimes reaching temperatures near boiling point." This hot water then flows into storage tanks underneath the house and the heat is "transferred to a surrounding bed of stones." Air circulating through the stones picks up heat and is blown through the ducts to warm the house. At the same time, the hot water is also used for domestic purposes. Mr. Henry further explains that the cool water is pumped back to the roof, where the cycle repeats itself to keep the water constantly hot. In the summer months, the system is reversed; water is cooled by refrigeration coil and pumped to the northeast side of the roof. The air that is blown through the stones around the water tank is also used to air–condition the house.[5] This kind of dwelling is classified as a solar–heated, solar–cooled home.

5   By contrast, there are over two dozen solar–powered homes now in existence. The difference between a solar–powered home and a solar–heated home is that a solar–powered home operates almost entirely on free sunlight and generates its own electricity for lighting and for the operation of washing machines, dishwashers, and other electrical appliances. The newest solar–powered model is located on the Connecticut coast off Long Island Sound.[6] Another solar–powered house worth mentioning is located in Wilmington, Delaware. Statistics reveal that this house, built in 1973 and studied by scientists at the University of Delaware, produced more than twenty kilowatt–hours of electricity a day, which is more than enough for an average home's daily requirement of eighteen kilowatt–hours.[7]

6   Almost everyone is aware that the sun does not shine every day; because it shines in some regions of the United States more than others,

The writer identifies her source of information at the beginning of the presentation and mentions again that she is quoting from Mr. Henry's explanation. Because of source acknowledgment in the body of the paper, one footnote at the conclusion of the discussion provides adequate formal documentation.

This ¶ continues the discussion of the actual use of solar energy systems by contrasting a solar-heated home with solar-powered homes. The writer has combined information from two sources in this ¶ and has eliminated irrelevant information taken in her original note about the occupants of the Connecticut home.

3

one is apt to question what happens to solar-heated homes on sunless days. An experiment conducted by scientists at the Delaware house previously mentioned revealed that each day enough unused energy is stored in the heating reservoir to last several days. When there is no sunshine, an auxiliary heat pump can be turned on to boost the temperature in the reservoir. As a further supplement, the scientists said "an external power from a public utility can be switched on" if sunless days continue.[8]

7   The low cost of solar energy is one advantage that cannot be ignored. Owners of private solar-heated homes, construction companies and researchers all seem to agree that, despite the initial high cost, the system offers tremendous savings over a period of years.[9] Nevertheless, the high initial outlay may be one of the few drawbacks of solar energy for the small home owner. In 1972 and 1973 homeowners reported that installation of the system cost from two thousand to twenty-five hundred dollars.[10] But many agree that this initial high cost still represents a savings over fossil fuel. Wilson Clark, consultant to the Environmental Policy Center of Washington, D.C., and author of the book Energy for Survival, states that one of the most impressive features of solar energy is the low cost. He referred to a study done by the National Science Foundation and NASA which indicated that solar energy heating and cooling could save the United States one hundred and eighty million dollars in fuel cost over a ten-year period.[11] Another testament that solar energy provides low-cost heating is cited in the article by Omer Henry. He states that Dr. Harry Thomason, the owner of a solar-heated home located in the Washington, D.C., area,

The student anticipates a reader's question: "What happens when the sun doesn't shine?"

In this ¶ the writer shifts to another advantage of solar-energy systems—low cost. She points out fairly that the initial cost of a solar-energy system is higher than that of a fossil fuel or electrical energy system, but that in the long run the solar-energy system is cheaper.

4

confirms that for the first year he spent seven dollars for oil. Mr. Henry also mentioned that in Coos Bay, Oregon, where winters are more severe, builders of solar-heated homes had monthly heating bills "averaging only seven to twelve dollars, while neighbors complained about monthly heating bills of sixty to seventy dollars for oil."[12] With the rising cost of fuel, these low heating bills are encouraging to the consumer.

8   Private home owners and builders are not the only ones who are experimenting with solar energy systems. Several government buildings, including schools, are testing this new form of heating and cooling. For example, the Timonium Elementary School in Baltimore, Maryland, is conducting an experiment with a newly installed [1974] solar heating and air-conditioning system. The first month after the system was in operation, the National Science Foundation (which is still responsible for conducting the experiments at this school) announced that, for a thirty-three day period the system saved approximately six hundred and forty-two gallons of fuel oil which would ordinarily cost four hundred and twenty-five dollars to run the entire building.[13] The above evidence seems to indicate that, while initial costs are high, the use of solar energy for heating would be cheaper than using fossil fuel. In desert areas such as Phoenix, Arizona, and parts of California, where the temperature is moderate, it would be cheaper to have the system than in places like Oregon or Vermont where the winters are harsh and where a back-up conventional system would have to be used.

9   The prospects of solar energy seem so promising that many cities and states are beginning to plan for its increased use. One example is the city of Santa Clara, California,

The first sentence of this ¶ provides a smooth transition from the previous emphasis on the uses of solar-energy systems in private homes to their uses in public facilities and the actions of governments in support of solar-energy systems for the future, topics which comprise the rest of the paper.

Square brackets are used to clarify the expression "newly installed" in the third sentence.

The writer not only presents information but concludes her ¶ with an evaluation of it.

5

which is planning to open a new solar-powered recreation building by the summer of 1975. Santa Clara's city officials are also planning to have solar equipment installed on all new buildings. Consumers will pay a monthly fee for the maintenance of the system.[14] In addition, the state of Florida passed a new law requiring all new single family residences to be built for future use of solar water heating equipment. Further, the state of Indiana exempts solar equipment from property taxation, and the state of Arizona allows businesses to deduct a higher depreciation off solar hardware. The California Coastal Conservation Committee has "recommended that all new construction in the coastal zone contain solar-assisted heating and cooling systems as soon as the necessary equipment is on the market."[15]

10   In voicing promise for the future of solar energy, and in reporting on the study done by Westinghouse, Peter Barnes in The New Republic asserts that scientists at the National Science Foundation are optimistic that the sun will provide more than one-third of the energy used for heating and cooling, and an additional twenty to thirty percent for electrical purposes.[16]

11   Last but not least is the support and recognition that members of Congress are giving to the further development of solar energy. Alan Cranston, Senator from California, acknowledges authorship of new legislation authorizing research on the feasibility of solar heating and cooling systems. The result is a new law referred to as the "1974 Solar Heating and Cooling Act." The law, says Senator Cranston, "involves the Department of Housing and Urban Development and NASA in a $60 million government-sponsored demonstration of solar heating and cooling for residential and

While these ¶s continue the focus on public or governmental action, the emphasis on the future for solar-energy systems carries out the paper's general organizational plan of moving from past to present to future.

6

commercial buildings." The National Science Foundation is the official research agency set up by the federal government to fund and evaluate research projects involving solar energy. It is hoped that the new legislation will open further avenues to make solar heating and cooling a reality within the next five years.[17]

12 It is evident that the idea of utilizing solar energy is not as far-fetched as it seemed years ago. With the continued support of government, plus the enthusiasm of research groups, environmentalists, private industry, and other citizens, solar energy may become a household word quite soon; with the increasing high cost of fossil fuel, the time could not be better for exploring this use of the sun.

The student's concluding ¶ is short, to the point, and not repetitious. She stresses the growing and diversified interest in solar energy and reminds the reader once more of the chief advantage of solar energy.

NOTES

[1] Aden B. Meinel, "Is It Time for a New Look at Solar Energy?" Science and Public Affairs, 27 Oct. 1971, p. 32.

[2] Joseph W. Kayne, "Solar Energy Revived," Science and Public Affairs, 20 Oct. 1971, p. 27.

[3] Allen L. Hammond, "Solar Energy: The Largest Resource," Science, 117 (Sept. 1972), 1088.

[4] Peter Barnes, "The Solar Derby," New Republic, 1 Feb. 1975, p. 18.

[5] Omer Henry, "The House That Has Its Furnace in the Sky," Popular Mechanics, June 1973, p. 151.

[6] Wilson Clark, "A Solar—House Primer," New York Times, 7 April 1974, Sec. 4, p. 92.

[7] Sheldon M. Gallager, "Switching on the Sun," Popular Mechanics, Oct. 1973, pp. 190—91.

[8] Gallager, p. 192.

[9] Hammond, p. 1089.

[10] Henry, "House," p. 153.

[11] Clark, Sec. 4, p. 94.

[12] Henry, "House," pp. 152—53.

[13] Omer Henry, "Timonium's Solar—Heated School," American Education, Oct. 1974, p. 33.

[14] Barnes, p. 17.

The footnotes have been placed after the last page of text. The first page of footnotes is titled "NOTES." Footnotes which run to more than one line of type are double-spaced. Triple-spacing is used between each footnote.

8

[15] Barnes, p. 19.

[16] Barnes, p. 17.

[17] Alan Cranston, "A Bright Future for Solar Energy," <u>National Parks and Conservation Magazine</u>, Oct. 1974, p. 13.

LIST OF WORKS CITED

Barnes, Peter. "The Solar Derby." <u>The New Republic</u>, 1 Feb. 1975, pp. 17–19.

Clark, Wilson. "A Solar-House Primer." <u>The New York Times</u>, 7 April 1974, pp. 92–95.

Cranston, Alan. "A Bright Future for Solar Energy." <u>National Parks and Conservation Magazine</u>, Oct. 1974, pp. 10–13.

Gallager, Sheldon M. "Switching on the Sun." <u>Popular Mechanics</u>, Oct. 1973, pp. 190–92.

Hammond, Allen. L. "Solar Energy: The Largest Resource." <u>Science</u>, 177 (Sept. 1972), 1088–90.

Henry, Omer. "The House That Has Its Furnace in the Sky." <u>Popular Mechanics</u>, June 1973, pp. 150–54.

———. "Timonium's Solar-Heated School." <u>American Education</u>, Oct. 1974, pp. 30–33.

Kayne, Joseph W. "Solar Energy Revived." <u>Science and Public Affairs</u>, 20 Oct. 1971, pp. 27–28.

Meinel, Aden Baker. "Is It Time for a New Look at Solar Energy?" <u>Science and Public Affairs</u>, 27 Oct. 1971, pp. 32–37.

Note that the list of works cited is an alphabetical list of only those sources actually used in the paper. Each citation is presented with *hanging indentation:* the first line is flush with the margin and subsequent lines are indented.

Section 4

A
COLLECTION
OF READINGS

RHETORICAL TABLE OF CONTENTS (with a brief explanation of rhetorical types)

Development by Examples

Providing examples is the most typical pattern of developing an essay. Examples need to be given regardless of the style of development (comparison/contrast, cause/effect), but many writers also use them as the primary method of development. Often writers will group examples by type; they first analyze their subject (divide it into parts) and then organize the examples according to the analysis. For instance, Harrington groups examples of American advertisements to show attitudes toward sex and cleanliness, and to depict fears.

Development by examples, whatever the organizational plan of the essay, is basic to good writing. A writer who offers examples explains, develops, and supports generalizations; if he wants to show a trend, he will need many examples. Examples must be relevant to the writer's thesis, and must also make the thesis convincing. Barnes gives numerous examples of the language of bureaucracy; Miller and Swift show specific ways in which our language is sexist. Sometimes one longer example, an extended illustration, is an effective technique if the writer convinces us that it is representative; both McGill and Goodwin demonstrate the effective use of extended illustration.

Examples may be drawn from a study of the topic (Asimov studies science fiction), from general knowledge (Epstein discusses the many sports figures he has admired), and from personal experience (Chisholm writes about the discrimination she experienced in her political activities). Essays developed largely from the personal experience of the writer (Roiphe describes the attitudes toward men that she was taught; Wylie talks about his mother-in-law's cooking) are called *familiar essays*; they often have an informal quality, and the personality of the writer emerges. Examples from personal experience need enough context so that the reader can understand their significance to the issue being discussed.

Ralph McGill, "Kluxers Flee Americans"

Norman Cousins, "Are You Making Yourself Clear?"

Henry A. Barnes, "The Language of Bureaucracy"

Richard N. Goodwin, "Incident at Kennebunk"

Process

Process essays are characterized by their use of *time sequence* (chronological order) as the organizational strategy and by their purpose: explaining how to do something (how to bake a cake, tune up a car), explaining how something was done (how the Golden Gate Bridge was constructed), or explaining how something can be done (how to establish a more responsible local government). The successful process paper depends upon the writer's ability to explain the separate steps in the process and to present them in the appropriate order. A good process paper will provide the reader with the directions he needs to reproduce a process or to understand how a task was accomplished. Reeves describes each unit in his course on advertising so that interested teachers can create a similar course.

Several essays in this collection illustrate variations of process analysis to suit different purposes. In his case study, Bettelheim uses a process strategy to explain the steps in Joey's therapy. Asimov explains the process by which science fiction writers create their imagined futures out of a known present. While Merrill's purpose is to show *Time*'s stereotyping of three presidents, he uses a process organization as part of his formal scientific report writing: he presents in chronological order the process of formulating an hypothesis, establishing methods for information gathering, analyzing the information, and drawing conclusions. Thus the most familiar organizational pattern, time sequence, can effectively serve the diverse purposes of serious essayists.

Bruce Reeves, "Ad-Man, Business-Man, Teacher-Man"

Bruno Bettelheim, "Joey: A 'Mechanical Boy' "

Isaac Asimov, "How Easy to See the Future!"

John C. Merrill, "How *Time* Stereotyped Three U.S. Presidents"

Comparison/Contrast

Comparison (pointing out likenesses) and contrast (pointing out differences) are familiar methods of development. A writer usually organizes comparison/contrast in one of three ways: whole by whole (a country school and a city school), part by part (classrooms in each school, materials in each school, teachers in each school), or likenesses and differences (similarity of goals and subjects, differences in facilities and materials).

Sometimes a writer compares or contrasts to evaluate; Norman Cousins makes a whole by whole comparison/contrast of poets and computers to demonstrate which he thinks is more valuable to society. Sometimes a writer compares or contrasts material to prove a point; John Merrill contrasts part by part (attribution, adjective, adverbial, and other biases) *Time's* attitudes toward three U. S. presidents. Anne Roiphe explains women's prejudices by comparing them to those of minorities; Gloria Steinem implies a contrast between the present and the future to show that the greater involvement of women in society will improve the quality of life; Julian Huxley relies on comparisons and contrasts between man and other living things to further his definition of war.

Norman Cousins, "The Computer and the Poet"

Anne Richardson Roiphe, "Confessions of a Female Chauvinist Sow"

Gloria Steinem, "What It Would Be Like If Women Win"

John C. Merrill, "How *Time* Stereotyped Three U. S. Presidents"

Julian Huxley, "War as a Biological Phenomenon"

Definition

Definition helps explain meaning. A writer might define only a word or term, using the dictionary method of *classification plus differentiation* (a horse is a large mammal that is four-footed, solid-hoofed, and herbivorous). At other times, a writer might explain a concept in greater detail, and then write an *extended definition* to prove a point. The extended definition may require examples, comparisons, contrasts, descriptions, analyses. Ralph Nader, Julian Huxley, and Henry Barnes define abstractions (patriotism, war, bureaucratic language) primarily through examples and analysis. Hayakawa's definition of contexts also includes numerous smaller definitions necessary to an understanding of the larger subject. TRB and Vernon Jordan undertake difficult definitions of an age and a class of people—often using negation (explaining what a subject is *not*). Ralph McGill implies a definition of 100% Americans by applying the term to different groups, thus causing the reader to examine his own definition.

S. I. Hayakawa, "Contexts"

Vernon E. Jordan, Jr., "The Truth About the Black Middle Class"

Ralph McGill, "Kluxers Flee Americans"

TRB, "The Tarnished Age"

Ralph Nader, "We Need a New Kind of Patriotism"

Henry A. Barnes, "The Language of Bureaucracy"

Julian Huxley, "War as a Biological Phenomenon"

Cause/Effect

Cause/effect describes or defines a particular kind of analysis or a particular purpose rather than a pattern of organization. The writer who explains causes is explaining why something happened (what economic conditions produced the Great Depression) or failed to happen (why the top-seeded player lost the tennis tournament); he may also analyze the conditions that will produce a desired future effect (what changes in company policy will increase profits). For example, Mannes asserts that TV advertising produces psychological and social problems.

The writer who examines effects is explaining the results of particular events or conditions (the impact on the environment of a new dam; the physical and emotional benefits of regular exercise). Steinem, for example, begins with a cause, the women's liberation movement, and predicts the effects of its success.

Whether a writer is explaining the reasons for, or predicting the results of, an event or condition, he will need to think carefully, keep his mind open to all possibilities, and use various strategies to develop his essay: reasoning from particular to general or general to particular, examples, perhaps comparison/contrast. Harrington, for instance, provides many examples to show what values and fears cause certain ads to be produced. Complete and accurate causal analysis requires attention to multiple causes (or effects) to avoid oversimplification; it requires a distinction between immediate and ultimate causes, or immediate and long-range effects; and it requires a full explanation of the sequence of causes (or effects) so that the reader can understand the connections perceived by the writer. For example, Epstein discusses and then discards several possible causes before settling on one acceptable to him.

> Stephanie Harrington, "Enticers, 1970; On TV, Who Do They Think You Are?"
>
> Joseph Epstein, "Obsessed with Sport"
>
> Marya Mannes, "Television Advertising: The Splitting Image"
>
> Bruno Bettelheim, "Joey: A 'Mechanical Boy' "
>
> Gloria Steinem, "What It Would Be Like If Women Win"
>
> Philip Wylie, "Science Has Spoiled My Supper"
>
> Walter Cronkite, "What It's Like to Broadcast News"
>
> Richard Goodwin, "Incident at Kennebunk"

Argumentation

Argumentation involves convincing the reader that the writer's point is valid and/or persuading him to take action or to change his attitude. Some argument is logical and factual; some is not. Some argument is moving and emotional; some is not. A complete argument usually includes clearly stating the problem, discussing the writer's proposed solution, anticipating and answering opponents' probable objections, and confirming the writer's solution. The most effective arguments are based on evidence that a reader may verify through his own observation, experience, or study. This anthology contains a wide variety of arguments ranging from weak to strong. Two special types of arguments are Martin Luther King's oration and Irving Fang's and Vernon Jordan's refutations. A full discussion of the problems of, and strategies for, writing and understanding arguments appears in Section 2.

Norman Cousins, "The Computer and the Poet"

Vernon E. Jordan, Jr., "The Truth About the Black Middle Class"

Casey Miller and Kate Swift, "One Small Step for Genkind"

Marya Mannes, "Television Advertising: The Splitting Image"

Russell Kirk, "Textbooks as Brainwashers"

Shirley Chisholm, "I'd Rather Be Black Than Female"

Helen Lawrenson, "The Feminine Mistake"

Martin Luther King, Jr., "I Have a Dream"

Ralph McGill, "Kluxers Flee Americans"

TRB, "The Tarnished Age"

Ralph Nader, "We Need a New Kind of Patriotism"

Eric Sevareid, "Illusions About America"

Lewis S. Feuer, "Why Not a Commentary on Sevareid?"

Walter Cronkite, "What It's Like to Broadcast News"

Irving E. Fang, "It *Is* Your Business, Mr. Cronkite"

Norman Cousins, "Are You Making Yourself Clear?"

THEMATIC TABLE OF CONTENTS

I. *Language*
S. I. Hayakawa, "Contexts"
Casey Miller and Kate Swift, "One Small Step for Genkind"
Bruce Reeves, "Ad-Man, Business-Man, Teacher-Man"
Russell Kirk, "Textbooks as Brainwashers"
John C. Merrill, "How *Time* Stereotyped Three U. S. Presidents"
Norman Cousins, "Are You Making Yourself Clear?"
Henry A. Barnes, "The Language of Bureaucracy"

II. *Advertising*
Bruce Reeves, "Ad-Man, Business-Man, Teacher-Man"
Stephanie Harrington, "The Enticers, 1970; On TV, Who Do They Think You Are?"

Marya Mannes, "Television Advertising: The Splitting Image"

III. *The News Media*
Lewis S. Feuer, "Why Not a Commentary on Sevareid?"
Walter Cronkite, "What It's Like to Broadcast News"
Irving E. Fang, "It *Is* Your Business, Mr. Cronkite"
John C. Merrill, "How *Time* Stereotyped Three U.S. Presidents"

IV. *Feminist Issues*
Casey Miller and Kate Swift, "One Small Step for Genkind"
Russell Kirk, "Textbooks as Brainwashers"
Shirley Chisholm, "I'd Rather Be Black Than Female"
Helen Lawrenson, "The Feminine Mistake"
Anne Richardson Roiphe, "Confessions of a Female Chauvinist Sow"
Gloria Steinem, "What It Would Be Like If Women Win"

V. *Minority Issues*
Vernon E. Jordan, Jr., "The Truth About the Black Middle Class"
Shirley Chisholm, "I'd Rather Be Black Than Female"
Martin Luther King, Jr., "I Have a Dream"
Ralph McGill, "Kluxers Flee Americans"

VI. *Patriotism*
Martin Luther King, Jr., "I Have a Dream"
Ralph McGill, "Kluxers Flee Americans"
TRB, "The Tarnished Age"
Ralph Nader, "We Need a New Kind of Patriotism"
Eric Sevareid, "Illusions About America"
Richard N. Goodwin, "Incident at Kennebunk"

VII. *Political Issues*
Shirley Chisholm, "I'd Rather Be Black Than Female"
Gloria Steinem, "What It Would Be Like If Women Win"
Ralph McGill, "Kluxers Flee Americans"
TRB, "The Tarnished Age"
Ralph Nader, "We Need a New Kind of Patriotism"
Henry A. Barnes, "The Language of Bureaucracy"
Richard Goodwin, "Incident at Kennebunk"
Julian Huxley, "War as a Biological Phenomenon"
Blue Ridge Material

VIII. *Science, Technology, and Modern Culture*
Norman Cousins, "The Computer and the Poet"
Joseph Epstein, "Obsessed with Sport"
Bruno Bettelheim, "Joey: A 'Mechanical Boy' "
Isaac Asimov, "How Easy to See the Future!"

READINGS

Epstein, the author of Divorced in America *and various articles, is editor of* The American Scholar. *The essay appeared in* Harper's *in July 1976.*

Obsessed with Sport: On the Interpretation
of a Fan's Dreams
Joseph Epstein

1   I cannot remember when I was not surrounded by sports, when talk of sports was not in the air, when I did not care passionately about sports. As a boy in Chicago in the late Forties, I lived in the same building as the sister and brother-in-law of Barney Ross, the welterweight champion. Half a block away, down near the lake, the Sullivan High School football team worked out in the spring and autumn. Summers the same field was given over to baseball and men's softball on Sundays. A few blocks to the north was the Touhy Avenue Fieldhouse, where basketball was played, and lifeguards trained, and behind which, in a softball field frozen over in winter, crack-the-whip, hockey, and speed skating took over. To the west, a block or so up Morse Avenue, was the Morse Avenue "L" Recreations, a combined pool hall and bowling alley. Life, in short, was games.

2   My father had no interest in sports. He had grown up, one of the ten children of Russian Jewish immigrant parents, on tough Notre Dame Street in Montreal, where the major sports were craps, poker, and petty larceny. He left Montreal at seventeen to come to Chicago, where he worked hard and successfully so that his sons might play. Two of his boyhood friends from Notre Dame Street, who had the comic-book names of Sammy and Danny Spunt, had also come to Chicago, where they bought the Ringside Gym on Dearborn Street in the Loop. All the big names worked out at Ringside for their Chicago fights: Willie Pep, Tony Zale, Joe Louis. At eight or nine I would take the El downtown to the Ringside, be introduced around by Danny Spunt ("Tony Zale, I'd like you to meet the son of an old friend of mine. Kid, I'd like you to meet the middleweight champion of the world"), and return home with an envelope filled with autographed 8-by-10 glossies of Gus Lesnevich, Tammy Mauriello, Kid Gavilan, and the wondrous Sugar Ray.

3   I lived on, off, and in sports. *Sport* magazine had recently begun publication, and I gobbled up its issues cover to cover, soon becoming knowledgeable not only about the major sports—baseball, football, and basketball—but about golf, hockey, tennis, and horse racing, so that I scored reputably on the Sport Quiz, a regular department at the front of the magazine. Another regular department was the Sport Classic, which featured longish profiles of the legendary figures in the history of sports: Ty Cobb, Jim Thorpe, Bobby Jones, Big Bill Tilden, Red Grange, Man o' War. I next moved on to the sports novels of John R. Tunis—*All-American, The Iron Duke, The Kid from Tomkinsville, The Kid Comes Back, World Series,* the lot—which I read with as much excitement as any books I have read since.

4   The time was, as is now apparent, a splendid era in sports. Ted Williams, Joe DiMaggio, and Stan Musial were afield; first Jack Kramer, then Pancho Gonzales, dominated tennis; George Mikan led the Minneapolis Lakers, and the Harlem Globetrotters could still be taken seriously; Doc Blanchard and Glen Davis, Mr. Inside and Mr. Outside, were playing for Army, Johnny Lujack was at Notre Dame; in the pros, Sammy Baugh, Bob Waterfield, and Sid Luckman were the major T-formation quarterbacks; Joe Louis and Sugar Ray Robinson fought frequently; the two Willies, Mosconi and Hoppe, put in regular appearances at Bensinger's in the Loop; Eddie Arcaro seemed to ride three, four winners a day. Giants, it truly seemed, walked the earth.

5   All learning of craft—which sport, like writing, most assuredly is— involves imitation, especially in the early stages; and I was an excellent mimic. By the time I was ten years old I had mastery over all the big-time moves: the spit in the mitt, the fluid infield chatter, the knocking of dirt from the spikes; the rhythmic barking out of signals, hands high under the center's crotch to take the ball; the three bounces and deep breath before shooting the free throw (on this last, I regretted not being a Catholic, so that I might be able to make the sign of the cross before shooting, as was then the fashion among Catholic high-school and college players). I went in for athletic haberdashery in a big way, often going beyond mimicry to the point of flat-out phoniness—wearing, for example, a knee pad while playing basketball, though my knees were always, exasperatingly, intact.

6   I always looked good, which was important, because form is intrinsic to sports; but in my case it was doubly important, because the truth is that I wasn't really very good. Or at any rate not good enough. Two factors accounted for this. The first was that, without being shy about body contact, I lacked a certain indispensable aggressiveness; the second, connected closely to the first, was that, when it came right down to it, I did not care enough about winning. I would rather lose a point attempting a slashing cross-court backhand than play for an easier winner down the side; the long jump shot always had more allure for me than the safer drive to the basket. Given a choice between the two vanities of winning and looking good, I almost always preferred looking good.

7   I shall never forget the afternoon, sometime along about my thirteenth year, when, shooting baskets alone, I came upon the technique for shooting the hook. Although today it has nowhere near the consequence of the jump shot—an innovation that has been to basketball what the jet has been to air travel—the hook is still the single most beautiful shot in the game. The rhythm and grace of it, the sway of the body off the pivot, the release of the ball behind the head and off the fingertips, the touch and instinct involved in its execution, make the hook altogether a balletic thing, and to achieve it is to feel one of the most delectable sensations in sports. That afternoon, on a deserted side street, shooting on a rickety wooden backboard and a black rim without a net, I felt it and grew nearly drunk on the feeling. Rain came down, dirt washed in the gutters, flecks of it spattering my clothes and arms and face, but, soaked and cold though I was, I do not think I would have left that basket on that afternoon for anything. I threw up hook after hook, from every angle, from farther and farther out, off the board, without the board, and hook after hook went in. Only pitch darkness drove me home.

8   I do not say that not to have shot the hook is never to have lived, but only that, once having done so, the pleasure it gives is not so easily forgotten. Every sport offers similar pleasures, the pleasures taken differing by temperament: the canter into the end zone to meet a floating touchdown pass, or the clean, crisp feel of a perfect block or tackle; the long straight drive or the precisely played approach shot to the green; the solid overhead; the pickup on the tricky short hop or the long ball down one of the power alleys. Different sports, different pleasures. But so keen are these pleasures—pleasures of execution, of craft completed—that, along with being unforgettable, they are also worth recapturing in any available way, and the most available way, when reflexes have slowed, when muscle no longer responds so readily to brain, is from the grandstand or, perhaps more often nowadays, from the chair before the television.

Pleasures of the Spectator

9   I have put in days on the bench, but years in my chair before the television set. Recently it has occurred to me that over the years I have heard more hours of talk from the announcer Curt Gowdy than from my own father, who is not a reticent man. I have been thoroughly Schenkeled, Mussbergered,

Summeralled, Coselled, DeRogotissed, and Garagiolaed. How many hundreds—thousands?—of hours have I spent watching sports of all sorts, either at parks or stadiums or over television? I am glad I shall never have a precise answer. Yet neither apparently can I get enough. What is the fascination? Why is it that, with the prospect of a game to watch in the evening or on the weekend, the day seems lighter and brighter? What do I get out of it?

10   What I get out of it, according to one fairly prominent view, is an outlet for my violent emotions. Knee-wrenching, rib-cracking, head-busting, this view has it, is what sports are really about, with sports fans being essentially sadists, and cowardly sadists at that, for they take their violence not at firsthand but at second remove. Enthusiasm for sports among Americans is little more than a reflection of the national penchant for violence. Military men talk about game plans; the long touchdown pass is called the bomb. The average pro-football fan, seeing a quarterback writhing on the ground at midfield as a result of the ministrations of Joe Green, Carl Eller, or Lyle Alzado, twitters with glee, finds his ultimate reward, and declares a little holiday in the blackest corner of his heart.

11   But this is a criticism that comes at sports by way of politics. To believe it one has to believe that the history of the United States is chiefly one of rape, expropriation, and aggressive imperialism. To dismiss it, however, one need only know something about sports. Violence is indubitably a part of some sports; in some—hockey is an example—it sometimes comes close to being featured. But in no sport—not even boxing, that most rudimentary of sports—is it the main item, and in many other sports it plays no part at all. A distinction worth insisting on is that between violence and roughness. Roughness, a willingness to mix it up, to take if need be an elbow in the jaw, is part of rebounding in basketball, yet violence is not. Even in pro football, most maligned of modern American sports, more of roughness than of violence is involved. Roughness raises the stakes, provides the pressure, behind execution. A splendid-because-true phrase has come about in pro football to cover the situation in which a pass receiver, certain that he will be tackled upon the instant he makes his reception, drops a ball he should otherwise have caught easily—the phrase, best delivered in a Southern accent such as Don Meredith's, is "He heard footsteps on that one, Howard." Although a part of the attraction, it is not so much those footsteps that fill the stands and the den chairs on Sunday afternoons as it is those men who elude them: the Lynn Swanns, the Fran Tarkentons, the O.J. Simpsons. The American love of violence theory really will not wash. Dick Butkus did not get us into Vietnam.

12   Many who would not argue that sports reflect American violence nevertheless claim that they imbue one with the competitive spirit. In some who are already amply endowed with it, sports doubtless do tend to refine (or possibly brutalize) the desire to win. Yet sports also teach a serious respect for craft. Competition, though it flourishes as always, is in bad odor nowadays; but craft, officially respected, does not flourish greatly outside the boutique.

13   If the love of violence or the competitive urge does not put me in my chair for the countless games I watch, is it, then, nostalgia, a yearning to regain the more glowing moments of adolescence? Many argue that this is precisely so, that American men exist in a state of perpetual immaturity, suspended between boy- and manhood. "The difference between men and boys," says Liberace, "is the price of their toys." (I have paid more than $300 for two half-season tickets to the Chicago Bulls games, parking fees not included.) Such unending enthusiasm for games may have something to do with adolescence, but little, I suspect, with regaining anything whatever. Instead, it has more to do with watching men do regularly and surpassingly what, as an adolescent, one did often bumblingly though with an occasional flash of genius. To have played these games oneself as a boy or a young man helps immeasurably the appreciation that in watching a sport played at professional caliber one is witnessing the extraordinary made to look ordinary. That a game may have no consequence outside itself—no effect on history, on one's own life, on anything, really—does not make it trivial but only makes the enjoyment of it all the purer.

14   The notion that men watch sports to regain their adolescence pictures them sitting in the stands or at home watching a game and, within their psyches, muttering, "There, but for the lack of grace of God, go I." And it is true that a number of contemporary authors who are taken seriously have indeed written about sports with a strong overlay of yearning. In the men's softball games described in the fiction of Philip Roth, center field is a place akin to Arcady. Arcadian, too, is the outfield in Willie Morris's memoir of growing up in the South, *North Toward Home*. In the first half of *Rabbit Run*, John Updike takes up the life of a man whose days are downhill all the way after hitting his peak as a high-school basketball star—and in the writing Updike himself evinces a nice soft touch of undisguised longing. In *A Fan's Notes*, a book combining yearning and self-disgust in roughly equal measure, Frederick Exley makes plain that he would much prefer to have been born into the skin of Frank Gifford rather than into his own.

15   But most men who are enraptured by sports do not think any such thing. I should like to have Kareem Abdul-Jabbar's sky hook, but not, especially for civilian life, the excessive height that is necessary to its execution. I should like to have Jimmy Connors's ground strokes, but no part of his mind. These are men born with certain gifts, gifts honed by practice and determination, that I, and millions along with me, enjoy seeing on display. But the reality principle is too deeply ingrained, at least in a man of my years, for me to even imagine exchanging places with them. One might as well imagine oneself in the winner's circle at Churchill Downs as the horse.

16   Fantasy is an element in sports when they are played in adolescence—an alley basket becomes the glass backboard at Madison Square Garden, a concrete park district tennis court with grass creeping out of the service line becomes center court at Wimbledon—but fantasy of this kind is hard to come by. Part of this has to do with age; but as large a part has to do with the age in which we live. Sport has always been a business but never more so than currently, and nothing lends itself less to fantasy than business. Reading the sports section has become rather like reading the business section—mergers, trades, salary negotiations, contract disputes, options, and strikes fill the columns. Along with the details of business, those of the psychological and social problems of athletes have come to the fore. The old *Sport* magazine concentrated on play on the field, with only an occasional digressive reference to personal life. ("Yogi likes plenty of pizza in the off-season and spends a lot of his time at his teammate Phil Rizzuto's bowling alley," is a rough facsimile of a sentence from its pages that I recall.) But the magazine in its current version, as well as the now more popular *Sports Illustrated,* expends much space on the private lives of athletes—their divorces, hang-ups, race relations, need for approval, concern for security, potted philosophies—with the result that the grand is made to seem small.

17 On the other side of the ledger, there is a view that finds a shimmering significance in everything having to do with sports. Literary men in general are notoriously to be distrusted on the subject. They dig around everywhere, and can be depended upon to find much treasure where none is buried. Norman Mailer mining metaphysical ore in every jab of Muhammad Ali's, an existential nugget in each of his various and profuse utterances, is a particularly horrendous example. Even the sensible William Carlos Williams was not above this sort of temptation. In a poem entitled "At the Ball Game," we find the lines "It is the Inquisition, the /Revolution." Dr. Williams could not have been much fun at the ball park.

The Real Thing

18 If enthusiasm for sports has little to do with providing an outlet for violent emotions, regaining adolescence, discovering metaphysical truths, the Inquisition or the Revolution, then what, I ask myself, am I doing past midnight, when I have to be up at 5:30 the next morning, watching on television what will turn out to be a seventeen-inning game between the New York Mets and the St. Louis Cardinals? The conversation coming out of my television set is of a very low grade, even for sports announcing. But even the dreary talk cannot put me off—the rehash of statistics, the advice to youngsters to keep their gloves low when in the field, the thin jokes. Neither the Mets nor the Cards figure to be contenders this year. The only possible effect that this game can have on my life is to make me dog-tired the next day. Yet I cannot pull myself away. I want to know how it is going to end. True, the score will be available in the morning paper. But that is not the same thing. What is going on here?

19 One thing that is going on is the practice of craft of a very high order, which is intrinsically interesting. But something as important is involved, something rarer in contemporary life, the spectacle of which gives enormous satisfaction. To define this satisfaction negatively, it is the absence of fraudulence and fakery. No small item, this, when one stops to think that in nearly every realm of contemporary life fraud and fakery have an established—some would say a preponderant—place. Advertising, politics, business, and journalism are only the most obvious examples. Fraud seems similarly pervasive in modern art: in painters whose reputations rest on press agentry; in writers who write one way and live quite another; in composers who are taken seriously but whose work cannot be seriously listened to. At a time when *image* is one of the most frequently used words in American speech and writing, one does not too often come upon the real thing.

20   Sport may be the toy department of life, but one of its abiding compensations is that, at least on the field, it is the real thing. Much has been done in recent years in the attempt to ruin sport—the ruthlessness of owners, the greed of players, the general exploitation of fans. But even all this cannot destroy it. On the court, down on the field, sport is fraud-free and fakeproof. With a full count, two men on, his team down by one run in the last of the eighth, a batter (as well as a pitcher) is beyond the aid of public relations. At match point at Forest Hills a player's press clippings are of no help. Last year's earnings will not sink a twelve-foot putt on the eighteenth at Augusta. Alan Page, galloping up along a quarterback's blind side, figures to be neglectful of that quarterback's image as a swinger. In all these situations, and hundreds of others, a man either comes through or he doesn't. He is alone out there, naked but for his ability, which counts for everything. Something there is that is elemental about this, and something greatly satisfying.

21   Another part of the satisfaction to be got from sports—from playing them, but also from watching them being played—derives from their special clarity. Sports offer clarity of a kind sufficient to engage the most serious minds. That the Cambridge mathematician G. H. Hardy closely followed cricket and avidly read cricket scores is not altogether surprising. Numbers in sports are ubiquitous. Scores, standings, averages, times, records—comfort is found in such numbers. ERA, RBIs, FGP, pass completions, turnovers, category upon category of statistics are kept for nearly every aspect of athletic activity. (Why, I recently heard someone ask, are records not kept for catchers throwing out runners attempting to steal? Because, the answer is, often runners steal on pitchers, and so it would be unfair to charge these stolen bases against catchers.) As perhaps in no other sphere, numbers in sports tell one where things stand. No loopholes here, where figures, for once, do not lie. Nowhere else is such specificity of result available.

22   Clarity about character is also available in sports. "You Americans hold to the proposition that it is self-evident that all men are created equal," I not long ago heard an Englishman say, adding, "it had better be self-evident, for no other evidence for it exists." Sport coldly demonstrates physical inequalities—there are the larger, the faster, the stronger, the more graceful athletes—but it also throws up human types who have devised ways to redress these inequalities. One such type is the hustler. In every realm but that of sports the word *hustle* is pejorative, whereas in sports it is approbative. Two of the hustler breed, Pete Rose of the Cincinnati Reds and Jerry Sloan of the Chicago Bulls, are men who supplement reasonably high levels of ability with unreasonably high levels of courage and desire. Other athletes—Joe Morgan and Oscar Robertson come to mind—bring superior athletic intelligence to bear upon their play. And Bill Russell, late of the Boston Celtics, who if the truth be known was not an inherently superior athlete, blended hustle and intelligence with what abilities he did have and through force of character established supremacy.

23   Whence do hustle, intelligence, and character in sports derive, especially since they apparently do not necessarily carry over into life? Joe DiMaggio and Sugar Ray Robinson, two of the most instinctively intelligent and physically elegant athletes, brought little of either of these qualities over into their business or personal activities. Some athletes can do all but one important thing well: Wilt Chamberlain at the free-throw line, for those who recall his misery there, leaves a permanent picture of a mental block in action. Other athletes—Connie Hawkins, Ilie Nastase, Dick Allen—have all the physical gifts in superabundance, yet, because of some insufficiency of character, some searing flaw, never come near to fulfilling their promise. Coaches supply yet another gallery of human types, from the fanatical Vince Lombardi to the comical Casey Stengel to the measured and aptly named John Wooden. The cast of characters in sport, the variety of situations, the complexity of behavior it puts on display, the overall human exhibit it offers—together these supply an enjoyment akin to that once provided by reading interminably long but inexhaustibly rich nineteenth-century novels.

24   In a wider sense, sport is culture. For many American men it represents a common background, a shared interest. It has a binding power that transcends social class and education. Some years ago I found myself working in the South among men with whom I shared nothing in the way of region, religion, education, politics, or general views; we shared nothing, in fact, but sports, which was enough for us to get along and grow to become friends, in the process showing how superficial all the things that might have kept us apart in fact were. More recently, in Chicago, at a time when race relations were in a particularly jagged state, I recall emerging from an NBA game, in which the Chicago Bulls in overtime beat the Milwaukee Bucks, into a snowy night and an aura of common good feeling that, for a time, submerged the enmity between races; laughing, throwing snowballs, exuberant generally, the crowd leaving the Chicago Stadium that night was not divided by being black and white but unified by being Bull fans. Last year's Boston-Cincinnati World Series, one of the most gratifying in memory, coming hard upon a year of extreme political divisiveness, performed, however briefly, something of the same function. How much better it felt to agree about the mastery of Luis Tiant than to argue about the wretchedness of Richard Nixon.

25   In sports, as in life, character does not much change. I have recently begun to play a game called racquet ball, and I find I would still rather look good than win, which is what I usually do: look good and lose. I beat the rum-dums but go down before quality players. I get compliments in defeat. Men who beat me admire the whip of my strokes, my wrist action, my anticipation, the power I get behind the ball. When this occurs I feel like a woman who is complimented for the shape of her bottom when it is her mind she craves admiration for, though of course she will take what praise she can get.

26 R. H. Tawney, the great historian of religion and capitalism, once re-marked that the only progress he could note during the course of his lifetime was in the deportment of dogs. For myself, I would say that the chief progress in the course of my lifetime has been in the quality and variety of athletic gear. Racquets made of metal, aluminum, wood, and fiberglass, balls of differ-ent colors, sneakers of all materials and designs, posh warm-up suits, tube socks, sweatbands for the head and wrist in various colors and pipings; only the athletic supporter, the old jockstrap, remains unornamented, but perhaps even now Vera or Peter Max is at the drawing board. In any event, with all this elegant plumage available, it is a nice time to be playing ball again.

27 Sports can be impervious to age. My father-in-law, a man of style, seri-ousness, and great good humor who died a year ago in his late sixties, was born in South Bend, Indiana, and in his early manhood left the Catholic Church—two facts that conjoined to give him an intense interest in the for-tunes of the teams from Notre Dame. He loved to see them lose. The torch has been passed on. I now love to see Notre Dame lose, and when it does I think of him and remember his smile.

28 When I was a boy I had a neighbor, a man who, after retirement, had a number of strokes. An old man and a young boy, we had in common a love of sports, which, when we met on the street, was our only topic of conversation. He once inspected a new glove of mine, and instructed me to rub it down with neat's-foot oil, place a ball firmly in the pocket, wrap string tightly around the glove, and leave it like that for the winter. I did, and it worked. After his last stroke but one, he seldom left his house. Afternoons he spent in a chair in his bedroom, a blanket over his lap, listening to Cub games over the radio. It was while listening to a ball game that he quietly died. I cannot imagine a better way.

VOCABULARY

haberdashery 5
intrinsic 6
allure 6
pivot 7
balletic 7
reticent 9
sadists 10
penchant 10
ministrations 10
expropriation 11
rudimentary 11
maligned 11

imbue 12
psyches 14
Arcady 14
evinces 14
honed 15
metaphysical 17
preponderant 19
ubiquitous 21
pejorative 22
approbative 22
enmity 24
conjoined 27

QUESTIONS

1. To what type of audience is this essay directed? How can you tell?
2. What is the effect of the numerous proper names in the opening paragraphs?
3. What do the details in the last part of ¶7 contribute to the explanation?
4. What is the purpose of the questions in ¶9?
5. What does the assertion of the last sentence in ¶11 imply?
6. What is the effect of ¶18?
7. The writer offers, and then refutes, three explanations for the love of sport. What are they? Are his refutations convincing?
8. What is his final explanation for the love of sport? Do you agree?
9. Except for the comparison in ¶25, the writer does not include women in his discussion. What does this omission imply about his thinking?

Marya Mannes (b. 1904) is well-known as an essayist, lecturer, and guest on radio and television talk shows. She is also a columnist for McCall's *and* Book Week *and a frequent contributor to other magazines. This essay originally appeared in* Saturday Review *(November 14, 1970).*

Television Advertising: The Splitting Image
Marya Mannes

1   A bride who looks scarcely fourteen whispers, "Oh, Mom, I'm so *happy*!" while a doting family adjust her gown and veil and a male voice croons softly, "A woman is a harder thing to be than a man. She has more feelings to feel." The mitigation of these excesses, it appears, is a feminine deodorant called Secret, which allows our bride to approach the altar with security as well as emotion.

2   Eddie Albert, a successful actor turned pitchman, bestows his attention on a lady with two suitcases, which prompt him to ask her whether she has been on a journey, "No," she says, or words to that effect, as she opens the suitcases. "My two boys bring back their soiled clothes every weekend from college for me to wash." And she goes into the familiar litany of grease, chocolate, mud, coffee, and fruit-juice stains, which presumably record the life of the average American male from two to fifty. Mr. Albert compliments her on this happy device to bring her boys home every week and hands her a box of Biz, because "Biz *is* better."

3   Two women with stony faces meet cart to cart in a supermarket as one takes a jar of peanut butter off a shelf. When the other asks her in a voice of nitric acid why she takes that brand, the first snaps, "Because I'm choosy for my family!" The two then break into delighted smiles as Number Two makes Number One taste Jiffy for "mothers who are choosy."

4   If you have not come across these dramatic interludes, it is because you are not home during the day and do not watch daytime television. It also means that your intestinal tract is spared from severe assaults, your credibility unstrained. Or, for that matter, you may look at commercials like these every day and manage either to ignore them or find nothing—given the fact of advertising—wrong with them. In that case, you are either so brainwashed or so innocent that you remain unaware of what this daily infusion may have done and is doing to an entire people as the long-accepted adjunct of free enterprise and support of "free" television.

5   "Given the fact" and "long-accepted" are the key words here. Only socialists, communists, idealists (or the BBC) fail to realize that a mass television system cannot exist without the support of sponsors, that the massive cost of maintaining it as a free service cannot be met without the massive income from selling products. You have only to read of the unending struggle to provide financial support for public, noncommercial television for further evidence.

6   Besides, aren't commercials in the public interest? Don't they help you choose what to buy? Don't they provide needed breaks from programming? Aren't many of them brilliantly done, and some of them funny? And now, with the new sexual freedom, all those gorgeous chicks with their shining hair and gleaming smiles? And if you didn't have commercials taking up a good part of each hour, how on earth would you find enough program material to fill the endless space/time void?

7   Tick off the yesses and what have you left? You have, I venture to submit, these intangible but possibly high costs: the diminution of human worth, the infusion and hardening of social attitudes no longer valid or desirable, pervasive discontent, and psychic fragmentation.

8   Should anyone wonder why deception is not an included detriment, I suggest that our public is so conditioned to promotion as a way of life, whether in art or politics or products, that elements of exaggeration or distortion are taken for granted. Nobody really believes that a certain shampoo will get a certain swain, or that an unclogged sinus can make a man a swinger. People are merely prepared to hope it will.

9   But the diminution of human worth is much more subtle and just as pervasive. In the guise of what they consider comedy, the producers of television commercials have created a loathsome gallery of men and women patterned, presumably, on Mr. and Mrs. America. Women liberationists have a major target in the commercial image of woman flashed hourly and daily to the vast majority. There are, indeed, only four kinds of females in this relentless sales procession: the gorgeous teen-age swinger with bouncing locks; the young mother teaching her baby girl the right soap for skin care; the middle-

aged housewife with a voice like a power saw; and the old lady with dentures and irregularity. All these women, to be sure, exist. But between the swinging sex object and the constipated granny there are millions of females never shown in commercials. These are—married or single—intelligent, sensitive women who bring charm to their homes, who work at jobs as well as lend grace to their marriage, who support themselves, who have talents or hobbies or commitments, or who are skilled at their professions.

10   To my knowledge, as a frequent if reluctant observer, I know of only one woman on a commercial who has a job; a comic plumber pushing Comet. Funny, heh? Think of a dame with a plunger.

11   With this one representative of our labor force, which is well over thirty million women, we are left with nothing but the full-time housewife in all her whining glory: obsessed with whiter wash, moister cakes, shinier floors, cleaner children, softer diapers, and greaseless fried chicken. In the rare instances when these ladies are not in the kitchen, at the washing machine, or waiting on hubby, they are buying beauty shops (fantasy, see?) to take home so that their hair will have more body. Or out at the supermarket being choosy.

12   If they were attractive in their obsessions, they might be bearable. But they are not. They are pushy, loud-mouthed, stupid, and—of all things now—bereft of sexuality. Presumably, the argument of the tenets of advertising is that once a woman marries she changes overnight from plaything to floor-waxer.

13   To be fair, men make an equivalent transition in commercials. The swinging male with the mod hair and the beautiful chick turns inevitably into the paunchy slob who chokes on his wife's cake. You will notice, however, that the voice urging the viewer to buy the product is nearly always male: gentle, wise, helpful, seductive. And the visible presence telling the housewife how to get shinier floors and whiter wash and lovelier hair is almost invariably a man: the Svengali in modern dress, the Trilby (if only she were!) his willing object.

14   Woman, in short, is consumer first and human being fourth. A wife and mother who stays home all day buys a lot more than a woman who lives alone or who—married or single—has a job. The young girl hell-bent on marriage is the next most susceptible consumer. It is entirely understandable, then, that the potential buyers of detergents, foods, polishes, toothpastes, pills, and housewares are the housewives, and that the sex object spends most of *her* money on cosmetics, hair lotions, soaps, mouthwashes, and soft drinks.

15   Here we come, of course, to the youngest class of consumers, the swinging teen-agers so beloved by advertisers keen on telling them (and us) that they've "got a lot to live, and Pepsi's got a lot to give." This affords a chance to show a squirming, leaping, jiggling group of beautiful kids having a very loud high on rock and—of all things—soda pop. One of commercial TV's most dubious achievements, in fact, is the reinforcement of the self-adulation characteristic of the young as a group.

16   As for the aging female citizen, the less shown of her the better. She is useful for ailments, but since she buys very little of anything, not having a husband or any children to feed or house to keep, nor—of course—sex appeal to burnish, society and commercials have little place for her. The same is true, to be sure, of older men, who are handy for Bosses with Bad Breath or Doctors with Remedies. Yet, on the whole, men hold up better than women at any age—in life or on television. Lines on their faces are marks of distinction, while on women they are signatures of decay.

17 There is no question, in any case, that television commercials (and many of the entertainment programs, notably the soap serials that are part of the selling package) reinforce, like an insistent drill, the assumption that a woman's only valid function is that of wife, mother, and servant of men: the inevitable sequel to her earlier function as sex object and swinger.

18 At a time when more and more women are at long last learning to reject these assumptions as archaic and demeaning, and to grow into individual human beings with a wide option of lives to live, the sellers of the nation are bent upon reinforcing the ancient pattern. They know only too well that by beaming their message to the Consumer Queen they can justify her existence as the housebound Mrs. America: dumber than dumb, whiter than white.

19 The conditioning starts very early: with the girl child who wants the skin Ivory soap has reputedly given her mother, with the nine-year-old who brings back a cake of Camay instead of the male deodorant her father wanted. (When she confesses that she bought it so she could be "feminine," her father hugs her, and, with the voice of a child-molester, whispers, "My little girl is growing up on me, huh.") And then, before long, comes the teen-aged bride who "has feelings to feel."

20 It is the little boys who dream of wings, in an airplane commercial; who grow up (with fewer cavities) into the doers. Their little sisters turn into *Cosmopolitan* girls, who in turn become housewives furious that their neighbors' wash is cleaner than theirs.

21 There is good reason to suspect that this manic obsession with cleanliness, fostered, quite naturally, by the giant soap and detergent interests, may bear some responsibility for the cultivated sloppiness of so many of the young in their clothing as well as in their chosen hideouts. The compulsive housewife who spends more time washing and vacuuming and polishing her possessions than communicating to, or stimulating her children creates a kind of sterility that the young would instinctively reject. The impeccably tidy home, the impeccably tidy lawn are—in a very real sense—unnatural and confining.

22 Yet the commercials confront us with broods of happy children, some of whom—believe it or not—notice the new fresh smell their clean, white sweatshirts exhale thanks to Mom's new "softener."

23 Some major advertisers, for that matter, can even cast a benign eye on the population explosion. In another Biz commercial, the genial Eddie Albert surveys with surprise a long row of dirty clothes heaped before him by a young matron. She answers his natural query by telling him gaily they are the products of her brood of eleven "with one more to come!" she adds as the twelfth turns up. "That's great!" says Mr. Albert, curdling the soul of Planned Parenthood and the future of this planet.

24 Who are, one cannot help but ask, the writers who manage to combine the sales of products with the selling-out of human dreams and dignity? Who people this cosmos of commercials with dolts and fools and shrews and narcissists? Who know so much about quirks and mannerisms and ailments and so little about life? So much about presumed wants and so little about crying needs?

25   Can women advertisers so demean their own sex? Or are there no women in positions of decision high enough to see that their real selves stand up?

26   Do they not know, these extremely clever creators of commercials, what they could do for their audience even while they exploit and entertain them? How they could raise the levels of manners and attitudes while they sell their wares? Or do they really share the worm's-eye view of mass communication that sees, and addresses, only the lowest common denominator?

27   It can be argued that commercials are taken too seriously, that their function is merely to amuse, engage, and sell, and that they do this brilliantly. If that were all to this wheedling of millions, well and good. But it is not. There are two more fallouts from this chronic sales explosion that cannot be measured but that at least can be expected. One has to do with the continual celebration of youth at the expense of maturity. In commercials only the young have access to beauty, sex, and joy in life. What do older women feel, day after day, when love is the exclusive possession of a teen-age girl with a bobbing mantle of hair? What older man would not covet her in restless impotence?

28   The constant reminder of what is inaccessible must inevitably produce a subterranean but real discontent, just as the continual sight of things and places beyond reach has eaten deeply into the ghetto soul. If we are constantly presented with what we are not or cannot have, the dislocation deepens, contentment vanishes, and frustration reigns. Even for the substantially secure, there is always a better thing, a better way, to buy. That none of these things makes a better life may be consciously acknowledged, but still the desire lodges in the spirit, nagging and pulling.

29   This kind of fragmentation works in potent ways above and beyond the mere fact of program interruption, which is much of the time more of a blessing than a curse, especially in those rare instances when the commercial is deft and funny: the soft and subtle sell. Its overall curse, due to the large number of commercials in each hour, is that it reduces the attention span of a people already so conditioned to constant change and distraction that they cannot tolerate continuity in print or on the air.

30   Specifically, commercial interruption is most damaging during that 10 per cent of programing (a charitable estimate) most important to the mind and spirit of a people: news and public affairs, and drama.

31   To many (and among these are network news producers), commercials have no place or business during the vital process of informing the public. There is something obscene about a newscaster pausing to introduce a deodorant or shampoo commercial between an airplane crash and a body count. It is more than an interruption; it tends to reduce news to a form of running entertainment, to smudge the edges of reality by treating death or disaster or diplomacy on the same level as household appliances or a new gasoline.

32   The answer to this would presumably be to lump the commercials before and after the news or public affairs broadcasts—an answer unpalatable, needless to say, to the sponsors who support them.

33   The same is doubly true of that most unprofitable sector of television, the original play. Essential to any creative composition, whether drama, music or dance, are mood and continuity, both inseparable from form and meaning. They are shattered by the periodic intrusion of commercials, which have become intolerable to the serious artists who have deserted commercial television in droves because the system allows them no real freedom or autonomy. The selling comes first, the creation must accommodate itself. It is the rare and admirable sponsor who restricts or fashions his commercials so as to provide a minimum of intrusion or damaging inappropriateness.

34   If all these assumptions and imponderables are true, as many suspect, what is the answer or alleviation?

35   One is in the course of difficult emergence: the establishment of a public television system sufficiently funded so that it can give a maximum number of people an alternate diet of pleasure, enlightenment, and stimulation free from commercial fragmentation. So far, for lack of funds to buy talent and equipment, this effort has been in terms of public attention a distinctly minor operation.

36   Even if public television should, hopefully, greatly increase its scope and impact, it cannot in the nature of things and through long public conditioning equal the impact and reach the size of audience now tuned to commercial television.

37   Enormous amounts of time, money, and talent go into commercials. Technically they are often brilliant and innovative, the product not only of the new skills and devices but of imaginative minds. A few of them are both funny and endearing. Who, for instance, will forget the miserable young man with the appalling cold, or the kids taught to use—as an initiation into manhood—a fork instead of a spoon with a certain spaghetti? Among the enlightened sponsors, moreover, are some who manage to combine an image of their corporation and their products with accuracy and restraint.

38   What has to happen to mass medium advertisers as a whole, and especially on TV, is a totally new approach to their function not only as sellers but as social influencers. They have the same obligation as the broadcast medium itself: not only to entertain but to reflect, not only to reflect but to enlarge public consciousness and human stature.

39   This may be a tall order, but it is a vital one at a time when Americans have ceased to know who they are and where they are going, and when all the multiple forces acting upon them are daily diminishing their sense of their own value and purpose in life, when social upheaval and social fragmentation have destroyed old patterns, and when survival depends on new ones.

40   If we continue to see ourselves as the advertisers see us, we have no place to go. Nor, I might add, has commercial broadcasting itself.

VOCABULARY

litany 2	self-adulation 15
BBC 5	archaic 18
diminution 7	manic 21
psychic fragmentation 7	benign 23
swain 8	cosmos 24
bereft 12	dolts 24
Svengali 13	narcissists 24
Trilby 13	subterranean 28

QUESTIONS

1. What does the title suggest? How does it relate to the essay?

2. What is Mannes's attitude toward television advertising? What is the tone of the essay? How does tone help to reinforce attitude? Consider her word choice.

3. Where is her thesis stated? The thesis statement suggests an order for the essay; does she follow it?

4. How would you describe her style? What is the effect of ¶s 1–3? What is the effect of her use of questions (¶s 6, 24–26)? Examine her vocabulary; what is the effect of such a mix?

5. What is the purpose of her essay? How do the examples help? What causes does she espouse? What evidence does she provide?

6. Do you find any examples of logical fallacies in this essay? Examine, for instance, ¶s 4 and 5. How would you refute ¶9?

7. What is your reaction to ¶s 29–31?

8. How specific and plausible are the solutions proposed in ¶s 34–38?

Bruce Reeves teaches in the English department at Acalanes High School, Lafayette, California. He has been a member of the National Council of Teachers of English Committee on Public Doublespeak. He delivered this essay as a paper at the 1971 NCTE Convention; it was then published in English Journal *in May 1972.*

Ad-Man, Business-Man, Teacher-Man
Bruce Reeves

1   "You can trust advertising to mess with words. You can look to business and advertising together to play a word game with the consumer, for the

benefit of the ad-man and business-man, and the detriment of everyone else"—so wrote one of my students at the beginning of a semester called Mass Media and Propaganda.

2   Over the past three years, I have seen my students in this course come into the classroom distrusting the package on the shelf, the prices on the rack, and almost all the advertisements that bombard them from TV and radio and the printed media. Yet somehow, during the semester, their attitude shifts dramatically in the direction of increasing trust that the products they purchase will turn out to be as advertised. A description of the course unit that leads to this shift—including a proposal to English teachers and advertising-men and business-men in the United States based in part on that shift—is the subject of this talk.

3   The course looks closely at newspapers, television, and advertising. We try to determine, for example, if the *Chronicle* is more or less biased than the *Examiner,* or whether they both offer the same stuff. We mailed out requests to

Acalanes Mass Media Classes

Study of Effect on Students' Attitudes of Testing the
Claims of Advertisements

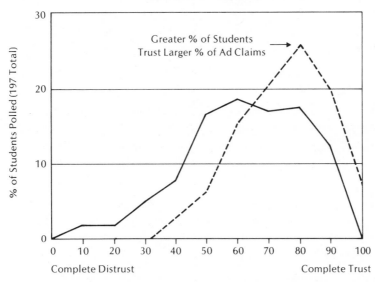

% of Products Purchased Which Students Feel Will Be "As Advertised"

The question: "What per cent of the goods you purchase will turn out to be 'as advertised'?"

Response at start of course: ————————

Response at end of course: — — — — — — —

Verification: Written evidence of above statistics will be produced on request. Above chart is for all courses, 1969–Fall 1971.

over one hundred newspapers all over the country, and the seventy or so which came back are being compared first for regional variations in reporting the news, and second for the treatment—or mistreatment—of wire-service copy. Our work with advertising and advertising claims—about which I'll tell you more shortly—got the Breck shampoo people so turned on that they're putting up $700 in a competition between Acalanes and two other high schools (University High School in Urbana, Illinois, and High School of Art and Design in New York) to encourage our teenagers to create their own full-page Breck ad which will run in the spring issue of a number of teenage magazines. The kids conduct attitude surveys in their neighborhoods, analyze short-wave radio propaganda broadcasts from places like Russia, Holland, Cuba, and Voice of America, write storyboards for and produce TV ads, and—they test advertising claims.

4   On the first day of school I ask the students to fill out a questionnaire, one part of which reads: "If you went into a store and bought one hundred items, what per cent of those items would turn out to be 'as advertised'?" The results, to me at least, were predictable, and have remained pretty much the same at the start of each new semester. Some of the kids don't trust anybody, most distrust the larger part of what they hear—and a few are gung ho trusters of everything. But this profile (see chart) undergoes quite a change during the course, largely, I believe, because of the claim-testing project which each student embarks on. The project works this way:

1. The student finds a testable advertising claim from any medium.

2. He works out a procedure for testing the claim, using the scientific method, and submits the claim and testing procedure to me.

3. I verify that the ad is testable (and not something like "Yummy Dog Biscuits are better than ever"), and the procedure a rational and safe one.

4. The student then runs his test, makes his observations, and concludes the product is *as advertised, somewhat misleading,* or *not as advertised.*

5. At this point he presents his results to the class orally, and gets a thorough going-over. What he is about to do next is a bit cheeky, and both student and teacher want the report to be logical, clear, and honest.

6. Regardless of the results of the testing, the student then writes a covering letter for the report and sends both to the manufacturer and ad agency. The letter states clearly the nature of the class and the results of the test; and it asks for a response to the whole process, promising that any such response will get the complete attention of the class.

7. And then the wait. If we are lucky, about half the letters are answered. But those that do arrive are a great conclusion to the process.

5   Here are some examples of projects, including portions of the correspondence evolving from them:

6   *ZEREX ANTI-FREEZE:* Dana Giles tested Zerex's claim that "Zerex is guaranteed not to run out on you." This test was run, by the way, on October 27 of last year—it is not the current ad. The can is punched, and liquid spurts out, only to stop within seconds. Her observations? "One of the holes stopped squirting out after a minute and a half, but the other two holes took over two and three minutes to stop squirting. Even after the squirting stopped, liquid continued to dribble out slowly. After five minutes, all liquid had stopped leaking, but would readily start dribbling again if the hole was touched."

7   Dana went on to observe that "the television commercial had more to it than met the eye. Photographic techniques altered the reality of what happened. On the basis of my test, I would conclude that this ad is somewhat misleading in its presentation. It is true that Zerex seals leaks; however, it does not do so as quickly or as completely as the public would be given to believe."

8   Soon after Dana's letter went to DuPont—but not, I hasten to add, as a result of it—the Federal Trade Commission clamped down on this can-stabbing commercial. Recently you may have seen the ad, saying "We're back!" And in small print you can now read the words "Contents 50 per cent Zerex, 50 per cent water under pressure."

9   Dana had mixed reactions to DuPont's response. The letter read in part: "I have read your data and conclusions and there are several questions that arise. I think when you answer them and make the necessary adjustments, you will want to reconsider your conclusions. (1) What size was the puncture you put in the can? (2) What form did the puncture take? A round hole or was it a slit? (4) How much pressure did you use? (6) How did you control the puncture for reproducibility?

10   "I can assure you there were no photographic techniques used to alter the reality that occurred. The conditions used to make the commercial reproduce that of an operating, circulating, pressurized automobile.

11   "I would be interested in your results after you rerun your test with some small refinements: (1) Circulation—30 G.P.M., (2) Pressure—15 P.S.I., (3) Puncture—20-30 mils wide slit. A slit is the most common radiator opening and not a round hole. You can use a modified automatic center punch. (4) Concentration—50 per cent with water.

12   "Thank you again for your interest in our product. Sincerely, etc."

13   Not an offhand reply. Defensive, to be sure. But can we expect anything else? Informative. Perhaps impatience suppressed. Instructive, too, since Dana had obviously overlooked some things.

14   *IVORY LIQUID:* Sandy Young tested Ivory Liquid's claim that it is so rich and thick, "it even whips." She indeed found that it whipped. But she took this a step further. As she writes:

15   "To find out if there was any particular value or significance involved with soap being able to whip, or that any type of soap is able to do it, I selected two other brands of liquid soap, Trend and Brocade. I then made the same test for these two types of soap. . . . Each type of soap was whipped for two and one-half minutes. The results were as follows:

16   "Ivory Liquid's claim was proved true. One cup of liquid was whipped for two and one-half minutes and grew stiffer and thicker and formed peaks. I found no real value or significance in the fact that Ivory Liquid could whip because the other two dishwashing liquids I used also whipped and proved actually to whip better than the Ivory Liquid."

17   Proctor & Gamble Company replied: "As you discovered, Ivory Liquid does, indeed, whip as mentioned in our advertising. Today's Ivory Liquid is the creamiest-feeling, mildest Ivory Liquid ever and our advertising was designed to emphasize that creamy Ivory Liquid can help the hands to the creamy complexion of youth. In this connection, we know, of course, that Ivory Liquid is not the only dishwashing detergent which whips, but we simply were equating its creamy consistency to its mildness by way of a visual, memorable demonstration."

18   It was signed by W. S. Carter of Public Relations who, by the way, will sign all letters to consumers from the PR department. It's a pseudonym used by the people whose job it is to answer letters like Sandy's.

19   *DENNISON'S CHILI:* Four students ended up working on the claim that "there are 106 chunks of beef in every can" of Dennison's Chili. They worked separately, and came up with different conclusions, a fact which led to an extra step which I thought put some zing into their report. After sieving and separating the chili sauce and beans from the "chunks," three of the students stated that they came up with far less than 106 chunks. One had many more. The problem, of course, lay with the definition of "chunk." How big did a piece of meat have to be—or how small—before it could be called a "chunk"?

20   The four of them took to the masses, and conducted a survey among one hundred students asking what size came to mind when people thought of a chunk of wood, meat, and rock. Using the rather clear-cut results, the students concluded that nothing smaller than a cube of meat, ¼'' on a side, could be called a chunk. Armed with this, then, they wrote American Home Products, the manufacturer, and stated that they felt the claim was somewhat misleading.

21   The gist of a thoughtful letter from the company's president, Mr. J. B. Shortlidge, was as follows: "What consumers . . . receive is meat in the form of chunks—we can't think of a more descriptive term—as distinguished from minute meat particles, and, because of our advertising, at least 106 of them. Your students may feel these chunks are small but we can only say that, given the nature of the product and the size of the can in which it is packed, they are appropriate. . . . The slogan with which your students take issue has been in use for five years and no consumer has ever asserted to us that she was misled by it. . . . We hope this letter clarifies the picture. If your students need additional information, please have them contact us. And, while we reach a different conclusion with respect to our advertising from that expressed by your students in their letter, we do wish to congratulate them for their efforts . . . in consumer advertising."

22   There have been others, too: one boy tested the claim that Zip-coded mail arrives faster—it didn't; another tested the money-back guarantee of five firms—each returned his money; another tested the ketchup claim, "comes out slowest"—it did! And another, a bit desperate for a project, counted to see whether there are indeed over six hundred tiny time pills in each capsule—(there are).

23 This business of testing claims and telling an advertiser that he passed or failed the test involves exposure to words with people behind them. And even more important, the student, by writing to someone in the heretofore faceless world of big business, gets to know what it's like to compose for someone who might just snap back to him "Go to hell" instead of "John, you can do better than this. Work on your gerunds." The return communication is the most revealing part of the whole project: there *are* the words, addressed to *him,* the student, in all their sincerity or hypocrisy or vagueness or excitement. And the student *knows!* He knows right away whether he is being taken or sloughed off or listened to.

24 Many ad claims are untestable at the high school level, either because they indulge in what my students now so easily recognize as "puffery," or because we don't have the technical facilities or know-how to assess the claim. About 80 per cent of the ads tested turned out to be "as advertised"; about 15 per cent turned out to be "somewhat misleading"; and about 5 per cent are found "not as advertised." The fact that the *students themselves* reach these conclusions on the basis of their own tests and find 80 per cent of the ads tested "as advertised"—plus the gratifying response to the project from business and advertising—results in a shift in attitude (based on the earlier questionnaire administered toward the end of the course), which shows that the students' attitude toward business and advertising is one of increased trust.

25 I would like, therefore, to urge English teachers in courses similar to this one, to start introducing their students to the semantics of advertising by testing ad claims and sending the results to business and advertising agencies. For further information on this process write Bruce Reeves, 1025 Hacienda Drive, Walnut Creek, CA 94598.

QUESTIONS

1. This essay was first an address to other teachers at a convention. Examine the sentence structure and word choice. Would you describe the essay as formal or informal? On what evidence? Is the level of formality appropriate to the context?

2. What is Reeves' attitude toward his subject? How do you know?

3. What is the purpose of ¶2?

4. In ¶23, what does Reeves mean by "puffery"?

5. Were you surprised by the students' change in attitude after they completed the course? How reliable do you think most advertising is?

6. Why does Reeves use student names when he describes some specific projects? Is this device effective?

7. Examine the letters from the manufacturers. Do you agree with Reeves' analysis of their tone? Are any manufacturers guilty of the "language of bureaucracy" (see Barnes, "The Language of Bureaucracy," pp. 349–55)?

Russell Kirk (b. 1918) has lectured and written extensively on conservative thought, educational theory, and literary topics. He writes a column on education for National Review, in which the following essay appeared on October 24, 1975.

Textbooks as Brainwashers
Russell Kirk

1 The publishers of school textbooks are blown about by every wind of doctrine. Eager for adoptions at whatever cost to candor, they trim their sails to the ideological wind. Just now they are slavishly sedulous to please NOW and other anti-feminine feminists.

2 Several of the major publishers have gone so far as to issue formal printed directives to authors, editors, illustrators, and other hirelings; practically all textbook publishers have genuflected before NOW and the like by admitting representatives of these outfits to sit in judgment on their publications.

3 McGraw-Hill Book Company has its "Guidelines for Equal Treatment of the Sexes in McGraw-Hill Book Company Publications." This begins by informing those subject to the authority of McGraw-Hill that "the word *sexism* was coined, by analogy to *racism*, to denote discrimination based on gender. In its original sense, *sexism* referred to prejudice against the female sex. In a broader sense, the term now indicates any arbitrary stereotyping of males and females on the basis of their gender."

4 Sexism is to be eliminated from McGraw-Hill publications. Humane letters, true, will be exempted: "We realize that the language of literature cannot be prescribed. The recommendations in these guidelines, thus, are intended primarily for use in teaching materials, reference works, and nonfiction works in general." I had thought previously that much "nonfiction" was literature too; but it is some comfort that Lady Macbeth is not to be transformed into Lord Macbeth, despite her expressed desire to be unsexed.

5 "Characteristics that have been traditionally praised in males—such as boldness, initiative, and assertiveness—should also be praised in females," McGraw-Hill informs us. "Characteristics that have been praised in

females—such as gentleness, compassion, and sensitivity—should also be praised in males." Everybody's just like everybody else, you know.

6   "It is hoped that these guidelines have alerted authors and staff members to the problems of sex discrimination and to various ways of solving them," the McGraw-Hill publication concludes. They better have been alerted, or else. There's only one real reason for textbooks, you know, and that's to make money, and we don't want any howls from NOW.

7   Scott, Foresman, and Company presents us with "Guidelines for Improving the Image of Women in Textbooks." Its line is much the same as McGraw-Hill's, but perhaps sillier: "Both men and women should be shown cooking, cleaning, making household repairs, doing laundry, washing the car, and taking care of children. Both men and women should be shown making decisions; participating in sports; writing poetry; working in factories, stores, and offices; playing musical instruments; practicing medicine and law; serving on boards of directors; and making scientific discoveries." As examples of sexist language, Scott, Foresman cites: "early man; Neanderthal man; when man invented the wheel . . . ; *History of the Black Man in America; Man and His World.*" Can it be that the editors of Scott, Foresman really remain unaware that "man" and "mankind" are generic terms, including both males and females? No, it cannot be: Scott, Foresman merely cowers before any militant bully, however illiterate.

8   Scott, Foresman is zealous against "sex-role stereotyping." This is a sexist sentence: "In New England, the typical farm was so small that the owner and his sons could take care of it by themselves." One is supposed to write "family members could take care of it by themselves." Presumably it would be well to include a sketch showing women and girls guiding the New England plow, or perhaps pulling it.

9   Macmillan Publishing Company has released a booklet of nearly a hundred pages, "Guidelines for Creating Positive Sexual and Racial Images in Educational Materials." A female vice-president of Macmillan hopes that these guidelines "will be useful to school boards in selecting textbooks and to local community groups working with their schools to promote quality education materials." Macmillan would avoid "businessman," and promote "business person, entrepreneur, manager, speculator, investor, group leader, trader, business leader." And down with womanhood! "The romantic image of ideal womanhood has been so overplayed that most girls grow up believing they must attain it to be acceptable as women. Binding young women with such demands can cripple them as severely as did binding their feet in old China."

10   Conversely, of course, we ought to denigrate manhood; but that's unnecessary: the typical school anthology has already done that, as C. S. Lewis points out in *The Abolition of Man.*

11   Macmillan laments the absence of American Indians (what! not Native Americans?) from photographs of classrooms. Weren't Samoset and Cornstalk in the second grade with us? Moreover, in the section on textbook art, we are instructed never to show just "one black face in a crowd of white faces . . .

Group scenes should not portray one minority person, or in other ways make blacks stand out as the exception." In fine, every classroom scene should include 50 per cent Indians, 50 per cent blacks, 50 per cent Jews, 50 per cent Spanish-surname folk, and even a number of Caucasians.

12   Macmillan people are forbidden to exhibit Jewish people always "working as small shopkeepers, doctors, lawyers, jewelers, to the exclusion of other professions." Play up those Jewish lettuce-pickers and cowboys!

13   The trouble with all this publisher's pablum, aside from its insolence toward the folk who write and illustrate textbooks, is that it makes textbooks into a tissue of new stereotypes and falsehoods. Any reflective pupil will be moved to think, "The people who wrote this textbook are either fools, or liars, or both. Life isn't like this." And the pupil will be correct.

VOCABULARY

sedulous 1	generic 7
NOW 1	entrepreneur 9
genuflected 2	denigrate 10
Lady Macbeth 4	pablum 13
Neanderthal 7	

QUESTIONS

1.   What is Kirk's thesis? Who is his audience? Does he anticipate a sympathetic audience? How do you know?

2.   Describe the tone. How is it created?

3.   Are Kirk's comments in ¶s 4 and 5 an adequate analysis and evaluation of the quotes from McGraw-Hill?

4.   In ¶7 Kirk's only comment about the first quote (from Scott, Foresman) is that it is silly. Is the passage obviously silly? Is this a helpful evaluation?

5.   In ¶8, Kirk's comments about the sexist quote represent what logical fallacy? What logical fallacy does Kirk commit in ¶12?

6.   How does Kirk portray the book publishers?

7.   Is the conclusion an overstatement?

8.   What would be the response of Miller and Swift ("One Small Step for Genkind") to Kirk's assertion that "man" and "mankind" are terms which include both males and females?

9.   What is Kirk's attitude toward feminists? How do you know? List all of the evidence you can find to support your decision.

Professor of education, psychology, and psychiatry at the University of Chicago, Bruno Bettelheim (b. 1903) has specialized in child psychoanalysis and development. His sensitive case study of "Joey" appeared in the March 1959 issue of Scientific American.

Joey: A "Mechanical Boy"
Bruno Bettelheim

1   Joey, when we began our work with him, was a mechanical boy. He functioned as if by remote control, run by machines of his own powerfully creative fantasy. Not only did he himself believe that he was a machine but, more remarkably, he created this impression in others. Even while he performed actions that are intrinsically human, they never appeared to be other than machine-started and executed. On the other hand, when the machine was not working we had to concentrate on recollecting his presence, for he seemed not to exist. A human body that functions as if it were a machine and a machine that duplicates human functions are equally fascinating and frightening. Perhaps they are so uncanny because they remind us that the human body can operate without a human spirit, that body can exist without soul. And Joey was a child who had been robbed of his humanity.

2   Not every child who possesses a fantasy world is possessed by it. Normal children may retreat into realms of imaginary glory or magic powers, but they are easily recalled from these excursions. Disturbed children are not always able to make the return trip; they remain withdrawn, prisoners of the inner world of delusion and fantasy. In many ways Joey presented a classic example of this state of infantile autism. In any age, when the individual has escaped into a delusional world, he has usually fashioned it from bits and pieces of the world at hand. Joey, in his time and world, chose the machine and froze himself in its image. His story has a general relevance to the understanding of emotional development in a machine age.

3   Joey's delusion is not uncommon among schizophrenic children today. He wanted to be rid of his unbearable humanity, to become completely automatic. He so nearly succeeded in attaining this goal that he could almost convince others, as well as himself, of his mechanical character. The descriptions of autistic children in the literature take for their point of departure and comparison the normal or abnormal human being. To do justice to Joey I would have to compare him simultaneously to a most inept infant and a highly complex piece of machinery. Often we had to force ourselves by a conscious act of will to realize that Joey was a child. Again and again his acting-out of his delusions froze our own ability to respond as human beings.

4   During Joey's first weeks with us we would watch absorbedly as this at once fragile-looking and imperious nine-year-old went about his mechanical existence. Entering the dining room, for example, he would string an imaginary wire from his "energy source"—an imaginary electric outlet—to the

table. There he "insulated" himself with paper napkins and finally plugged himself in. Only then could Joey eat, for he firmly believed that the "current" ran his ingestive apparatus. So skillful was the pantomime that one had to look twice to be sure there was neither wire nor outlet nor plug. Children and members of our staff spontaneously avoided stepping on the "wires" for fear of interrupting what seemed the source of his very life.

5   For long periods of time, when his "machinery" was idle, he would sit so quietly that he would disappear from the focus of the most conscientious observation. Yet in the next moment he might be "working" and the center of our captivated attention. Many times a day he would turn himself on and shift noisily through a sequence of higher and higher gears until he "exploded," screaming "Crash, crash!" and hurling items from his ever present apparatus—radio tubes, light bulbs, even motors or, lacking these, any handy breakable object. (Joey had an astonishing knack for snatching bulbs and tubes unobserved.) As soon as the object thrown had shattered, he would cease his screaming and wild jumping and retire to mute, motionless nonexistence.

6   Our maids, inured to difficult children, were exceptionally attentive to Joey; they were apparently moved by his extreme infantile fragility, so strangely coupled with megalomaniacal superiority. Occasionally some of the apparatus he fixed to his bed to "live him" during his sleep would fall down in disarray. This machinery he contrived from masking tape, cardboard, wire and other paraphernalia. Usually the maids would pick up such things and leave them on a table for the children to find, or disregard them entirely. But Joey's machine they carefully restored: "Joey must have the carburetor so he can breathe." Similarly they were on the alert to pick up and preserve the motors that ran him during the day and the exhaust pipes through which he exhaled.

7   How had Joey become a human machine? From intensive interviews with his parents we learned that the process had begun even before birth. Schizophrenia often results from parental rejection, sometimes combined ambivalently with love. Joey, on the other hand, had been completely ignored.

8   "I never knew I was pregnant," his mother said, meaning that she had already excluded Joey from her consciousness. His birth, she said, "did not make any difference." Joey's father, a rootless draftee in the wartime civilian army, was equally unready for parenthood. So, of course, are many young couples. Fortunately most such parents lose their indifference upon the baby's birth. But not Joey's parents. "I did not want to see or nurse him," his mother declared. "I had no feeling of actual dislike—I simply didn't want to take care of him." For the first three months of his life Joey "cried most of the time." A colicky baby, he was kept on a rigid four-hour feeding schedule, was not touched unless necessary and was never cuddled or played with. The mother, preoccupied with herself, usually left Joey alone in the crib or playpen during the day. The father discharged his frustrations by punishing Joey when the child cried at night.

9   Soon the father left for overseas duty, and the mother took Joey, now a year and a half old, to live with her at her parents' home. On his arrival the

grandparents noticed that ominous changes had occurred in the child. Strong and healthy at birth, he had become frail and irritable; a responsive baby, he had become remote and inaccessible. When he began to master speech, he talked only to himself. At an early date he became preoccupied with machinery, including an old electric fan which he could take apart and put together again with surprising deftness.

10   Joey's mother impressed us with a fey quality that expressed her insecurity, her detachment from the world and her low physical vitality. We were struck especially by her total indifference as she talked about Joey. This seemed much more remarkable than the actual mistakes she made in handling him. Certainly he was left to cry for hours when hungry, because she fed him on a rigid schedule; he was toilet-trained with great rigidity so that he would give no trouble. These things happen to many children. But Joey's existence never registered with his mother. In her recollections he was fused at one moment with one event or person; at another, with something or somebody else. When she told us about his birth and infancy, it was as if she were talking about some vague acquaintance, and soon her thoughts would wander off to another person or to herself.

11   When Joey was not yet four, his nursery school suggested that he enter a special school for disturbed children. At the new school his autism was immediately recognized. During his three years there he experienced a slow improvement. Unfortunately a subsequent two years in a parochial school destroyed his progress. He began to develop compulsive defenses, which he called his "preventions." He could not drink, for example, except through elaborate piping systems built of straws. Liquids had to be "pumped" into him, in his fantasy, or he could not suck. Eventually his behavior became so upsetting that he could not be kept in the parochial school. At home things did not improve. Three months before entering the Orthogenic School he made a serious attempt at suicide.

12   To us Joey's pathological behavior seemed the external expression of an overwhelming effort to remain almost nonexistent as a person. For weeks Joey's only reply when addressed was "Bam." Unless he thus neutralized whatever we said, there would be an explosion, for Joey plainly wished to close off every form of contact not mediated by machinery. Even when he was bathed he rocked back and forth with mute, engine-like regularity, flooding the bathroom. If he stopped rocking, he did this like a machine too; suddenly he went completely rigid. Only once, after months of being lifted from his bath and carried to bed, did a small expression of puzzled pleasure appear on his face as he said very softly: "They even carry you to your bed here."

13   For a long time after he began to talk he would never refer to anyone by name, but only as "that person" or "the little person" or "the big person." He was unable to designate by its true name anything to which he attached feelings. Nor could he name his anxieties except through neologisms of word contaminations. For a long time he spoke about "master paintings" and "a master painting room" (i.e., masturbating and masturbating room). One of his machines, the "criticizer," prevented him from "saying words which have unpleasant feelings." Yet he gave personal names to the tubes and motors in his collection of machinery. Moreover, these dead things had feelings; the tubes bled when hurt and sometimes got sick. He consistently maintained this reversal between animate and inanimate objects.

14   In Joey's machine world everything, on pain of instant destruction, obeyed inhibitory laws much more stringent than those of physics. When we came to know him better, it was plain that in his moments of silent with-drawal, with his machine switched off, Joey was absorbed in pondering the compulsive laws of his private universe. His preoccupation with machinery made it difficult to establish even practical contacts with him. If he wanted to do something with a counselor, such as play with a toy that had caught his vague attention, he would not do so: "I'd like this very much, but first I have to turn off the machine." But by the time he had fulfilled all the requirements of his preventions, he had lost interest. When a toy was offered to him, he could not touch it because his motors and his tubes did not leave him a hand free. Even certain colors were dangerous and had to be strictly avoided in toys and clothing, because "some colors turn off the current, and I can't touch them because I can't live without the current."

15   Joey was convinced that machines were better than people. Once when he bumped into one of the pipes on our jungle gym he kicked it so violently that his teacher had to restrain him to keep him from injuring himself. When she explained that the pipe was much harder than his foot, Joey replied: "That proves it. Machines are better than the body. They don't break; they're much harder and stronger." If he lost or forgot something, it merely proved that his brain ought to be thrown away and replaced by machinery. If he spilled something his arm should be broken and twisted off because it did not work properly. When his head or arm failed to work as it should, he tried to punish it by hitting it. Even Joey's feelings were mechanical. Much later in his therapy, when he had formed a timid attachment to another child and had been rebuffed, Joey cried: "He broke my feelings."

16   Gradually we began to understand what had seemed to be contradictory in Joey's behavior—why he held on to the motors and tubes, then suddenly destroyed them in a fury, then set out immediately and urgently to equip himself with new and larger tubes. Joey had created these machines to run his body and mind because it was too painful to be human. But again and again he became dissatisfied with their failure to meet his need and rebellious at the way they frustrated his will. In a recurrent frenzy he "exploded" his light bulbs and tubes, and for a moment became a human being—for one crowning instant he came alive. But as soon as he had asserted his dominance through the self-created explosion, he felt his life ebbing away. To keep on existing he had immediately to restore his machines and replenish the electricity that supplied his life energy.

17   What deep-seated fears and needs underlay Joey's delusional system? We were long in finding out, for Joey's preventions effectively concealed the secret of his autistic behavior. In the meantime we dealt with his peripheral problems one by one.

18   During his first year with us Joey's most trying problem was toilet behav-ior. This surprised us, for Joey's personality was not "anal" in the Freudian

sense; his original personality damage had antedated the period of his toilet-training. Rigid and early toilet-training, however, had certainly contributed to his anxieties. It was our effort to help Joey with this problem that led to his first recognition of us as human beings.

19   Going to the toilet, like everything else in Joey's life, was surrounded by elaborate preventions. We had to accompany him; he had to take off all his clothes, he could only squat, not sit, on the toilet seat; he had to touch the wall with one hand, in which he also clutched frantically the vacuum tubes that powered his elimination. He was terrified lest his whole body be sucked down.

20   To counteract this fear we gave him a metal wastebasket in lieu of a toilet. Eventually, when eliminating into the wastebasket, he no longer needed to take off all his clothes, nor to hold on to the wall. He still needed the tubes and motors which, he believed, moved his bowels for him. But here again the all-important machinery was itself a source of new terrors. In Joey's world the gadgets had to move their bowels, too. He was terribly concerned that they should, but since they were so much more powerful than men, he was also terrified that if his tubes moved their bowels, their feces would fill all of space and leave him no room to live. He was thus always caught in some fearful contradiction.

Fig. 1.   Joey's Drawing of a House. The elaborate sewage system in Joey's drawing of a house reflects his long preoccupation with excretion. His obsession with sewage reflected intense anxieties produced by his early toilet-training, which was not only rigid but also completely impersonal.

21   Our readiness to accept his toilet habits, which obviously entailed some hardship for his counselors, gave Joey the confidence to express his obsessions in drawings. Drawing these fantasies was a first step toward letting us in, however distantly, to what concerned him most deeply. It was the first step in a year-long process of externalizing his anal preoccupations. As a result he began seeing feces everywhere; the whole world became to him a mire of excrement. At the same time he began to eliminate freely wherever he happened to be. But with this release from his infantile imprisonment in compulsive rules, the toilet and the whole process of elimination became less dangerous. Thus far it had been beyond Joey's comprehension that anybody could possibly move his bowels without mechanical aid. Now Joey took a further step forward; defecation became the first physiological process he could perform without the help of vacuum tubes. It must not be thought that he was proud of this ability. Taking pride in an achievement presupposes that one accomplishes it of one's own free will. He still did not feel himself an autonomous person who could do things on his own. To Joey defecation still seemed enslaved to some incomprehensible but utterly binding cosmic law, perhaps the law his parents had imposed on him when he was being toilet-trained.

22   It was not simply that his parents had subjected him to rigid, early training. Many children are so trained. But in most cases the parents have a deep emotional investment in the child's performance. The child's response in turn makes training an occasion for interaction between them and for the building of genuine relationships. Joey's parents had no emotional investment in him. His obedience gave them no satisfaction and won him no affection or approval. As a toilet-trained child he saved his mother labor, just as household machines saved her labor. As a machine he was not loved for his performance, nor could he love himself.

23   So it had been with all other aspects of Joey's existence with his parents. Their reactions to his eating or noneating, sleeping or wakening, urinating or defecating, being dressed or undressed, washed or bathed did not flow from any unitary interest in him, deeply embedded in their personalities. By treating him mechanically his parents made him a machine. The various functions of life—even the parts of his body—bore no integrating relationship to one another or to any sense of self that was acknowledged and confirmed by others. Though he had acquired mastery over some functions, such as toilet-training and speech, he had acquired them separately and kept them isolated from each other. Toilet-training had thus not gained him a pleasant feeling of body mastery; speech had not led to communication of thought or feeling. On the contrary, each achievement only steered him away from self-mastery and integration. Toilet-training had enslaved him. Speech had left him talking in neologisms that obstructed his and our ability to relate to each other. In Joey's development the normal process of growth had been made to run backward. Whatever he had learned put him not at the end of his infantile development toward integration but, on the contrary, farther behind than he was at its very beginning. Had we understood this sooner, his first years with us would have been less baffling.

24   It is unlikely that Joey's calamity could befall a child in any time and culture but our own. He suffered no physical deprivation; he starved for human contact. Just to be taken care of is not enough for relating. It is a necessary but not a sufficient condition. At the extreme where utter scarcity reigns, the forming of relationships is certainly hampered. But our society of mechanized plenty often makes for equal difficulties in a child's learning to relate. Where parents can provide the simple creature-comforts for their children only at the cost of significant effort, it is likely that they will feel pleasure in being able to provide for them; it is this, the parents' pleasure, that gives children a sense of personal worth and sets the process of relating in motion. But if comfort is so readily available that the parents feel no particular pleasure in winning it for their children, then the children cannot develop the feeling of being worthwhile around the satisfaction of their basic needs. Of course parents and children can and do develop relationships around other situations. But matters are then no longer so simple and direct. The child must be on the receiving end of care and concern given with pleasure and without the exaction of return if he is to feel loved and worthy of respect and consideration. This feeling gives him the ability to trust; he can entrust his well-being to persons to whom he is so important. Out of such trust the child learns to form close and stable relationships.

25   For Joey relationship with his parents was empty of pleasure in comfort-giving as in all other situations. His was an extreme instance of a plight that sends many schizophrenic children to our clinics and hospitals. Many months passed before he could relate to us; his despair that anybody could like him made contact impossible.

26   When Joey could finally trust us enough to let himself become more infantile, he began to play at being a papoose. There was a corresponding change in his fantasies. He drew endless pictures of himself as an electrical papoose. Totally enclosed, suspended in empty space, he is run by unknown, unseen powers through wireless electricity.

27   As we eventually came to understand, the heart of Joey's delusional system was the artificial, mechanical womb he had created and into which he had locked himself. In his papoose fantasies lay the wish to be entirely reborn in a womb. His new experiences in the school suggested that life, after all, might be worth living. Now he was searching for a way to be reborn in a better way. Since machines were better than men, what was more natural than to try rebirth through them? This was the deeper meaning of his electrical papoose.

28   As Joey made progress, his pictures of himself became more dominant in his drawings. Though still machine-operated, he has grown in self-importance. Another great step forward is represented in a picture in which he has acquired hands that do something, and he has had the courage to make a picture of the machine that runs him. Later still the papoose became a person, rather than a robot encased in glass.

29   Eventually Joey began to create an imaginary family at the school: the "Carr" family. Why the Carr family? In the car he was enclosed as he had been in his papoose, but at least the car was not stationary; it could move.

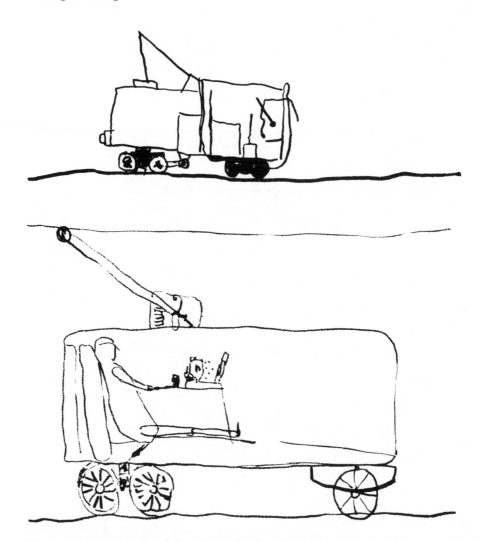

Fig. 2. Joey's Drawings of the "Carr" Family. Growing autonomy is shown in Joey's drawings of the imaginary "Carr" family. First drawing shows a machine which can move but is unoccupied. Second drawing is occupied, but by a passive figure. In the third drawing [see facing page] the figure has gained control of the machine.

More important, in a car one was not only driven but also could drive. The Carr family was Joey's way of exploring the possibility of leaving the school, of living with a good family in a safe, protecting car.

30   Joey at last broke through his prison. In this brief account it has not been possible to trace the painfully slow process of his first true relations with other human beings. Suffice it to say that he ceased to be a mechanical boy and became a human child. This newborn child was, however, nearly 12 years old. To recover the lost time is a tremendous task. That work has occupied

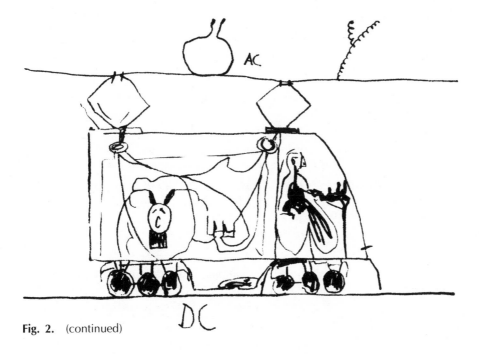

Fig. 2. (continued)

Joey and us ever since. Sometimes he sets to it with a will; at other times the difficulty of real life makes him regret that he ever came out of his shell. But he has never wanted to return to his mechanical life.

31   One last detail and this fragment of Joey's story has been told. When Joey was 12, he made a float for our Memorial Day parade. It carried the slogan: "Feelings are more important than anything under the sun." Feelings, Joey had learned, are what make for humanity; their absence, for a mechanical existence. With this knowledge Joey entered the human condition.

VOCABULARY

autism 2	ambivalently 7	inhibitory 14
schizophrenic 3	fey 10	peripheral 17
imperious 4	pathological 12	Freudian 18
megalomaniacal 6	neologisms 13	autonomous 21

QUESTIONS

1. What are your feelings about Joey? How does Bettelheim help to shape your response to Joey and his autism?

2. Who is Bettelheim's anticipated audience: specialists? knowledgeable non-specialists? Does he write effectively to that audience?

3. What, according to Bettelheim, were the causes of Joey's autism? Describe his parents and his early childhood experiences.

4. How, exactly, did Joey become a machine? Summarize the key details of his defense system.

5. Examine Bettelheim's assertion (¶24) that Joey's illness probably would not occur in another time or culture. Does he provide convincing evidence? Is that his purpose in this essay?

6. What are the characteristics of our time that Bettelheim sees as causes of more Joey's? Do you agree? In a machine age, how can we avoid becoming machines?

Shirley Chisholm (b. 1924) has been a member of the United States House of Representatives from the 12th Congressional District in New York (Brooklyn) since 1968. Her special interests include the problems of the poor, minorities, and women. Her article appeared in McCall's magazine, August 1970.

I'd Rather Be Black Than Female
Shirley Chisholm

1   Being the first black woman elected to Congress has made me some kind of phenomenon. There are nine other blacks in Congress; there are ten other women. I was the first to overcome both handicaps at once. Of the two handicaps, being black is much less of a drawback than being female.

2   If I said that being black is a greater handicap than being a woman, probably no one would question me. Why? Because "we all know" there is prejudice against black people in America. That there is prejudice against women is an idea that still strikes nearly all men—and, I am afraid, most women—as bizarre.

3   Prejudice against blacks was invisible to most white Americans for many years. When blacks finally started to "mention" it, with sit-ins, boycotts, and freedom rides, Americans were incredulous. "Who, us?" they asked in injured tones. *"We're* prejudiced?" It was the start of a long, painful reeducation for white America. It will take years for whites—including those who think of themselves as liberals—to discover and eliminate the racist attitudes they all actually have.

4   How much harder will it be to eliminate the prejudice against women? I am sure it will be a longer struggle. Part of the problem is that women in America are much more brainwashed and content with their roles as second-class citizens than blacks ever were.

5   Let me explain. I have been active in politics for more than twenty years. For all but the last six, I have done the work—all the tedious details that make the difference between victory and defeat on election day—while men reaped the rewards, which is almost invariably the lot of women in politics.

6   It is still women—about three million volunteers—who do most of this work in the American political world. The best any of them can hope for is the honor of being district or county vice-chairman, a kind of separate-but-equal position with which a woman is rewarded for years of faithful envelope stuffing and card-party organizing. In such a job, she gets a number of free trips to state and sometimes national meetings and conventions, where her role is supposed to be to vote the way her male chairman votes.

7   When I tried to break out of that role in 1963 and run for the New York State Assembly seat from Brooklyn's Bedford-Stuyvesant, the resistance was bitter. From the start of that campaign, I faced undisguised hostility because of my sex.

8   But it was four years later, when I ran for Congress, that the question of my sex became a major issue. Among members of my own party, closed meetings were held to discuss ways of stopping me.

9   My opponent, the famous civil-rights leader James Farmer, tried to project a black, masculine image; he toured the neighborhood with sound trucks filled with young men wearing Afro haircuts, dashikis, and beards. While the television crews ignored me, they were not aware of a very important statistic, which both I and my campaign manager, Wesley MacD. Holder, knew. In my district there are 2.5 women for every man registered to vote. And those women are organized—in PTAs, church societies, card clubs, and other social and service groups. I went to them and asked their help. Mr. Farmer still doesn't quite know what hit him.

10   When a bright young woman graduate starts looking for a job, why is the first question always: "Can you type?" A history of prejudice lies behind that question. Why are women thought of as secretaries, not administrators? Librarians and teachers, but not doctors and lawyers? Because they are thought of as different and inferior. The happy homemaker and the contented darky are both stereotypes produced by prejudice.

11   Women have not even reached the level of tokenism that blacks are reaching. No women sit on the Supreme Court. Only two have held Cabinet rank, and none do at present. Only two women hold ambassadorial rank. But women predominate in the lower-paying, menial, unrewarding, dead-end jobs, and when they do reach better positions, they are invariably paid less than a man gets for the same job.

12   If that is not prejudice, what would you call it?

13   A few years ago, I was talking with a political leader about a promising young woman as a candidate. "Why invest time and effort to build the girl up?" he asked me. "You know she'll only drop out of the game to have a couple of kids just about the time we're ready to run her for mayor."

14   Plenty of people have said similar things about me. Plenty of others have advised me, every time I tried to take another upward step, that I should go back to teaching, a woman's vocation, and leave politics to the men. I love teaching, and I am ready to go back to it as soon as I am convinced that this country no longer needs a woman's contribution.

15   When there are no children going to bed hungry in this rich nation, I may be ready to go back to teaching. When there is a good school for every child, I may be ready. When we do not spend our wealth on hardware to murder people, when we no longer tolerate prejudice against minorities, and when the laws against unfair housing and unfair unemployment practices are enforced instead of evaded, then there may be nothing more for me to do in politics.

16   But until that happens—and we all know it will not be this year or next—what we need is more women in politics, because we have a very special contribution to make. I hope that the example of my success will convince other women to get into politics—and not just to stuff envelopes, but to run for office.

17   It is women who can bring empathy, tolerance, insight, patience, and persistence to government—the qualities we naturally have or have had to develop because of our suppression by men. The women of a nation mold its morals, its religion, and its politics by the lives they live. At present, our country needs women's idealism and determination, perhaps more in politics than anywhere else.

VOCABULARY

empathy   17   dashikis   9

QUESTIONS

1. What does the opening paragraph accomplish? What is Chisholm's thesis?

2. Who is her audience? How do you know?

3. What sort of personality emerges? Through what devices?

4. Chisholm supports her thesis by examining the problems in removing prejudice against females. What problem is presented in ¶2? In ¶4?

5. What kind of evidence does Chisholm present in ¶s 5–9? ¶10? Is the evidence effective?

6. What contribution does Chisholm think women can make in politics? Does she support these assertions with evidence? Is ¶17 sexist?

7. Compare the views of Steinem and Roiphe with Chisholm on the issue of women in politics. Which one is most convincing? What is the basis for your judgment?

A free-lance writer who publishes in popular magazines, Helen Lawrenson (b. 1907) is the author of several books, including her autobiography, Stranger at the Party *(1975). What follows is a slightly condensed version of an essay published by* Esquire *in January 1971.*

The Feminine Mistake
Helen Lawrenson

1   You might have to go back to the Children's Crusade in 1212 A.D. to find as unfortunate and fatuous an attempt at manipulated hysteria as the Women's Liberation movement. For six months I have been reading their literature and listening to their strident speeches, and I had hoped that by now these sick, silly creatures would have huffed and puffed themselves out.

2   Instead, the movement is spreading, not only in America but in Europe; more and more women are letting themselves be worked up to a splenetic frenzy of hatred for men; and the latter, in cowardly panic lest they be labeled male chauvinists, are ignominiously making placatory noises. Male magazine editors, to a mouse, have jumped on the bandwagon, and every militant feminist with a typewriter is banging away on it. The books they produced last year sold so well that many bookstores have set up special Women's Lib sections in anticipation of increasing demand for the more than a dozen titles steaming off the presses this winter, with more to come, all contracted for by leading male publishers who fell over each other to compete for the authors. Last summer, the New York Shakespeare Festival put on a Women's Lib musical gawkishly entitled *Mod Donna,* written by two females and described as dealing with "women's sexual subjugation to Penis Power"; a group called the Feminist Repertory Theatre produced plays containing such fustian lines as "Have you made my body the incubator of your artificial passion?"; and actress Barbara Harris promised to direct a dramatic presentation of selected feminist writings from Susan B. Anthony on down, a theatrical event to be awaited with muted anticipation. The commercial lampreys of the cinema world will surely not be dilatory in latching on, just as they did with the youth revolution, so that before long we can expect to see a spate of films exploiting Women's Lib in different versions—comic, serious, sexy, and, of course, Cary Grant and Katharine Hepburn in the geriatric version.

3   It's a phony issue and a phony movement. Demands for equal political and legal rights, for child-care centers and equal pay for equal work are reasonable enough—although even in these areas some of the more belligerent feminists tend to go off the beam—but these have been submerged in a hair-raising emotional orgy of hatred as vicious as it is ludicrous, directed at love, marriage, children, the home, and encompassing en route, with wild catholicity, the penis, the Pill, false eyelashes, brassieres, Barbie dolls, Freud,

Dr. Spock, the Old Left, the New Left, detergent advertisements, and such despicable male gallantries as opening doors for women and helping them on with their coats. What they are demanding is not equality but the absolute subjugation of men, or even their elimination.

4   These are not normal women. I think they are freaks. Besides, they are dead wrong in their assumption that most women detest men, marriage and housework so much that they can't wait to be liberated from them so they can rush out to work all day in factory, shop or office. Where do they get this lunatic idea that women had rather work for a boss than stay home and run their own domain? All orthodox Lib members seethe with bile at the thought of housework, to which they constantly refer as "shitwork," and rant continuously about the dreadful degradation of cooking meals, making beds, bathing babies. But the average normal woman derives a very basic happiness from performing these tasks. Most women have a strong nesting instinct and they *like* taking care of their homes. It may get tiresome at times but it sure as hell beats working. They get satisfaction from cooking special dishes to please their families, from polishing their best furniture and washing their grandmother's china, from planning new curtains or refurbishing an old chair. Even if they own nothing valuable or grand, what they have are Their Own Things and they enjoy taking care of them. Housework is not degrading, and there is nothing demeaning about caring for your home, your husband, your children. Besides, who do these Women's Lib characters think ought to do this "degrading" housework? Other women? Their husbands? One of them, Caroline Bird, in an article in *Signature,* the Diners Club magazine, suggests an end to the family system, which might be replaced by some sort of commune, and adds, "If women are totally liberated, more men and women would remain single," thus ignoring the fact that most women *want* to get married. Discussing the effect on industry, she writes, "The market for nursery furniture and child gear would taper off" (What? No more little pink or blue crib mattresses with bunnies and kittens on them?), and prophesies that "convenience foods" (whatever they are) and takeout-food shops would replace home-cooked meals and that "Home furnishings would give way to portable or disposable furniture" *Disposable furniture.* Can she really be kidding herself that this is what women want in their homes?

5   The worst thing about the movement is that it is distracting the attention of thousands of women from more urgent and important questions. They should get their priorities straight. Instead of yapping about men treating them as "sex objects" (and, personally, I have always *liked* being treated as a sex object), they might better devote themselves to more socially useful protests: against the war in Indochina, against nuclear, chemical and biological weapons, against environmental pollution, to name a few of the more obvious. Or the exploitation of migrant workers, the oppression of the blacks, the American Indians, the Alaskan Eskimos. Or any one of at least several hundred other projects more immediate and more deserving than the issue of whether or not women should do housework and let men whistle at them in the streets. There is only so much time and energy that each person has

available to devote to causes. To try to persuade people to concentrate this time and energy on something as capricious and spurious as Women's Lib is not only wasteful but truly evil. . . .*

6   American women have more freedom and more material advantages than any other women on earth. They are also notorious for their tendency to dominate their menfolk. As Dr. Spock remarked when he appeared on British television a few months ago, "If you liberate women in America one more inch, man will be completely subjugated." Sentiments like this have aroused the rage of Women's Lib groups: one of their publications portrayed him as a penis (obviously the most hateful object they could imagine) in a drawing, and a *Newsweek* journalist talking to Lib groups reported that they hissed at the mention of his name.

7   He was only confirming what many psychiatrists and sociologists have said previously. Dr. Theodore S. Weiss, formerly a senior psychiatrist of the New York City Department of Hospitals, once told me, "America is becoming a matriarchy." The American wife, he claimed, treats her husband as a combination of problem child and indentured servant. She expects him to be escort, meal ticket, handyman, errand boy and mother's helper. She is always trying to remodel and improve him. She supervises his manners and language, dictates how he shall dress, what friends he shall have, and how he shall spend his leisure time. Customarily, it is she who determines the decor of their home, the extent of their social orbit, and where they go on holidays. In public, she does not hesitate to interrupt him, contradict him, or attempt to regulate his habits. ("Don't give him any more to drink. He's had enough.") If he rebels, she nags him, bosses him, belittles him and tries to make him feel so inadequate that he would no more think of asserting his male authority as head of the family than he would dare wipe his hands on the guest towels in the bathroom. Increasingly, he suffers from nervous breakdowns, ulcers, premature heart attacks, insomnia, alcoholism. On the other hand, American women not only live longer than their men but they own more than fifty percent of the money in the country, they have sixty-five percent of the savings accounts, they control fifty-seven percent of listed securities, have title to seventy-four percent of suburban homes, and, according to The New York Sunday *Times,* control eighty-seven and a half percent of the total buying power.

8   So what are they bitching about? Careers? If a woman is sufficiently ambitious, determined *and* gifted, there is practically nothing she can't do. We have been judges, legislators, bank presidents, college presidents, publishers, ambassadors, doctors, lawyers, scientists, Cabinet members, auditors, bond traders, tax experts, bullfighters, bartenders, plumbers, taxi drivers, riveters and even, some twenty-odd years ago, six percent of the total number of the country's paperhangers. [Recently,] we have [had] a woman Director of the Mint, U.S. Treasurer, Chairman of the Federal Maritime Commission, as

---

*The deleted paragraphs examine the range and influence of women's liberation groups in a number of countries throughout the world.

well as a couple of ambassadors. There is only one woman Senator but ten women in the House. That there are not more of us in the top echelons is due to personal choice rather than denial of opportunity. The main life interest of the average woman quite simply lies in other directions: love, marriage, children, home. Men start work with the intention of working all their lives, often with the goal of rising to the top. The majority of women take their first jobs with the intention of working only until they get married, or, if they continue after marriage, until they have children. There are 29,500,000 women in the U.S. labor force today and those of that number who continue to work after marriage usually do so for reasons more economic than feminist. A Department of Labor questionnaire some years ago asked the motives of married women workers. The typical answer was: "Because my husband does not earn enough to support our family with the cost of living what it is." They did not say: "Because I'm just crazy about the factory assembly line."

9   There is, too, the matter of ability—or talent. (I'm not going into the question of genius here, although certainly the absence of any female equivalent to Beethoven, Shakespeare, Leonardo da Vinci or all the other great composers, writers and painters cannot be blamed on male oppression.) If women have it and are sufficiently dedicated to its advancement, they can make the grade. They do not always have it, or if they do, they sometimes lack the driving urge, the single-minded perseverance to exploit it. Furthermore, as far as politics go, whatever makes the feminists think that women could run the world any better than men? We got the vote, kiddo, and a fat lot of good we've done with it.

10   What they want is Everything—and they can't even agree on that. Although most of the groups who demonstrated last August on the fiftieth anniversary of the women's suffrage constitutional amendment listed free abortions among their demands, Women, Inc. of San Francisco, opposes abolition of the abortion laws, while Roxanne Dunbar, a leading Liberation spokeswoman, has been quoted as saying she feels support of abortion reform is "basically racist." Nor do they approve of the Pill, which they have denounced as "the final pollution, the exact analogue of DDT," or of douches—"another billion-dollar industry off our bodies"—while at the same time they attack the supposed hardships of motherhood. For years, feminists have railed against the sexual freedom of men and the double standard in morals, but now that the sexual revolution is here, they don't like it. Robin Morgan, a founder of W.I.T.C.H., is only one of those who claim that the new sexual freedom "never helped us—just made us more available," and someone else has written, "Women have gone from private property to public property—she's fair game." (This brings to mind the same question I had when I read Sally Kempton's statement, "In my adolescence I screwed a lot of guys I didn't much like." Doesn't it ever occur to any of these girls that they can always say No?) Some of them are even against the newly acclaimed clitoral orgasm: "The hullabaloo over the female clitorally stimulated orgasm has further done nothing to liberate women because male domination of all women has not changed. Men are heard gloating over the power trip of 'I can make my girl go off like a machine gun.'"

11   To these women, a man is always wrong, no matter what. Although some feminists speak glowingly of the examples of communal nurseries and equality of work in Communist countries, others claim that "socialism in Cuba, China, the Soviet Union is a more advanced stage of male supremacy in which the means of production are owned by all men collectively." Many Lib members quit American radical groups because women had to type, answer telephones, run mimeograph machines and get coffee when what they thought they should have been doing, of course, was making the speeches and dictating the policy. As one of them has written, "The average student male wants a passive sex object . . . while he does all the fun things [like getting his head clubbed?] and bosses her around . . . he plays either big-shot male executive or Che Guevara—and he is my oppressor and my enemy." A manifesto issued on the West Coast by Redstockings refers to revolutionary groups as all "run by men and, consequently, interested in destroying us." Another complaint cites the "male supremacy rampant in white, male, anti-war groups" and says that women must "begin to demand control of these groups." (Note—not equal rights but *control*.)

12   Women like these will never be satisfied, no matter what rights they gain, because they are incapable of coming to terms with their own natures as females. Many of the Lib leaders are divorced or separated from their husbands (one deserted her husband and baby when the child was only one year old); many are childless; many more state flatly that they never want children or marriage. Those are their problems, but they should not try to impose them on other women, nor should they blame men for their own deficiencies. In nature, the basic, primary function of woman is to mate for the purpose of reproduction. Everything else has been superimposed, and women deny this at their peril. No matter what kind of political, economic or social setup we may have in the future, nothing is going to change the biological facts. Kate Millett can claim that gender identity is imposed by society, not genes, till she's blue in the face, but this doesn't make it true, as several anthropologists and psychiatrists have recently remarked. Even Simone de Beauvoir, top-drawer member of feminist hagiology, has written, "The division of the sexes is a biological fact, not an event in history." After treating us to a survey of the sex habits of ants, termites (Did you know that a termite queen lays up to 4000 eggs a day? Well, now you do.) and toads, she works her way up to birds, fishes and mammals and admits that "it is unquestionably the male who takes the female—she is *taken* . . . the male deposits his semen, the female receives." Even among female humans, she says, the "reproductive function is as important as the productive capacity." This doesn't mean that she approves of marriage or motherhood. Speaking with all the assurance of one who has experienced neither, she feels that "the tragedy of marriage is not that it fails to assure woman the promised happiness—there is no such assurance in regard to happiness—but that it mutilates her. . . . Real activities, real work, are the prerogative of her man . . . she is betrayed from the day he marries her." This contempt for the wife-mother role is as major a Women's Lib theme as hatred of men (the producer of a Lib radio program on New York's WBAI claimed that "to be a woman is to be nothing" and described the lives of

housewives and mothers as "nothingness, total nothingness"). Simone thinks that marriage should be prohibited as a career for women. Man should free woman, she writes, and "give her something to *do* in the world" (a statement which could only have been written by a nullipara), although even she confesses that women enjoy marketing and cooking: "there is a poetry in making preserves ... cooking is revelation and creation; and a woman can find special satisfaction in a successful cake." (She'd better retract that or they'll tear off all her buttons and drum her out of the movement.)

13   Women also dearly love cosmetics and it is idiotic for Lib members to say they should renounce them because they are degrading. Women enjoy using makeup, trying out new kinds, playing around with it. They always have, primarily to make themselves desirable in the eyes of men (a goal which is anathema to Lib members) and, secondarily, for the sheer pleasure of self-adornment. Women's Lib sneers at this and their members plaster stickers reading "This Ad Insults Women" across posters which play up feminine sex appeal. It is an insult, they say, to assume that women are thinking of sex when they buy soap or perfume (Oh, but they are, honey) and in many cities Lib groups have publicly burned lipsticks, false eyelashes, bras and girdles, along with assorted objects like wedding certificates, birth-control pills, a Barbie doll and a book by Norman Mailer. (They lambaste Mailer and D. H. Lawrence as "male supremacist sexists," but have a kind word for Jean Genet.) The Barbie doll was included because they consider that "toys are, like abortion laws, deadly earnest instruments of women's oppression" dreamed up by fiendish male toy manufacturers who foist dolls, miniature stoves, refrigerators, mops and brooms on innocent and helpless little girl children. This, of course, is piffle. Little girls play with dolls, etc. because they love them, just as they love helping around the kitchen, dreaming of the day when they will be housewives and mothers, themselves. Why not? There is probably no career in the world as basically rewarding for a woman, from an emotional and psychological point of view, as that of wife and mother. And what about love? Even the most emancipated career woman can fall in love; and love is not only when the bush becomes the burning bush, but it is also caring more about someone else than you do about yourself. When a woman falls madly in love with a man, she *wants* to wait on him and please him and be bossed by him and make a home for him and bear his children. Anyone who says otherwise is talking rubbish.

14   Women's Lib members who, for whatever personal reasons, find this idea loathsome are bucking nature. Women are the lunar sex. They do menstruate and they do have the babies. This is not the fault of men. It is asinine, as well as useless, to try to reverse the genders or to mount a venomous hate campaign against men for fulfilling the role for which nature made them. Men and women today should be working together to try to make the earth a better and a safer place. Any movement that tends to set them against each other by drumming up false sexual controversies is stupid and wrong. I cannot even feel sorry for these neurotic, inadequate women, because they are so appallingly selfish. They shriek about the monotony of housework with never a

thought for the millions of men working their balls off at far more monotonous jobs in order to support their wives and children. Housework in America, despite all the labor-saving gadgets and easily prepared foods, may be boring at times, but it can't compare with the ego-destructive, soul-deadening boredom of standing in one spot on an assembly line, repeating one motion over and over, all day, every day.

15   Come off it, girls. Who is kidding whom? Besides, hasn't it ever dawned on you that whatever equality women get is given to them by men? So you see, no matter how you slice it, it's the same old sex game. Liberate me, daddy, eight to the bar.

VOCABULARY

fatuous   1
strident   1
splenetic   2
ignominiously   2
placatory   2
fustian   2
lampreys   2
dilatory   2

catholicity   3
capricious   5
spurious   5
matriarchy   7
analogue   10
nullipara   12
anathema   13

QUESTIONS

1. What is Lawrenson's attitude toward the women's liberation movement? What words and statements convey this attitude?

2. Who is her anticipated audience? How does her audience affect the tone of her essay? How would you characterize her tone?

3. The range of word choice is wide; what is its effect?

4. What is the purpose of ¶1? of ¶2?

5. What argument does she present in ¶4 to support her thesis? Is it convincing?

6. In ¶5 Lawrenson argues that there are more important issues. What are they? Do you think they are more important? Does she offer criteria for deciding what issues are important?

7. In ¶6 Lawrenson asserts that "American women have more freedom. . . ." Assuming that this is a provable fact, is it relevant to the issue being debated?

8. What evidence does she provide to support the assertion that women have not been denied career opportunities? Is the evidence relevant?

9. Lawrenson questions that women would make better politicians than men. How would Chisholm or Steinem respond to her?

10. Lawrenson says that the "primary function of woman is to mate for the purpose of reproduction." Could we not say the same for men? Lawrenson makes a similar statement at the end of ¶13. Her assumption is that men do not want the same things as women when they fall in love. Is this assumption valid? If so, is it biologically determined or socially conditioned?

11. What logical fallacy occurs in sentence 1, ¶13? What logical fallacy occurs in the last ¶?

12. How convincing is Lawrenson's argument?

Anne Roiphe (b. 1935) is the author of Digging Out *(1968),* Up the Sandbox *(1971), and* Long Division *(1973). This essay was printed in the October 30, 1972, issue of* New York *magazine.*

Confessions of a Female Chauvinist Sow
Anne Richardson Roiphe

1 I once married a man I thought was totally unlike my father and I imagined a whole new world of freedom emerging. Five years later it was clear even to me—floating face down in a wash of despair—that I had simply chosen a replica of my handsome daddy-true. The updated version spoke English like an angel but—good God!—underneath he was my father exactly: wonderful, but not the right man for me.

2 Most people I know have at one time or another been fouled up by their childhood experiences. Patterns tend to sink into the unconscious only to reappear, disguised, unseen, like marionette strings, pulling us this way or that. Whatever ails people—keeps them up at night, tossing and turning— also ails movements no matter how historically huge or politically important. The women's movement cannot remake consciousness, or reshape the future, without acknowledging and shedding all the unnecessary and ugly baggage of the past. It's easy enough now to see where men have kept us out of clubs, baseball games, graduate schools; it's easy enough to recognize the hidden directions that limit Sis to cake-baking and Junior to bridge-building; it's now possible for even Miss America herself to identify what *they* have done to us, and, of course, *they* have and *they* did and *they* are. . . . But along the way we also developed our own hidden prejudices, class assumptions and an anti-male humor and collection of expectations that gave us, like all oppressed groups, a secret sense of superiority (co-existing with a poor self-image— it's not news that people can believe two contradictory things at once).

3   Listen to any group that suffers materially and socially. They have a lexicon with which they tease the enemy: ofay, goy, honky, gringo. "Poor pale devils," said Malcolm X loud enough for us to hear, although blacks had joked about that to each other for years. Behind some of the women's liberation thinking lurk the rumors, the prejudices, the defense systems of generations of oppressed women whispering in the kitchen together, presenting one face to their menfolk and another to their card clubs, their mothers and sisters. All this is natural enough but potentially dangerous in a revolutionary situation in which you hope to create a future that does not mirror the past. The hidden anti-male feelings, a result of the old system, will foul us up if they are allowed to persist.

4   During my teen years I never left the house on my Saturday night dates without my mother slipping me a few extra dollars—mad money, it was called. I'll explain what it was for the benefit of the new generation in which people just sleep with each other: the fellow was supposed to bring me home, lead me safely through the asphalt jungle, protect me from slithering snakes, rapists and the like. But my mother and I knew young men were apt to drink too much, to slosh down so many rye-and-gingers that some hero might well lead me in front of an oncoming bus, smash his daddy's car into Tiffany's window or, less gallantly, throw up on my new dress. Mad money was for getting home on your own, no matter what form of insanity your date happened to evidence. Mad money was also a wallflower's rope ladder; if the guy you came with suddenly fancied someone else, well, you didn't have to stay there and suffer, you could go home. Boys were fickle and likely to be unkind; my mother and I knew that, as surely as we knew they tried to make you do things in the dark they wouldn't respect you for afterwards, and in fact would spread the word and spoil your rep. Boys like to be flattered; if you made them feel important they would eat out of your hand. So talk to them about their interests, don't alarm them with displays of intelligence—we all knew that, we groups of girls talking into the wee hours of the night in a kind of easy companionship we thought impossible with boys. Boys were prone to have a good time, get you pregnant, and then pretend they didn't know your name when you came knocking on their door for finances or comfort. In short, we believed boys were less moral than we were. They appeared to be hypocritical, self-seeking, exploitative, untrustworthy and very likely to be showing off their precious masculinity. I never had a girl friend I thought would be unkind or embarrass me in public. I never expected a girl to lie to me about her marks or sports skill or how good she was in bed. Altogether—without anyone's directly coming out and saying so—I gathered that men were sexy, powerful, very interesting, but not very nice, not very moral, humane and tender, like us. Girls played fairly while men, unfortunately, reserved their honor for the battlefield.

5   Why are there laws insisting on alimony and child support? Well, everyone knows that men don't have an instinct to protect their young and, given half a chance, with the moon in the right phase, they will run off and disappear. Everyone assumes a mother will not let her child starve, yet it is necessary to legislate that a father must not do so. We are taught to accept the idea that men are less than decent; their charms may be manifold but their characters are riddled with faults. To this day I never blink if I hear that a man has gone to find his fortune in South America, having left his pregnant wife, his blind mother and taken the family car. I still gasp in horror when I hear of a woman leaving her asthmatic infant for a rock group in Taos because I can't seem to avoid the assumption that men are naturally heels and women the ordained carriers of what little is moral in our dubious civilization.

6   My mother never gave me mad money thinking I would ditch a fellow for some other guy or that I would pass out drunk on the floor. She knew I would be considerate of my companion because, after all, I was more mature than the boys that gathered about. Why was I more mature? Women just are people-oriented; they learn to be empathetic at an early age. Most English students (students interested in humanity, not artifacts) are women. Men and boys—so the myth goes—conceal their feelings and lose interest in anybody else's. Everyone knows that even little boys can tell the difference between one kind of a car and another—proof that their souls are mechanical, their attention directed to the nonhuman.

7   I remember shivering in the cold vestibule of a famous men's athletic club. Women and girls are not permitted inside the club's door. What are they doing in there, I asked? They're naked, said my mother, they're sweating, jumping up and down a lot, telling each other dirty jokes and bragging about their stock market exploits. Why can't we go in? I asked. Well, my mother told me, they're afraid we'd laugh at them.

8   The prejudices of childhood are hard to outgrow. I confess that every time my business takes me past that club, I shudder. Images of large bellies resting on massage tables and flaccid penises rising and falling with the Dow Jones average flash through my head. There it is, chauvinism waving its cancerous tentacles from the depths of my psyche.

9   Minorities automatically feel superior to the oppressor because, after all, they are not hurting anybody. In fact, they feel morally better. The old canard that women need love, men need sex—believed for too long by both sexes—attributes moral and spiritual superiority to women and makes of men beasts whose urges send them prowling into the night. This false division of good and bad, placing deforming pressures on everyone, doesn't have to contaminate the future. We know that the assumptions we make about each other become a part of the cultural air we breathe and, in fact, become social truths. Women who want equality must be prepared to give it and to believe in it, and in order to do that it is not enough to state that you are as good as any man, but also it must be stated that he is as good as you and both will be humans together. If we want men to share in the care of the family in a new way, we must assume them as capable of consistent loving tenderness as we.

10   I rummage about and find in my thinking all kinds of anti-male prejudices. Some are just jokes and others I will have a hard time abandoning. First, I share an emotional conviction with many sisters that women given power would not create wars. Intellectually I know that's ridiculous; great

queens have waged war before; the likes of Lurleen Wallace, Pat Nixon and Mrs. General Lavelle can be depended upon in the future to guiltlessly condemn to death other people's children in the name of some ideal of their own. Little girls, of course, don't take toy guns out of their hip pockets and say "Pow, pow" to all their neighbors and friends like the average well-adjusted little boy. However, if we gave little girls the six-shooters, we would soon have double the pretend body count.

11   Aggression is not, as I secretly think, a male-sex-linked characteristic: brutality is masculine only by virtue of opportunity. True, there are 1,000 Jack the Rippers for every Lizzie Borden, but that surely is the result of social forms. Women as a group are indeed more masochistic than men. The practical result of this division is that women seem nicer and kinder, but when the world changes, women will have a fuller opportunity to be just as rotten as men and there will be fewer claims of female moral superiority.

12   Now that I am entering early middle age, I hear many women complaining of husbands and ex-husbands who are attracted to younger females. This strikes the older woman as unfair, of course. But I remember a time when I thought all boys around my age and grade were creeps and bores. I wanted to go out with an older man: a senior or, miraculously, a college man. I had a certain contempt for my coevals, not realizing that the freshman in college I thought so desirable, was some older girl's creep. Some women never lose that contempt for men of their own age. That isn't fair either and may be one reason why some sensible men of middle years find solace in young women.

13   I remember coming home from school one day to find my mother's card game dissolved in hysterical laughter. The cards were floating in black rivers of running mascara. What was so funny? A woman named Helen was lying on a couch pretending to be her husband with a cold. She was issuing demands for orange juice, aspirin, suggesting a call to a specialist, complaining of neglect, of fate's cruel finger, of heat, of cold, of sharp pains on the bridge of the nose·that might indicate brain involvement. What was so funny? The ladies explained to me that all men behave just like that with colds, they are reduced to temper tantrums by simple nasal congestion, men cannot stand any little physical discomfort—on and on the laughter went.

14   The point of this vignette is the nature of the laughter—us laughing at them, us feeling superior to them, us ridiculing them behind their backs. If they were doing it to us we'd call it male chauvinist pigness; if we do it to them, it is inescapably female chauvinist sowness and, whatever its roots, it leads to the same isolation. Boys are messy, boys are mean, boys are rough, boys are stupid and have sloppy handwriting. A cacophony of childhood memories rushes through my head, balanced, of course, by all the well-documented feelings of inferiority and envy. But the important thing, the hard thing, is to wipe the slate clean, to start again without the meanness of the past. That's why it's so important that the women's movement not become anti-male and allow its most prejudiced spokesmen total leadership. The much-chewed-over abortion issue illustrates this. The women's-liberation position, insisting on a woman's right to determine her own body's destiny, leads in fanatical extreme to a kind of emotional immaculate conception in which the father is not judged even half-responsible—he has no rights, and no consideration is to be given to his concern for either the woman or the fetus.

15   Woman, who once was abandoned and disgraced by an unwanted pregnancy, has recently arrived at a new pride of ownership or disposal. She has traveled in a straight line that still excludes her sexual partner from an equal share in the wanted or unwanted pregnancy. A better style of life may develop from an assumption that men are as human as we. Why not ask the child's father if he would like to bring up the child? Why not share decisions, when possible, with the male? If we cut them out, assuming an old-style indifference on their part, we perpetuate the ugly divisiveness that has characterized relations between the sexes so far.

16   Hard as it is for many of us to believe, women are not really superior to men in intelligence or humanity—they are only equal.

VOCABULARY

lexicon 3
empathetic 6
psyche 8
canard 9
Lurleen Wallace 10
Mrs. General Lavelle 10

Jack the Ripper 11
Lizzie Borden 11
masochistic 11
coevals 12
vignette 14
cacophony 14

QUESTIONS

1. What is the function of ¶1? How does Roiphe make the transition between ¶1 and ¶2? What is being compared?

2. What is Roiphe's thesis? Where is it stated?

3. What is the implied comparison in ¶3?

4. Summarize ¶s 4-9; what anti-male prejudice is described? What anti-male prejudice is described in ¶s 11-12?

5. What point does Roiphe want to make through the scene presented in ¶13? What behavior and attitudes characteristic of oppressed groups does Roiphe find in women?

6. What is Roiphe's chief source of evidence, chief means of developing her thesis? How does she make that evidence convincing?

7. Both Lawrenson and Roiphe discuss the negative attitudes of many women toward men; in what terms and with what word choice does each writer discuss the issue? How does each discussion affect you

intellectually and emotionally? Which discussion is most likely to gain your attention and respect? How much does your reaction depend on your opinions?

8. Characterize Roiphe's style. Is it appropriate?

A speaker and writer of feminist issues, Gloria Steinem (b. 1936) is currently editor of Ms. *magazine. The following article appeared in* Time *on August 31, 1970.*

What It Would Be Like If Women Win
Gloria Steinem

1   Any change is fearful, especially one affecting both politics and sex roles, so let me begin these Utopian speculations with a fact. To break the ice.

2   Women don't want to exchange places with men. Male chauvinists, science-fiction writers and comedians may favor that idea for its shock value, but psychologists say it is a fantasy based on the ruling-class ego and guilt. Men assume that women want to imitate them, which is just what white people assumed about blacks. An assumption so strong that it may convince the second-class group of the need to imitate, but for both women and blacks that stage has passed. Guilt produces the question, what if they could treat us as we have treated them?

3   That is not our goal. But we do want to change the economic system to one more based on merit. In Women's Lib Utopia, there will be free access to good jobs—and decent pay for the bad ones women have been performing all along, including housework. Increased skilled labor might lead to a four-hour workday, and higher wages would encourage further mechanization of repetitive jobs now kept alive by cheap labor.

4   With women as half the country's elected representatives, and a woman President once in a while, the country's *machismo* problems would be greatly reduced. The old-fashioned idea that manhood depends on violence and victory is, after all, an important part of our troubles in the streets, and in Viet Nam. I'm not saying that women leaders would eliminate violence. We are not more moral than men; we are only uncorrupted by power so far. When we do acquire power, we might turn out to have an equal impulse toward aggression. Even now, Margaret Mead believes that women fight less often but more fiercely than men, because women are not taught the rules of the war game and fight only when cornered. But for the next 50 years or so, women in politics will be very valuable by tempering the idea of manhood into something less aggressive and better suited to this crowded, post-atomic planet. Consumer protection and children's rights, for instance, might get more legislative attention.

5   Men will have to give up ruling-class privileges, but in return they will no longer be the only ones to support the family, get drafted, bear the strain of power and responsibility. Freud to the contrary, anatomy is not destiny, at least not for more than nine months at a time. In Israel, women are drafted, and some have gone to war. In England, more men type and run switchboards. In India and Israel, a woman rules. In Sweden, both parents take care of the children. In this country, come Utopia, men and women won't reverse roles; they will be free to choose according to individual talents and preferences.

6   If role reform sounds sexually unsettling, think how it will change the sexual hypocrisy we have now. No more sex arranged on the barter system, with women pretending interest, and men never sure whether they are loved for themselves or for the security few women can get any other way. (Married or not, for sexual reasons or social ones, most women still find it second nature to Uncle-Tom.) No more men who are encouraged to spend a lifetime living with inferiors; with housekeepers, or dependent creatures who are still children. No more domineering wives, emasculating women, and "Jewish mothers," all of whom are simply human beings with all their normal ambition and drive confined to the home. No more unequal partnerships that eventually doom love and sex.

7   In order to produce that kind of confidence and individuality, child rearing will train according to talent. Little girls will no longer be surrounded by air-tight, self-fulfilling prophecies of natural passivity, lack of ambition and objectivity, inability to exercise power, and dexterity (so long as special aptitude for jobs requiring patience and dexterity is confined to poorly paid jobs; brain surgery is for males).

8   Schools and universities will help to break down traditional sex roles, even when parents will not. Half the teachers will be men, a rarity now at preschool and elementary levels; girls will not necessarily serve cookies or boys hoist up the flag. Athletic teams will be picked only by strength and skill. Sexually segregated courses like auto mechanics and home economics will be taken by boys and girls together. New courses in sexual politics will explore female subjugation as the model for political oppression, and women's history will be an academic staple, along with black history, at least until the white-male-oriented textbooks are integrated and rewritten.

9   As for the American child's classic problem—too much mother, too little father—that would be cured by an equalization of parental responsibility. Free nurseries, school lunches, family cafeterias built into every housing complex, service companies that will do household cleaning chores in a regular, businesslike way, and more responsibility by the entire community for the children: all these will make it possible for both mother and father to work, and to have equal leisure time with the children at home. For parents of very young children, however, a special job category, created by government and unions, would allow such parents a shorter workday.

10   The revolution would not take away the option of being a housewife. A woman who prefers to be her husband's housekeeper and/or hostess would receive a percentage of his pay determined by the domestic relations courts. If divorced, she might be eligible for a pension fund, and for a job-training

allowance. Or a divorce could be treated the same way that the dissolution of a business partnership is now.

11   If these proposals seem farfetched, consider Sweden, where most of them are already in effect. Sweden is not yet a working Women's Lib model; most of the role-reform programs began less than a decade ago, and are just beginning to take hold. But that country is so far ahead of us in recognizing the problem that Swedish statements on sex and equality sound like bulletins from the moon.

12   Our marriage laws, for instance, are so reactionary that Women's Lib groups want couples to take a compulsory written exam on the law, as for a driver's license, before going through with the wedding. A man has alimony and wifely debts to worry about, but a woman may lose so many of her civil rights that in the U.S. now, in important legal ways, she becomes a child again. In some states, she cannot sign credit agreements, use her maiden name, incorporate a business, or establish a legal residence of her own. Being a wife, according to most social and legal definitions, is still a 19th century thing.

13   Assuming, however, that these blatantly sexist laws are abolished or reformed, that job discrimination is forbidden, that parents share financial responsibility for each other and the children, and that sexual relationships become partnerships of equal adults (some pretty big assumptions), then marriage will probably go right on. Men and women are, after all, physically complementary. When society stops encouraging men to be exploiters and women to be parasites, they may turn out to be more complementary in emotion as well. Women's Lib is not trying to destroy the American family. A look at the statistics on divorce—plus the way in which old people are farmed out with strangers and young people flee the home—shows the destruction that has already been done. Liberated women are just trying to point out the disaster, and build compassionate and practical alternatives from the ruins.

14   What will exist is a variety of alternative lifestyles. Since the population explosion dictates that childbearing be kept to a minimum, parents-and-children will be only one of many "families": couples, age groups, working groups, mixed communes, blood-related clans, class groups, creative groups. Single women will have the right to stay single without ridicule, without the attitudes now betrayed by "spinster" and "bachelor." Lesbians or homosexuals will no longer be denied legally binding marriages, complete with mutual-support agreements and inheritance rights. Paradoxically, the number of homosexuals may get smaller. With fewer overpossessive mothers and fewer fathers who hold up an impossibly cruel or perfectionist idea of manhood, boys will be less likely to be denied or reject their identity as males.

15   Changes that now seem small may get bigger:

Men's Lib

Men now suffer from more diseases due to stress, heart attacks, ulcers, a higher suicidal rate, greater difficulty living alone, less adaptability to change and, in general, a shorter life span than women. There is some scientific evidence that what produces physical problems is not work itself, but the inability to choose which work, and how much. With women bearing half the financial responsibility, and with the idea of "masculine" jobs gone, men might well feel freer and live longer.

Religion

Protestant women are already becoming ordained ministers; radical nuns are carrying out liturgical functions that were once the exclusive property of priests; Jewish women are rewriting prayers—particularly those that Orthodox Jews recite every morning thanking God they are not female. In the future, the church will become an area of equal participation by women. This means, of course, that organized religion will have to give up one of its great historical weapons: sexual repression. In most structured faiths, from Hinduism through Roman Catholicism, the status of women went down as the position of priests ascended. Male clergy implied, if they did not teach, that women were unclean, unworthy and sources of ungodly temptation, in order to remove them as rivals for the emotional forces of men. Full participation of women in ecclesiastical life might involve certain changes in theology, such as, for instance, a radical redefinition of sin.

Literary Problems

Revised sex roles will outdate more children's books than civil rights ever did. Only a few children had the problem of a *Little Black Sambo,* but most have the male-female stereotypes of "Dick and Jane." A boomlet of children's books about mothers who work has already begun, and liberated parents and editors are beginning to pressure for change in the textbook industry. Fiction writing will change more gradually, but romantic novels with wilting heroines and swashbuckling heroes will be reduced to historical value. Or perhaps to the sado-masochist trade. *(Marjorie Morningstar,* a romantic novel that took the '50s by storm, has already begun to seem as unreal as its '20s predecessor, *The Shiek.)* As for the literary plots that turn on forced marriages or horrific abortions, they will seem as dated as Prohibition stories. Free legal abortions and free birth control will force writers to give up pregnancy as the *deus ex machina.*

Manners and Fashion

Dress will be more androgynous, with class symbols becoming more important than sexual ones. Pro- or anti-Establishment styles may already be more vital than who is wearing them. Hardhats are just as likely to rough up antiwar girls as antiwar men in the street, and police understand that women are just as likely to be pushers or bombers. Dances haven't required that one partner lead the other for years, anyway. Chivalry will transfer itself to those who need it, or deserve respect: old people, admired people, anyone with an armload of packages. Women with normal work identities will be less likely to attach their whole sense of self to youth and appearance; thus there will be fewer nervous breakdowns when the first wrinkles appear. Lighting cigarettes and other treasured niceties will become gestures of mutual affection. "I like to be helped on with my coat," says one Women's Lib worker, "but not if it costs me $2,000 a year in salary."

16 For those with nostalgia for a simple past, here is a word of comfort. Anthropologist Geoffrey Gorer studied the few peaceful human tribes and discovered one common characteristic: sex roles were not polarized. Differences of dress and occupation were at a minimum. Society, in other words, was not using sexual blackmail as a way of getting women to do cheap labor, or men to be aggressive.

17 Thus Women's Lib may achieve a more peaceful society on the way toward its other goals. That is why the Swedish government considers reform to bring about greater equality in the sex roles one of its most important concerns. As Prime Minister Olof Palme explained in a widely ignored speech delivered in Washington this spring: "It is *human beings* we will emancipate. In Sweden today, if a politician should declare that the woman ought to have a different role from man's, he would be regarded as something from the Stone Age." In other words, the most radical goal of the movement is egalitarianism.

18 If Women's Lib wins, perhaps we all do.

VOCABULARY

machismo 4	sado-masochist 15
Margaret Mead 4	*deus ex machina* 15
Uncle-Tom 6	androgynous 15
emasculating 6	polarized 16
reactionary 12	egalitarianism 17

QUESTIONS

1. What is Steinem's purpose in writing? What is her thesis? Is it stated or implied?

2. What is the function of ¶s 1 and 2? What attitudes does Steinem expect at least some of her anticipated audience to hold?

3. What political changes does Steinem anticipate? What changes in marriage and family relationships? in job selection? in religious institutions and dress? in men's lives?

4. Steinem anticipates the argument of anti-feminists that the feminist movement will destroy the institution of marriage. What are her reasons for asserting that marriage will continue? Do you agree? Do you have any evidence to support your opinion?

5. How concrete and specific is Steinem's picture of the future? Are her proposals adequately supported with evidence? Given her purpose in writing, is it reasonable to expect full documentation?

6. Look at Steinem's style. Are her sentences usually long or short? simple or complex? Is her word choice generally simple, sophisticated, slangy?

7. What is the tone of the essay? Does the tone seem appropriate for her audience, purpose, and subject?

Isaac Asimov (b. 1920) was born in Russia and is now a naturalized American citizen. He is well-known as a scholar and writer in physics, biochemistry, and genetics, and as a science-fiction novelist. Asimov is currently Associate Professor of Biochemistry at Boston University School of Medicine. This essay appeared in Natural History *magazine, April 1975.*

How Easy to See the Future!
Isaac Asimov

1   If we were to glance over the thousands of years of history of *Homo sapiens,* we might make the following generalizations: As time passed, the human way of life continually changed. The change has generally resulted from a technological advance—a new tool, a new technique, a new energy source. As each technological advance broadened the base of human technological capacity, further advances became more frequent and were made in a greater number of directions, so that the rate of change has, in the course of history, continually increased.

2   Until modern times, the rate of change was so slow that the process was unnoticeable in the course of any one person's lifetime. Mankind had the illusion, therefore, that change did not take place. When, in the face of that illusion, a change had clearly taken place, the response was to view it as something that should not have happened—as something that represented a degeneration from the "good old days."

3   The steadily increasing rate of change reached the stage, about 1800, of becoming clearly visible to many thoughtful individuals. The Industrial Revolution was under way, and those affected by it could detect change in the course of their own lifetimes.

4   For the first time, people grew to understand that not only was change taking place but that it would continue to take place after their death. It meant there would be changes still greater than a person could live to see, changes that he would never see. This gave rise to a new curiosity—perhaps the first

really new curiosity in historic times—that of wondering what life on earth would be like after one was no longer alive. The literary response to that new curiosity was what we call science fiction. Science fiction can be defined as that branch of literature that deals with the reactions of human beings to changes in science and technology.

5   The reference can be to *any* changes, of course, and the science fiction writer chooses those that provide him with a dramatic situation out of which he can weave an exciting plot. There is usually no deliberate attempt to predict what will actually happen, but a science fiction writer is a creature of his times, and in trying to imagine a change in science and technology, he is quite likely to base it on those changes he already sees in embryo.

6   Often this means an extrapolation of the present, an extrapolation that is so clear and obvious as to forecast something that is inevitable. When this happens, the science fiction writer does make a successful prediction. Usually, this astonishes almost everyone, for mankind generally, even today, takes it for granted that things do not change.

7   Here is an example. As the twentieth century opened, oil was coming into use as a source of energy and, thanks to the internal-combustion engine, was beginning to gain on coal. Now oil, like coal, is a fossil fuel. Even if our entire planet were solid coal and oil, there is only so much of it in the ground—and new supplies are being formed at an entirely trivial rate. If oil and coal are being constantly burned, then someday the natural supply in the ground will be used up. That is not a matter of argument at all; it is inevitable. The only question is when.

8   Mankind, generally, assuming that since there is oil in the ground today, there will be oil in the ground forever (the doctrine of no change) is not concerned with the matter. The science fiction writer, however, avidly seeking out change as a matter of artistic necessity, takes up the possibility of an end of our fossil fuel supply. It then becomes possible for a writer to say: "Coal is the key to metallurgy and oil to transit. When they are done we shall either have built up such a fabric of apparatus, knowledge, and social organization that we shall be able to manage without them . . . or we shall have travelled a long way down the slopes of waste towards extinction. . . . Today, in getting, in distribution, in use, we waste enormously. . . . As we sit there all the world is wasting fuel . . . fantastically."

9   That certainly sounds familiar in this year of 1975, but it wasn't said in 1975. The writer was H. G. Wells, the book was *Secret Places of the Heart* (not even science fiction, strictly speaking), and the year of publication was 1921.

10   Imagine Wells foreseeing the energy crunch half a century before it happened! Well, don't waste your admiration. He saw the obvious and foresaw the inevitable. What is really amazing and frustrating is mankind's habit of *refusing* to see the obvious and inevitable, until it is there, and then muttering about unforeseen catastrophes.

11   The science fiction writer Laurence Manning wrote a story called *The Man Who Awoke* about a man who invented a potion that would place him

in suspended animation for three thousand years. He would then awake and see the world of the future. When he carried this through, he found the world of three thousand years hence was energy poor. They explained to him that this was a result of what they called the Age of Waste. They said, "But for what should we thank the humans of three thousand years ago? For exhausting the coal supplies of the world? For leaving us no petroleum for our chemical factories? For destroying the forests on whole mountain ranges and letting the soil erode into the valleys?"

12   The story appeared in the March, 1933, issue of *Wonder Stories*, and I read it when it appeared and I had just turned thirteen. Science fiction, everyone said, was "escape literature." Reading it was disgraceful, for it meant turning away from the hard realities of life to a never-never fantasy land of the impossible.

13   But who lived in a never-never fantasy land? I, who began worrying about our oil and coal in 1933 as a result of Manning's story? Or the rest of mankind, who as always, were convinced that tomorrow would be exactly like today and who waited for the day when the long lines at the gas station came before deciding that there might some day be long lines at the gas station.

14   Yes, science fiction can have its fantasy aspects. I have written stories about galactic empires, about faster-than-light speeds, about intelligent robots that eventually became God, about time-travel. I don't consider that any of these have predictive value; they weren't intended for that. I was just trying to write entertaining stories about the might-be, not at all necessarily about the would-be.

15   But sometimes . . .

16   In the July, 1939, issue of *Astounding Science Fiction,* there appeared one of my stories. It was called "Trends," and it dealt with the first flight to the moon (silly escape literature, of course). I got all the details childishly and ludicrously wrong, including having it happen ten years later than it really did happen.

17   Even at the age of nineteen, however, I was aware that all those technological advances in the past that had significantly ruffled the current of human custom had been attacked by important segments of the population, who, for one reason or another, found it difficult to accept change. It occurred to me, then, that this would surely be true of the development of space flight as well. My story "Trends," therefore, dealt primarily with opposition to space flight. It was, as far as I know, the first description of ideological opposition to mankind's advance into space. Until then, all those who had looked forward to the new development had either ignored the reaction of humanity or had assumed it would be favorable. When there did indeed arise ideological opposition, in the late 1960s, I found myself accepting credit as a seer, when I had merely foreseen the inevitable.

18   Once uranium fission was discovered, a nuclear bomb was an easy extrapolation, and through the years of World War II, the science fiction

stories dealing with nuclear bombs nestled as thickly as snowflakes in the pages of the science fiction magazines. One of them, "Deadline," by Cleve Cartmill, which appeared in the March, 1944, issue of *Astounding Science Fiction,* came so close to the actual facts that both the author and the editor of the magazine were interviewed by intelligence agents. But when the bomb dropped on Hiroshima, the world was astonished.

19 More remarkable still was a story—"Solution Unsatisfactory," by Anson Macdonald (a pseudonym of Robert A. Heinlein)—that appeared in the May, 1941, issue of *Astounding Science Fiction.* Written and published before Pearl Harbor, Heinlein described a vast gathering of scientists called together to develop a nuclear weapon. The weapon was invented, used to end World War II, and a nuclear stalemate developed thereafter.

20 It all made sense, you see, in the light of what was already known in 1940, but who else foresaw it but science fiction writers?

21 Today we face the most predictable of all disasters, that of the consequences of over-population. The population of the earth is now 4,000,000,000, and that population is increasing at the rate of 2 percent a year, which means that each day there are 220,000 more mouths to feed. In the course of the last thirty years, during which population has risen by 1,500,000,000, the food supply has managed to keep up, thanks to the spreading use of farm machinery and irrigation pumps, of fertilizers and pesticides, and of an extraordinary run of good weather.

22 But now weather is taking a turn for the worse, and the energy shortage is slowing the machinery and raising the price of fertilizers and pesticides. The food supply will not be increasing any more; it will probably go down—and with the population going up at a rate of 220,000 per day, isn't it the easiest and surest thing in the world to predict great and spreading famines? Yet whenever I do, I am greeted with amused disbelief. After all, people look around and see no famine today, so why should there be famine tomorrow?

23 Now let's consider this: If science fiction writers foresee the problems and catastrophes that will come to face mankind, do they also foresee solutions? Not necessarily. Science fiction writers foresee the inevitable, and although problems and catastrophes may be inevitable, solutions are not. Writers are all too often forced to pull solutions out of thin and implausible air—or leave the matter with no solution and end the story in dramatic disaster.

24 The best way to defeat catastrophe is to take action to prevent it long before it happens: to conserve the oil and work for alternate sources of energy in time; to consider the international effects of the nuclear bomb before it ever is invented; to lower the birthrate before the population grows dangerously high.

25 To do that one must foresee the catastrophe in time, but who listens to those who do the foreseeing? "Escape literature," says the world and turns away.

VOCABULARY

Homo sapiens 1   galactic 14
embryo 5   ideological 17
extrapolation 6   fission 18
metallurgy 8   pseudonym 19

QUESTIONS

1. How would you characterize Asimov's anticipated audience?

2. Does Asimov assume that his readers have read the science fiction works he mentions?

3. What is the purpose of Asimov's introduction?

4. Is Asimov's purpose in the essay to test out his definition of science fiction? Is that his only purpose?

5. What is Asimov's thesis? Where is it stated?

6. How fully has the thesis been proven? Examine the evidence.

7. Why are the dates of the works often mentioned after they are summarized?

8. What is the purpose of ¶23?

9. What is his tone? How does he create it?

Philip Wylie (1902-71), an American novelist, essayist, and short story writer, is best-known as the author of A Generation of Vipers *(1942). The following essay was published in* The Atlantic Monthly, *April 1954.*

Science Has Spoiled My Supper
Philip Wylie

1   I am a fan for Science. My education is scientific and I have, in one field, contributed a monograph to a scientific journal. Science, to my mind, is applied honesty, the one reliable means we have to find out truth. That is why, when error is committed in the name of Science, I feel the way a man would if his favorite uncle had taken to drink.

2   Over the years, I have come to feel that way about what science has done to food. I agree that America can set as good a table as any nation in the world. I agree that our food is nutritious and that the diet of most of us is

well-balanced. What America eats is handsomely packaged; it is usually clean and pure; it is excellently preserved. The only trouble with it is this: year by year it grows less good to eat. It appeals increasingly to the eye. But who eats with his eyes? Almost everything used to taste better when I was a kid. For quite a long time I thought that observation was merely another index of advancing age. But some years ago I married a girl whose mother is an expert cook of the kind called "old-fashioned." This gifted woman's daughter (my wife) was taught her mother's venerable skills. The mother lives in the country and still plants an old-fashioned garden. She still buys dairy products from the neighbors and, insofar as possible, she uses the same materials her mother and grandmother did—to prepare meals that are superior. They are just as good, in this Year of Grace, as I recall them from my courtship. After eating for a while at the table of my mother-in-law, it is sad to go back to eating with my friends—even the alleged "good cooks" among them. And it is a gruesome experience to have meals at the best big-city restaurants.

3   Take cheese, for instance. Here and there, in big cities, small stores and delicatessens specialize in cheese. At such places, one can buy at least some of the first-rate cheeses that we used to eat—such as those we had with pie and in macaroni. The latter were sharp but not too sharp. They were a little crumbly. We called them American cheeses, or even rat cheese; actually, they were Cheddars. Long ago, this cheese began to be supplanted by a material called "cheese foods." Some cheese foods and "processed" cheese are fairly edible; but not one comes within miles of the old kinds—for flavor.

4   A grocer used to be very fussy about his cheese. Cheddar was made and sold by hundreds of little factories. Representatives of the factories had particular customers, and cheese was prepared by hand to suit the grocers, who knew precisely what their patrons wanted in rat cheese, pie cheese, American and other cheeses. Some like them sharper; some like them yellower; some liked anise seeds in cheese, or caraway.

5   What happened? Science—or what is called science—stepped in. The old-fashioned cheeses didn't ship well enough. They crumbled, became moldy, dried out. "Scientific" tests disclosed that a great majority of the people will buy a less-good-tasting cheese if that's all they can get. "Scientific marketing" then took effect. Its motto is "Give the people the least quality they'll stand for." In food, as in many other things, the "scientific marketers" regard quality as secondary so long as they can sell most persons anyhow; what they are after is "durability" or "shippability."

6   It is not possible to make the very best cheese in vast quantities at a low average cost. "Scientific sampling" got in its statistically nasty work. It was found that the largest number of people will buy something that is bland and rather tasteless. Those who prefer a product of a pronounced and individualistic flavor have a variety of preferences. Nobody is altogether pleased by bland foodstuff, in other words; but nobody is very violently put off. The result is that a "reason" has been found for turning out zillions of packages of something that will "do" for nearly all and isn't even imagined to be superlatively good by a single soul!

7   Economics entered. It is possible to turn out in quantity a bland, impersonal, practically imperishable substance more or less resembling, say, cheese—at lower cost than cheese. Chain groceries shut out the independent stores and "standardization" became a principal means of cutting costs.

8   Imitations also came into the cheese business. There are American duplications of most of the celebrated European cheeses, mass-produced and cheaper by far than the imports. They would cause European food-lovers to gag or guffaw—but generally the imitations are all that's available in the supermarkets. People buy them and eat them.

9   Perhaps you don't like cheese—so the fact that decent cheese is hardly ever served in America any more, or used in cooking, doesn't matter to you. Well, take bread. There has been (and still is) something of a hullabaloo about bread. In fact, in the last few years, a few big bakeries have taken to making a fairly good imitation of real bread. It costs much more than what is nowadays called bread, but it is edible. Most persons, however, now eat as "bread" a substance so full of chemicals and so barren of cereals that it approaches a synthetic.

10   Most bakers are interested mainly in how a loaf of bread looks. They are concerned with how little stuff they can put in it—to get how much money. They are deeply interested in using chemicals that will keep the bread from molding, make it seem "fresh" for the longest possible time, and so render it marketable and shippable. They have been at this monkeyshine for a generation. Today a loaf of "bread" looks deceptively real; but it is made from heaven knows what and it resembles, as food, a solidified bubble bath. Some months ago I bought a loaf of the stuff and, experimentally, began pressing it together, like an accordion. With a little effort, I squeezed the whole loaf to a length of about one inch!

11   Yesterday, at the home of my mother-in-law, I ate with country-churned butter and home-canned wild strawberry jam several slices of actual bread, the same thing we used to have every day at home. People who have eaten actual bread will know what I mean. They will know that the material commonly called bread is not even related to real bread, except in name.

12   For years, I couldn't figure out what had happened to vegetables. I knew, of course, that most vegetables, to be enjoyed in their full deliciousness, must be picked fresh and cooked at once. I knew that vegetables cannot be over-cooked and remain even edible, in the best sense. They cannot stand on the stove. That set of facts makes it impossible, of course, for any American restaurant—or, indeed, any city-dweller separated from supply by more than a few hours—to have decent fresh vegetables. The Parisians managed by getting their vegetables picked at dawn and rushed in farmers' carts to market, where no middleman or marketman delays produce on its way to the pot.

13   Our vegetables, however, come to us through a long chain of command. There are merchants of several sorts—wholesalers before the retailers, commission men, and so on—with the result that what were once edible products become, in transit, mere wilted leaves and withered tubers.

14   Homes and restaurants do what they can with this stuff—which my mother-in-law would discard on the spot. I have long thought that the famed

blindfold test for cigarettes should be applied to city vegetables. For I am sure that if you puréed them and ate them blindfolded, you couldn't tell the beans from the peas, the turnips from the squash, the Brussels sprouts from the broccoli.

15 It is only lately that I have found how much science has had to do with this reduction of noble victuals to pottage. Here the science of genetics is involved. Agronomists and the like have taken to breeding all sorts of vegetables and fruits—changing their original nature. This sounds wonderful and often is insane. For the scientists have not as a rule taken any interest whatsoever in the taste of the things they've tampered with!

16 What they've done is to develop "improved" strains of things for every purpose but eating. They work out, say, peas that will ripen all at once. The farmer can then harvest his peas and thresh them and be done with them. It is extremely profitable because it is efficient. What matter if such peas taste like boiled paper wads?

17 Geneticists have gone crazy over such "opportunities." They've developed string beans that are straight instead of curved, and all one length. This makes them easier to pack in cans, even if, when eating them, you can't tell them from tender string. Ripening time and identity of size and shape are, nowadays, more important in carrots than the fact that they taste like carrots. Personally, I don't care if they hybridize onions till they are big as your head and come up through the snow; but, in doing so, they are producing onions that only vaguely and feebly remind you of onions. We are getting some varieties, in fact, that have less flavor than the water off last week's leeks. Yet, if people don't eat onions because they taste like onions, what in the name of Luther Burbank do they eat them for?

18 The women's magazines are about one third dedicated to clothes, one third to mild comment on sex, and the other third to recipes and pictures of handsome salads, desserts, and main courses. "Institutes" exist to experiment and tell housewives how to cook attractive meals and how to turn leftovers into works of art. The food thus pictured looks like famous paintings of still life. The only trouble is it's tasteless. It leaves appetite unquenched and merely serves to stave off famine.

19 I wonder if this blandness of our diet doesn't explain why so many of us are overweight and even dangerously so. When things had flavor, we knew what we were eating all the while—and it satisfied us. A teaspoonful of my mother-in-law's wild strawberry jam will not just provide a gastronome's ecstasy: it will entirely satisfy your jam desire. But, of the average tinned or glass-packed strawberry jam, you need half a cupful to get the idea of what you're eating. A slice of my mother-in-law's apple pie will satiate you far better than a whole baker pie.

20 That thought is worthy of investigation—of genuine scientific investigation. It is merely a hypothesis, so far, and my own. But people—and their ancestors—have been eating according to flavor for upwards of a billion years. The need to satisfy the sense of taste may be innate and important. When food is merely a pretty cascade of viands, with the texture of boiled cardboard and the flavor of library paste, it may be the instinct of *genus homo*

to go on eating in the unconscious hope of finally satisfying the ageless craving of the frustrated taste buds. In the days when good-tasting food was the rule in the American home, obesity wasn't such a national curse.

21   How can you feel you've eaten if you haven't tasted, and fully enjoyed tasting? Why (since science is ever so ready to answer the beck and call of mankind) don't people who want to reduce merely give up eating and get the nourishment they must have in measured doses shot into their arms at hospitals? One ready answer to that question suggests that my theory of overeating is sound: people like to taste! In eating, they try to satisfy that like.

22   The scientific war against deliciousness has been stepped up enormously in the last decade. Some infernal genius found a way to make biscuit batter keep. Housewives began to buy this premixed stuff. It saved work, of course. But any normally intelligent person can learn, in a short period, how to prepare superb baking powder biscuits. I can make better biscuits, myself, than can be made from patent batters. Yet soon after this fiasco became an American staple, it was discovered that a half-baked substitute for all sorts of breads, pastries, rolls, and the like could be mass-manufactured, frozen—and sold for polishing off in the home oven. None of these two-stage creations is as good as even a fair sample of the thing it imitates. A man of taste, who had eaten one of my wife's cinnamon buns, might use the premixed sort to throw at starlings—but not to eat! Cake mixes, too, come ready-prepared—like cement and not much better-tasting compared with true cake.

23   It is, however, "deep-freezing" that has really rung down the curtain on American cookery. Nothing is improved by the process. I have yet to taste a deep-frozen victual that measures up, in flavor, to the fresh, unfrosted original. And most foods, cooked or uncooked, are destroyed in the deep freeze for all people of sense and sensibility. Vegetables with crisp and crackling texture emerge as mush, slippery and stringy as hair nets simmered in Vaseline. The essential oils that make peas peas—and cabbage cabbage—must undergo fission and fusion in freezers. Anyhow, they vanish. Some meats turn to leather. Others to wood pulp. Everything, pretty much, tastes like the mosses of tundra, dug up in midwinter. Even the appearance changes, oftentimes. Handsome comestibles you put down in the summer come out looking very much like the corpses of wooly mammoths recovered from the last Ice Age.

24   Of course, all this scientific "food handling" tends to save money. It certainly preserves food longer. It reduces work at home. But these facts, and especially the last, imply that the first purpose of living is to avoid work—at home, anyhow.

25   Without thinking, we are making an important confession about ourselves as a nation. We are abandoning quality—even, to some extent, the quality of people. The "best" is becoming too good for us. We are suckling ourselves on machine-made mediocrity. It is bad for our souls, our minds, and our digestion. It is the way our wiser and calmer forebears fed, not people, but hogs: as much as possible and as fast as possible, with no standard of quality.

26   The Germans say, "*Mann ist was er isst*—Man is what he eats." If this be true, the people of the U.S.A. are well on their way to becoming a faceless

mob of mediocrities, of robots. And if we apply to other attributes the criteria we apply these days to appetite, that is what would happen! We would not want bright children any more; we'd merely want them to look bright—and get through school fast. We wouldn't be interested in beautiful women—just a good paint job. And we'd be opposed to the most precious quality of man: his individuality, his differentness from the mob.

27 There are some people—sociologists and psychologists among them—who say that is exactly what we Americans are doing, are becoming. Mass man, they say, is on the increase. Conformity, standardization, similarity—all on a cheap and vulgar level—are replacing the great American ideas of colorful liberty and dignified individualism. If this is so, the process may well begin, like most human behavior, in the home—in those homes where a good meal has been replaced by some-thing-to-eat-in-a-hurry. By something not very good to eat, prepared by a mother without very much to do, for a family that doesn't feel it amounts to much anyhow.

28 I call, here, for rebellion.

VOCABULARY

monograph 1		Luther Burbank 17
guffaw 8		satiate 19
tubers 13		viands 20
victuals 15		*genus homo* 20
pottage 15		fiasco 22
agronomists 15		tundra 23
hybridize 17		comestibles 23

QUESTIONS

1. What is Wylie's thesis?

2. What is the tone of the essay? What techniques create this tone?

3. Why does Wylie discuss his wife and mother-in-law?

4. Wylie makes some sweeping generalizations: "The 'scientific market-ers' regard quality as secondary as long as they can sell most persons," "Most bakers are interested mainly in how a loaf of bread looks," "The scientists have not as a rule taken any interest whatsoever in the taste of the things they've tampered with!" For what purpose does he make these assertions? Are they justified?

5. What is the purpose of the cause-and-effect discussion in ¶19-21?

6. What is effective about the descriptions of frozen foods in ¶23?

7. What is the effect of ¶s 26-28?

MY COUNTRY, RIGHT OR WRONG?

In the following five essays writers examine their feelings about America. When you have finished reading all five, answer the following questions:

1. Which essay appeals most to you? In what way does its appeal depend on your beliefs and biases? What else influences you?

2. How does the style and tone of each writer reflect his purpose and audience? Are the styles and tones different?

3. Is each argument well-reasoned and logical? Must each be logical to be effective, given the writer's purpose and audience?

Martin Luther King (1929-68), Baptist minister, civil rights leader dedicated to nonviolence, president of the Southern Christian Leadership Conference, and Nobel Peace Prize winner in 1964, was assassinated in 1968. He was an important influence in the August 1963 March on Washington, where he delivered his speech "I Have a Dream" from the steps of the Lincoln Memorial.

I Have a Dream
Martin Luther King, Jr.

1   Five score years ago, a great American, in whose symbolic shadow we stand, signed the Emancipation Proclamation. This momentous decree came as a great beacon light of hope to millions of Negro slaves who had been seared in the flames of withering injustice. It came as a joyous daybreak to end the long night of captivity.

2   But one hundred years later, we must face the tragic fact that the Negro is still not free. One hundred years later, the life of the Negro is still sadly crippled by the manacles of segregation and the chains of discrimination. One hundred years later, the Negro lives on a lonely island of poverty in the midst of a vast ocean of material prosperity. One hundred years later, the Negro is still languishing in the corners of American society and finds himself an exile in his own land. So we have come here today to dramatize an appalling condition.

3   In a sense we have come to our nation's capital to cash a check. When the architects of our republic wrote the magnificent words of the Constitution and the Declaration of Independence, they were signing a promissory note to which every American was to fall heir. This note was a promise that all men would be guaranteed the unalienable rights of life, liberty, and the pursuit of happiness.

4   It is obvious today that America has defaulted on this promissory note

insofar as her citizens of color are concerned. Instead of honoring this sacred obligation, America has given the Negro people a bad check; a check which has come back marked "insufficient funds." But we refuse to believe that the bank of justice is bankrupt. We refuse to believe that there are insufficient funds in the great vaults of opportunity of this nation. So we have come to cash this check—a check that will give us upon demand the riches of freedom and the security of justice. We have also come to this hallowed spot to remind America of the fierce urgency of *now*. This is not time to engage in the luxury of cooling off or to take the tranquilizing drug of gradualism. *Now* is the time to make real the promises of Democracy. *Now* is the time to rise from the dark and desolate valley of segregation to the sunlit path of racial justice. *Now* is the time to open the doors of opportunity to all of God's children. *Now* is the time to lift our nation from the quicksands of racial injustice to the solid rock of brotherhood.

5   It would be fatal for the nation to overlook the urgency of the moment and to underestimate the determination of the Negro. This sweltering summer of the Negro's legitimate discontent will not pass until there is an invigorating autumn of freedom and equality. 1963 is not an end, but a beginning. Those who hope that the Negro needed to blow off steam and will now be content will have a rude awakening if the nation returns to business as usual. There will be neither rest nor tranquility in America until the Negro is granted his citizenship rights. The whirlwinds of revolt will continue to shake the foundations of our nation until the bright day of justice emerges.

6   But there is something I must say to my people who stand on the warm threshold which leads into the palace of justice. In the process of gaining our rightful place we must not be guilty of wrongful deeds. Let us not seek to satisfy our thirst for freedom by drinking from the cup of bitterness and hatred. We must forever conduct our struggle on the high plane of dignity and discipline. We must not allow our creative protest to degenerate into physical violence. Again and again we must rise to the majestic heights of meeting physical force with soul force. The marvelous new militancy which has engulfed the Negro community must not lead us to a distrust of all white people, for many of our white brothers, as evidenced by their presence here today, have come to realize that their destiny is tied up with our destiny and their freedom is inextricably bound to our freedom. We cannot walk alone.

7   And as we walk, we must make the pledge that we shall march ahead. We cannot turn back. There are those who are asking the devotees of civil rights, "When will you be satisfied?" We can never be satisfied as long as the Negro is the victim of the unspeakable horrors of police brutality. We can never be satisfied as long as our bodies, heavy with the fatigue of travel, cannot gain lodging in the motels of the highways and the hotels of the cities. We cannot be satisfied as long as the Negro's basic mobility is from a smaller ghetto to a larger one. We can never be satisfied as long as a Negro in Mississippi cannot vote and a Negro in New York believes he has nothing for which to vote. No, no, we are not satisfied, and we will not be satisfied until justice rolls down like waters and righteousness like a mighty stream.

8   I am not unmindful that some of you have come here out of great trials and tribulations. Some of you have come fresh from narrow jail cells. Some of you have come from areas where your quest for freedom left you battered by the storms of persecution and staggered by the winds of police brutality. You have been the veterans of creative suffering. Continue to work with the faith that unearned suffering is redemptive.

9   Go back to Mississippi, go back to Alabama, go back to South Carolina, go back to Georgia, go back to Louisiana, go back to the slums and ghettoes of our northern cities, knowing that somehow this situation can and will be changed. Let us not wallow in the valley of despair.

10   I say to you today, my friends, that in spite of the difficulties and frustrations of the moment I still have a dream. It is a dream deeply rooted in the American dream.

11   I have a dream that one day this nation will rise up and live out the true meaning of its creed: "We hold these truths to be self-evident, that all men are created equal."

12   I have a dream that one day on the red hills of Georgia the sons of former slaves and the sons of former slaveowners will be able to sit down together at the table of brotherhood.

13   I have a dream that the state of Mississippi, a desert state sweltering with the heat of injustice and oppression, will be transformed into an oasis of freedom and justice.

14   I have a dream that my four little children will one day live in a nation where they will not be judged by the color of their skin but by the content of their character.

15   I have a dream today.

16   I have a dream that the state of Alabama, whose governor's lips are presently dripping with the words of interposition and nullification, will be transformed into a situation where little black boys and black girls will be able to join hands with little white boys and white girls and walk together as sisters and brothers.

17   I have a dream today.

18   I have a dream that one day every valley shall be exalted, every hill and mountain shall be made low, the rough places will be made plain, and the crooked places will be made straight, and the glory of the Lord shall be revealed, and all flesh shall see it together.

19   This is our hope. This is the faith with which I return to the South. With this faith we will be able to hew out of the mountain of despair a stone of hope. With this faith we will be able to transform the jangling discords of our nation into a beautiful symphony of brotherhood. With this faith we will be able to work together, to pray together, to struggle together, to go to jail together, to stand up for freedom together, knowing that we will be free one day.

20   This will be the day when all of God's children will be able to sing with new meaning,

My country, tis of thee
Sweet land of liberty,
  Of thee I sing:
Land where my fathers died,
Land of the pilgrims' pride,
From every mountainside
  Let freedom ring.

21   And if America is to be a great nation this must become true. So let freedom ring from the prodigious hilltops of New Hampshire. Let freedom ring from the mighty mountains of New York. Let freedom ring from the heightening Alleghenies of Pennsylvania!

22   Let freedom ring from the snowcapped Rockies of Colorado!

23   Let freedom ring from the curvacious peaks of California!

24   But not only that; let freedom ring from Stone Mountain of Georgia!

25   Let freedom ring from Lookout Mountain of Tennessee!

26   Let freedom ring from every hill and molehill of Mississippi. From every mountainside, let freedom ring.

27   When we let freedom ring, when we let it ring from every village and every hamlet, from every state and every city, we will be able to speed up that day when all of God's children, black men and white men, Jews and Gentiles, Protestants and Catholics, will be able to join hands and sing in the words of the old Negro spiritual, "Free at last! free at last! thank God almighty, we are free at last!"

VOCABULARY

manacles 2	inextricably 16
promissory 3	interposition 16
defaulted 4	nullification 16
gradualism 4	prodigious 21

QUESTIONS

1. How is the context of the speech (date and circumstances of delivery, audience, background of speaker) apparent?

2. How does the language reflect King's vocation as a minister?

3. Is there a single audience?

4. What is the purpose of the speech?

5. How do the language and the line of argument indicate that "I Have a Dream" was originally a speech?

6. Examine the appropriateness of concrete language in ¶s 1, 3-4, 5, and 19.

7. One of King's major devices is repetition. Where do you find repetition? What is its effect?

8. What techniques does he use to build up the drama of his message? Where do you hear strong emotion expressed?

9. How would you define "creative suffering"?

Winner of a Pulitzer Prize for editorial writing, Ralph McGill (1898-1969) was editor of the Atlanta Constitution *from 1942-60 and publisher from 1960-69. This essay appeared in a selection of his daily columns entitled* A Church, a School, *published in 1959.*

Kluxers Flee Americans
Ralph McGill

1   Yes, sir, you can count on the 100-per-cent Americans! They can spot the pretenders to Americanism with an unfailing eye. A group of these 100-per-cent Americans, Lumbee or Croatan Indians, chased the Ku Klux pretenders to Americanism into the swamps, over the hills, and across the dales. It was, altogether, one of the most hilarious and satisfying incidents of recent years.

2   The Klan, which prostitutes the cross of Christ by burning it to advertise its meetings and to attract the suckers, also exploits Americanism. By paying a necessary sum a fellow can become a 100-per-cent American. The Ku Klux mentality also prostitutes the Christian religion by making over the New and Old Testaments into a KKK revised version. This justifies hate and twists the great commandment to love thy neighbor as thyself to apply only to 100-per-cent Americans, excluding most Protestants, all Roman Catholics and Jews, and all colored peoples. To the Kluxer mentality the Christian communion cup must be a Dixie cup.

3   Their claim to 100-per-cent Americanism is their major one. And it is entertaining, indeed, to read that in their first encounter with American Indians they fled in panic. The Indians were concerned about encroachment on human rights—their rights.

4   In this battle of the flying coattails, the Klan leader flung down his sacred banner.

5   Simeon Oxendine, son of the mayor of Pembroke, community leader, commander of the Veterans of Foreign Wars, who flew on thirty bombing missions over Germany, took the deserted Kluxer flag into Charlotte and walked into the leading hotel lobby wearing it like a scarf.

6   "It's mine," said Chief Oxendine, who had done more fighting for his country than all the Kluxers put together. "And it will never fly over America if I can prevent it"—to which every truly 100-per-cent American will say "Amen."

7   There always is the yapping, sometimes snarling, feistpack to cry "Nazi" or "Red" at those who stand for human rights and who persist in affirming that for Christians the great commandment has validity. But history moves on, and history gives answer to them.

8   The second chapter in this astonishing story of Indians on the warpath in the year 1958 is that the sheriff of the county sought an indictment against the Kluxers for inciting riot. It was they who pushed into the Indian domain against advice of the law-enforcement officers, and the fact the Indians fired into the air, and not at the Kluxers, doesn't change the story.

9   The Lumbee Indians have supplied a moment of laughter to a continuing story which has been somber, if exciting. They also have provided an example of forthright and effective action against un-American mob action. North Carolina is a much healthier place, and the air smells sweet, because of the coattail war.

10   A dip into a North Carolina guide reveals that the Indians make up one fourth of the population of Robeson County, the largest and one of the more prosperous counties in the United States. It early had its own health and agricultural departments. Its first settlers were English, French, and Scottish Highlanders.

11   Lumberton, the county seat, lies on both sides of Lumber River, to which settlers gave the name Drowning Creek. The Indian name was Lumbee.

12   Raleigh sent out in 1587 a colony of one hundred settlers, including seventeen women and nine children. They settled at Roanoke Island. The commander, John White, returned to England. In 1590 he returned to find only a few pieces of broken, rusting armor and carved on one tree the word "Croatan" and on another the letters CRO. The rest was—and to this day is—silence.

13   A romantic legend has it that these Indians at Lumbee are descendants of that last colony which, starving and ill, either was taken by the Indians or joined them.

14   That is legend.

15   But it is a 100-per-cent fact that the real 100-per-cent Americans believe in decent Americanism.

VOCABULARY

pretenders 1	feistpack 7
encroachment 3	domain 8

QUESTIONS

1. What point of view did you expect McGill to have when you first examined the context of the editorial? Were you correct?

2. What is the effect of the opening sentence?

3. What language shows McGill's attitude toward the Ku Klux Klan? toward the Indians? What other devices reveal his attitude?

4. Describe McGill's style. Is it appropriate?

5. How many meanings can you find for "100-per-cent Americans"?

6. What is the meaning of the last sentence in ¶7?

7. Why do you think McGill, in ¶8, characterizes his story as "astonishing"?

8. What is the effect of ¶s 10-14?

Richard Lee Strout (b.1898) writes a regular column in The New Republic *under the pseudonym "TRB." Strout is a longtime correspondent for the Washington Bureau of* The Christian Science Monitor. *This column appeared in* The New Republic, *October 24, 1974.*

The Tarnished Age
TRB

1   Richard Nixon is pardoned, Leon Jaworski is gone. Anybody can see how Watergate is going to end. It's going to be smudged. That's the story of the era between Kennedy and Nixon. There have been good times, great times, but so many of them flawed. And then smudged. That's how we do things.

2   Take the war. In 1964, just 10 years ago exactly, LBJ was telling us that we couldn't trust Goldwater—he would escalate. Lyndon said the war should be fought by Asian boys, not American boys. He said it in New York, New Hampshire, Texas: "We are not going to send American boys nine or 10 thousand miles away from home to do what Asian boys ought to be doing for themselves!" So then he got a landslide and he sent American boys. That was the story of the era. Treat the people as children. Don't trust them. Johnson had been on his way to a place in history as a great President with his vision of the Great Society but he cooked up the Tonkin Gulf incident, and emergency war powers, and the vote in Congress was 504 to two. Only two men

voted against him. Neither was returned to the Senate. Who will put up a plaque for Gruening and Morse in the Capitol?

3 We were lied into the war; we elected Nixon to lie us out of it, to get us "peace with honor." We couldn't face the fact that we had made a mistake. It was better to keep the war going that extra four years than to lose face. The 1968-72 heroes who gave their lives, 20,000 of them, didn't die to spread liberty. You couldn't do that with Thieu as dictator. They didn't die to make America stronger; the war gave us roaring inflation; they died so we wouldn't have to admit that we had made a mistake.

4 But it was embarrassing too. There was a draft system in which the rich boys went to college and the poor boys went to Vietnam. There were demonstrations and some people were shot, as at Kent State (embarrassing). And it was embarrassing that the most powerful nation couldn't break the will of a backward little country whose soldiers wore black pajamas. The pictures of little children running bawling with their clothes burnt off by napalm; that was embarrassing. And the Mylai massacre was embarrassing, but we smudged that. The brass was let off and we'll get Lt. Calley off too; give us time.

5 For a decade it was like that. Always something bitter, like aloes. And then Watergate. Your son will ask you what it was like in those days. Embarrassing, you will tell him. Voters gave Nixon the biggest majority in history. They rejected McGovern because he was too soft, and then discovered that Nixon had been lying to them all the time. The latest tape says he told Haldeman to sacrifice some subordinate: "Give the investigators an hors d'oeuvre," he chuckled, "maybe they won't come back for the main course" (meaning Nixon). He embarrassed the Republicans who voted for him, the Democrats who respected the presidency and his defenders in Congress.

6 All the way from Kennedy to Nixon it was the same; it was in many ways a good era; it might have been a great era, but always it was flawed. "For once there was a fleeting wisp of glory—called Camelot." That ended with a shot. There was the Great Society. That ended with a war. There was Bobby Kennedy, who grew before our eyes from a tough boy to a strong man, and that ended with another murder. And in the civil rights battle the blacks produced a great prophet-leader, Martin Luther King. He had to go too. Always there was a flaw at the center of things.

7 Where did it start? From many causes, of course. One was from living in an unreal world. It was there in the belief that we were always victorious and always righteous. Over generations, a belief grew that Asiatics were a special mission of the US, as historian Eric Goldman said, under the laws of history. Sen. Kenneth Wherry (R, Neb.) put it prettily when he told a wildly cheering crowd in 1940, "With God's help, we will lift Shanghai up and up, ever up, until it is just like Kansas City."

8 Then suddenly we had to change our patronizing vision of Asiatics as little deferential yellow men perpetually smiling, to treacherous cruel Orientals making up part of a menacing communistic monolith. We had "lost"

China; evidently we were betrayed. Joe McCarthy used that charge and Nixon too. Historian Sam Morison wrote, "McCarthy himself collapsed, but the poisonous suspicion he injected into the body politic will take many years to leach out."

9   Exactly; hear young congressman Nixon describing the Acheson-Hiss relationship: "Traitors in the high councils of our own government have made sure that the deck is stacked on the Soviet side of the diplomatic tables." Respectables like Bob Taft and Gen. Eisenhower encouraged the rising Nixon to denounce "Dean Acheson's College of Cowardly Communist Containment." Tell the public anything.

10   Mark Twain looked at the period after the Civil War, the era of wealth and expansion, the era of Jay Gould and Jim Fisk and the scandals of Grant, and he came up with a name for it: it wasn't real gold, he said; it was the Gilded Age. What are we going to call this one?

11   It was so good in so many ways! We saw social improvements and a lift in living standards, and an awakening of conscience about environment and our incredible waste: six percent of world population using a third of its energy. There were magnificent moments—the landing on the Moon! Yet at the same time we could not impose our will on Congress to reform the tax system. Always the surface that might have shone so brightly never seemed to.

12   In our embarrassment and malaise we couldn't face things squarely; we had to smudge things. There was the elaborate falsification of the bombing runs in Cambodia, we smudged that; and the CIA in Chile, we smudged that; and the lies former Attorney General Richard Kleindienst told the grand jury, we smudged that; and the knavery of the Vice President, we smudged that good. The man LBJ wanted as chief justice left under the cloud of an indiscretion; the men Nixon wanted on the high court, what's-his-name and you-know-who, they were dropped. And then Nixon quit and Jerry fixed it with the best smudge of all: the pardon smudge.

13   Mark Twain knew the trick: you can pillory with a name. That was so in the days of dross—the Gilded Age. This is the age that might have been sterling-bright and wasn't. The Tarnished Age.

VOCABULARY

Gruening 2	Jay Gould 10
Morse 2	Jim Fisk 10
napalm 4	gilded 10
Mylai 4	malaise 12
Lt. Calley 4	pillory 13
aloes 5	dross 13
monolith 8	

QUESTIONS

1. How does the expected audience affect the essay?

2. Describe the style. Is it appropriate to the writer's purpose?

3. What is the effect of the repeated words "smudged," "embarrassing," "lie," and "flawed"?

4. Why does the writer refer to Presidents Johnson and Ford as "Lyndon" and "Jerry," but never to Nixon and Kennedy as "Dick" and "Jack"?

5. How thorough is TRB's analysis of the causes of the flawed society (¶7)?

6. Examine the validity of the writer's statements on the draft (¶4, sen. 2), the reason for McGovern's loss (¶5, sen. 7), Johnson's attitude toward the people (¶2, sens. 6-8). What is the purpose of these assertions?

7. To whom does "we" refer in ¶12?

Ralph Nader (b. 1934), a lawyer and author, is best-known for his activism in legal, public safety, and environmental issues. This essay was published in Life *magazine, July 9, 1971.*

We Need a New Kind of Patriotism
Ralph Nader

1   At a recent meeting of the national PTA, the idealism and commitment of many young people to environmental and civil rights causes were being discussed. A middle-aged woman, who was listening closely, stood up and asked: "But what can we do to make young people patriotic?"

2   In a very direct way, she illuminated the tensions contained in the idea of patriotism. These tensions, which peak at moments of public contempt or respect for patriotic symbols such as the flag, have in the past few years divided the generations and pitted children against parents. Highly charged exchanges take place between those who believe that patriotism is automatically possessed by those in authority and those who assert that patriotism is not a pattern imposed but a condition earned by the quality of an individual's, or a people's, behavior. The struggle over symbols, epithets, and generalities impedes a clearer understanding of the meaning and value of patriotism. It is time to talk of patriotism, not as an abstraction steeped in nostalgia, but as

behavior that can be judged by the standard of "liberty and justice for all."

3   Patriotism can be a great asset for any organized society, but it can also be a tool manipulated by unscrupulous or cowardly leaders and elites. The development of a sense of patriotism was a strong unifying force during our Revolution and its insecure aftermath. Defined then and now as "love of country," patriotism was an extremely important motivating force with which to confront foreign threats to the young nation. It was no happenstance that *The Star Spangled Banner* was composed during the War of 1812 when the Redcoats were not only coming but already here. For a weak frontier country beset by the competitions and aggressions of European powers in the New World, the martial virtues were those of sheer survival. America produced patriots who never moved beyond the borders of their country. They were literally defenders of their home.

4   As the United States moved into the 20th century and became a world power, far-flung alliances and wars fought thousands of miles away stretched the boundaries of patriotism. "Making the world safe for democracy" was the grandiose way Woodrow Wilson put it. At other times and places (such as Latin America) it became distorted into "jingoism." World War II was the last war that all Americans fought with conviction. Thereafter, when "bombs bursting in air" would be atomic bombs, world war became a suicidal risk. Wars that could be so final and swift lost their glamour even for the most militaristically minded. When we became the most powerful nation on earth, the old insecurity that made patriotism into a conditioned reflex of "my country right or wrong" should have given way to a thinking process; as expressed by Carl Schurz: "Our country . . . when right, to be kept right. When wrong, to be put right." It was not until the Indochina war that we began the search for a new kind of patriotism.

5   If we are to find true and concrete meaning in patriotism, I suggest these starting points. First, in order that a free and just consensus be formed, patriotism must once again be rooted in the individual's own conscience and beliefs. Love is conceived by the giver (citizens) when merited by the receiver (the governmental authorities). If "consent of the governed" is to have any meaning, the abstract ideal of country has to be separated from those who direct it; otherwise the government cannot be evaluated by its citizens. The authorities in the State Department, the Pentagon, or the White House are not infallible; they have been and often are wrong, vain, misleading, shortsighted or authoritarian. When they are, leaders like these are shortchanging, not representing, America. To identify America with them is to abandon hope and settle for tragedy. Americans who consider themselves patriotic in the traditional sense do not usually hesitate to heap criticism in domestic matters over what they believe is oppressive or wasteful or unresponsive government handling of their rights and dignity. They should be just as vigilant in weighing similar government action which harnesses domestic resources for foreign involvements. Citizenship has an obligation to cleanse patriotism of the misdeeds done in its name abroad.

6   The flag, as the Pledge of Allegiance makes clear, takes its meaning from that "for which it stands"; it should not and cannot stand for shame, injustice and tyranny. It must not be used as a bandanna or a fig leaf by those unworthy of this country's leadership.

7   Second, patriotism begins at home. Love of country in fact is inseparable from citizen action to make the country more lovable. This means working to end poverty, discrimination, corruption, greed and other conditions that weaken the promise and potential of America.

8   Third, if it is unpatriotic to tear down the flag (which is a symbol of the country), why isn't it more unpatriotic to desecrate the country itself—to pollute, despoil and ravage the air, land and water? Such environmental degradation makes the "pursuit of happiness" ragged indeed. Why isn't it unpatriotic to engage in the colossal waste that characterizes so many defense contracts? Why isn't it unpatriotic to draw our country into a mistaken war and then keep extending the involvement, with untold casualties to soldiers and innocents, while not telling Americans the truth? Why isn't the deplorable treatment of returning veterans by government and industry evaluated by the same standards as is their dispatch to war? Why isn't the systematic contravention of the U.S. Constitution and the Declaration of Independence in our treatment of minority groups, the poor, the young, the old and other disadvantaged or helpless people crassly unpatriotic? Isn't all such behavior contradicting the innate worth and the dignity of the individual in America? Is it not time to end the tragic twisting of patriotism whereby those who work to expose and correct deep injustices, and who take intolerable risks while doing it, are accused of running down America by the very forces doing just that? Our country and its ideals are something for us to uphold as individuals and together, not something to drape, as a deceptive cloak, around activities that mar or destroy these ideals.

9   Fourth, there is no reason why patriotism has to be so heavily associated, in the minds of the young as well as adults, with military exploits, jets and missiles. Citizenship must include the duty to advance our ideals actively into practice for a better community, country and world, if peace is to prevail over war. And this obligation stems not just from a secular concern for humanity but from a belief in the brotherhood of man—"I am my brother's keeper"—that is common to all major religions. It is the classic confrontation—barbarism *vs.* the holy ones. If patriotism has no room for deliberation, for acknowledging an individual's sense of justice and his religious principles, it will continue to close minds, stifle the dissent that has made us strong, and deter the participation of Americans who challenge in order to correct, and who question in order to answer. We need only to recall recent history in other countries where patriotism was converted into an epidemic of collective madness and destruction. A patriotism manipulated by the government asks only for a servile nod from its subjects. A new patriotism requires a thinking assent from its citizens. If patriotism is to have any "manifest destiny," it is in building a world where all mankind is our bond in peace.

VOCABULARY

epithets 2	consensus 5	servile 9
happenstance 3	contravention 8	manifest destiny 9
jingoism 4	crassly 8	

QUESTIONS

1. What does the date of publication (July 9, 1971) suggest about the purpose of the essay?

2. What sort of audience did read *Life?* How is Nader's awareness of this audience reflected in his language?

3. Why does Nader present the country's historical background primarily through its wars?

4. In ¶5, what does Nader mean by the phrase "patriotic in the traditional sense"?

5. Does Nader suggest changing the basic definition of patriotism (love of country)?

6. In ¶6, what does the allusion to a fig leaf suggest?

7. What does Nader see as distortions in the current concept of patriotism?

8. The accepted pattern of a definition is categorizing something and then specifying the qualities that differentiate it from other members of that category—a pencil is a writing instrument with a shaft of graphite encased in wood. Does the essay (an extended definition) reflect this pattern?

9. Nader suggests four "starting points" for reconsidering patriotism. How fully developed are they? Are some suggestions more useful than others? Would you add any to the list?

Eric Sevareid (b. 1912), long a well-known commentator for CBS News, presented this essay as a television commentary in October 1961.

Illusions About America

Eric Sevareid

1   We are seeing the end of our adolescence. In its reincarnation as guardian, advisor and donor to half the world the United States is emerging from

its teens. A certain glow begins to fade. The hard, gray thoughts of maturity take possession and there is some danger of the cynicism that is itself immature.

2   In our relations with allied, neutral and client countries we are like the half-boy, half-man who is chagrined to learn that his own best image of himself is not really shared by others, that many he has helped feel no particular gratitude or even obligation and that some he has trusted return the trust only when the occasion serves them.

3   We will persevere, no doubt, learning that we can re-make very little of the world in our own image, losing many illusions about others and ourselves. But one thing we dare not lose—our essential self-confidence, now shaken under strong assault from within and without. Every other consequential country save Russia and possibly China has already lost this. Not one of them really knows where it is going or how to get there.

4   In a profound sense the United States is alone in this world. Most Americans who grasp this hard fact have only recently grasped it, as it has dawned upon them that our major alliance *may* be pulled apart, beginning with loss of faith and will among the Germans; as they learn that the neutrals are not going to be "won over" to our side; as they learn that bringing internal stability to a long list of backward countries is a much, much more difficult, drawn-out and expensive task than ever faintly imagined by the advisors who inserted that paragraph called "Point Four" in Mr. Truman's inaugural speech of January 1949.

5   It is time we ceased clutching illusions to our breast. We have to let them go if our hands are to be free. Some were of a self-denigrating nature, in any case, and it ought to be a pleasure to let them go, a source of greater confidence. Such, at least, have been my own sensations as various items of impediments sloughed off during the two past years in Europe, Africa and Latin America. A few may be worth the mention:

6   *Americans are materialistic.* We are, in fact, as furiously moralistic and idealistic as any people left on earth. We are swamped by the materials, but their simple possession fills no hollow in our souls, as it seems to do with the French. For pure money and possession lust I think I would put the black Africans first.

7   *We are status seekers.* The most ironclad pecking orders of my observance exist among Africans and Arabs. The average well-off Latin American is so riven by class and status that he wants nothing to do with the poor, even in his thoughts. Some members of my English shooting syndicate, which hunted on Wednesdays, were young businessmen who felt obliged to demonstrate that they could afford a mid-week day off, which they could not. One stockbroker carried the *Financial Times* in his cartridge case and consulted it between flights of partridge.

8   *America is a conformist society.* The reason for our fantastic profusion of laws and regulations is the fantastic variety of our manners, ambitions and desires. The true conformist societies, of course, are the primitive societies.

9   *We have neglected Latin America.* The neglecters of Latin America are

Latin Americans. Somewhere between $5 and $10 billion owned by Latin businessmen is salted away in New York, London and Swiss banks, while their governments demand grants and soft-currency loans from us as a matter of ecclesiastical right.

10   *Europeans understand the Communist threat more clearly than we.* Less clearly, if anything, because we have to measure it in its worldwide framework. Not even the able British diplomatic establishment possess Russian experts of the eminence of Charles Bohlen or George Kennan. No European provincial city boasts a hard-working citizens group comparable to the Foreign Policy Study organization in Cleveland or in a dozen other American towns. No academic centers of Russian study in Europe are superior to those at Harvard or Columbia.

11   *America is too impatient.* We have been, in my reluctant judgment, far too patient with allies, neutrals and clients alike. This has won us no affection and now is losing us respect.

12   Goodness without power is impotent in this world. Power itself is impotent when there is no belief in the will to use it, if need be.

VOCABULARY

reincarnation 1	sloughed 5
chagrined 2	ecclesiastical 9
self-denigrating 5	Charles Bohlen 10
impediments 5	George Kennan 10

QUESTIONS

1. How effective is Sevareid's analogy about America's development?

2. Pick out the phrases in which Sevareid expresses an abstraction in concrete terms. What does this device contribute?

3. What elements of sound contribute to the style? What is their effect?

4. Summarize briefly the main points of Sevareid's commentary.

5. What evidence supports the conclusion in the last two sentences of ¶3?

6. What reasoning led to the conclusions of ¶12?

7. Why are the first sentences in ¶s 6-11 italicized?

8. Examine and evaluate the evidence given to support the assertions in ¶s 6-11. What does this tell you about the purpose and limitations of television commentary? Do you listen to television commentary expecting to hear a fully reasoned argument?

THE RESPONSIBILITY OF NEWSCASTERS

The following three essays deal with a newscaster's responsibility to the public. When you have read them, answer the following questions:

1. Which essay appeals most to you? Why? How does its appeal depend on your beliefs and biases? What else influences you?

2. How does the style and tone of each writer reflect his purpose and audience? Are the styles and tones different?

3. Is each a well-reasoned, logical argument?

Lewis Feuer (b. 1912), author of books on philosophy and social science, is a frequent contributor to professional journals. His latest book is Ideology and the Ideologists. *Feuer currently teaches sociology at the University of Toronto. This essay was published in* National Review, *August 15, 1975.*

Why Not a Commentary on Sevareid?
Lewis S. Feuer

1   An old Latin proverb queries: *"Quis custodiet ipsos custodes?"* Who will watch the watchmen themselves? That, in brief, is the problem of the "mass media": the power of the television networks, the radio, and the newspapers, and its misuse. As oligopoly in the electro-magnetic media has grown, it has become clear that it is not the medium that dictates the message, but rather a handful of "telegogues" who select and edit the news and deliver themselves of two-minute capsules of what they call "analysis." A handful of men, especially of the Columbia Broadcasting System, have an awesome grid with which to magnetize the opinions of many millions of people; the effects of their oligopoly, with those of NBC and ABC, have been of a kind that Adam Smith would have predicted. The free market for ideas continues to be steadily undermined by the oligopolistic power of the networks.

2   Who has ever heard the "analysts" of one network take issue with those of another? The last thing a policeman likes to do is to investigate other policemen; the last thing a newsman likes to do is to investigate other newsmen (that defines the limit of what they call "investigative reporting"); and the last thing an analyst wants to do is to "analyze" other analysts. In politics, it is taken for granted that the background of every politician will be scrutinized; every act of his public career and private life is regarded as material to be probed. But to do the same with "analysts" is to conjure forth a staged indignation that freedom of publication is being menaced. The reality is that one class in American society, the newsmen, like the medieval church, still enjoys an immunity despite the fact that it is, of all the political elites, the

most continuous. Legislators, Presidents, and Cabinet secretaries come and go, but Eric Sevareid, for instance, is always there, emitting exordia, pronouncements, and sermonettes.

3   I have been listening more closely in recent weeks to Eric Sevareid. He dominates the screen with "jutting jaw," gimlet-like gaze, all groomed with the skills of makeup men; his imperious assertions are never alloyed with a trace of doubt. Lately he has been concerned with avoiding what are called "recriminations" over Vietnam. Can it be that he wants no discussion as to whether he contributed to the American defeat?

4   Sevareid, as he relates in an early book, *Not So Wild A Dream,* had his formative political experience at the University of Minnesota. This banker's son found himself a member of the Jacobin Club, where he shared a hatred for the existing society, especially its Army: "Of all the instruments designed to uphold the existing order, I think we most hated the military establishments." Eric was ready to be shaped as a revolutionist by the student movement: "With my college generation a new thing developed: the 'student movement,' long a serious political factor in China and many European countries, became for a time a reality in American affairs." It had a "definite effect," wrote Sevareid, on our lives: "We were in revolt," not in the sense of the old-fashioned reformers, but against "the whole underlying motivation of public affairs." While not adhering strictly to any party line, "we frequently worked with them [the Communists]." And after he had lent his support to the Trotskyite-led truckdrivers in their clash with the police, "I went home, as close to becoming a practicing revolutionary as one of my noncombative instincts could ever get." He clashed with his father, and together with a couple of hundred other students, took the Oxford Pledge, that symbol of his generation's revolution. "We refuse to support any war which the United States Government may undertake."

5   And lastly Eric Sevareid learned in the Jacobin Club the cardinal imperative of modern political action: to get control of the media of communication, "the really vital instruments—the daily newspaper, the literary review, the law review, the board of publication, the student council." Soon ten or twelve Jacobins were running campus life, and Eric himself was a syndicated student columnist for 130 college papers.

6   Sevareid's enthusiasm for student activism, for the younger generation, has been rekindled. But where, one wonders, has the All-Knowing Media Man been all these years? Has he visited campuses and heard of the crimes, the drugs, the ripoffs, the sale of academic papers, the corruption of grades? While academic budgets are being slashed, the only allocations that flourish are those for security guards, a category which even in Mr. Sevareid's Jacobin days was minuscule. And what lies behind the attack mounted for several years on the so-called "work ethic" and its replacement by the "ego-trip"?

7   Surely the privileged purveyor of such "analyses" should himself have to face challenge in a public forum. Upward of sixty million people listen to Mr. Sevareid several evenings a week. His persuasive potential far exceeds that of almost any United States senator or public official; the latter, however, are

obliged to face questions and debate in legislative chambers and committee hearings. Our Constitution is being virtually amended so that we have a fourth branch of government; to the legislative, judicial, and executive, we now must add the communicational. The newsmen reiterate the demand that all public figures submit to the interpellation of press conferences. A Prime Minister in Britain has a much easier time with his interpellations than a President of the United States. The questions are sent to him in advance; his replies are never *ex tempore;* and above all, he can always challenge the questioner to state the grounds for an alternative policy. The opposition in Britain has a responsibility analogous to that of the scientist who has to provide an alternative theory instead of merely engaging in a critical assault. And this responsibility alone is what tempers an opposition into what we mean by a "responsible opposition."

8   But in American press conferences, the successful newsman is the man who can "make the news" by provoking indiscreet, emotional, or cantankerous phrases for headlines; he advances his career if he can elicit some sensational remark, some careless comment by a tired man, some slip of speech which would have been repudiated after quieter reflection but which, once rendered, has public consequences that are in part irreversible. Always aware of the news value of personality, he is less mindful of the complexities of policy and of his responsibilities in discussing it.

9   The institution of the press conference (now televised) was really the creation of Franklin D. Roosevelt, who with his extraordinary charm, bonhomie, and zest sought to cultivate the good will of newsmen. He felt capable of using them as a kind of counterforce to propagandize against a hostile Court and Congress. Abraham Lincoln never had a press conference. (Think of Lincoln being prepared in the television room by the makeup men, the conferences over his warts and the trim of his beard.) Was Lincoln's electorate really any less reflective or any less able to discuss the logic of his carefully reasoned speeches? Will the like of a Gettysburg Address ever emerge from the media milieu of the press conference?

10   In Rome the Pretorian Guard grew to have the power if not to make, at least to unmake an Emperor. Our media are close to accumulating such power. The political views of a couple of network presidents and their ace staff-men and commentators outweigh the significance of any similar combination of trade union leaders or corporation executives.

11   The Imperial Media have a command over opinion-making far more potent than that possessed by any Imperial Presidency. Moreover, they can shape the national ethics with a multitude of stimuli. James Reston may wring his hands about it but the suborning of informers in the government goes on apace. The two *Washington Post* correspondents awarded a Pulitzer Prize for their investigative reporting called their informer "Deep Throat"; it requires little psychoanalytical acumen to see what this appellation signified as to their unconscious opinion of the official who was betraying his pledged word. A few years ago the *New York Times* was boasting of the "brilliant investigative reporting" of Neil Sheehan on the matter of the Pentagon papers. Then it transpired that this "brilliant investigative reporting" consisted in Daniel Ellsberg's carting the papers over to his favorite, friendly newspaper. When Ellsberg was tried, his defense was that there was really nothing new in the papers, that it had all been actually known before. Then what, we may ask, made the *New York Times* so eager to print these papers—which, when published in book form, were one of the colossal failures of the industry? Evidently what the *Times* wanted was its very own venture into the fringes of civil disobedience, and indeed, it almost ran afoul of the United States Supreme Court.

12   A hundred years ago, in the crisis of the Civil War, the editors of the *New York Times* and *New York Tribune* had a conception of patriotism which seems to have all but vanished among their successors. In 1864, Horace Greeley, the editor of the *Tribune,* and Henry J. Raymond, the editor of the *Times,* wanted to publish the papers concerning a secret meeting with a Confederate mission; this meeting to explore a negotiated peace had collapsed under Lincoln's intransigence. Greeley, himself a presidential aspirant, insisted to President Abraham Lincoln that "nine-tenths of the whole American people, North and South, are anxious for peace—peace on almost any terms . . ." And indeed Lincoln himself at that time had almost despaired of a Union victory. He was prepared to approve the publication of the papers provided that "a few passages" that he red-penciled himself were suppressed. As Lincoln explained with candor, they were those parts which, if published, might "give too gloomy an aspect to our cause, and those which present the carrying of elections as a motive of action." For all his hostility to President Lincoln, Greeley never published the secret Civil War papers and neither did the *New York Times.* Whose moral standards were higher: those of Greeley and Raymond, or those of Arthur Ochs Sulzberger and his cohort?

13   The issues of media bias and electronic oligopoly remain unresolved. It may be that there are no adequate solutions, and that we shall prefer to live with one set of problems rather than abet the creation of the far worse ones that arise with increased state control. But the issues must once more be debated; they were only prorogued by the Watergate imbroglio. When the American Society of Newspaper Editors met last year, the hope was freely expressed "that Watergate had saved" the newspapers, albeit the fear was also voiced as to what might happen after the "post-Watergate euphoria" had evaporated. There remained the disquieting testimony that three-quarters of the people, according to a Gallup poll, felt that "newspapers are not careful about getting their facts straight."

14   It is hard, of course, to evaluate the basic trend of newspaper credibility; has it gone up or down during the last fifty years, or have the American people always had a certain cynicism about their press? Daniel Schorr complained bitterly a couple of years ago that the profession of a newsman was being sullied by reprisal-seeking Administration officials. Possibly a far more powerful factor in the public's estimate may be its repugnance toward a journalism that thrives on "Deep Throats," that makes the cultivation of informers a primary factor in news-collecting. Inevitably, the public becomes

suspicious about the relations between newsmen and informers and surmises that "leaks" are made to win a most favored status from privileged, powerful newsmen. And all this is claimed to be sacrosanct and protected by the First Amendment.

15   There are some practicable steps, which might well be considered, that would not involve the risks and unforeseen consequences of a large-scale reconstruction of the media oligopoly. For instance, once a week, instead of having politicians interviewed, one might have the newsmen themselves questioned, "confronted"—not by their fellow-newsmen, but by a "blue-ribbon" intellectual panel. This latter panel could be drawn from professors of political science, economics, contemporary history, from the echelons of the business, labor, and professional communities; its members could be chosen on a rotating basis to avoid a selective bias. They would query such tele-gogues as Eric Sevareid about their "analyses." Nothing has been so salutary in making for a realistic view of journalists than such interviews as those which took place with newsmen returned from Communist China, like James Reston, aglow as he told of acupuncture—as if Chinese medieval medicine proved something about the Communist system.

16   The glib speaker of rehearsed lines often turns out to be a political stutterer who needs lots of Scotch-tape to hold his arguments together. To be sure, at the height of listeners' discontent with their news programs, CBS began to serve up selected tidbits from viewers' letters, but this sort of pre-edited criticism and praise is no substitute for the interpellation of the media-managers. Of course, as Walter Cronkite told an audience, if you don't like the program, you can always turn it off. But Cronkite knows very well, as do the advertisers, that the appeal of pictures is such that many viewers tend to swallow the ideological additive along with it. If there were a large number of competing, equally wealthy, national networks, if there were always available someone like the ever-rational Howard K. Smith, said to be ostracized by fanatical colleagues, then Cronkite's sage reminder of the freedom to choose would be well grounded. But the oligopoly narrowly limits the choice. Hence it is all the more imperative that the competitive debate be extended to include the privileged opinion makers of the oligopoly themselves.

VOCABULARY

oligopoly 1	purveyor 7	intransigence 12
Adam Smith 1	interpellation 7	prorogued 13
exordia 2	*ex tempore* 7	imbroglio 13
imperious 3	bonhomie 9	sullied 14
recriminations 3	milieu 9	sacrosanct 14
Jacobin 4	suborning 11	echelons 15
allocations 6	acumen 11	ideological 16
minuscule 6	appellation 11	

QUESTIONS

1. Who is Feuer's audience? How do they affect his style and his argument?

2. What is his attitude toward his subject? What techniques reveal it?

3. What does Feuer mean by his word "telegogues" in ¶1?

4. Is Sevareid Feuer's only target? Why might Feuer have chosen Eric Sevareid as his primary subject?

5. Do you agree with the point made in ¶7? Should newscasters be able to (or be required to) suggest alternatives to the ideas they are questioning? In Feuer's analogy, is it clear who is meant by "the opposition"?

6. How convincing is Feuer's point in ¶8?

7. What is the purpose of the statements and questions about Lincoln in ¶9?

8. Is the conclusion of ¶11 demonstrated by the facts presented?

9. Examine the comparison developed in ¶12 and the conclusion drawn from it.

10. Does Feuer offer a plausible solution?

11. How responsible is the argument?

Walter Cronkite (b. 1916) is the longtime anchorman of the CBS Evening News. This article, printed in Saturday Review, *December 12, 1970, was adapted by Cronkite from an address which he delivered to a convention of Sigma Delta Chi, a national journalism fraternity.*

What It's Like to Broadcast News
Walter Cronkite

1   When Vice President Agnew, in November 1969, unleashed his attack upon the news media, he was following, albeit with unique linguistic and philosophic departures, a long line of predecessors. Somewhere in the history of our Republic there may have been a high government official who said he had been treated fairly by the press, but for the life of me, however, I can't think of one.

2   Mr. Agnew's attacks, of course, were particularly alarming because of their sustained virulence and intimidating nature. But the Vice President was

simply joining the chorus (or, seeing political opportunity, attempting to lead it) of those who have appointed themselves critics of the television medium. Well, I don't like everything I see on television either, but I am frank to say I'm somewhat sick and mighty tired of broadcast journalism being constantly dragged into the operating room and dissected, probed, swabbed, and needled to see what makes it tick.

3   I'm tired of sociologists, psychologists, pathologists, educators, parents, bureaucrats, politicians, and other special interest groups presuming to tell us what is news or where our responsibilities lie.

4   Or perhaps I'm phrasing this wrong. It is not those who squeeze us between their slides and hold us under their microscopes with whom my patience has grown short. The society *should* understand the impact of television upon it. There are aspects of it that need study so that the people can cope with an entirely revolutionary means of communication. Those who disagree with our news coverage have every right to criticize. We can hardly claim rights to a free press and free speech while begrudging those rights to our critics. Indeed, that would seem to be what some of them would like to do to us. So believing, it clearly cannot be the responsible critics or serious students of the TV phenomenon with whom I quarrel. I am provoked more by those in our craft who, like wide-eyed country yokels before the pitchman, are losing sight of the pea under the shell.

5   We must expose the demagogues who would undermine this nation's free media for personal or partisan political gain. That is news. And we should not withhold our cooperation from serious studies of the medium. But we must not permit these matters to divert us from our task, or confuse us as to what that task is.

6   I don't think it is any of our business what the moral, political, social, or economic effect of our reporting is. I say let's get on with the job of reporting the news—and let the chips fall where they may. I suggest we concentrate on doing our job of telling it like it is and not be diverted from that exalted task by the apoplectic apostles of alliteration.

7   Now, a fair portion of what we do is not done well. There are things we are not doing that we ought to do. There are challenges that we have not yet fully met. We are a long way from perfection. Our problems are immense, and they are new and unique.

8   A major problem is imposed by the clock. In an entire half-hour news broadcast we speak only as many words as there are on two-thirds of one page of a standard newspaper. Clearly, the stricture demands tightness of writing and editing, and selection, unknown in any other form of journalism. But look what we do with that time. There are twenty items in an average newscast—some but a paragraph long, true, but all with the essential information to provide at least a guide to our world that day. Film clips that, in a way available to no other daily medium, introduce our viewers to the people and the places that make the news; investigative reports (pocket documentaries) that expose weakness in our democratic fabric (not enough of these, but we're coming along), feature film reports that explore the byways of America and assure us that the whole world hasn't turned topsy-turvy; graphics that in a

few seconds communicate a great deal of information; clearly identified analysis, or commentary, on the news—I think that is quite a package.

9   The transient, evanescent quality of our medium—the appearance and disappearance of our words and pictures at almost the same instant—imposes another of our severe problems. Most of us would agree that television's greatest asset is the ability to take the public to the scene—the launch of a spaceship, a Congressional hearing, a political convention, or a disaster (in some cases these are not mutually exclusive). Live coverage of such continuing, developing events presents the radio-television newsman with a challenge unlike any faced by the print reporter. The newspaper legman, rewrite man, and editor meet the pressure of deadlines and must make hard decisions fast and accurately. But multiply their problems and decisions a thousandfold and you scarcely have touched on the problems of the electronic journalist broadcasting live. Even with the most intensive coverage it still is difficult and frequently impossible to get all the facts and get all of them straight as a complex and occasionally violent story is breaking all around. We do have to fill in additional material on subsequent broadcasts, and there is the danger that not all the original audience is there for the fuller explanation.

10   When a television reporter, in the midst of the riot or the floor demonstration or the disaster, dictates his story, he is not talking to a rewrite man but directly to the audience. There is no editor standing between him and the reader. He will make mistakes, but his quotient for accuracy must be high or he is not long for this world of electronic journalism. We demand a lot of these on-the-scene television reporters. I for one think they are delivering in a magnificent fashion.

11   Directors of an actuality broadcast, like newspaper photo editors, have several pictures displayed on the monitors before them. But they, unlike their print counterparts, do not have ten minutes, or five, or even one minute to select the picture their audience will see. Their decision is made in seconds. Theirs is a totally new craft in journalism, but they have imbued it with all the professionalism and sense of responsibility and integrity of the men of print. Of course we make mistakes, but how few are the errors compared to the fielding chances!

12   Our profession is encumbered, even as it is liberated, by the tools of our trade. It is a miracle—this transmission of pictures and voices through the air, the ability to take the whole world to the scene of a single event. But our tools still are somewhat gross. Miniaturization and other developments eventually will solve our problem, but for the moment our cameras and our lights and our tape trucks and even our microphones are obtrusive. It is probably true that their presence can alter an event, and it probably also is true that they alter it even more than the presence of reporters with pad and pencil, although we try to minimize our visibility. But I think we should not be too hasty in adjudging this as always a bad thing. Is it not salutary that the government servant, the politician, the rioter, the miscreant knows that he is operating in the full glare of publicity, that the whole world is watching?

13 Consider political conventions. They have been a shambles of democratic malfunction since their inception, and printed reports through the years haven't had much effect in reforming them. But now that the voters have been taken to them by television, have sat through the sessions with the delegates and seen the political establishment operate to suppress rather than develop the democratic dialogue, there is a stronger reform movement than ever before, and the chances of success seem brighter.

14 I would suggest that the same is true of the race rioters and the student demonstrators, whatever the justice of the point they are trying to make. Of course they use television. Hasn't that always been the point of the demonstrator—to attract attention to his cause? But the *excesses* of the militants on ghetto streets and the nation's campuses, shown by television with almost boring repetition, tend to repel rather than enlist support, and this is a lesson I hope and *believe* that rational leaders are learning.

15 Scarcely anyone would doubt that television news has expanded to an immeasurable degree the knowledge of many people who either cannot or do not read. We have broadened the interests of another sizable group whose newspaper reading is confined to the headlines, sports, and comics. We are going into homes of the untutored, teaching underprivileged and disadvantaged who have never known a book. We are exposing them to a world they scarcely knew existed, and while advertisements and entertainment programing whet their thirst for a way of life they believe beyond them, we show them that there are people and movements, inside and outside the Establishment, that are trying to put the good things within their reach.

16 Without any intent to foster revolution, by simply doing our job as journalists with ordinary diligence and an extraordinary new medium, we have awakened a sleeping giant. No wonder we have simultaneously aroused the ire of those who are comfortable with the status quo. Many viewers happily settled in their easy chairs under picture windows that frame leafy boughs and flowering bushes and green grass resent our parading the black and bearded, the hungry and unwashed through their living rooms, reminding them that there is another side of America that demands their attention. It is human nature to avoid confronting the unpleasant. No one *wants* to hear that "our boys" are capable of war crimes, that our elected officials are capable of deceit or worse. I think I can safely say that there are few of us who want to report such things. But as professional journalists we have no more discretion in whether to report or not to report when confronted with the facts than does a doctor in deciding to remove a gangrenous limb.

17 If it *happened,* the people are entitled to know. There is no condition that can be imposed on that dictum without placing a barrier (censorship) between the people and the truth—at once as fallible and corrupt as only self-serving men can make it. The barrier can be built by government—overtly by dictatorship or covertly with propaganda on the political stump, harassment by subpoena, or abuse of the licensing power. Or the barrier can be built by the news media themselves. If we permit our news judgment to be colored by godlike decisions as to what is good for our readers, listeners, or viewers, we are building a barrier—no matter how pure our motives. If we permit friendship with sources to slow our natural reflexes, we also build a barrier. If we lack courage to face the criticism and consequences of our reporting, we build barriers.

18   But of all barriers that we might put between the people and the truth, the most ill-considered is the one that some would erect to protect their profits. In all media, under our precious free enterprise system, there are those who believe performance can only be measured by circulation or ratings. The newspaper business had its believers long before we were on the scene. They practiced editing by readership survey. Weak-willed but greedy publishers found out what their readers *wanted* to read and gave it to them—a clear abdication of their duties as journalists and, I would submit, a nail in the coffin of newspaper believability.

19   Today, before the drumfire assault of the hysterical Establishment and the painful complaints of a frightened populace, there are many in our business who believe we should tailor our news reports to console our critics. They would have us report more good news and play down the war, revolution, social disturbance. There certainly is nothing wrong with good news. In fact, by some people's lights we report quite a lot of it: an anti-pollution bill through Congress, a report that the cost of living isn't going up as fast as it was last month, settlement of a labor dispute, the announcement of a medical breakthrough, plans for a new downtown building. There isn't anything wrong either with the stories that tell us what is right about America, that reminds us that the virtues that made this nation strong still exist and prosper despite the turmoil of change.

20   But when "give us the good news" becomes a euphemism for "don't give us so much of that bad news"—and in our business one frequently means the other—the danger signal must be hoisted.

21   It is possible that some news editors have enough time allotted by their managements to cover all the significant news of their areas—much of it, presumably, in the "bad" category—and still have time left over for a "good news" item or two. But for many and certainly those at the network level, that is not the case. To crowd in the "happy" stories would mean crowding out material of significance. Some good-news advocates know this, and it is precisely what they want: to suppress the story of our changing society in the hope that if one ignores evil it will go away.

22   Others simply are tired of the constant strife. They would like a little relief from the daily budget of trouble that reminds them of the hard decisions they as citizens must face. But can't they see that pandering to the innocent seeking relief is to yield to those who would twist public opinion to control our destiny?

23   It is no coincidence that these manipulative methods parallel those adopted half a century ago by Russian revolutionaries also seeking the surest means to bend the population to their will. You will not find bad news in

Russian newspapers or on broadcast media. There are no reports of riots, disturbances of public order, muggings or murders, train, plane, or auto wrecks. There are no manifestations of race prejudice, disciplinary problems in army ranks. There is no exposure of malfeasance in public office—other than that which the government chooses to exploit for its own political purposes. There is no dissent over national policy, no argument about the latest weapons system.

24   There is a lot of good news—factories making their quotas, happy life on the collective farm, successes of Soviet diplomacy, difficulties in the United States. The system works. Without free media—acerbic, muckraking, irreverent—the Soviet people are placid drones and the Soviet Establishment runs the country the way it wants it run.

25   Since it is hard to know the real motives in others' minds—indeed, it is hard sometimes to know our own motives—and since few are likely to admit that they would seek to suppress dissent from Establishment norms, it would be wrong to ascribe such Machiavellian connivance to the good-news advocates. The only trouble is that the other, more likely motive—profiting from the news by pandering to public taste—is almost as frightening. To seek the public's favor by presenting the news it wants to hear is to fail to understand the function of the media in a democracy. We are not in the business of winning popularity contests, and we are not in the entertainment business. It is not our job to please anyone except Diogenes.

26   The newsman's purpose is contrary to the goal of almost everyone else who shares the airwaves with us, and perhaps we should not be too harsh with those executives with the ultimate responsibility for station and network management. We are asking a great deal of them. For seventeen of the eighteen hours during an average broadcast day their job is to win friends and audience. They and we live on how successfully they do this difficult job.

27   But then we ask them to turn a deaf ear to the complaints of those dissatisfied with what we present in the remaining minutes of the day. We ask them to be professionally schizoid—and that would seem to be a lot to ask. But is it, really? After all, in another sense, as journalists we live this life of dual personality. There is not a man who can truthfully say that he does not harbor in his breast prejudice, bias, strong sentiments pro and con on some if not all the issues of the day.

28   Yet it is the distinguishing mark of the professional journalist that he can set aside these personal opinions in reporting the day's news. None of us succeeds in this task in all instances, but we know the assignment and the pitfalls, and we succeed far more often than we fail or than our critics would acknowledge. We have a missionary duty to try to teach this basic precept of our craft to those of our bosses who have not yet learned it. We in broadcasting, at least, cannot survive as a major news medium if we fail.

29   We were well on the way before the current wave of politically inspired criticism. In my twenty years in broadcasting I have seen more and more station owners taking courage from their news editors, tasting the heady fruit of respect that can be won by the fearless conveyer of the truth. Some years ago William Allen White wrote that "nothing fails so miserably as a cowardly newspaper." I suspect he spoke not only of commercial failure but of the greater failure: not winning the confidence of the people. A radio or television station also can fail this test of courage, and when it does its owner wins not a community's respect and gratitude but its contempt.

30　Broadcast management is going to need a stiff backbone in the days ahead—not only for its own well-being but for the good of us all. We are teetering on the brink of a communications crisis that could undermine the foundation of our democracy that is a free and responsible press. We all know the present economic background. We in radio and television with our greater impact and our numerous outlets have forced many of our print competitors out of business. It is a rare American city today that has more than one newspaper. And yet I think most of us will acknowledge that we are not an adequate substitute for the newspapers whose demise we have hastened. We cannot supply the wealth of detail the informed citizen needs to judge the performance of his city, county, or state. If we do our jobs thoroughly, however, we can be a superb monitor over the monopoly newspaper, assuring that it does not by plot, caprice, or inadvertence miss a major story.

31　We *can* be, that is, if we are left alone to perform that essential journalistic function. The trouble is that broadcast media are not free; they are government licensed. The power to make us conform is too great to lie forever dormant. The ax lies there temptingly for use by any enraged administration, Republican, Democrat, or Wallaceite. We are at the mercy of the whim of politicians and bureaucrats, and whether they choose to chop us down or not, the mere existence of their power is an intimidating and constraining threat.

32　So on one side there is a monopoly press that may or may not choose to present views other than those of the domineering majority, on the other side a vigorously competitive but federally regulated broadcast industry, most of whose time is spent currying popular—that is, majority—favor. This scarcely could be called a healthy situation. There is a real danger that the free flow of ideas, the vitality of minority views, even the dissent of recognized authorities could be stifled in such an atmosphere.

33　We newsmen, dedicated as we are to freedom of press and speech and the presentation of all viewpoints no matter how unpopular, must work together, regardless of our medium, to clear the air while there is still time. We must resist every new attempt at government control, intimidation, or harassment. And we must fight tenaciously to win through Congress and the courts guarantees that will free us forever from the present restrictions. We must stand together and bring the power of our professional organizations to bear against those publishers and broadcast managers who fail to understand the function of a free press. We must keep our own escutcheons so clean that no one who would challenge our integrity could hope to succeed.

34　If we do these things, we can preserve, and reestablish where it has faded, the confidence of the people whose freedom is so indivisibly linked with ours.

VOCABULARY

demagogues 5
apoplectic apostles
  of alliteration 6
stricture 8
evanescent 9
quotient 10
gangrenous 16
euphemism 20

malfeasance 23
acerbic 24
muckraking 24
Diogenes 25
Machiavellian 25
schizoid 27
Wallaceite 31
escutcheons 33

QUESTIONS

1. Does the style reveal that the essay was originally a speech? How would you describe the style? What is the effect of the figure of speech in ¶4? in ¶16?

2. What differences between the original audience and a *Saturday Review* audience might lead Cronkite to revise the speech before publication?

3. What is Cronkite's attitude toward his subject? Is it what you expected?

4. What is his thesis? Where is it stated? Which best indicates the purpose of his essay: the title or the thesis?

5. How does Cronkite organize his essay? Does his organization help his argument?

6. What is the effect of ¶7? Does he develop these assertions with examples?

7. Is the argument in ¶s 9-11 convincing?

8. Is the argument from cause to effect in ¶13 convincing?

9. Examine ¶s 16-17; is it true that newscasters do not select the news to report? Consider ¶s 20-25.

10. Study ¶s 20-25; how fairly and effectively does Cronkite anticipate the arguments of others? What techniques does he use?

11. Who are Cronkite's opponents? Does he name them?

12. Is ¶28 convincing? Why?

13. Compare the assertions in ¶15 with those in ¶28 of Mannes' essay.

Irving Fang (b. 1929) was a television newsman for nine years and is now Associate Professor in the School of Journalism and Mass Communication at the University of Minnesota. This article appeared in Saturday Review, *January 9, 1971.*

It Is Your Business, Mr. Cronkite

Irving E. Fang

1   Walter Cronkite, in a recent article adapted from a speech to the Sigma Delta Chi national convention, stated, "I don't think it is any of our business what the moral, political, social, or economic effect of our reporting is" ["What It's Like to Broadcast the News," *SR,* Dec. 12, 1970].

2   I disagree with Mr. Cronkite. It *is* the journalist's concern to consider the consequences of his work, just as it is the physician's, the attorney's, the minister's, the professor's, and indeed every professional man's concern.

3   Of course, Cronkite is not heedless of public reaction. If an obscenity were part of an important news story (for example, what the Chicago Seven were really saying in court), he would not repeat it on the air. Nor would he repeat a blasphemy. Nor would he use pornography to illustrate a national concern. No responsible journalist does these things, whether or not they might be news.

4   The journalist operates as he does because society chooses that he do so. Our society, based on the libertarian ideals of a democracy, chooses wisely that journalists should, within certain bounds, "tell it like it is." Besides obscenity, blasphemy, and pornography, news that lies out of bounds includes certain military secrets, indefensible libels, matters of personal privacy, and unsubstantiated rumor. While broad, the rights of free speech and freedom of the press are not absolute.

5   To the left and to the right of our democracy lie the censored societies.

6   Lenin asked:

> Why should freedom of speech and freedom of the press be allowed? Why should a government which is doing what it believes to be right allow itself to be criticized? It would not allow opposition by lethal weapons. Ideas are much more fatal things than guns. Why should any man be allowed to buy a printing press and disseminate pernicious opinions calculated to embarrass the government?

7   And Franco's former foreign minister, Alberto Martin Artajo, stated:

> There are certain substantive freedoms derived from natural law—man's freedom to worship his God, to found a home, to educate his children, to work, and to act with self-respect and independence. These freedoms [in Spain] once succumbed to the action of license, as a result of the excess of other freedoms, like freedom of the press, of party, of trade unions, of strikes, which are not of

the same nature and degree, because they are, so to speak, secondary freedoms, "adjective" freedoms, of a lower order. That is why the [Franco] regime has in some way repressed these other political freedoms, which, because they are secondary, must be the safeguard of the previous ones.

8   Some Americans can always be found who would like more restrictions on what may now be broadcast or printed. I have even heard this from a few men who make their living in the news business. (I am reluctant to call them journalists.) Vice President Agnew's Des Moines speech has less significance than the apparent support it received across the land. Many, many Americans honestly believe that television network news isn't telling it as it is. I sometimes ask for a show of hands in a college classroom to learn how many students believe that television newscasts, network and local, report news in an unbiased manner, without fear or favor. The voting usually runs 4 to 1 against the newscasters. The reasons vary. Some students, supporting the Vice President, see a liberal bias. Some students see a conservative, Establishment bias. Some students are convinced that broadcast journalists do not report news harmful to advertisers. And so on.

9   If such an erosion of faith exists among university students, who are among the most libertarian members of our society, can the journalist argue that it is not his business what the effect of his reporting is?

10   Let us look beyond journalism for a moment. When a society feels itself sufficiently threatened, it reacts. Lenin and Franco felt sufficiently threatened by freedom of speech and freedom of the press to crush them. If those Americans who would restrict freedom of speech and freedom of the press take action, will the rest of America rise up in indignation or fury to stop them?

11   We hope so. We hope these freedoms matter to enough Americans. But should not the journalist be aware of the effect he is having? Should he not buttress his hope that most Americans value freedom of the press, even when the news is upsetting or grim or pleases their political opponents or undercuts their moral philosophy or appears to give aid and comfort to their nation's enemies? In short, news which shows us what we are, warts and all?

12   Mr. Cronkite may have expressed himself here more broadly than he intended. If he meant to argue that the journalist has a responsibility to report significant news, even if it upsets us, then he ought to have the support of all who regard the right to know as paramount.

13   The distinction between the journalist judging an individual story on its merits and the journalist ignoring the impact of news upon his audience is obviously far more than hairsplitting. To cite one example, riot news was once reported on television newscasts purely on its merits as news. But it soon became evident that the impact of riot news on television viewers—including the rioters themselves—was so great that television news departments trimmed their sails. Broadcast journalists had to make the effects of riot news their business. They did so voluntarily, behaving as responsible members of our society. To ignore the effects of this news would have been unacceptable, and everyone knew it.

14   In his article, Mr. Cronkite stated:

> . . . I'm somewhat sick and mighty tired of broadcast journalism being constantly
> dragged into the operating room and dissected, probed, swabbed, and needled
> to see what makes it tick.
>
> I'm tired of sociologists, psychologists, pathologists, educators, parents,
> bureaucrats, politicians, and other special interest groups presuming to tell us
> what is news or where our responsibilities lie.

15   He immediately qualified this by saying the researchers really have a right to research, "But we must not permit these matters to divert us from our task, or confuse us as to what that task is."

16   To his statement, I would say "Amen," if the journalists would undertake their own research instead. Who is better qualified to study journalism than the journalist? I don't mean every journalist should undertake a research project, any more than every lawyer does legal research and every physician does medical research. But some should, and others should support them. (To argue that journalism is merely a craft and not a profession is quibbling with definitions. Journalism is too powerful to ignore professional responsibilities.)

17   The networks and large television stations now have sales research departments. A few of the largest news departments also employ a "researcher" or two, usually a girl whose job it is to look things up and make telephone calls for information. That, plus some intelligently managed survey research for network election coverage and some polling, is about it for news operations, so far as I know.

18   Networks and large stations ought to engage in basic and applied mass communications research, using university facilities where needed. And the results of their research should influence their work. Other professions benefit from their own research. Why not journalism?

19   For example, I should like to see research on the effect of visual images on auditory news information. When film of a farmyard is used to illustrate a story about farm legislation, it is possible that the picture of a cow munching hay overwhelms what the newscaster is reporting. I don't know that this is so, but I venture to guess that neither does the news director who ordered the film shot.

20   If this rustic example sounds simple, there is more complex and sensitive research to be done, not only by sociologists and psychologists who often don't know the territory, but by trained and concerned television journalists. How can film of a riot or a demonstration or strike violence best be put into perspective (the viewer's perspective, not the newscaster's) by words? How can war coverage be improved in the only way that really matters—the information being imparted?

21   The list is long, maybe endless, and the questions are not trifling. If electronic journalism is to have the future we hope for, continued growth in freedom, the men who practice it must make it their business to analyze the effects of what they do upon the tens of millions of Americans who watch television newscasts daily.

VOCABULARY

libertarian 4

Lenin 6

pernicious 6

Franco 7

liberal 8

conservative 8

auditory 19

QUESTIONS

1. Who is Fang's audience? Is it Walter Cronkite, or is it a larger audience?

2. What is the effect of the title?

3. What is the effect of the abrupt beginning?

4. Where is the thesis stated?

5. Why is the last sentence of ¶3 not an overstatement?

6. How do the quotations in ¶s 6 and 7 relate to the thesis? Is ¶8 contrary to Fang's thesis?

7. Why does Fang frame the ideas in ¶s 9-11 as questions?

8. What is the purpose of ¶12? of ¶13?

9. Is the last sentence of ¶13 overstated?

10. Where does Fang anticipate counterarguments?

11. Does Fang offer an effective solution?

John Merrill (b. 1924) is a professor of journalism at the University of Missouri and the author of Media, Messages and Men *(1971) and* Journalistic Autonomy: A Philosophy of Press Freedom *(1974). This essay appeared in* Journalism Quarterly *(Autumn 1965).*

How <u>Time</u> Stereotyped Three U.S. Presidents
John C. Merrill

1   The suggestion that *Time* magazine selects, aligns and explains (*i.e.,* "subjectivizes") information will certainly not startle many persons. In fact, its editors have insisted from the magazine's founding in 1923 that objectivity in news presentation is impossible and that *Time* writers should "make a judg-

ment" in their articles.[1] This study investigates some of the techniques used by the publication to subjectivize its news and to try to determine what stereotyped pictures of three American Presidents were presented. The study is not concerned with the "ethics" of a newsmagazine's "subjectivizing" its news content, although some writers have been critical in this respect.[2]

2   This study[3] was undertaken primarily to answer this question: What kind of stereotyped image of each of the Presidents—Truman, Eisenhower, and Kennedy—was presented by the magazine? Rather cursory and non-analytical readings of *Time* had given the impression that the magazine was anti-Truman and pro-Eisenhower. And during the Kennedy administration, there were many surface indications that *Time* was at least more objective (or neutral) toward the late President. What would be the stereotypes of the three Presidents presented by *Time* and how would the magazine go about creating them?

3   Would the "newsstories" in the magazine indicate political bias? Would the stories provide clear-cut examples of subjective, judgmental or opinionated reporting? If so, what were these techniques of subjectivizing? This study would at least be a beginning in a systemized critique.

The Method

4   Ten consecutive issues of *Time* were chosen for study from each of the three Presidential administrations. The beginning date of each consecutive issue period was chosen by the random method of selection. First, the years of each administration were chosen: for Truman, 1951; for Eisenhower, 1955; for Kennedy, 1962. Successive procedures determined the month and the week which would be used as the beginning date for the 10 issues in each administration. The Truman beginning date was April 2, 1951; the Eisenhower date was January 24, 1955, and the Kennedy beginning date was November 23, 1962.

5   It was decided that there was no need to compare space treatment given the three Presidents, since space in itself has no necessary bearing on subjectivity or bias. What was considered important was the language used to describe each President, with special emphasis on the presence or absence of

---

[1]John Kobler, "Luce: The First Tycoon and the Power of His Press," *Saturday Evening Post* (Jan. 16, 1965), pp. 28-45. Cf. James Playsted Wood, *Magazines in the United States* (New York: Ronald Press, 1956), pp. 205-6, and *The Story of an Experiment* (New York: Time, Inc., 1948).

[2]Almost the entire first issue of *FACT* (Jan.-Feb., 1964) was devoted to a series of highly critical essays by important personages, all deploring the practices of *Time*. Another criticism of *Time*, even more harsh, perhaps, was the entire issue of *UAW Ammunition* (Dec., 1956). Yet another, couched in more intellectual though hardly less cutting language, was "Time: the Weekly Fiction Magazine" by Jigs Gardner in *The Nation* (Aug. 15, 1959), pp. 65-67.

[3]Sponsored in part by the Fund for Organized Research, Texas A&M University.

"loaded" words and expressions and on general contextual impressions presented.

6   Six *bias categories* were set up: 1) attribution bias, 2) adjective bias, 3) adverbial bias, 4) contextual bias, 5) outright opinion, and 6) photographic bias. In considering these categories, as they related to the 30 issues of *Time* studied, instances of bias were noted either as *positive* (favorable) or as *negative* (unfavorable). Advanced journalism students served as an evaluative panel. Indications of bias (either positive or negative) thought dubious (borderline cases) were not counted as bias in this study.

The Bias Categories

7   *Attribution Bias* designates bias which stems from the magazine's means of attributing information to the President. In other words, this is bias which is contained in the synonym for the word "said" used by the magazine. An attribution verb such as "said" is neutral (not opinionated and evokes no emotional response) and was ignored in the study. An attribution verb such as "snapped" (negatively affective) is a word designed to appeal to the reader's emotions, to give a judgmental stimulus. An attribution verb such as "smiled" is counted as a "favorable" term, for it is positively affective.

8   *Adjective Bias* is a type which, like attribution bias, attempts to build up an impression of the person described; this is accomplished by using adjectives, favorable or unfavorable, in connection with the person. While use of adjectives is quite common in news reporting, they must be used with extreme care or subjectivity will creep in and the mere use of the adjectives will create a favorable or unfavorable impression. Or, as Rudolf Flesch points out, "the little descriptive adjectives" of *Time* "tend to blot out" the other words because of their "overpotency." This results, says Flesch, in the reader getting "a wrong impression or, at least, an emphasis that isn't there."[4]

9   An example of "favorable" bias in adjective use: "*serene* state of mind." An example of "unfavorable" bias in adjective use: "*flat, monotonous* voice." Not only do these adjectives tend to prejudice the reader for or against the person described, but they are actually *subjective* in nature; they are opinions of the writer. They might be called "judgmental" adjectives; at any rate they are quite different from adjectives which might be called "neutral" or "objective"—such as "the *blue* sky."

10   *Adverbial Bias* depends on qualifiers or magnifiers—adverbs—to create an impression in the reader's mind. Often this adverbial bias is a sort of reinforcing of another bias expression already present (e.g., when an adverb reinforces an attribution bias as in this case: "He barked *sarcastically*.") This is

---

[4]*How to Write, Speak and Think More Effectively* (New York: Signet Books, 1963). pp. 68-9. Dr. Flesch says that these adjectives, according to *Time* editors, help the reader get a better picture of what's going on. Dr. Flesch takes issue with this and says that it is "quite obvious that *Time* readers are apt to learn a lot about the faces, figures, hands, lips and eyes of world leaders, but are liable to misread or skip what these people do" (p. 69).

a technique by which the magazine creates a favorable or unfavorable impression in the mind of the reader by generally telling *how* or *why* a person said or did something.

11   *Contextual Bias* cannot be notated in neat lists. It is the bias in whole sentences or paragraphs or in other (and larger) units of meaning, even an entire story. The purpose is to present the person reported on in a favorable or an unfavorable light by the overall meaning or innuendo of the report, not by specific words and phrases alone. The whole context must be considered. Since one's own biases or interpretations might very well determine what he considers contextually biased, it was necessary to get the opinions of a panel.[5] Contextual bias was counted *only* when there was agreement among the panelists.

12   *Outright Opinion,* of course, is the most blatant and obvious type of bias or subjectivity in newswriting. The expression of opinion by the publication might be called "presenting a judgment," which S. I. Hayakawa says should be kept out of reports.[6] Dr. Hayakawa defines "judgments" as "all expressions of the writer's approval or disapproval of the occurrences, persons, or objects he is describing." Readers do not expect to find the judgments or opinions of the writer in a newspaper or a newsmagazine except in a signed column or editorial. *Time* does use outright opinion. Examples: "His (Eisenhower's) powers of personal persuasion are strong" and "He has an aversion to stirring up unnecessary national crises."

13   The expression of opinion is sometimes disguised. In other words, through semantic tricks *Time* permits someone else (or the whole United States) to say or believe something about the President, thus presenting its own opinion indirectly. Example: "Few at home in the U.S. seemed to begrudge the President his trip, however inauspicious the timing." In addition, *Time* projects its opinion by explaining *why* people in the news do as they do. As one writer puts it: "*Time* reads men's motives—good for friends, bad for enemies—with that Olympian supremacy and aloofness which prompted Commager to speak of the period 'before *Time* became omniscient.' "[7]

14   *Photographic Bias,* it is granted, might possibly result from inability to get other photographs or from no real desire to prejudice the reader. In other words, it could be unintentional. However, intention is not considered in the treatment of this or any other category, for there is no real way to know intent. These questions were asked in trying to determine this bias: What overall impression does the photograph give? How is the President presented in the picture—dignified, undignified; angry, happy; calm, nervous, etc.? What does the caption say/imply?

---

[5]Six advanced journalism students at Texas A&M composed the panel to decide on these cases of possible contextual bias.

[6]*Language in Thought and Action* (New York: Harcourt, Brace and Company, 1940), pp. 38, 42-44.

[7]Garry Wills, "Timestyle," *National Review* (Aug. 3, 1957), p. 130.

A Selected Week: Truman

15   *Issue of April 23, 1951:* Of the 10 weeks of *Time* studied from the Truman administration, this issue of April 23 contains more obvious indications of bias and subjectivity than any of the others. It is one of the several issues which dealt with Truman's relieving General MacArthur of his post as Supreme Commander in the Far East. *Time* is obviously in sympathy with the general, and in this week's issue makes some of its more biased statements. Some examples of the magazine's opinions can be seen in the following paragraph (p. 24):

> Seldom had a more unpopular man fired a more popular one. Douglas MacArthur was the personification of the big man, with the many admirers who look to the great man for leadership, with the few critics who distrust and fear a big man's domineering ways. Harry Truman was almost a professional little man, with admirers who like the little man's courage, with the many critics who despise a little man's inadequacies.

16 Not satisfied with the then-current issue, *Time* quickly and in broad strokes presents the readers with a "flash-back" to an administration filled with six years of "shabby politicking and corruption" and "doubts about his State Department" coupled with "distaste for his careless government-by-crony."

17   *Time* in this issue, *however,* does not stop here; it goes further and gives the impression that the nation shares its opinion of President Truman. Says *Time* (p. 25): "A few days later, over the morning coffee, the nation read of Harry Truman's reply and fumed." (This followed a report by the magazine that Truman had "replied curtly" to a critic of his MacArthur action.) Also in this issue readers were reminded that "probers were still unearthing new evidence of skulduggery in the RFC" and that Truman was a President who "stubbornly protected shoddy friends."

A Selected Week: Eisenhower

18   *Issue of Feb. 7, 1955:* In this week's issue, *Time* quite typically provides vivid examples of subjective and biased reporting and evidences a strong pro-Eisenhower slant. According to the magazine: "The strong leadership of President Eisenhower and the near-unanimity of the Congress in backing him in the Formosa resolution undoubtedly retrieved much of the U.S. prestige and influence that had been recently lost in Asia." As described by *Time*, Ike's resolution that the U.S. would fight was "evidence of the President's patience and peacefulness" (p. 9).

19   A few further quotes from this story might serve to indicate the magazine's bias toward *Eisenhower* and give good examples of subjective reporting:

> A few days before the President's message to Congress last week, the whole anti-Communist position in the Far East seemed to be coming apart. Ike stopped the rot, and the U.S. emerged in a better light than it had enjoyed in several weeks. (P. 9)

> He (Eisenhower) wanted to demonstrate national unity behind the policy; he wanted to keep his 1952 campaign promise that he would submit to Congress any proposed steps to use U.S. forces in combat. (P. 10)
>
> For Dwight Eisenhower, the week's events were demonstration of forceful and skillful presidental leadership. He had used his prestige to score a political and policy victory, and placed Capitol Hill—its Republicans and Democrats alike—in the position of sharing the decision. (P. 10)

A Selected Week: Kennedy

20 *Issue of Dec. 28, 1962:* Again in this issue *Time* presented the President as a confident person, one who "bluntly voiced his growing impatience with British and European bellyaching about U.S. contributions to the common defense," one who was behind the ransom payments to Castro's government, and one whose TV interview "from the rocking chair" showed the President "at his informal confident best" (pp. 13-15). Over in the "Business" section (pp. 50-55), the Presidential image turned more unpleasant. Recounting the business year of 1962, *Time* dealt at some length with JFK's part in the steel crisis. The magazine referred to "John F. Kennedy's hasty and whitelipped counterattack" against U.S. Steel Chairman Roger Blough, who was trying to raise steel prices $6 a ton. According to *Time*, "virtually all U.S. businessmen were outraged by the tactics Kennedy used against Blough." But, added the magazine later in the story, "in board rooms around the country, businessmen were impressed that President Kennedy had talked even tougher to Khrushchev than to Roger Blough" (p. 62).

The Presidential Stereotypes

21 It was found in this study that from week to week *Time,* through the skillful use of devices described earlier, creates and reinforces a stereotype of the President in office. The personality of the President gets more emphasis through the colorful and subjective language of the magazine than does his news activities. As Jigs Gardner wrote in *The Nation,* it is the "reduction of news to emotional conflicts of personalities."[8] One reason for this, obviously, is that "conflicts of personalities" make strong appeal to emotions. This appeal is far greater for the general reader than is the appeal of straight, neutralist reporting.

22 The following paragraph from *Time* (June 16, 1952) serves as an example:

> They saw Ike, and liked what they saw. They liked him for his strong, vigorous manner of speech . . . and for an overriding innate kindliness and modesty. But most of all, they liked him in a way they could scarcely explain. They liked Ike because, when they saw him and heard him talk, he made them proud of themselves and all the half-forgotten best that was in them and the nation.

---

[8]Gardner, *op. cit.,* p. 66.

23   This example is typical of the way *Time* creates and develops its presidential images or stereotypes. Below, in brief profiles taken from *Time*-treatment, are re-created the stereotypes of the three Presidents which the reader of the magazine had developed for him week by week during the three administrations. These stereotypes, although naturally abstractions even of *Time*-images, picture each president as seen through the verbal lenses of the "weekly newsmagazine."

Truman: A bouncy man, sarcastic and shallow. A very unpopular man, a "little" man with many inadequacies. A President who condoned all types of "shabby politicking and corruption" in his administration. A man who practiced "careless government-by-crony." A petulant President who "stubbornly protected shoddy friends," one who had "grown too touchy to make judicious decisions." A President who failed to give firm leadership to the country. A man whose State Department was full of homosexuals. A man who evaded issues and refused to face an argument. A President who "breathed cocky belligerence," and bounced on his heels while he launched off-the-cuff oratory. A President who when he spoke, generally sputtered, barked, cracked, droned, or "popped a gasket." A person who "grinned slyly," and "preached the Truman sermon" and "probed with a blunt finger." A man whose speeches had a "thin, overworked and flat quality" as he spoke with a "flat, monotonous voice." A man who stirred up national crises and who left the nation's nervous system "jangled and jumpy." A man who was blunt, sarcastic, belligerent, cocky, petulant, irascible, harried, lazy, vain, angry, sly, curt, and cold.

Eisenhower: A smiling, warm-hearted, sincere leader. A man of "earnest demeanor." A President whose strong leadership brought united determination. A patient and peaceful man, and one who wanted to keep his campaign promises. A skillful leader who was a statesman rather than a politician. One who was humble and who took his duties very seriously. One who was "on top of his job." A President who when he moved, moved "quietly." One who was sensitive to "the mood of the nation," and who did not like to stir up crises. A person who loved children, one who was forgiving and religious. One who brushed away misunderstandings and insisted on facts and the truth. A President who was cautious, warm, charitable, modest, happy, amiable, firm, cordial, effective, serene, frank, calm, skillful, and earnest. A person who talked with a happy grin, who pointed out cautiously, spoke warmly, and chatted amiably.

Kennedy: A President who was wealthy but generous in charity. A man who liked much social life in the White House, and who travelled extensively. A versatile man—who wore "many hats." A President who fostered a kind of "forced togetherness of New Frontier society." A man whose mistake it was not to censor the press, but "to talk out loud" about it. A confident person, usually pleasant. A happy man with a "cheery look." A man who seldom showed irritation, but who could launch a "hasty and whitelipped counterattack." A President who would bring full force of his power to bear to get his way. A President who talked tough to Khrushchev. A man whose presence had great impact on crowds, one who was willing to take risks, who had a "conviction of correctness." A speaker who, when he spoke, said, reaffirmed, announced, promised, concluded, and insisted. He usually simply "said." A man who was usually confident, informed, emphatic, cheery, social, versatile, energetic, youthful, impressive, determined, and well-informed.

Table 1 Bias Category Breakdown for the Three Presidents in Each 10-Issue Period

Bias Category	Truman	Eisenhower	Kennedy
Attribution Bias	9	11	5
Adjective Bias	21	22	3
Adverbial Bias	17	7	4
Contextual Bias	33	20	13
Outright Opinion	8	17	12
Photographic Bias	5	5	8
Total Bias	93	82	45
Total Positive Bias	1	81	31
Total Negative Bias	92	1	14

Examples and Commentary

24   Following is a group of selected examples of subjective and biased reportorial quotations taken from the sample study periods. After each example is the author's comment[9] on the example. These examples offer insight into the kind of techniques used by *Time* in its reporting during the periods studied:

> If the Administration had ever toyed with the idea of appeasement, it had been forced to a public renunciation. (May 21, 1951, p. 19.)
>
> *Here is the case of implicating somebody or something where nothing—so far as* Time *knew—really existed. This is possibly the most questionable type of reporting used by the magazine.*
>
> Harry Truman had worn a harried and rumpled air during General MacArthur's three days of testimony before Congress. (May 21, 1951, p. 19.)
>
> *Here there is an insinuation of a guilty conscience, of someone afraid something unpleasant will leak out about him. A case of implication by appearance.*
>
> History would remember this day and this man, and mark him large. (April 30, 1951, p. 23.)
>
> *Here is a case of pure opinion and doubtful syntax. The quote relates to MacArthur.*
>
> It was a neat bit of off-the-cuff campaigning, and was calculated—like his "hope" of making a cross-country give-'em-hell speaking tour this spring or summer—to gladden the hearts of Democrat bigwigs who met in Denver last week to beat the drums for '52. (June 4, 1951, p. 19.)
>
> *Here is the case of* Time *telling the reader why Truman greeted a group of young people at the White House; this is purely the magazine's conjecture stated as fact.*
>
> The State Department was still clearing homosexuals out of its woodwork. . . . Total number of homosexuals dismissed as bad security risks since 1947: 146 men and two women. (May 7, 1951, p. 26.)
>
> *Here is a case of imputing corruption to an administration by pointing out and playing up a certain "scandal" in one department.*
>
> A few days later, over the morning coffee, the nation read of Harry Truman's reply and fumed. (April 23, 1951, p. 25.)

---

[9]These comments by the author dealing with the examples from *Time* are certainly themselves "subjective." But there is one thing in their favor: they are *said to be comments* and are not hidden in a factual context.

Table 2   Subjective Expressions Used by *Time* in Reporting Speeches
of the Three Presidents

Truman:	Eisenhower:
"said curtly"	"said with a happy grin"
"said coldly"	"cautiously pointed out"
"barked Harry S. Truman"	"chatted amiably"
"cracked Harry Truman"	"said warmly"
"with his voice heavy with sarcasm"	"paused to gather thought"
"preached the Truman sermon"	"equanimity and inner ease"
"flushed with anger"	"sensitive to the mood of the nation"
"grinning slyly"	"devastatingly effective"
"petulant, irascible President"	"serene state of mind"
"had worn a harried and rumpled air"	"calm and confident"
"made his familiar, chopping motions"	"frankness was the rule"
"cocky as ever"	"skillfully refused to commit himself"
"publicly put his foot in his mouth"	"obviously a man with a message"
"with a blunt finger he probed"	"brushing aside misunderstanding"

Kennedy:
"President Kennedy said" (10 t.)
"President Kennedy announced"
"Concluded the President"
"stated the case in plain terms"
"the President urged"
"Kennedy argued"
"concluded Kennedy"
"he suggested"
"President Kennedy recommended"
"Kennedy insisted"
"Kennedy contended"
"Kennedy maintained"
"The President promised"

Time here projects it omniscience over the entire nation and tells the reader what the country read and even how it reacted after reading it.

The strong leadership of President Eisenhower and the near-unanimity of the Congress in backing him in the Formosa resolution undoubtedly retrieved much of the U.S. prestige and influence that had been recently lost in Asia. (Feb. 7, 1955, p. 9.)

This example is interesting not only for the clever way positive bias is packed in, but for the use of the subjective key-word "undoubtedly."

He (Eisenhower) has an aversion to stirring up unnecessary national crises, has deliberately tried to soothe the nation's nervous system—left jangled and jumpy by an unbroken procession of Truman crises. (Feb. 28, 1955, p. 13.)

Here is the implication that other presidents might like to stir up trouble, but not Ike. Also Truman's "crises" are dragged in and the reader is informed that this is the reason for the "nation's nervous system" being "jumpy."

Conclusions

25   Because of its racy style, its clever use of captions and pictures and its smooth integration of separated (in space and time) incidents and speeches, *Time* is understandably a popular publication for the general reader. However, the careful and thoughtful reader who is looking for proper perspective and serious backgrounding instead of entertainment and polemic will probably not find the magazine very satisfying.[10] This is not to imply that *Time* contains no *facts;* certainly its pages abound with facts. But it is the popularization of these facts, the constant weaving of these facts into semi-fictionalized language patterns and the constant evidence of preferential or prejudicial treatment of news subjects that would probably be unpalatable to the reader seeking the "true picture."

26   This study indicated that *Time* editorialized in its regular "news" columns to a great extent, and that it used a whole series of tricks to bias the stories and to lead the reader's thinking. Mostly, in its Presidential treatment, the magazine presented the reader with highly loaded essays of a subjective type.

27   In addition to isolating several interesting types of subjectivizing procedure, the study showed that *Time* 1) was clearly anti-Truman, 2) was strongly pro-Eisenhower, and 3) was neutral or certainly moderate toward Kennedy. Stereotypes of the three Presidents built up by the magazine during the periods studied were quite vivid—especially in the cases of Truman and Eisenhower.

28   By way of summary, the following principal techniques were used by *Time* in subjectivizing its reports: 1) deciding which incidents, which remarks, etc., to play up and which ones to omit completely or to play down; 2) failing to tell the whole story; 3) weaving opinion into the story; 4) imputing wisdom and courage and other generally admired qualities by use of adjectives, adverbs and general context and by quoting some friend of the person; 5) dragging into the story past incidents unnecessary to the present report; 6) using one person's opinion to project opinion to this person's larger group— the "one-man cross-section device."

29   7) Imputing wide acceptance, such as "the nation believed" without presenting any evidence at all; 8) transferring disrepute to a person by linking him or his group to some unpopular person, group, cause or idea; 9) playing up certain phrases or descriptions which tend to point out possible weaknesses, paint a derogatory picture or create a stereotype (e.g., "small-town boy," "off-the-cuff oratory").

30   10) Creating an overall impression of a person by words, an impression which is reinforced from issue to issue (e.g., to show an active and healthy President when the nation was concerned about his health, *Time* would have him "yelling tirelessly," "playing a wicked game of golf," "enjoying himself tremendously," "waving happily," and "stepping lightly"); 11) explaining motives for Presidential actions, and 12) telling the reader what "the people" think or what the nation or public thinks about almost anything.

---

[10]It should be noted, however, that some critics seem to feel that *Time* in 1965 has become more responsible in its news reporting; see, for example William Forbis, "The March of Time; Curt, Clear and More Complete," *Montana Journalism Review* (Spring 1965), pp. 6-8. This article contrasts sharply with the negative criticism about *Time* made by David Halberstam in his *The Making of a Quagmire* (New York: Random House, 1964). pp. 35-37.

VOCABULARY

cursory   2
critique   3
random   4
contextual   5
attribution   6
notated   11

innuendo   11
semantic   13
inauspicious   13
Olympian   13
skulduggery   17

reportorial   24
conjecture   24
omniscience   24
polemic   25
imputing   28.

QUESTIONS

1. How has Merrill's audience affected his style?

2. Where do you find the thesis? the statement of purpose? How do they differ?

3. What is the purpose of the questions asked in ¶s 2 and 3?

4. Why has Merrill used subtitles?

5. Why does Merrill spend fourteen paragraphs explaining how he proceeded with the study?

6. What purpose does each footnote serve?

7. Does Merrill approve or disapprove of the subjective reporting he demonstrates in *Time*? How can you tell?

8. Do you approve or disapprove? Why?

9. Are you convinced by the study? Why? What techniques have been used to convince the reader?

Here is another editorial essay ("The Computer and the Poet" appears in Section 2) by Norman Cousins, editor of Saturday Review. *This essay was published in* SR *on February 22, 1969.*

Are You Making Yourself Clear?
Norman Cousins

1   In the present scratchy and undiscriminating national mood, education is an easy target. I deplore the tendency but would like to get into the act nonetheless. One of the prime weaknesses of education, it seems to me, is that it doesn't give enough attention to the need for developing the individu-

al's communications skills. It is concerned with his ability to absorb knowledge but it assigns somewhat lesser importance to his need to make himself clear. This is less a matter of vocabulary range than of vocabulary control. It has to do with the entire process by which an individual organizes his thoughts for purposes of transmission.

2   The prime element in this process is sequence. Ideas have to be fitted together. The movement of a concept or an image from the mind of the speaker to the mind of the listener is retarded when words become random chunks rather than sequential parts of an ordered whole. This doesn't rule out unhurried allusions; these can give color to an account and help to make a claim on the imagination and memory. But it does rule out ungoverned circling and droning, reminiscent of buzzards hovering and swooping over a victim until he drops.

3   It contributes nothing to a conversation to have an individual interrupt himself in order to insert sudden thoughts. The abuse is compounded when these obtrusive thoughts are invaded by yet others so that nothing is complete, neither the sentence, nor the paragraph, nor any of the vagrant incidents or ideas that are strewn around like fragments of an automobile wreck.

4   The following quotation is a fair approximation drawn from a recent conversation:

5   "This book I want to talk to you about," a visitor told me, "is one of the finest novels that I—well, let me put it this way, when I first heard about it I said to myself—actually, I told my wife, who asked me if we were publishing anything exciting; you know, my wife is one of the finest assets I have in my job. She doesn't come to the office or anything like that, you know, but—well, she does have a reputation in the shop for being a good critic and she—well, first let me tell you that she did disagree with me about two manuscripts I turned down and they were published by another house and of course they became best sellers. First let me tell you I once had a manuscript reader who was working for me and, well, she was two years out of Radcliffe but she had taken Levin's course in writing at Yale. I don't agree that writing can't be taught. I remember my own lit course with Jenney, who told me—well, you know, he had the highest standards and I was very pleased to see him published last month in *Saturday Review*. What I meant was, someone always publishes the manuscript that everyone considers unpublishable, and this is what one always hears about and it is what always comes up in conversation. One always hears about *A Tree Grows in Brooklyn*—it was rejected by a dozen publishers—or *The Naked and the Dead*—it must have been turned down by ten publishers. Of course, Norman Mailer has turned out to be quite different from what everyone expected. His report on the Chicago convention was one of the finest—I don't know whether you saw it in *Harper's*—it was better, you know, than his piece on the Pentagon riots in *Commentary* which—well, let me put it this way, the best writing is being done by—I mean the best reporting—no one has come close, you know, to Truman Capote and this is where we go, you know, when we want to find out

what is really—you know, nothing in any of the newspapers can tell us what it is like, especially if you want to know what the real facts were. . . ."

6 He was at least two hundred words and three minutes beyond his topic sentence, and I had yet to hear the title of the book. The passage quoted is not a parody. If you want its equivalent, I suggest you take a tape recording of a cross section of an average day's office interviews or serious conversations. Chances are you will be appalled by the sprawling and fragmented character of the transcript. Complete sentences will be largely nonexistent; central ideas will emerge as from a deep mist. The surprise will not be that the meaning should be as obscured as it is by the unrelated turnings and self-interruptions, but that there should be any meaning at all. Oral communication in our society comes close to being a complete bust.

7 Let me be a little crotchety at this point. During the course of an average work week, it is necessary for me to see perhaps forty or fifty people. Most of them come on matters related to the business of the magazine. Some may have ideas for articles or have projects for which they seek *SR*'s sponsorship. I value these meetings; they bring a rich supply of information and opinions. They widen our editorial options.

8 Having said this, I must also confess that not all our callers know how pressing and persistent magazine deadlines can be. Nothing is more fatiguing than to be pinned down in a chair on a busy day while a visitor seeks through sheer volume of words to get a message across. After a while I have to quell a raging desire to terminate a "conversation" with someone who has talked for forty minutes without making his purpose known—or, what is even worse, who has talked for forty minutes *after* making his purpose known. But the compulsion to walk away is downed. Such things just aren't done.

9 I see that recent medical research indicates that a wide variety of maladies, including rheumatoid arthritis and adrenal exhaustion, are sometimes directly related to the intense frustration and restlessness a man suffers when subjected to mindless and predatory assaults on his time by people who don't know how to come to the point. It is astounding that otherwise well-educated men should have so little awareness of their obligation to make themselves clear and to stay within reasonable time limits. My heart sinks whenever a caller takes out a note pad on which he has listed a dozen or more separate items for our conversation. When, fifteen minutes later, he is still in the middle of item one, I make a hasty calculation and realize that at this rate we won't be through for a couple of days. That is when the corticoids and all the other stress chemicals in the body begin racing up and down.

10 Not long ago a man arrived at *SR,* identified himself as a charter subscriber, and asked to see the editor for a few minutes. He came into my office and proceeded to talk volubly and obscurely. Finally, I perceived he was telling me about his daughter's book, published by a firm unknown to me. As a father who likes to think his own daughters are bursting with literary ability, I was impressed by my visitor's determination to do everything he could to herald his child's talents. Unfortunately, he continued to herald long past the

point of reasonable persuasion. Finally, I broke in and told him we would be glad to look at the book in order to determine whether it could be sent out for review.

11   "I don't want you to review it," he said. "I want you to buy it. It costs only $4.95 and. . . ."

12   I gave him the $4.95. It was an inexpensive way of terminating a conversation, considering the price I would otherwise have had to pay in suppressed anguish over the delay in getting back to my desk.

13   If there is no excuse for blurring and meandering in conversation, there is even less excuse for it in written forms of communication. The daily correspondence basket is a greater source of fatigue than anything that has been invented to harass a man whose work requires him to be in almost constant communication. I have a vivid picture in my mind of Dr. Albert Schweitzer at the age of eighty-four spending most of his time struggling with his correspondence. Every day two sacks of mail would arrive at the hospital at Lambaréné—letters from people who wanted to visit the hospital or work there; letters from Schweitzer Fellowship members all over the world; letters from admirers and readers of his books; letters from doctors and theologians, musicologists and scientists, all of them writing on matters within his professional competence.

14   Late at night, long after the hospital was put to bed, Schweitzer would be bent over his desk, working on his correspondence. One night, during my visit in 1958, I was unable to sleep. I left my bunk and walked toward the river. I saw a light in Dr. Schweitzer's quarters and peeked in. There was Le Grand Docteur, struggling with his correspondence at 2 A.M.

15   We discussed the matter the next day.

16   "My correspondence is killing me," he said. "I try to answer all my letters, but I keep falling further and further behind. I get great joy out of reading my letters. It keeps me in touch with the outside world. I like to hear from people. But most of the time, I don't really know what my letters are trying to tell me. They wander so, ach!"

17   Is it unreasonable to expect education to attach primary importance to the techniques of clarity, either oral or written? Is it unreasonable to suggest that respect for the next man's time is one of the most essential and useful lessons a person can learn? Time is capital. Time is finite. Clarity is a coefficient of time.

18   I should like to think that the school provides an environment conducive to the development of habits of clarity. But I am troubled by what I know. A recent high school test in English composition that came to my attention called upon the student to write descriptive material of 1,000 words or more in ninety minutes. If the school allowed (or even required) the student to spend half a day thinking about such a writing assignment, and a full day for the actual writing, the time would not be excessive. A writer like Thomas Mann felt he had put in a productive day if he had been able to write 500 words. Good writing, most of all, is clear writing. This is painstaking and often painful work. It requires time. It requires sustained and sequential thought.

19   But the school itself is not yet a model of organization, either in its internal structure or in its relationship to the student. I see very little evidence of total time-management in the demands made by the school on the student. Each course of study has its own claim. Unable to get it all in, the student is often under pressure to cut corners. He finds himself forced into a strategy of intellectual merchandising and packaging; he becomes more concerned with the voluminous trappings and the appurtenances of surface scholarship than with genuine achievement. He learns the tricks of glibness.

20   It is difficult to understand why the school should foster habits of juggling and fragmentation rather than of concentration. Why is so little consideration given to the coordination of work assignments for students? Why is it considered good educational practice to compel a student to work on more than one major paper at a time? Why shouldn't the full mobilization of an individual's intelligence, rather than his capacity for sustaining diffusion, engage the aims of the school? Some of the greatest feats of the human intelligence have proceeded out of total focus on a single problem. Charles Darwin was riding on a London bus top when some key thoughts of his theory of evolution burst upon him. This doesn't mean that there is something about the topside of a London omnibus that triggers profound ideas on the origin of species. What it does mean is that Darwin had allowed his mind to fill up with a complex problem until it spilled over to the subconscious; the result was that, even when he did not consciously direct his thoughts, his mind kept working away at the problem, sorting all the factors that were being accumulated, weighing them, making correlations, and engaging in all the operations leading to a deduction or a discovery. It was the gestative process of ideas, rather than the environment of a bus top, that was reponsible for the flash that electrified Darwin. Socrates had no particular liking for the term "teacher" when it was applied to himself; he preferred to think of himself as an intellectual midwife who helped bring ideas to birth out of laboring minds. What is most valuable in the Socratic method is the painstaking and systematic development of a thought from its earliest beginnings to its full-bodied state. The mind was fully engaged; this was what was most vital to the process.

21   What I am trying to suggest is that the natural requirements of thought are the essential and prior business of education. No teacher I knew had a better understanding of this basic purpose than Harold Rugg. He never wavered in his confidence in the ability of the mind to create its own optimum environment. His belief in the importance of integrative education was directly related to this concept.

22   My apprehension about modern education is that it is scatter-prone, even as it promotes overspecialization. That is, it lacks a philosophy of education to go along with the education it provides. It has yet to come to terms with the constant accretion of new knowledge. The result is that we are producing a generation of idea-hoppers. It is not necessarily true that the school is helpless to cope with the onrush of increasing specialization. Major emphasis can be given to the interrelationships of knowledge and to the points of contact and convergence. It may not be possible to keep the student up-to-date in the accumulation of new knowledge—or even to instruct him fully in the old. But what is possible is to define the significance of what is happening and to identify the juncture at which different areas of knowledge come together.

23   All this has to do with the student's ability to organize his time, to give his total attention to a difficult problem or objective, and to make himself clear. The school is not the only conditioning agent in the thought patterns and habits of the student, but it is possibly the dominant one.

24   Meanwhile, there is the ongoing problem of all those who are beyond the reach of the school. It is churlish and absurd to take the position that a poor communicator is locked into his low-level condition. The key to his liberation is the realization that effective communications, oral or written, depend absolutely on a clear understanding of his purpose. That purpose should be clearly identified. It should not be cluttered with extensive comment or side excursions. It should be developed point by point, with the rigorous attention to sequence of a professional bead-stringer at work.

25   In verbal communication, the prime requisite is to anticipate the circumstances of a meeting or encounter. If it seems likely that the time available for meeting will be limited, then it is obviously suicidal to use up most of the time in clearing one's throat. Nor does it seem especially perspicacious to have an overly long agenda, saving the most important items for last, when there is every likelihood that time will run out long before the main event.

26   In written communication, no better advice can be offered than to cite the favorite six-word question of Harold Ross, late editor of *The New Yorker:* "What the hell do you mean?" Ross was a great editor because he was death on ambiguities. Though he edited one of the most sophisticated magazines in the nation, he cherished the simplicities. He insisted on identifications for all names and places. And he hated extraneous words or observations. Under his rule, *The New Yorker* became a model of clear, effective writing.

27   My purpose here is not to drum up business for *The New Yorker* (I have a drum of my own), but to point out that institutions can be built on clarity. Also, that clarity is one of the truly distinguishing characteristics of the educated man.

VOCABULARY

allusions 2
obtrusive 3
rheumatoid arthritis 9
predatory 9
adrenal 9
Dr. Albert Schweitzer 13
Lambaréné 13
coefficient 17
glibness 19
appurtenances 19

Charles Darwin 20
Socrates 20
integrative 21
optimum 21
accretion 22
churlish 24
perspicacious 25
ambiguities 26
extraneous 26

QUESTIONS

1. What is Cousins' thesis? Where does he state it?

2. How does he develop his thesis?

3. What kinds of examples does Cousins provide?

4. Examine several of Cousins' examples, for instance, the "conversation" in ¶s 4–6, the "conversation" in ¶ 10–12, and the Schweitzer example in ¶s 13–16. What characterizes these examples? Why are they effective?

5. What is the point of the Darwin example in ¶20?

6. What problem does Cousins see in modern education? What does he think schools ought to be teaching?

7. Characterize Cousins' word choice; is it difficult or simple? abstract or concrete? Are his sentences generally long, short, or a combination? Are the long ones difficult to read? How are the short ones used? Look at his metaphors in ¶s 2, 3, 9, 19, 20, 22, 24; are they vivid and original? What contribution do they make to the quality of his writing?

8. What is the tone of the essay? How is that tone achieved?

9. Describe the voice used in the essay. What sort of personality comes through? What techniques help to create that voice?

10. Do you agree with Cousins (¶18) that good writing requires time? Are you surprised to find that a professional writer finds writing painful?

Henry Barnes (1906–1968) was Commissioner of Traffic for New York City and a contributor to professional journals and magazines. He wrote the following essay for the anthology Language in America *(1969).*

The Language of Bureaucracy
Henry A. Barnes

1   The word *bureau* has grown in significance for me over the past half century. Its earliest meaning was a chest of drawers for the bedroom, intended for the storage of personal gear unsuited to hanging in a closet or hiding under a bed.

2   Family ground rules demanded that the lower drawers of a bureau be maintained in reasonably orderly array, but tradition permitted the top drawer to be reserved for clutter. The top drawer was a catchall for baseball cards, pencil stubs, watch fobs, unmated shoestrings, 23-skiddoo buttons, and similar miscellany.

3   Unaware as I was of any other kind of bureau, I was, nevertheless, learning many useful facts for my later years spent among the bureaus of public life. Early experience taught me that a bureau requires constant supervision lest it become a mare's-nest of disorder. Another lesson fixed in memory is the knowledge that the periodic reorganizing of a bureau can become a refuge from reality, a dawdler's delight which provides the aimless with endless hours of seemingly productive endeavor.

4   An early organizing technique was to divide the bureau into divisions. This might be accomplished in the lower drawers, but never in the top drawer. The attempt was usually made with the aid of partitions consisting of discarded cigar and candy boxes. The boxes were seldom suitable for the job, being selected to fit the space rather than the purpose. The result resembled the printed forms of modern bureaucracy—small boxes for long items and big boxes for short items.

5   *Bureaucrat* and *bureaucracy* were words I had never heard. I probably would have associated them with *aristocrat* and *aristocracy,* and concluded that a bureaucrat was a boy who didn't have to share a bureau with his brother. A bureaucracy would, no doubt, have been a fanciful state in which such affluent isolation prevailed.

6   Since those days of innocence, I have learned that many words have more than one meaning—*bureau* among them. Many such words have been directed my way—*bureaucrat* among them. These confrontations lose their jolt with time, but I am still dismayed when anyone, in evident compliment, refers to me as a "top-drawer bureaucrat."

7   Bureaucracy generally carries the connotation of an impersonal governmental agency insulated from reality and responsibility by layers of red tape. It is in this context that I intend to pursue the subject of the language of bureaucracy. It would be unrealistic, however, to ignore the fact that bureaucracy arises also in private enterprise, and its language is spoken wherever an organization becomes so large and complex and detached that it loses the common urge to communicate in the common tongue with others.

8   The grating voice of bureaucracy's jargon may be heard in any organization, public or private, which feels itself free of the need to share a bureau with its brothers.

9   When the profits of industry go down, the towers of bureaucratic babel go up. I have read corporation reports which were based on the assumption that the stockholder has at his disposal as many lawyers, accountants, and word-splitters as the firm itself. I have heard executives from the "private sector of the economy" spatter audiences with such eloquent nonsense as: "This is a novel innovation of such dimension, scope, and proportion that, without a certain doubt, it is a boon and benefit not only to all mankind but to every customer, employee, and stockholder of this enterprise."

10   While much of the language of bureaucracy defies precise decipherment, it will be found that about 50 percent of the spoken language, including the foregoing example, consists of variations of a single sentence—"Keep your eye on the girl with the pretty legs while I prepare to pull another rabbit out of the hat."

11   At this point it may be to my advantage to state that the examples of the language of bureaucracy presented here have been subjected to considerable paraphrasing to protect the guilty.

12   One very useful method of translating the spoken language of bureaucracy is to commit it to print. In the following example, truth crushed to earth in a bureaucrat's dictation rose again, inadvertently, in his secretary's typing.

> *Example:*
> This little-publicized program has been endorsed by a hundred-odd officials.
> *Translation:*
> This little, publicized program has been endorsed by a hundred odd officials.

13   It will be noted that the hidden meaning of the dictated version was revealed in the typing by simple revision of punctuation. One who has worked for an appreciable time in areas where the jargon of bureaucracy prevails learns other simple translation devices. For instance, all expressions of confidence should be interpreted as evidences of doubt. A simple way to remember this rule is to bear in mind the true significance of *confidence man*.

14   As indicated below, a little practice with simple words and phrases of assurance and conviction will enable the student to move quickly to more complex sentences.

> *Example:*
> Doubtless
> *Translation:*
> Unverified
>
> *Example:*
> Interesting fact
> *Translation:*
> Drivel
>
> *Example:*
> Universally recognized principle
> *Translation:*
> A risky proposition
>
> *Example:*
> We are assigning major priority to the early completion of the preliminary stages of the program.
> *Translation:*
> With any luck we can forget the matter completely.

15   It must not, however, be assumed that translations may always be accomplished so readily. Since the technique of the bureaucrat is to pour more words than light on his subject, all surplus words must be deleted before any translation can be attempted. To fully understand this principle, one must remember that an important rule of the language of bureaucracy requires, wherever possible, the use of two or more difficult words selected by sound, rather than one simple word chosen for meaning.

Example:
The respondent correspondent gave expression to the unqualified opinion that the subject missive was anterior to his facile comprehension.
Translation:
He replied that he didn't understand our letter.

16   The thought presents itself here that English grammarians can be rather bureaucratic in their insistence on conformity. Some of the most interesting addresses I have heard have been among the least grammatical. But this is a subject of a different discussion.

17   The language of bureaucracy is essentially a professional jargon. Like other professional jargons it lends itself to exclusiveness, defensiveness, and laziness. A thorough study of this or any other private language would require psychological and sociological analyses of the structure, functions, conditions, and mentality which created the desire for a special lingo. Two difficulties to this approach present themselves—the space limitations of this article, and the author's inability to understand the professional jargons of the psychologists and sociologists. So without extensive examination of the motivational aspects, let us consider a few of the factors bearing on the formation of the private bureaucratic jargon.

18   Bureaucracy is often called "The System." This is, perhaps, some small recognition of the fact that a bureaucracy has its origin in the good intention of achieving systematic operation. All "inside" languages begin with a group's desire to foster efficiency. It is only when the group loses or discards its initial motivation to serve the general public that the "outside" language falls into discard. The "inside" tongue now develops in direct proportion to the group's new inclination to isolate itself and deceive or confuse outsiders.

19   Contrary to popular belief, the language of bureaucracy is not essential to success in public life. The names of Adlai Stevenson and Robert Moses come readily to mind as examples of public figures who have used the common English language with grace, skill, and effectiveness.

20   Such men have no need for the protective cover of an "inside" language. The jargon of bureaucracy developed from the needs of lesser men to make their lives easier, shield their shortcomings, or cover the drabness of their operations with some tawdry gloss.

21   The desire to make life easier fosters the growth of routine phrasing to fit routine situations. Clichés replace original thought. Perfunctory phrases chill response. Dullness is mistaken for dignity. Ready-made replies are stockpiled to handle recurring questions.

22   The form letter is, perhaps, the most exasperating evidence of this tendency. From the standpoint of the bureaucrat, the form letter is a survival kit on the barren mountain of correspondence. To the citizen with a unique problem, the form letter is an abomination.

23   Originating as bureaucracy's fence against avalanches of official correspondence, the form letter becomes in time a despotic protector against work and worry. The periodic attempts of committees to revise form letters or to make them applicable to new types of correspondence often succeed only in spreading the same old ineffective unction more thinly over additional wounds. The time-saving device now becomes a time-wasting irritant as bureaucracy vainly attempts to channel the warm pulsings of civic life into cold classifications like so many columns of want ads.

24   Heavy reliance on ready-made replies eventually reduces bureaucracy's ability to express itself clearly when a tailor-made reply is required. New constructions are introduced into its language to mask its deficiencies. Emphasis is sought by stacking superlative on superlative. Unpleasant facts are hidden behind the screens of flamboyant words. Tautology impedes meaning. The plague of -*ants*—pursu*ant,* cogniz*ant,* convers*ant,* result*ant*—is turned loose. Ideas are lost in the maze of complex sentences. A shortage of meaning develops in direct proportion to the surplus of words.

25   Just as bureaucracy feeds on carbon copies, its language fattens on the repetition of words. Adjectives must always be accompanied by their identical twins and all known relatives. To a bureaucrat, the United States is not merely a big country, it is a huge, vast, and spacious nation. Certain words in the bureaucrat's vocabulary may not decently appear in public without their chaperons. The story is told of an agency which could not prepare a notice for an employees' social because it was impossible to separate *social* from *political* and *economic* in an official document.

26   Some of the long and legalistic phrasing in the language of bureaucracy results from the public servant's duty to protect the public interest. If any fault attaches to it, the special jargon of the law should be held accountable. Contracts are prime examples. In a contract which I signed for my department recently was a sentence composed of 279 words. This lengthy sentence merely stated that the contractor could lose his contracts and be barred from further bidding if he refused to testify in any legal proceedings. Although the thought can be stated here in a couple of dozen words, this simple version would be powerless to withstand the attacks of an astute attorney. Loophole-stuffing of this kind accounts for a considerable amount of the padding in official correspondence.

27   In my years in public service, I have noted a gradual improvement in the language of bureaucracy as used externally. Internally, however, where committee reports rise like magnificent tombstones over the remains of the English language, improvements have been scarce.

28   Much of the fault lies in bureaucracy's passion for prepackaged decisions—advance planning to remove all possibility of personal judgment and initiative. Although as an individual man is seldom gifted with prophetic vision, as a member of a committee he feels himself equal to any future emergency. With his co-oracles, he finds no difficulty in producing such dogma as this:

PROCEDURES, EMERGENCY
Instruction #20973 A-3 (1964)
Section 794—Attack, Atomic

In the possible event of an atomic attack, the senior administrative officer in effective attendance (see Personnel Order 000.06) shall proceed in strict compliance and accordance with applicable provisions of General Circular #87 (1951), paragraphs 843 to 976 as amended by General Circular #103 (1952), paragraphs 237 to 743 and 821 to 934.

Due care must be exercised to comply completely and fully with Office Procedure Manual #1 (1901) Section F-103 (Catastrophes, major) Section V-19 (Absence, excused) and Section W-47 (Routines, timecards).

Reference may profitably be made to Emergency Procedures—Instruction #45678 R-7 (1964) under the subsequently following headings:

Cave-in, roof (Section 279)
Pipes, steam, broken (Section 293)
Pipes, water, broken, hot (Section 483-A)
Pipes, water, broken, cold (Section 483-J)
Elevators, service, none (Section 791)
Stairways, use of (Section 904)

Reports will be made in quadruplicate to the executive office on Forms #3290R (1904), #5280 (1907) and 7654321-G (1960). Separate forms will be completed for each employee concerned. Filing of reports is mandatory and required during the work day on which emergency occurs.

Note: The above enumeration of forms is not to be construed or interpreted to excuse the senior administrative officer from using all other appropriate forms applicable to the circumstance obtaining.

Important: No disbursements of agency funds will be permitted nor may agency vehicles be used by other than assigned personnel without prior approval in writing from the bureau head or his duly appointed representative on written request to be filed at least two (2) weeks in advance of the date upon which permission shall become operative.

29   Assuming that the documents, pertinent, have not been consumed in a holocaust, fiery, the officer, administrative, senior, need spend only an hour or two decoding the instructions and another few hours in preparing reports to emerge as the hero, unquestioned, of the situation.

30   A word might be said for the public servant who struggles daily through this jungle of bureaucratic entanglements. His pretentious phrasings are often the reflection of a dull and repetitive existence rather than a pompous personality. Frequent flowery redundancies in the language of bureaucracy are comparable to the sports writer's thesaurus-like reports. A person doomed to tell the same story daily deserves some commendation for his efforts to tell it in a new way.

31   All the elements for continual growth persist, but one small peril to the language of bureaucracy has begun to develop. This is a problem of bureaucracy's own making—the long evasive answer. For years this technique permitted a bureaucrat the advantage of a revolving door of words from which he

could emerge on either side at his own convenience. A classic instance of its use is in the final moments of a radio or TV interview to prevent the moderator from asking the question he was saving for the final discomfiture of the bureaucrat. Moderators are now learning to counter this tactic with the long evasive question which leaves the bureaucrat only seconds to answer a query he probably doesn't understand. Thus a medium of communications with major influence on the development of language patterns begins to veer toward the language of bureaucracy. If the trend continues, bureaucracy may be forced for self-protection to return to the use of the English language.

VOCABULARY

fobs 2	jargon 13	abomination 22
miscellany 2	lingo 17	despotic 23
bureaucrat 5	Adlai Stevenson 19	unction 23
babel 9	Robert Moses 19	tautology 24
decipherment 10	perfunctory 21	thesaurus 30
confidence man 13		

QUESTIONS

1. What is accomplished by the long introduction (¶ 1-6) that examines the words "bureau" and "bureaucrat"? What image of bureaucracy is created by the analogy to dresser drawers?

2. What is Barnes's attitude toward his subject? How do you know? How does the introduction help to establish attitude and create tone?

3. Where does Barnes define his subject?

4. What reasons does Barnes suggest for the creation of a language of bureaucracy? What reason is suggested by comparing a bureaucrat to a magician in ¶10?

5. Examine the examples of bureaucratic language; what are its characteristics?

6. What is the relevance of ¶16?

7. What techniques does Barnes use to make his essay humorous?

8. Barnes also examines "in-house" reports and directives. How does he account for the absurdity of the directions for emergencies (¶28)? Are these ideas new to you? Does his explanation make sense? Are bureaucrats (or people in general) more often foolish than vicious?

9. Cousins and Barnes are both concerned with the failure of writers to communicate thoughts with clarity and precision. Do you see any solutions to the problem either stated or implied in their essays? Do you have any solutions to offer?

Richard Goodwin (b. 1931), lawyer and former assistant to President Kennedy, is the author of several books (The Sower's Seed: A Tribute to Adlai Stevenson, *1965;* Triumph or Tragedy: Reflections on Vietnam, *1966). The following essay is an excerpt from his latest book,* The American Condition *(1974).*

Incident at Kennebunk
Richard N. Goodwin

1   A newspaper account recorded the angered dismay of the citizenry of Kennebunk, Maine, upon arising one morning to find that the town's Centennial Plot—a remnant of the original village green—has been "removed by state highway crews to make way for new traffic islands." Outrage provoked an inquiry which established that the removal was pursuant to a state highway project approved not too long ago by the town citizens themselves. The green was the most important and visible link with the Kennebunk past, having been enjoyed and admired by more than five generations. It was maintained by a special trust fund established in 1920. And in recent years, a display of flowers had been continually renewed by a town museum entrusted with the nostalgic bequest of the late Colonel Harry A. Naples. It was gone before anyone even noticed. However, the paper tells us, the decision of the town selectmen to request "grassed-over islands rather than the hard-topped type" was expected to "ease the situation—if the grass plots are approved by the state Highway Commission."

2   Who destroyed the Centennial Plot?

3   Not the highway crew. They only followed instructions. Most of them weren't even from Kennebunk. Not the voters of Kennebunk. They merely approved a recommendation for a new road to ease the obviously congested traffic on its way to other parts of Maine. Although the engineering plans were on file in the engineer's office at the state capital of Augusta—about eighty miles away—they did not appear on any ballot. Nor could many have understood them if they had. In any event, the subsequent protest clearly proves that the citizens would have rejected the design had they been aware of its consequence.

4   The state Highway Commission was not responsible. It was only carrying out its assigned task to draw up plans for new roads which, according to conclusive studies, would benefit the entire area. Having submitted recommendations, they thereafter acted as the faithful agent of the expressed popular will. Moreover, since the particular engineer involved was from Bangor—at the other end of the state—he could hardly be expected to know of the passion and nostalgia attached to that one plot of grass, so like a thousand others on his surveys. The construction of this particular highway was stimu-

lated and assisted by federal funds flowing from that vast and visionary federal highway program initiated by President Eisenhower. Without these funds it would never have been built. Was it then President Eisenhower who destroyed Kennebunk's Centennial Plot? It seems unduly harsh to blame a man who may never even have heard of Kennebunk, and whose program, moreover, was the only logical response to the enormous postwar boom in automotive transportation. (Statistics reveal that, if they want to, the entire American population can fit into the front seats of its automobiles.) Perhaps we are now getting closer. There would have been no highway program without all the cars and thus—as radical theory predicts—the villains must be General Motors, Ford and Chrysler. The managers of these companies, however, would immediately counter any such accusation by pointing out that they built cars only because people wanted to buy them; acting as the admittedly well-paid economic servants of a free people making a free choice. The argument is unanswerable.

5   Yet common sense tells us that the millions of people who, year after year, drove their new acquisitions from a dealer's lot did not want to destroy the Centennial Plot. Clearly they didn't mean to. Had a poll been taken, and the issue explained, a majority would probably have supported preservation. Yet when they put their signature on a bill of sale, they helped initiate events which ultimately evoked the futile anger of a Maine town. It was that movement of circumstances, known as "the system," which forever erased the fine old Kennebunk Centennial Plot.

VOCABULARY

centennial 1   pursuant 1
remnant 1   selectmen 1

QUESTIONS

1. Whose fault was it?

2. In his discussion of an illogical situation, has Goodwin remained logical?

3. Does he state a thesis?

4. What is the effect of the parenthetical remark in ¶4?

5. What is Goodwin's attitude? What does his background suggest about his attitude and how has he expressed it?

6. This essay appeared in a book, *The American Condition*, in which Goodwin questions the direction our country seems to be taking. How does this essay contribute to the purpose of the book?

Julian Huxley (b. 1887), noted British biologist, is the author and/or editor of over forty books on both scientific and humanistic issues. This essay was published in On Living in a Revolution *in 1944.*

War as a Biological Phenomenon
Julian Huxley

1   Whenever we tend to become completely absorbed in an enterprise or an idea, it is a good thing to stand off from it now and again and look at it from the most dispassionate point of view possible. War is no exception. Quite rightly, all our major efforts must today be devoted to the urgent business of making sure that we win the war and win it as quickly as possible. We are for most purposes immersed in the war; however, it will not merely do no harm, but will actually be of service, if now and again we try to get outside it and to look at it as objectively as we can in long perspective.

2   The longest possible perspective is that of the biologist, to whom man is a single animal species among hundreds of thousands of others, merely one of the products (albeit the latest and the most successful) of millions of years of evolution.

3   How does war look when pinned out in the biologist's collection? In the first place, he is able to say with assurance that war is not a general law of life, but an exceedingly rare biological phenomenon. War is not the same thing as conflict or bloodshed. It means something quite definite: an organized physical conflict between groups of one and the same species. Individual disputes between members of the same species are not war, even if they involve bloodshed and death. Two stags fighting for a harem of hinds, or a man murdering another man, or a dozen dogs fighting over a bone, are not engaged in war. Competition between two different species, even if it involves physical conflict, is not war. When the brown rat was accidentally brought to Europe and proceeded to oust the black rat from most of its haunts, that was not war between the two species of rat; nor is it war in any but a purely metaphorical sense when we speak of making war on the malaria mosquito or the boll weevil. Still less is it war when one species preys upon another, even when the preying is done by an organized group. A pack of wolves attacking a flock of sheep or deer, or a peregrine killing a duck, is not war. Much of nature, as Tennyson correctly said, is "red in tooth and claw"; but this only means what it says, that there is a great deal of killing in the animal world, not that war is the rule of life.

4   In point of fact, there are only two kinds of animals that habitually make war—man and ants. Even among ants war is mainly practiced by one group, comprising only a few species among the tens of thousands that are known to science. They are the harvester ants, inhabitants of arid regions where there is

little to pick up during the dry months. Accordingly they collect the seeds of various grasses at the end of the growing season and store them in special underground granaries in their nests. It is these reserve supplies which are the object of ant warfare. The inhabitants of one nest set out deliberately to raid the supplies of another group. According to Forel and other students of ant life, they may employ quite elaborate military tactics, and the battles generally result in heavy casualties. If the attackers win, they remove the stores grain by grain to their own nest. Ant wars never last nearly so long as human wars. One campaign observed by the American myrmecologist McCook in Penn Square in the center of Philadelphia, lasted almost 3 weeks. The longest on record is 6½ weeks.

5   Harvesters are the only kind of ants to go in for accumulating property, as well as the chief kind to practice war. This association of property with war is interesting, as various anthropologists believe that in the human species war, or at any rate habitual and organized war, did not arise in human evolution until man had reached the stage of settled civilization, when he began to accumulate stores of grain and other forms of wealth.

6   Less deliberate wars may also occur in some other species, between communities whose nests are so close that they compete for the same food-territory. When similarly provoked conflicts occur between closely related species, the term war may perhaps be extended to them. On the other hand, the raids of the slave-making ants are not true war, but a curious combination of predation and parasitism.

7   There is another group of ants called army ants, which suggests military activity; but the phrase is really a misnomer, for these army ants are in reality simply predatory species which happen to hunt in packs: they are the wolves of the insect world, not the warmongers.

8   So much then for war as a biological phenomenon. The facts speak for themselves. War, far from being a universal law of nature, or even a common occurrence, is a very rare exception among living creatures; and where it occurs, it is either associated with another phenomenon, almost equally rare, the amassing of property, or with territorial rights.

9   Biology can help put war in its proper perspective in another way. War has often been justified on biological grounds. The program of life, say war's apologists, depends on the struggle for existence. This struggle is universal and results in what Darwin called "Natural Selection," and this in its turn results in the "Survival of the Fittest." Natural Selection, of course, works only in a mass way, so that those which survive in the struggle will merely have an average of fitness a little above those which perish or fail to reproduce themselves. But some of the qualities which make for success in the struggle, and so for a greater chance of survival, will certainly be inherited; and since the process continues generation after generation not merely for thousands but for millions of years, the average fitness and efficiency of the race will steadily and continuously be raised until it can be pushed no higher. In any case, say the believers in this doctrine, struggle is necessary to maintain fitness; if the pressure of competition and conflict is removed, biological efficiency will suffer, and degeneration will set in.

10 Darwin's principle of Natural Selection, based as it is on constant pressure of competition or struggle, has been invoked to justify various policies in human affairs. For instance, it was used, especially by politicians in late Victorian England, to justify the principles of *laisser-faire* and free competition in business and economic affairs. And it was used, especially by German writers and politicians from the late nineteenth century onwards, to justify militarism. War, so ran this particular version of the argument, is the form which is taken by Natural Selection and the Struggle for Existence in the affairs of the nations. Without war, the heroic virtues degenerate; without war, no nation can possibly become great or successful.

11 It turns out, however, that both the *laisser-faire* economists and the militarists were wrong in appealing to biology for justification of their policies. War is a rather special aspect of competition between members of the same species—what biologists call "intra-specific competition." It is a special case because it involves physical conflict and often the death of those who undertake it, and also because it is physical conflict not between individuals but between organized groups; yet it shares certain properties in common with all other forms of intra-specific struggle or competition. And recent studies of the way in which Natural Selection works and how the Struggle for Existence operates in different conditions have resulted in this rather surprising but very important conclusion—that intra-specific competition need not, and usually does not, produce results of any advantage to the species as a whole.

12 A couple of examples will show what I mean. In birds like the peacock or the argus pheasant, the males are polygamous—if they can secure a harem. They show off their gorgeous plumage before the hen birds in an elaborate and very striking display, at definite assembly grounds where males and females go for the purpose of finding mates. The old idea that the hen deliberately selects the male she thinks the most beautiful is putting the matter in human terms which certainly do not apply to a bird's mind; but it seems certain that the brilliant and exciting display does have an effect on the hen bird, stimulating her to greater readiness to mate. Individual male birds meet with different degrees of success in this polygamous love business: some secure quite a number of mates, others only one or a few, and some get none at all. This puts an enormous biological premium on success: the really successful male leaves many times more descendants than the unsuccessful. Here, then, is Natural Selection working at an exceedingly high pitch of intensity to make their display plumage and display actions more effective in their business of stimulating the hens. Accordingly, in polygamous birds of this kind, we often find the display plumage developed to a fantastic extent, even so far as to be a handicap to the species as a whole. Thus the display organ of the peacock, his train of enormously overgrown tail-covert feathers, is so long and cumbersome that it is a real handicap in flight. In the argus pheasant the chief display organs are the beautifully adorned wings which the male throws up and forward in display so that he looks like a gigantic bell-shaped flower. The business of display has been so important that it has overridden the business of flying, and now the male argus pheasant can fly only with difficulty, a few feet at a time.

13   Here are two good examples of how a purely intra-specific struggle, in this case between individual rival males, can produce results which are not merely useless, but harmful to the species as a whole in its struggle for existence against its enemies and the forces of nature. In general, selection for success in reproduction reaches greater intensities than selection for individual survival, for the simple reason that reproduction implies multiplication: the individual is a single unit, but, as we have just seen for polygamous birds, success in reproduction may give the individual's characteristics a multiple representation in later generations.

14   In flowering plants, the intra-specific struggle for reproduction between different individuals often produces results which, if not directly harmful to the species, are at least incredibly wasteful. We need only think of the fantastic profusion of bloom on flowering trees like dogwood or hawthorn or catalpa, or the still more fantastic profusion of pollen in trees which rely on fertilization by the wind, like pine and fir. The individual trees are competing for the privilege of surviving in their descendants; the species could certainly perpetuate itself with a much more modest expenditure of living material.

15   One final example. Naturalists have often noted the almost unbelievable perfection of the protective resemblance of certain insects to their surroundings. The most extraordinary cases are the resemblances of various butterflies, like the Kallima, to dead leaves. Not only do the folded wings perfectly resemble a dead leaf in shape and color, not only do they have a projection to imitate the stalk, and dark lines which perfectly simulate the veins, but some even go so far as to be marked with imitation mold-spots and holes!

16   Now, in all butterflies the survival of the species depends to a preponderant degree on the capacity of the defenseless and juicy caterpillar and chrysalis to survive. Selection presses with much greater intensity on the larval and pupal stages than on the adult. Furthermore, there is some sort of balance between the number of adults which survive to reproduce themselves and the intensity of selection which presses on the next generation of caterpillars. If more adults reproduce, there will be many more caterpillars, and they will be more easily found by their enemies, especially the tiny parasitic wasps which lay eggs inside the caterpillars, the eggs growing into grubs which devour the unfortunate animals from within. Conversely, if fewer adults reproduce, there are many fewer caterpillars, but each of them has a better chance of surviving to the butterfly stage. Accordingly, the protection of the adults is, from the point of view of the species, a secondary matter. Of course they must be protected sufficiently well for a reasonable number to survive and reproduce, but after this it is quite unimportant—for the species—if a slightly higher or a slightly lower proportion survives.

17   It is unimportant for the species but it remains important for the individual. If one kind of adult is better protected than another, it will automatically leave a higher average number of offspring; and so the intra-specific struggle for reproduction among the individual adult butterflies will continue

to push any protective devices they possess on toward ever greater efficiency, even though this may be quite immaterial to the survival of the species. The perfection of the Kallima's resemblance to a dead leaf is one of the marvels of nature; not the least marvelous part of it is that it is of no value to the species as a whole.

18   On the other hand, intra-specific competition and struggle need not always lead to results which are useless to the species. The competition between individuals may concern qualities which are also useful in the struggle of the species against its enemies, as in deer or zebra or antelope—the same extra turn of speed which gives one individual an advantage over another in escaping from wolf or lion or cheetah will also stand the whole species in good stead. Or it may concern qualities which help the species in surviving in a difficult environment; an extra capacity for resisting drought in an individual cactus or yucca will help the species in colonizing new and more arid regions. It will not be useless or harmful to the species unless the competition is directed solely or mainly against other individuals like itself.

19   Furthermore, the results will differ according to conditions. When there is competition for mates among male birds, it will become really intense only when polygamy prevails and the advantage of success is therefore multiplied. Monogamous birds also stimulate their mates with a display of bright plumage, but in this case the display plumage is never developed to a pitch at which it is actually harmful in the general struggle for existence; the balance is struck at a different level.

20   All these considerations apply to war. In the first place it is obvious that war is an example of intra-specific competition—it is a physical conflict between groups within the same species. As such, it might be not merely useless but harmful to the species as a whole—a drag on the evolutionary progress of humanity. But, further, it might turn out to be harmful in some conditions and not in others. This indeed seems to be the truth. Those who say that war is always and inevitably harmful to humanity are indulging in an unjustified generalization (though not nearly so unjustified as the opposite generalization of the militarists who say that war is both necessary and beneficial to humanity). Warfare between peoples living on the tribal level of early barbarism may quite possibly have been on balance a good thing for the species—by encouraging the manly virtues, by mixing the heritage of otherwise closed communities through the capture of women, by keeping down excessive population-pressure, and in other ways. War waged by small professional armies according to a professional code was at least not a serious handicap to general progress. But long-continued war in which the civilian population is starved, oppressed, and murdered and whole countries are laid waste, as in the Thirty Years War—that is harmful to the species; and so is total war in the modern German sense in which entire populations may be enslaved and brutalized, as with Poland or Greece today, whole cities smashed, like Rotterdam, the resources of large regions deliberately destroyed, as in the Ukraine. The more total war becomes, both intensively, as diverting more of the energies of the population from construction to destruc-

tion, and extensively, as involving more and more of the countries of the globe, the more of a threat does it become to the progress of the human species. As H. G. Wells and many others have urged, it might even turn back the clock of civilization and force the world into another Dark Age. War of this type is an intra-specific struggle from which nobody, neither humanity at large nor any of the groups engaged in the conflict, can really reap any balance of advantage, though of course we may snatch particular advantages out of the results of war.

21   But it is one thing to demonstrate that modern war is harmful to the species, another thing to do something about abolishing it. What has the biologist to say to those who assert that war is inevitable, since, they say, it is a natural outcome of human nature and human nature cannot possibly be changed?

22   To this the biologist can give a reassuring answer. War is not an inevitable phenomenon of human life; and when objectors of this type talk of human nature they really mean the expression of human nature, and this can be most thoroughly changed.

23   As a matter of observable fact, war occurs in certain conditions, not in others. There is no evidence of prehistoric man's having made war, for all his flint implements seem to have been designed for hunting, for digging, or for scraping hides; and we can be pretty sure that even if he did, any wars between groups in the hunting stage of human life would have been both rare and mild. Organized warfare is most unlikely to have begun before the stage of settled civilization. In man, as in ants, war in any serious sense is bound up with the existence of accumulations of property to fight about.

24   However, even after man had learned to live in cities and amass property, war does not seem to have been inevitable. The early Indus civilization, dating from about 3000 B.C., reveals no traces of war. There seem to have been periods in early Chinese history, as well as in the Inca civilization in Peru, in which war was quite or almost absent.

25   As for human nature, it contains no specific war instinct, as does the nature of harvester ants. There is in man's make-up a general aggressive tendency, but this, like all other human urges, is not a specific and unvarying instinct; it can be molded into the most varied forms. It can be canalized into competitive sport, as in our own society, or as when certain Filipino tribes were induced to substitute football for head-hunting. It can be sublimated into noncompetitive sport, like mountain-climbing, or into higher types of activity altogether, like exploration or research or social crusades.

26   There is no theoretical obstacle to the abolition of war. But do not let us delude ourselves with the idea that this will be easy. The first step needed is the right kind of international machinery. To invent that will not be particularly simple: sanctions against aggressors, the peaceful reconciliation of national interests in a cooperative international system, an international police force—we can see in principle that these and other necessary bits of anti-war machinery are possible, but it will take a great deal of hard thinking to design them so that they will really work.

27   The second step is a good deal more difficult. It is to find what William James called a "moral equivalent for war," while at the same time reducing the reservoir of potential aggressiveness which now exists in every powerful nation. This is a psychological problem. Thanks to Freud and modern psychology in general, we are now beginning to understand how the self-assertive impulses of the child may be frustrated and repressed in such a way as to drive them underground. There in the subconscious they may persist in the form of crude urges to aggression and cruelty, which are all the more dangerous for not being consciously recognized.

28   To prevent the accumulation of this store of psychological dynamite and to find ways in which our self-assertive impulses can issue along conscious and constructive channels is a big job. It means a better structure of social and family life, one which does not inflict such frustrations on the growing human personality; it means a new approach to education; it means providing outlets in the form of physical or mental adventure for the impulses which would otherwise be unused even if not repressed. It is a difficult task; but by no means an impossible one.

29   Thus in the perspective of biology war first dwindles to the status of a rare curiosity. Further probing, however, makes it loom larger again. For one thing, it is a form of intra-specific struggle, and as such may be useless or even harmful to the species as a whole. Then we find that one of the very few animal species which make war is man; and man is today not merely the highest product of evolution, but the only type still capable of real evolutionary progress. And, war, though it need not always be harmful to the human species and its progress, indubitably is so when conducted in the total fashion which is necessary in this technological age. Thus war is not merely a human problem; it is a biological problem of the broadest scope, for on its abolition may depend life's ability to continue the progress which it has slowly but steadily achieved through more than a thousand million years.

30   But the biologist can end on a note of tempered hope. War is not inevitable for man. His aggressive impulses *can* be canalized into other outlets; his political machinery *can* be designed to make war less likely. These things *can* be done: but to do them will require a great deal of hard thinking and hard work. While waging this particular war with all our might, we have a duty to keep a corner of our minds open, engaged on the job of thinking out ways and means of preventing war in general in the future.

VOCABULARY

dispassionate 1	predation 6	larval 16
immersed 1	parasitism 6	pupal 16
albeit 2	misnomer 7	canalized 25
metaphorical 3	*laisser-faire* 10	sublimated 25
granaries 4	polygamous 12	sanctions 26
myrmecologist 4	preponderant 16	indubitably 29
anthropologists 5	chrysalis 16	tempered 30

QUESTIONS

1. How would you characterize Huxley's anticipated audience? Does his style support your characterization? What else supports it?

2. What is the purpose of ¶3?

3. Why does Huxley discuss ants near the beginning of the essay?

4. What is Huxley's definition of war?

5. How does Huxley make his major points clear? What are they?

6. Why does Huxley spend so much time discussing plants, animals, and insects?

7. Does Huxley believe in Darwin's principle of Natural Selection?

8. Is it clear how the processes in ¶14 are wasteful?

9. What is Huxley's attitude toward war? Toward World War II? How is the date of publication relevant?

10. Explain more fully the distinction Huxley makes in ¶22.

11. Do you have any suggestions for a "moral equivalent for war" and for preventing the buildup of subconscious aggression?

THE NEW RIVER AND THE BLUE RIDGE PROJECT

In 1965 the Appalachian Power Company, a subsidiary of the American Electric Power Company, requested a permit from the Federal Power Commission to build two dams and a generating plant on the New River near the Virginia-North Carolina border. The following articles about the New River represent the opinions of the power company, environmentalists, and the federal government concerning the proposed project. On pp. 15 and 17 you will find pictures of the New River and the Kanawha River.

As you read, ask yourself these questions:

1. What might the writer's background suggest about his or her attitude toward the subject?

2. What is the purpose of the piece?

3. How fully has each point been documented?

4. How fair and reliable is each argument?

5. What techniques of persuasion has the writer used?

Elizabeth Watson lives in West Virginia and works as a guide for groups interested in traveling the New River. The following essay was published in February 1975 in National Parks and Conservation *magazine.*

New River Country: Wild and Scenic
Elizabeth Watson

1   Winding its way through the Appalachian foothills, the New River is one of the wildest and most scenic rivers in the eastern United States and is the oldest river on this continent. Once it was called "the river of death" by Indians who hunted and fished along its banks. Its quiet pools, where the rocky bottom drops away quickly to depths of thirty feet, and the boulder-strewn whitewater rapids were feared by the superstitious and became part of the local folklore.

2   Today the river still challenges all who seek to enjoy its beauty and power. Because the river flows through relatively undeveloped areas, its waters remain unpolluted, sparkling, and clear. During millions of years the river has cut a V-shaped valley along most of its course, and in many places the New River flows through steep-walled canyons. In summer, lush stands of broad-leaved trees hide the ruggedness of the terrain along the river. In winter, however, precipitous cliffs become visible and give the river's course its nickname, "Grand Canyon of the East."

3   Several measures have been proposed that would affect this ancient and wild river: one would study the New River for potential inclusion in the National Wild and Scenic Rivers System; Senator Jennings Randolph of West Virginia has officially requested the National Park Service to study the New River Gorge area for possible designation as a national park; and twin pumped-storage dams are planned near the river's headwaters.

4   The New River begins high in the Appalachian Mountains of Ashe County, North Carolina. There two smaller streams, the North Fork and the South Fork, join to form it. The river's direction of flow is predominantly north, an oddity for major rivers. It is part of the New–Kanawha drainage system, which in its entirety drains almost seven thousand square miles of land. Meandering for almost two hundred miles across western Virginia, the New River enters an area known as The Narrows. There the river has cut deeply through a high Allegheny ridge, forming a narrow gorge of special interest to paleontologists. The rocks exposed in the canyon walls contain many fossils, including some crinoids and trilobites, which help to reconstruct the geologic history of the area.

5   A short distance from The Narrows the New River crosses into West Virginia. Continuing its northward flow for approximately thirty miles, the river reaches the only major town along its banks in West Virginia. The

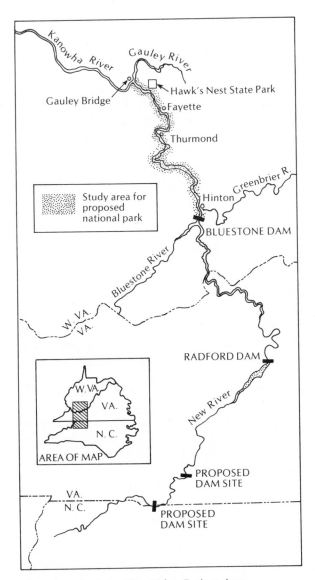

Fig. 1 Map of the Blue Ridge Project Area

community of Hinton fronts on the east side of the New River and is the home of approximately 4,500 people. The town was once a center for the lumber industry and remains today as a focus for railroad and trade activities.

6   Just upstream from Hinton are the confluences of the New River with its only two significant tributaries. The Bluestone River enters from the west through a spectacular narrow gorge. Numerous waterfalls dot the canyon walls and fall to a rocky, low-volume whitewater stream. From the east the beautiful Greenbrier River joins the New River and drains some of West

Virginia's most fertile farmlands. Together the two streams contribute considerably to the volume of the New River. With an average flow of 7,531 cubic feet per second, the New River ranks among the higher volume whitewater streams in the United States.

7   From Hinton downriver to Thurmond the New River is generally broad with a powerful current. The Brooks and Sandstone falls interrupt many long, flatwater pools. A secondary road and the main line of the Chesapeake and Ohio Railroad follow along one side of the river but are largely hidden from view. Below Thurmond the river quickly narrows to approximately one-third its upstream width. The funneling of water into this narrow channel results in the best series of whitewater that can be run year-round in the eastern United States. Second only to the Colorado River, the New River attracts boaters and rafters from all directions. This section of the river tumbles through its deepest canyon area—the New River Gorge. Massive blocks of rock lie strewn along the river's bed and banks. Although a few are angular, most are well rounded, reminding the keen observer of the river's erosive power and venerable age. Along the gorge, springs and waterfalls rush into the New River as do many minor tributaries, further enhancing the enchantment of the wild water. The rugged canyon walls and narrow course have allowed only the building of the Chesapeake and Ohio's main line through the gorge. No roads follow the river downstream from Thurmond to the New's confluence with the Gauley River at Gauley Bridge. There, about fifty miles east of Charleston, the two rivers form the Kanawha River and mark the end of the New River Gorge.

8   Geologically, the New River is the oldest river on the North American contintent. During most of the Paleozoic era, its present drainage area was inundated by a large saltwater sea. The result was massive depositions of sandstone, shale, bituminous coal, and conglomerates. Later, during the Mesozoic era, the area underwent two periods of major uplifting that drained the sea and created river systems. The major system created—a forerunner of the New River—was the Teays River. It flowed northwesterly, cutting across the Alleghenies toward the present Great Lakes before reaching the Mississippi delta. The history of the Teays system was one of continual erosion as the sedimentary rocks were being uplifted. During the Cenozoic era, then, the Teays system in large part was destroyed by the southward reaching glaciers of the Ice Age. The only remaining section of it in which a stream still flows is that portion of the New River upstream from Nitro, West Virginia.

9   Because the mountains on both sides of the New River are of nearly equal height, geologists feel that the Teays began downcutting as a small stream much as the Colorado River did when it formed the Grand Canyon in Arizona. The stream's gradient was great enough to survive the repeated uplifts of the Alleghenies and to cut a deep canyon. The canyon widened as house-size blocks of rock weakened from undercutting of the stream's erosive water and fell to the river's bed. Such activity continues at the present and has created a gorge along the New River in Fayette County, West Virginia, of strikingly similar proportions of height and width to the Inner Gorge of the Grand Canyon.

10   Originally, thick strands of white pine covered much of the New River's banks. Its commercial value led to large-scale cuttings during the 1870s when railroad transportation opened the forests to eastern markets. As a result, few areas of virgin timber remain. Revegetation is comprised largely of a wide variety of deciduous trees. White alder is found along the New River and many of its tributaries. River birch and sycamore grow in considerable numbers. Silver maple, black willow, and American elm are found on the silty soils of the river's edge and floodplain area. Together with a variety of oaks, hickorys, and ashes, these trees add the colors of a painter's palette to New River country during the autumn months.

11   In the spring a different group of trees lends the beauty of floral displays to the river banks. The white dogwood and pink redbud flourish in May. And southern catalpas are also found in blossom, having migrated so far north because of the river's northward flow.

12   The first wildflower to appear in the spring in New River country is usually the spring beauty. Mountain laurel and white-blossomed arbutus, blue violets, and orange wild azaleas follow. Throughout the summer months thick stands of pink and white and rose-purple rhododendron bedeck the river banks to such an extent that rhododendron is the state flower of West Virginia. Black-eyed Susans and daisies also bloom during the summer months and give way to goldenrod, asters, ironweed, and others in late summer and fall. Warm, humid conditions along the New River encourage heavy vegetation, and the river's physical location provides a setting for the meeting of northern and southern varieties of flora. The wide range of species of trees and flowers along the river not only adds to its natural splendor but also makes it a botanist's delight.

13   Similarly, a variety of animal life is found in and along the New River. Because of its unusually clean water the river provides excellent fishing. Small-mouthed bass are abundant in still, shaded, and weedy pools at the river's edge. On the bottom lurk exceptionally large channel catfish, the New's record catch being 110 pounds. Golden trout have been stocked in Manns Creek, a minor tributary to the New River in Fayette County, West Virginia, since the state's sesquicentennial in 1903, and provide an unusual catch for eastern fishermen. In addition, large-mouthed bass, carp, and wall-eyes are caught in the river. The use of the New River for recreational fishing is extensive, its banks being dotted with trout lines and fishing camps from early spring to late fall.

14   Many small furbearing animals live along the New River as well. The presence of beavers is evident from their gnawing of small trees along the banks. Raccoons, red foxes, minks, skunks, opossums, and woodchucks are still living along the river and its tributaries, although their numbers have diminished considerably since the first hunters began trapping in New River country in the 1600s. Squirrels, rabbits, mice, and moles are among the smaller mammals that live along the New River. Occasionally larger animals such as black bear and deer are seen, but their numbers are limited.

15   Several species of turtles, lizards, and snakes are found in New River country. Portions of the river's course are infested with rattlesnakes and copperheads; black snakes, water snakes, and garter snakes are common all along the river. In addition, a careful observer may spot many frogs, toads, and salamanders.

16   A colorful group of birds round out the wildlife along the New River. Robins, cardinals, wrens, sparrows, nuthatches, and thrushes provide song along the banks during the summer months. Some quail and pheasant are found, as are herons and crows. The main winged predators are hawks and great horned owls, and turkey vultures scavenge after spotting food from soaring heights above the river.

17   The native animals brought the first white men into New River country. The ruggedness of the surrounding land, however, delayed man's settlement into the area. Economic development did not get underway until the Chesapeake and Ohio Railroad decided to lay its main east-west line through the New River gorge.

18   In the early 1870s the route of the railroad, which would link Covington, Virginia, and Huntington, West Virginia, was finalized. The mainline would cross the Allegheny Mountains from Covington into the Greenbrier valley. It would proceed along the valley to the confluence of the New and Greenbrier rivers near where the infamous Big Bend tunnel would be blasted. Turning northward, the Chesapeake and Ohio Railroad would open the New River gorge and continue to the Kanawha's bottomlands. Then, crossing the Teays valley, it would join the Ohio River at Huntington.

19   When the railroad began its construction, most of the New River country, and especially the gorge area, was unopened wilderness. Working conditions for most of the laborers were harsh. Documented figures on the deaths resulting from the construction are difficult to obtain, but legends and folk songs suggest that hundreds of lives may have been involved. When the last spike was driven at Hawks Nest on January 29, 1873, however, a major change in the economy of the New River country was made possible.

20   The growing American industrial complex was steam-powered at that time, and coal was the chief fossil fuel. With completion of the railroad came an economical means of getting West Virginia's rich natural resources to market. Much logging was done to help build the nation's factories, and large quantities of timber were taken from along the New River. More important, however, was the opening of coal mines along the New River Gorge to remove the high grade bituminous coal from the Firecreek and Sewell seams. A town generally developed at each mine, and by 1900 thirteen towns had been established in the fifteen-mile stretch of New River between Thurmond and Fayette Station. Most of these towns housed several hundred miners and were accessible only by rail.

21   While coal was "king," activity in New River country flourished. Most of the mining was done by hand. Men and mules were the backbone of the industry. By the late 1920s many of the mines in the gorge itself had been dug out as much as was economically feasible by conventional means. So the miners were forced to load their households onto railroad cars and move on to new mines. Towns were abandoned as quickly as they had sprung up, leaving ghostly reminders of a past way of life. In the fifty years since, fires have claimed many of the towns. Others have fallen into ruin. Coal tipples, beehive ovens, some stone buildings and many foundations, cemeteries, and flat bottomlands cleared of their trees are all that remain. Only one person lives along the river between Thurmond and Fayette Station. For the most part, nature has moved in, its lush vegetation hiding much of man's cultural remains from view during the summer months. The gorge is quiet once more except for the teeming whitewater and an occasional haunting train whistle.

22   Ironically, the only major town along the New River during the coal era that did not have a coal mine is the one that has survived the passing of that bygone way of life. In its heyday Thurmond was a focus of gambling and scarlet night life. Miners in the New River area came to Thurmond to trade their scrip for goods at the company store and for entertainment. The town was also an important railroad center linking the Virginia Railway with the Chesapeake and Ohio Railroad. The closing of the mines along the river began Thurmond's decline. The original population of 500 to 600 people around 1900 has steadily decreased to its present 86. Most of its commercial buildings stand abandoned and in ruin. The C&O's maintenance shop in Thurmond employs a few people locally, but most of the economy is now based on miners' pensions and welfare. What Thurmond can offer now is only a glimpse of its colorful past, an important part of West Virginia's heritage.

23   At present most of the land along the New River is in private ownership, the railroad and large landholding companies being the chief owners. What development has been done by the states of Virginia and West Virginia has been mainly for recreational purposes, and the remaining land largely lies dormant.

24   Three major dams and their accompanying reservoirs now control the flow of the New River. The Radford Dam at Radford, Virginia, is a hydroelectric producer owned by the Appalachian Power Company and retains the waters of Claytor Lake. Downriver at Hinton, West Virginia, is the Bluestone Dam. Built by the Army Corps of Engineers for flood control purposes, the backwaters of the dam, Bluestone Reservoir, are the center of a large recreational area. And the dam at Hawks Nest State Park near Ansted, West Virginia, was constructed by Union Carbide Metals Company to provide power for its nearby smelting plant.

25   In addition, a fifty-year license has recently been granted to the Appalachian Power Company for development of the Blue Ridge Power Project along the New River near the Virginia–North Carolina line pending action by Congress on the wild and scenic river proposal. This project involves the construction of huge twin pumped-storage dams and reservoirs for power production. Completion of the project would result in the inundation of seventy miles of the river and 44,000 acres of adjoining land. Proponents of the project point out the need for additional energy sources for eastern cities, and they encourage regional development. Opponents defend preservation of the river in its natural state and are working to secure the inclusion of parts of it under the National Wildlife and Scenic Rivers System. (The National Wild and Scenic Rivers Act precludes water resource developments on water included in the system.)

26   The fate of the New River is being watched by both conservationists and industrialists. Few major rivers with such natural beauty and historic significance are left in the eastern United States. The river's struggle today is no longer against the uplifting Alleghenies but against pressures of a growing society. Hopefully, man's need for unspoiled nature will encourage preservation of the New River for future generations.

Raymond Janssen (b. 1903), a geologist, retired as chairman of the geology department at Marshall University, Huntington, West Virginia. He has written numerous books and articles in the field of geology. This essay appeared in National Parks and Conservation *magazine, August 1971.*

Blue Ridge Dams: The 'Pollution Dilution' Approach
Raymond E. Janssen

1   The heavy hand of man is threatening to change the character of one of the world's oldest rivers so that the pollution load dumped into it by industry will seem lighter.

2   Precursor of the Mississippi, the New River crosses the entire width of the Appalachian Mountains, from the Blue Ridge in North Carolina through western Virginia to West Virginia, where it joins the Gauley River to form the Kanawha, which flows into the Ohio. On its way to the Kanawha, the New River passes through some of the most beautiful and as yet least despoiled territory of the eastern United States. By unfortunate contrast, the Kanawha River passes a line of chemical plants along the banks near Charleston, West Virginia, where it absorbs a deadly dose of pollution, enough completely to remove the oxygen from the water for a length of 20 miles.

3   Over 150 miles upstream (toward the south), where the New River follows the border between North Carolina and Virginia, the Appalachian Power Company has proposed building a pumped storage and hydroelectric generating station, requiring the construction of two dams and two reservoirs. Conservationists are opposed for several reasons, the strongest of which is that the project would make water available to dilute the polluted water in Charleston.

4   The present controversy stems from a request in June 1962 by the Appalachian Power Company for permission to make preliminary studies of the Blue Ridge Hydroelectric Project. The site was in the midst of a tourist and recreational area just west of the Blue Ridge Parkway and more or less surrounded by three existing state parks—Hungry Mother, Claytor Lake, and

Mount Rogers. While the power company was formulating its construction proposal, a fourth such area was created. An act of Congress in May 1966 provided for the establishment of the Mount Rogers National Recreation Area, consisting of 154,000 acres to the north of the proposed reservoir sites.

5   Until then there was little opposition of consequence to the power project. However, as a result of the Congressional action creating the new area, the United States Department of the Interior entered the picture. The department raised the question of pollution control by contending that the Federal Power Commission should require the power company to increase the sizes of the proposed reservoirs sufficiently to store water for periodic release to improve the quality of water downstream in Charleston. Essentially, this would produce a flushing action whereby the purer upstream water would be used to dilute the polluted downstream water.

6   To provide the extra water, the proposed capacities of the reservoirs were doubled. Revised plans were made for an upper reservoir to be situated between Sparta, North Carolina, and Independence, Virginia, covering 26,000 acres, and a lower one near Galax and Fries, Virginia, of 12,800 acres.

7   In addition to the pollution control aspect, the Federal Power Commission recommended that the power company buy land for a new 3,900-acre park in North Carolina, a 2,400-acre park in Virginia, and 3,400 acres for a possible interstate park on the boundary of the two states.

8   In 1965 Appalachian Power Company requested a construction permit from the Federal Power Commission. Commission Examiner William C. Levy approved the request in October 1969, but by then opposition from environmentalists had gained strength. The full Commission decided to delay making the decision final until the environmentalists had filed briefs and delivered testimony explaining their opposition to the enlarged project.

9   Critics rested their opposition on several grounds: that increased flows due to pollution dilution requirements would disturb the river's ecosystems and its recreational uses; that pollution dilution is unnecessary and illegal; and that further consideration should be given to allowing a public group—in particular the federal government—to develop the power project.

10   A statement filed jointly by the Conservation Council of Virginia, the West Virginia Natural Resources Council, and the Izaak Walton League, and a separate brief filed by the Attorney General of West Virginia, pointed out that the increased water flows would virtually eliminate canoeing, wading, and associated fishing activities. The groups presented evidence that the maximum flow that allows wade-in fishing is 3,000 cubic feet per second. The project called for 4,000 cubic feet per second during the months from April through October and 5,000 cubic feet per second during the remaining months.

11   The same groups contended that sustained cold water flows would disturb the ecosystems of the stream by preventing some organisms from completing their life cycles and by reducing the food supply. For evidence they pointed to previous testimony by a federal fish biologist.

12   The case against pollution dilution was outlined most strongly by Edward

Berlin, counsel to the conservation coalition. In his brief he pointed out that the Federal Water Pollution Control Act of 1961 rules against pollution dilution in cases such as the Blue Ridge project. Section 1153 (b)(1) of the act states:

13   "In the survey or planning of any reservoir by the Corps of Engineers, Bureau of Reclamation, or other Federal agency, consideration shall be given to inclusion of storage for the purpose of water quality control, *except that any such storage and water releases shall not be provided as a substitute for adequate treatment or other methods of controlling waste at the source*" (emphasis supplied).

14   This passage is augmented by Section 1155 (d)(C), which instructs the Interior Secretary to study: "Methods and procedures for evaluating the effects on water quality and water uses of augmented streamflows to control water pollution *not susceptible to other means of abatement*" (emphasis supplied).

15   Berlin argued that processes exist now that could adequately clean up the effluent from the factories located along the Kanawha in Charleston. The industries, as their own testimony indicates, have been grossly negligent. With one exception, they admitted that some of their effluent could be treated, and most of them asserted that they will be able to comply with Phase III of West Virginia's cleanup program. Testimony by the Interior Department and others in support of low-flow augmentation did not calculate how much extra water, if any, would be needed after the completion of Phase III.

16   The state of West Virginia and the conservation groups asked that the power company be allowed to proceed with the original, smaller project. The original project would have covered 17,000 acres and displaced less than 500 people; the modified project would cover 40,000 acres and displace 5,000 people. Huge fluctuations of water in the lower reservoir would make it completely unsuitable for recreational uses. The requirements for low-flow augmentation threatened to cause large drawdowns in the upper reservoir as well.

17   Another group, the Appalachian Research and Defense Fund, filed a brief late in the proceedings that asked a question no one else had raised; should the project be built at all? Counsel Paul J. Kaufman assailed the Appalachian Power Company for its poor record of public service and its monopolistic tendencies, and suggested that the project might be better managed by a public agency. He asked for a complete study to determine alternatives to the project. As it is proposed, the project calls for both pumped storage and hydroelectric generation. Water falling from the upper reservoir would turn turbines to generate electricity. The water then would be contained in the lower reservoir, from which some of it would be dispensed downstream toward Charleston and some pumped back into the upper reservoir. The energy to accomplish this would be provided by a steam-powered plant that each year would burn 2 million tons of coal strip-mined from the hills of West Virginia. Kaufman estimated that for every 2 kilowatts of energy produced by the hydroelectric station, 3 kilowatts would be consumed in the pumping process.

18 FPC Examiner Levy issued a second decision on June 21, 1971, to allow the Blue Ridge Project to go forward with only minor changes. From April through October the pollution diluting flow would be restricted to 3,000 cubic feet per second rather than 4,000 as originally planned, pending further study. The total quantity of water contained for low-flow augmentation would be reduced from 650,000 acre-feet to 400,000 acre-feet.

19 To the conservationists' contention that flows of 3,000 cubic feet per second might disturb the ecosystems of the river and hurt canoeing and fishing, the Examiner's decision states that the "controlled river" may be "bigger and different," but that it will be "equally or probably more valuable in the long run." Regarding pollution dilution, the decision begs off from the restrictions of the Federal Water Pollution Control Act: "The purpose of this license proceeding is not to evaluate industry compliance with or governmental enforcement" of the Act. Examiner Levy claims that although presently the situation on the Kanawha in Charleston does not require "all the water-quality storage of which the project is capable and which can be provided without adverse effect downstream. . . . Comprehensive development of the river requires all the storage of which the reach is capable, compatible with optimum public benefits and project economics." He denies the request by the Appalachian Research and Defense Fund for study of the feasibility of public development and alternatives to the project because doing this would only "delay indefinitely construction of a project that is badly needed now in the public interest."

20 FPC rules provide 30 days following announcement of the Examiner's decision for exceptions to be filed. If exceptions are filed, the full commission is obliged to review the case, and at least two attorneys are planning to file exceptions. If the full commission approves the Blue Ridge Project as it now stands, Kaufman is considering bringing the matter to the public courts. Berlin said that he is "absolutely certain" that he will file a lawsuit. The full committee decision is not expected before the end of the year.

21 Examiner Levy wrote that if the Blue Ridge Project is built, "the dead hand of economic uncertainty and paralysis will be removed" from that part of the country. To this statement environmentalist Kaufman scoffed, for reasons understood by those who value natural systems over man-made money: "Hogwash."

This editorial was printed in The Washington Post *on December 18, 1975.*

The New River and the New Secretary

1 The new Secretary of Interior, Thomas S. Kleppe, has been in office for only a few weeks, but already he has an opportunity to begin making a positive record. The issue involves the long struggle to save the New River valley and the people along its banks. The New River, said to be the second oldest watercourse of its kind in the world (only the Nile is older), flows in part in northwest North Carolina, southern Virginia and southern West Virginia. It is an area of unrivaled beauty, but more important, it is an area where the citizens' instincts to preserve their land and culture are strong.

2   They need to be. The New River is under threat from the American Electric Power Company's plans to build a generating plant. According to conservationists, about 42,000 acres of land would be submerged; on this land now are 936 homesites, 10 industrial buildings, 23 commercial buildings, 15 churches, 12 cemeteries and five post offices. Some 4,000 citizens would be displaced.

3   The trade-off is unacceptable. Over the past 10 years, opposition to the power project has slowly grown to the point that the entire North Carolina congressional delegation has made a stand. In Congress itself, only the backwardness of the House Rules Committee—lobbied intensely by the power industry and the AFL-CIO—blocked legislation that would have protected the river. The opportunity now before Secretary Kleppe is to settle the dispute by including the New River in the National Wild and Scenic Rivers System.

4   Conceivably, there might be some merit in damming the New River if the case could be made that the power plant would contribute to easing the energy shortage. But, incredible as it may sound, it is argued by opponents that this project would actually consume more energy than it would produce and thus *would contribute to the energy shortage.* According to the Committee for the New River, "instead of burning three kilowatts of power (while pumping water upstream) to produce two for consumer use, as other projects do, it would burn four while producing three for consumers. That still leaves it, of course, a net user of power." There is an explanation for this, which has to do with the nature of pumped-storage projects—water must be pumped from a lower reservoir to a higher one to create a reserve of power for peak periods. But better ways exist to deal with this problem—ways which wouldn't involve despoiling a river and displacing people. One possibility being suggested is a steam plant, an operation that would meet energy needs while being socially and environmentally acceptable.

5   Such a possibility, joined with the havoc that this project would create, has bewildered many in light of the license the Federal Power Commission granted. The FPC decision is being challenged in the courts by the state of North Carolina, but a favorable ruling by the Interior Department would take precedence and block the project. With so large a coalition of citizens, conservationists and politicians lined up to save the river, Secretary Kleppe will not need immense amounts of political courage to act. Instead, he needs only a measure of normal bureaucratic resolve and common sense, qualities that he could reasonably be expected to have brought along when he took the job.

Donald Cook (b. 1909), president of the American Electric Power Company, Inc., since 1961, has published numerous articles on legal, financial, and accounting subjects. He wrote this letter to the editor of The Washington Post *in response to the* Post's *editorial of December 18, 1975, on the New River project.*

The New River Project
Donald C. Cook

1   In your December 18 editorial entitled "The New River and the New Secretary" opposing the Blue Ridge Project, the following statement appears: "Conceivably, there might be some merit in damming the New River if the case could be made that the power plant would contribute to easing the energy shortage. But, incredible as it may sound, it is argued by opponents that this project would actually consume more energy than it would produce and thus would contribute to the energy shortage."

2   Indeed it would be incredible if American Electric Power, the nation's most efficient electric utility system, proposed the construction of an energy project which actually contributed to the energy shortage! Indeed it would be even more incredible if the Federal Power Commission, the expert federal agency in the field, by unanimous (5–0) vote and on the basis of an exhaustive evidentiary record, granted a license for the construction of such a project. These obvious considerations should have alerted you to pause, reflect and perhaps even ask a few questions before giving such prominence to the partisan statements of a group of elitists who are intent upon preserving their "view of the mountain," regardless of the consequences to the nation.

3   The fact is that during its 50-year license period, Blue Ridge will produce more than 85 billion kilowatt hours of electric energy without the consumption of any oil or natural gas—our nation's scarcest fuels. The fact is that 16 billion of these kilowatt hours will be produced by natural stream flow without the consumption of any fuel at all. The remainder will be produced by coal—our nation's most abundant fuel. To produce the pumping energy, this coal will be burned off peak in the most efficient power plants of our nation's most efficient system—plants which otherwise would be sitting idle. Basically, the only cost is the cost of coal. Furthermore, an FPC study has demonstrated that the AEP System with Blue Ridge would burn less coal than would the AEP System with a coal-fired alternative to Blue Ridge. Thus, Blue Ridge is highly efficient not only in terms of energy production, but also in terms of the conservation of our nation's finite fuel resources—a much more meaningful criterion of efficiency than the kilowatt hours consumed in pumping.

This two-page advertisement paid for by the American Electric Power Company, Inc., appeared in national newsmagazines and newspapers in early 1976.

The Truth About the Blue Ridge Project
—in contrast to the abridged and biased version editorialized by a responsible press

1   The welfare of this entire nation is endangered by an energy shortage. The White House has ordered the development of all our energy resources—and Departments of Government are trying to do just that, in keeping with environmental standards. No selfish group which stands in the way can remain unchallenged—be they privileged elitists or a prejudiced press.

2   To help break away from the tyranny of a band of sheiks, Washington has called for the development of additional sites for the production of hydroelectric power, i.e., the generation of electricity by water power.

3   There are very, very few remaining in America.

4   There is one excellent, undeveloped site on a segment of the New River—a river that runs through West Virginia, Virginia and North Carolina—where we propose to develop the Blue Ridge Project.

5   This segment is not without some attractiveness. However, it is paralleled by 118 miles of highway, crossed by 47 bridges, contains two dams and nests two large industrial plants.

6   While the river is clear and unpolluted, it is not particularly biologically productive. Little recreational use is made of it, though it is easily accessible.

7   These are some of the reasons why the U.S. Department of the Interior could not propose the New River as "wild and scenic" when, in the mid 1960's it searched the country over for any which could possibly qualify under the law—in fact, stretched its list to accommodate 650 such rivers.

8   The New in North Carolina was not one.

9   Essentially, all that would be needed to have the New River contribute to America's critically needed energy supply would be two large dams. Behind them would be created two beautiful lakes in a lovely mountainous setting.

10   Surrounding them would be new State parks, and other recreational facilities, far surpassing in aesthetics and value the present, limited accommodations.

11   As far back as 1962 . . .13 long years ago . . . Appalachian Power Company, part of the AEP System, began investigating the possibilities of a hydro and pumped storage project, and applied for a license in 1965.

12   Then the Federal Power Commission—a body of experts expressly created by the U.S. Congress to investigate and decide such matters—went to work.

13   Its hearings were open to everyone from anywhere.

14   Though this was really a Virginia project, with all of the structures located there and only ⅓ of the lakes in North Carolina, absolutely no one with any interest . . . from the slight to the profound . . . was prevented from intervening in the proceeding.

15   Pro and con, they came in droves.

16   In over nine years of work the FPC expended 40,000 man hours and amassed 7,500 pages of sworn testimony—all subject to cross-examination.

17   Again and again it reopened the proceedings to hear from environmentalists and conservationists, the Department of Defense, U.S. Senators, the Izaak Walton League, the Interior Department, groups of private citizens, the Environmental Protection Agency, three State Governments, Highway Departments, private industry, two Farm Bureaus, county executives, and ecologists.

18   The Project was designed, revised and modified to assure a minimum of adverse impact and a maximum of benefit to the air, the water, and the people.

19   Every conceivable alternative . . . including no hydroelectric plant at all . . . was studied to exhaustion. None better was found to exist.

20   Three different times the Presiding Administrative Law Judge, with no personal attachment of any kind, recommended licensing. Only to have the FPC reopen the case again—particularly for environmental matters. Only to have it conclude that the adverse effects would be "more than balanced by the environmental benefits created."

21   Finally, the Commission found . . . unanimously . . . that the proposed 1,800,000 kilowatt Blue Ridge Project, estimated in 1973 to cost $430 million, is badly needed to help satisfy the power demands of the 1980's.

22   Blue Ridge:

- will conserve our national resources by consuming no oil and gas.
- will provide emergency reserve power for the East Central region of the United States.
- will provide 160,000 acre-feet of flood control capacity—endorsed by the U.S. Corps of Engineers—where none exists today.
- will assure water benefits downstream where, to improve recreation and fishing, the river flow is periodically in need of augmentation.
- will vastly increase the recreational potential of the area, turning it into one of the most appealing sites in the East.
- will facilitate the economic development of depressed Appalachia.
- will consume less fuel than any available alternative means of generation.

23   No project with these monumental benefits to so many is ever without some degree of impact on some individual families. Evidence those displaced by Federal highways, bridges, tunnels and military installations.

24   So, to minimize or eliminate any hardship to the 586 families affected by the Project, we willingly offered to do the following:

- pay fully for their present holdings.
- pay for a relocation advisory service.

- pay for their new dwellings.
- pay all increased interest rates.
- pay closing costs.
- pay for their moving.
- pay for any loss in personal property.

25 And we will periodically report the success of our efforts to the FPC.

26 And so, a license was granted—effective January 2, 1975.

27 The sum of the benefits to the American people was so demonstrably great that the Blue Ridge Project won the support of the States of Virginia and West Virginia, the Federal Power Commission, the Federal Energy Administration and for six long years ('67 to '73)—until a mysterious reversal—the State of North Carolina.

28 Many North Carolinians fully favor the project.

29 But, it is not welcomed by an affluent few. They shudder at the thought of intrusion by outsiders.

30 They have decided to resist the needs of this nation . . . to ignore the President's call . . . and to save the privileged status quo by killing the Blue Ridge Project.

31 Twice they tried in the U.S. Congress. Once with a rider on the Rivers and Harbors Bill.

32 They failed.

33 Once they actually tried to have this tame, this bridged and dammed river-along-the-highway made a component of the untouchable National Wild and Scenic Rivers System . . . a flagrant perversion of an Act of Congress. They failed.

34 Ironically, not one word of criticism of these actions appeared in the press.

35 And now . . . THE STING!

36 Although the people of North Carolina will benefit substantially from a strengthened power supply, our gift of 3,900 acres hand-picked by North Carolina for a lakefront State park, recreational facilities valued in the millions, and participation in a construction payroll of over $125,000,000 . . . the influential elitists are about to euchre them out of it with a tricky scheme.

37 Incredibly, North Carolina officials would circumvent the U.S. Congress by having a *limited stretch* of the New River incorporated into the National Wild and Scenic Rivers System . . . by administrative decree.

38 *Just enough of a stretch to block Blue Ridge!*

39 One editorialist took the bait.

40 He published the elitist pap that the Blue Ridge Project would contribute to the energy shortage(!) and asked Interior Secretary Thomas S. Kleppe to participate by using "bureaucratic resolve" in naming this river wild and scenic.

41 One might have expected pause, reflection and even the asking of a few penetrating questions about benefits to the people . . . and to the nation.

42 And now it looks as though The New York Times has been taken in, too.

43 Its editorial, orchestrated on the same theme, is a classic example of what every cub should avoid:

1. It breathes nary a word about energy shortage or President's mandate, but derides a needed hydroelectric project.
2. It writes no syllable about the 13 years of study or the 7,500 pages of sworn testimony, but hands down its own ill-founded judgement.
3. It calls the Blue Ridge lakes "ugly reservoirs," but avoids the experts' words that they'd be areas of great beauty.
4. It speaks of environmental "enormity," but not of the Commission's conclusion that the detriments are more than balanced by all the environmental benefits.
5. It cites "severe economic problems," but not the great economic gains due to parks and recreational—residential—commercial complexes where there is now only a depressed area.
6. It talks of "drown"ing the land, but not of scenic lakes, boating, or fishing.
7. It points to "displacing close to 3,000 people," but not that they'll be fully cared for and repaid.
8. It chortles over the North Carolina Assembly vote to put the New in the scenic rivers system, but never once asks, "who could have influenced such a vote when many people in the project area have stated they emphatically oppose any such designation . . . and especially since the net effects of Blue Ridge on North Carolina will be beneficial?"
9. It writes of "costly surplus energy" rather than of needed power more economically generated than by any other available method.
10. It talks of "alternative sources," but not that those alternative sources were studied to exhaustion and found unacceptable.
11. It cries out that the river will be "sacrificed," but not that the Commission stated the river will not be eliminated; 150 of its 220 miles will remain in its free-flowing state.
12. Finally, it succumbs to asking Secretary Kleppe to take part in the scheme by incorporating the New River into the Federal system, without mentioning that it is not—as it must be—primitive and inaccessible. Nor that it will be far more recreational, and more scenic for more people under the Blue Ridge Project.

44 We find this unbalanced journalistic presentation outrageous.
45 We find this biased attempt to influence a newly appointed Secretary distasteful.
46 The whole truth—in case some have forgotten—is fit to print.

American Electric Power Company, Inc.
2 Broadway, N.Y., N.Y. 10004

George Will (b. 1941) writes columns which appear regularly in the Washington Post *and* Newsweek. *This column was published in the* Post *on January 9, 1976.*

"Progress" Threatens Again
George F. Will

1   The New River Valley in North Carolina and Virginia resembles Washington Irving's "Sleepy Hollow": ". . . it is in such little retired . . . valleys . . . that population, manners, and customs, remain fixed; while the great torrent of migration and improvement, which is making such incessant change in other parts of this restless country, sweeps by them unobserved. They are little nooks of still water which border a rapid stream. . . ."

2   The New River Valley was settled centuries ago by ancestors of today's residents. It is a triumph of happy fixity in a restless nation. Valley residents are proud that "the names on the mailboxes match the names on the gravestones." Today it is threatened with destruction, drowning in the name of—what else?—"improvement," specifically, more electricity for people who live elsewhere.

3   Irreversible destruction of a river and a way of life will occur unless Interior Secretary Thomas Kleppe agrees to include the New River in the National Wild and Scenic Rivers System. Appalachian Power, a subsidiary of American Electric Power Company, the nation's largest private utility, wants to build a $430 million two-reservoir pumped storage generating plant in the Blue Ridge Mountains on the North Carolina border.

4   AEP's chairman Donald Cook says people oppose the project "because among other things, a species of snail might be endangered. . . . should we choose a snail over needed electric power which can contribute so much to the quality of human life?" This tendentious statement cannot obscure the real issues.

5   Cook's project would inundate about 40,000 acres and evict 3,000 people. It would flood residences, farms, churches, graveyards, and would ruin 70 miles of a river that is not only among the most beautiful in the world, but is, with the Nile, among the oldest. The New River is perhaps 100 million years old and contains at least 11 species of aquatic life found nowhere else.

6   The area that would be flooded has been occupied since about 8,000 B.C. and is among the nation's most significant archaeological sites. In one two-week survey a scholar found 1,459 pieces of pottery and 415 arrowheads and other items. Federal law requires that the Federal Power Commission, when licensing plant construction, show adequate concern for such aspects of our cultural heritage. The FPC did not do so.

7   The AEP plant would pump water into an upper reservoir and release it

into a lower reservoir, thereby generating 1,600 megawatts, but only for hours of peak demand, and would use four units of energy to produce three. So the plant would be a net energy consumer. And critics charge, plausibly, that AEP has not adequately considered measures—such as high prices at peak hours—that would dampen peak demand.

8   Today AEP has ample off-peak hour capacity: It sells 10 per cent of its power as excess to other utilities. AEP says it would cost $3.2 million more per year to produce the new "needed" megawatts in a coal-burning plant elsewhere. (AEP serves seven states but not North Carolina.) But $13.5 million of New River Valley agricultural products would be lost each year because of the flooding.

9   The Federal Power Commission says the plant's reservoirs would make dandy recreation areas. Yes, and Paris could demolish the Louvre to build a bowling alley. The "unimproved" New River offers splendid recreation, including white water canoeing. But the drawdown of water from the reservoirs for generating purposes would produce broad mudflats and bogs.

10   Cook says opposition to this project comes from a small number of people concerned only about their view of the mountains. That is typical of his respect for truth. Last year both houses of the North Carolina General Assembly voted—unanimously—in favor of rescuing the river from AEP by getting it included in the wild rivers system.

11   At his confirmation hearing Secretary Kleppe said: "We must keep in mind that the economic penalty for an error in the direction of over-protections can always be corrected, while the damage from resources abuse may be irreparable." The abuse of the New River would be irreparable, and there is no demonstrable "economic penalty" involved in protecting the river. This proposal, like the proposal's advocate, Cook, is an example of our economic system at its most predatory and least defensible.

Austin Scott (b. 1939) is a national correspondent for The Washington Post. *This article appeared in the* Post *on January 19, 1976.*

Power Struggle on Ancient River
Austin Scott

1   Mouth of Wilson, Va.—On the surface it seems to be just one more admittedly bitter but not all that uncommon dispute between a big company that wants to expand and rural landowners who don't want their lives and their land disrupted.

2   But here on the Virginia-North Carolina border, in rolling Appalachian hills that ripple along a bedrock shelf 3,000 feet above sea level, there is quite a bit more to it than that.

3   The nation's largest public utility holding company, American Electric Power, has been frustrated for 10 years in its attempt to dam an unusual river in order to build what would be the country's largest twin-dam, pumped storage electric generating system.

4   AEP, which serves the central Northeast from Illinois to Virginia as far south as Tennessee and is second in size only to the government-owned Tennessee Valley Authority in terms of generating capacity, has been struggling with some serious financial problems during the past few years.

5   Chairman Donald C. Cook said in June that his company, once one of the industry's healthiest, was forced to slash its proposed $1 billion 1975 construction budget in half and eliminate or postpone three large generating plants because "for the first time we clearly overestimated the demand of the economy in our area."

6   Nevertheless, Cook wants to build the Blue Ridge twin-dam project on the New River here. Although AEP now has such a surplus of generating capacity that it can sell up to 1.6 million kilowatt hours daily to other utilities, Cook says he is convinced that electricity is going to be in such short supply in the years ahead that major industrial shutdowns will begin in 1978 and will be widespread by 1980.

7   The project has stirred substantial opposition, in part because of the beauty of the New River and its largely unexplored but promising archeological sites, in part because AEP does not serve North Carolina where substantial portions of two counties would be flooded by the dams, and in part because the project would not contribute to the company's total sustained generating capacity.

8   A pumped storage project acts a bit like an enormous storage battery, helping to meet sharp fluctuations in demand, storing up energy pumped into it during the low-demand hours at night and on weekends for release during late afternoon peak load hours.

9   The company's biggest roadblock may prove to be the state of North Carolina, which has asked Interior Secretary Thomas S. Kleppe to declare 26.5 miles of the New River and its south fork part of the protected National Wild and Scenic Rivers System.

10   If Kleppe says yes, AEP could not build the project as now conceived.

11   Contrary to its name, the New River, estimated to be 100 million years old, may be the oldest river in North America, and perhaps one of the two oldest in the world, according to geological studies.

12   It is a perverse river, not just in its name, but also in the way it behaves. Unlike nearly every other northeastern river, it flows from south to north. Unlike every other Appalachian river, it crosses the mountains from east to west.

13   And unlike almost every other river in the country, it does not flow along the mountain ridges, but across them, leading geologists to theorize that it must have been there before the mountains, so it had time to keep cutting its own channel as the mountains rose slowly around it.

14   The dams AEP wants to build would create two lakes totaling 44 miles in length, displacing up to 3,000 people and flooding some of the richest food-producing bottomlands in the Blue Ridge Mountains.

15   Many of the people who would have to leave say they do not merely own their land. They say they are a part of it, and it is a part of them, in a way that is true in few sections of the country.

16   In the three affected counties—Grayson in Virginia, Ashe and Alleghany in North Carolina—some people trace their families living on the same land back nearly 100 years before the Civil War, and sometimes back to land grants obtained from King George III of England.

17   There is Gerald Crouse, who farms the land where four previous generations of his family were born and raised and now lie buried. His property would be partially flooded by the dams.

18   There is Elizabeth Jordan Cox, sharp and spry at 87, who lives alone in a home built by her husband's grandfather's father-in-law. The home contains so many family heirlooms that she often points to pieces of furniture and says:

19   "Oh, that's not old, it's only 75 years old . . . Now that's very old, that's over 100 years old." Among the relics on her 400 acres that would be flooded are the family blacksmith shop, with its bellows and equipment, and the old mill that was used to grind flour by families throughout the area from the late 1800s until the 1960s.

20   There is G. Cam Fields, 79, whose family owns the woolen mill, the private power company and the Ford auto agency that are the business community of tiny Mouth of Wilson (population: 500)—so named because it grew up from the crossroads at the mouth of Wilson Creek.

21   Fields says the dams would put the Mouth of Wilson post office under 160 feet of water.

22   "It's home," he said. "I don't know if you know what I mean by that . . . Always spend your old days where you spent your young days. If you've sunk down roots that's the way you feel."

23   While some 40,000 acres would be flooded, those opposed to the project estimate 60,000 acres would be affected because of the nature of farming in this area.

24   "You've got to grow feed for wintertime for cattle, and you try to grow it on level bottomland where it won't wash," said one farmer. "Then in the summertime you graze the cattle on these hills. If all you have left is the hills, because the bottomland is flooded, then you can't do anything."

25   Lorne Campbell, an attorney in nearby Independence, Va., is second vice president of the "Committee for the New River," an organization formed a year ago to fight the power company.

26   Now 67, Campbell claims to have fished every inch of the river in his younger days, and a drive with him along the dirt roads that twist and turn through forests near the riverbanks is an oral history lesson in local folklore.

27   He is deep into a story about two local brothers who had a falling out in their teens, and refused to speak to each other for the rest of their lives, but continued to cooperate, and would send their wives over to say, "John wants to know if you can help him plow today." But he interrupts the story to point to the walls of an ancient brick house.

28   "That old house was built about 1796, it belonged to old Black John Parsons," Campbell says. "He had 30-some children by two women, and the families associated with each other."

29   The Interior Department's draft environmental impact statement on North Carolina's request to have its part of the New declared a scenic river says projectile points dating back "several thousand years" have been recovered in the New River valley, indicating that it "was a major migration route and represents successive levels of Indian development from Paleo-Indian times to the arrival of the white man in the 15th and 16th centuries."

30   Dr. C. G. Holland of the Smithsonian Institution, who conducted two of four preliminary archeological surveys, says he thinks the New River valley may be one of the most important archeological sites in the eastern United States.

31   Dr. William Gardner, chairman of Catholic University's anthropology department, says, "At a minimum, the valley has been occupied since 8000 B.C., according to artifacts there."

32   North Carolina, its legislature, congressional delegation and governor are unanimously opposed to the Blue Ridge Project. The state lists 16 rare and endangered species of wildlife in the river area.

33   North Carolina has filed suit in U.S. District Court charging that the Federal Power Commission acted improperly when it granted AEP a 50-year license to build the project in June, 1974.

34   Among the state's arguments are insufficient consideration of the archeological and environmental impact and insufficient recognition of the state's desire to make the New River a federally protected scenic river.

35   AEP counters that the FPC acted unanimously after nine years of consideration, 40,000 hours of work, and 7,500 pages of sworn testimony at public hearings.

36   "The project was designed, revised and modified to assure a minimum of adverse impact and a maximum of benefit to the air, the water, and the people," the company said in a two-page New York Times advertisement Jan. 9.

37   AEP's ad called the North Carolinians who oppose the project "an affluent few." It added that "the influential elitists" are using "a tricky scheme" to try to "euchre" the people of North Carolina out of ". . . our gift of 3,900 acres . . . for a lake-front state park."

38   Opponents, the company said, never consider the energy-saving potential of a hydroelectric plant, the flood control benefits of the dams, or the need for an emergency power reserve.

39   AEP concedes that its Blue Ridge Project, estimated in 1973 to cost $430 million, is the cheapest way for it to get the kind of electrical buffer it needs for its expanding power network.

40   The FPC found during its investigation that the next best alternative would be another large, coal-fired power plant. But Joe Dowd, general counsel for AEP, admits that the two are not directly comparable.

41   A new coal-fired plant would be what is called a baseline plant, adding another million kilowatt hours of permanent, 24-hour-a-day generating capacity into AEP's power network.

42   The Blue Ridge Project would not do that. While it would be able to supply extra electrical energy to AEP for weeks if necessary, it would be a net consumer of electricity in the long run.

43   At night and on weekends, when electrical demands are normally low, AEP plans to feed power from its huge nuclear and coal-fired plants in Illinois and Ohio and Virginia to giant pumps that would lift water from the lake formed by the lower Blue Ridge dam into the lake formed by the upper one.

44   For AEP, that would have the added benefit of letting its biggest generators run 24 hours a day at their most efficient power output, which is close to maximum.

45   During the day, or in case of an emergency, water would be released from the upper dam to turn big hydroelectric generators for extra daytime power.

46   Used in that way, however, the Blue Ridge Project would consume overall four units of electricity for every three it produced, AEP said. And its capacity to generate would be only the length of time it took the water in the upper dam to drop too low to be useful.

47   Also, AEP counsel Dowd admits the shoreline of both lakes would fluctuate daily as AEP pumped water back and forth.

48   Opponents of the dam raise the spectre of vacationers arriving to be greeted by huge expanses of mud flats created by the fluctuating water level.

49   Although AEP estimates it has spent $17 million on the Blue Ridge Project over 10 years, including the purchase of substantial quantities of land that critics charged disrupted the local economy as it came out of production, the company has not started to build.

50   Its license was temporarily stayed while the North Carolina suit is considered. A ruling on the case is expected soon.

51   If the three-judge panel in Washington sends the matter back to the FPC for more study, that would delay the project several years but would not necessarily kill it.

52   The man with the power to kill it is Kleppe, who is expected to make his decision shortly after Feb. 21, when a 90-day comment period on North Carolina's scenic river proposal runs out.

53   AEP charges that the North Carolina proposal was "designed and tailored just to block the Blue Ridge project," a point some proposal supporters do not deny. They argue, however, that regardless of its timing, the proposal has more than enough merit to warrant approval by Kleppe.

54   AEP claims Congress considered a similar proposal in 1974 and turned it down. Actually, the 1974 bill died when House Rules Committee Chairman

Ray Madden (D-Ind.) held it hostage, refusing to schedule a vote on it because his committee would not approve a bill expanding the Indiana Dunes National Lakeshore.

55 The bill was then brought up on the House floor where it won a majority vote, 196 to 181, but not the two-thirds vote needed to pass a bill killed by the Rules Committee.

56 AEP has also argued that a number of bridges and roads, two small eight-foot dams built years ago for local milling and power operations, and two small industries not on the parts of the river that might be declared scenic, all make the river ineligible for such a designation.

57 The Interior Department has decided otherwise, ruling the river eligible. Interior has also decided the FPC did not make a sufficiently comprehensive environmental impact study.

58 "Our conclusion was that the FPC really hadn't given consideration to the no-build alternative," said a spokesman, adding he cannot predict what Kleppe will decide.

The following is a fact sheet which accompanied a news release on the New River project from the Interior Department on March 13, 1976.

Department of the Interior News Release Fact Sheet
Office of the Secretary of the Interior

1 The New River originates in North Carolina; it flows north through Virginia, and into West Virginia where it merges with the Gauley and Kanawha Rivers at the terminus of the spectacular New River Gorge. The 26.5-mile segment for which North Carolina seeks protection includes 4.5 miles of the main stem and 22 miles of the South Fork; the area extends southward from the North Carolina/Virginia border.

2 In February 1965 the Appalachian Power Company (AEP) filed a license application with FPC for a pumped storage hydroelectric project (Blue Ridge project) on the New River. Two dams would be built in Virginia. Water would be backed up along the River creating a reservoir that would extend into North Carolina and inundate the area for which the State now seeks Federal protection.

3 In June 1966 the Interior Department intervened, requesting modification of the project to provide for recreation development and public access, flow regulation for water quality control, flood control features, and fish and wildlife resource development. The project, as subsequently designed, satisfied most of Interior's requirements at that time. The project would generate 1.8 million kilowatts of power.

4 The New River had not been included in an initial list of 650 rivers considered as potential wild rivers during studies in the mid 1960's leading to the development of wild and scenic rivers legislation. The first such recognition of the North Carolina portion of the River came in 1974 when the Administration proposed to add new study rivers to the Wild and Scenic Rivers Act and include the entire New River, exclusive of reservoirs and the potential Blue Ridge project if licensed by the FPC. In House hearings on June 3, 1974, however, the Department supported a study of the River segment, contending that the Federal Power Commission's Environmental Impact Statement on the proposed Blue Ridge project license did not adequately consider the free-flowing character of the river. On June 14, 1974, eleven days after the hearings, FPC issued its license to the Appalachian Power Company authorizing construction of the Blue Ridge project, effective January 2, 1975, if Congress failed in the meantime to enact legislation protecting the River through the National Wild and Scenic Rivers System. A bill to study the River's eligibility for such designation passed the Senate but never reached a House vote.

5   North Carolina has challenged the validity of the FPC license on environmental grounds, and the U.S. Circuit Court of Appeals has enjoined construction of the Blue Ridge project pending its decision on the adequacy of the FPC Environmental Impact Statement.

6   On October 23, 1975, the court heard North Carolina's plea to void the license. If the court upholds the State, no dam can be built; if it upholds the FPC and the power company, the Wild and Scenic Rivers designation would not block a dam unless that decision was appealed to a higher court and subsequently overturned.

7   Meanwhile, on December 12, 1974, Governor Holshouser applied to have a 4.5-mile segment of the New River designated a State-administered component of the National rivers system. On June 11, 1975, that application was amended to add 22 additional miles on the South Fork making the total 26.5 miles, enough to meet minimum length requirements. Several technical questions were raised by Interior regarding the State's application. These were satisfactorily answered and the application and draft Environmental Impact Statement were circulated on November 28, 1975, for a 90-day review which ended February 28, 1976.

8   The Bureau of Outdoor Recreation subsequently prepared the final Environmental Impact Statement taking into consideration the views of Federal and State agencies, private organizations and individuals. The final EIS has been submitted to the Council on Environmental Quality for a 30-day review as required by law.

9   The North Carolina General Assembly has met the requirements of the Wild and Scenic Rivers Act by passing legislation designating the river segment as a component of the State Natural and Scenic Rivers System.

10   The Secretary of the Interior cannot formally take the implementing action on the River until that 30-day review has been completed, under CEQ guidelines.

11   The issue is essentially that of electrical power versus the environment.

12   *River advocates,* those opposing the power project, contend that the

River merits Federal protection under the Wild and Scenic Rivers Act because it is perhaps the oldest waterway in geological terms in the United States; because of potentially valuable archaeological sites that would be inundated by a power project reservoir; because upwards of 3,000 farmers and other landowners in North Carolina and Virginia (1,175 in North Carolina and 1,825 in Virginia) would be displaced by the reservoir (they would be financially compensated by the power company); because the power project would cause at least nominal air pollution; because valuable free-flowing river recreation opportunities, including fishing, canoeing, and floating would be preserved; and because 42,000 acres of land in North Carolina (14,200 acres) and Virginia (27,900 acres) would be flooded were the power project to be built as presently designed. Sixty-two percent (8,800 acres) of the land in North Carolina is actual or potential agricultural land. Public sentiment, as expressed through responses to appeals by the press and comments on the State application and EIS, has been heavy on both sides, with a majority favoring the State's application.

13   Interior's Bureau of Outdoor Recreation has found that the North Carolina segment meets the scenic river criteria of the Wild and Scenic Rivers Act.

14   *Power advocates,* those favoring construction of the Blue Ridge project, contend that the Nation's needs for electrical power override environmental objections. They point out that the project would generate 1.8 million kilowatts of peaking power through a highly efficient system. The project would use more power than it would generate, but the power it burns in refilling its reservoirs at night is essentially waste power of little dollar value, produced by generators which must run continuously. The peaking power produced by the hydro project during the day, on the other hand, is highly important and valuable energy, the lack of which could lead to brownouts and power disruptions. Power advocates point to the flat water recreation opportunities that would be created, including power boating, sailing, canoeing, water skiing, and picnicking. Second home development could occur around the reservoirs and the Appalachian Power Company would give 3,900 acres of land to North Carolina for a lakefront State park.

QUESTIONS

Now that you have read all eight pieces, consider these questions:

1. Where were your sympathies before you read this material?

2. Where do you stand now? Why?

3. Which arguments were most convincing? Why?

4. Which arguments were best written?

Acknowledgments (continued)

P. 120–23 Four letters to the editor by Leon A. Doughty, Howard G. Simkins, Neil and Eileen Katz, and Senator Mike Gravel, in the *Washington Post*, February 18, 1974 and January 1, 1975. © 1974, 1975, *The Washington Post*. Used by permission. Also used by permission of the authors.

P. 122 From "Senator Gravel Wins One," in the *Washington Post*, December 30, 1974. © 1974, *The Washington Post*. Used by permission.

P. 129 From "One Small Step for Genkind" by C. Miller & K. Swift, in *The New York Times Magazine*, April 16, 1972. © 1972, C. Miller & K. Swift. Used by permission.

P. 170 From *Readers' Guide to Periodical Literature* Copyright © 1975 by The H. W. Wilson Company. Material reproduced by permission of the publisher.

P. 171 © 1975 by The New York Times Company. Reprinted by permission.

P. 187 Reprinted by permission from TIME, The Weekly Newsmagazine; Copyright Time Inc.

P. 189 Copyright © 1944, 1945 by the American Historical Association. Reprinted by permission of Beacon Press.

P. 190 From *The First Five Years of Life* by Arnold Gesell, et al. © 1940, Harper & Row Publishers Inc. Used by permission.

P. 191 Reprinted from *Anthropology and Modern Life* by Franz Boas. By permission of W. W. Norton & Company, Inc. Copyright 1928 by W. W. Norton & Company, Inc. Copyright renewed 1956 by Norman Boas. Copyright 1932 by W. W. Norton & Company, Inc. Copyright renewed 1960 by Helen Boas Yampolsky. Copyright © 1962 by W. W. Norton & Company, Inc.

P. 193 From *The Cycle of American Literature* by Robert E. Spiller. Copyright © 1955, 1956 by Macmillan Publishing Co., Inc.

P. 203 From *Only Yesterday* by Frederick Lewis Allen. © 1931 (Perennial Library edition 1964), Harper & Row Publishers Inc. Used by permission.

P. 203 From *American Humor* by Constance Rourke. Used by permission of Harcourt Brace Jovanovich, Inc.

P. 239 "Obsessed with Sport," © by Joseph Epstein 1976.

P. 248 "Television Advertising: The Splitting Image" by Marya Mannes, in *Saturday Review*, November 14, 1970. © 1970, Saturday Review/World Inc. Used by permission.

P. 254 "Ad-Man, Business-Man, Teacher-Man" by Bruce Reeves, in *English Journal*, May 1972. Copyright © 1972 by National Council of Teachers of English. Reprinted by permission of the publisher and the author.

P. 260 "Textbooks as Brainwashers" by Russell Kirk, in *National Review*, October 24, 1975. © 1975 National Review, Inc. Used by permission.

P. 263 "Joey: A 'Mechanical' Boy" by Bruno Bettelheim, in *Scientific American*, March 1959. Reprinted with permission. Copyright © March, 1959 by Scientific American, Inc. All rights reserved.

P. 272 "I'd Rather Be Black Than Female" by Shirley Chisholm. © 1970, McCall's. Used by permission of the author.

P. 275   "The Feminine Mistake" by Helen Lawrenson. Reprinted by permission of *Esquire* Magazine. © 1970 by Esquire Inc.

P. 282   "Confessions of a Female Chauvinist Sow" by Anne Roiphe. Copyright © 1972 by the NYM Corp. Reprinted with the permission of NEW YORK Magazine.

P. 287   "What It Would Be Like if Women Win." Copyright © 1970 by Gloria Steinem. Reprinted by permission of The Sterling Lord Agency, Inc.

P. 292   "How Easy to See the Future" by Isaac Asimov. Reprinted with permission, from *Natural History* Magazine, April, 1975. Copyright © The American Museum of Natural History, 1975.

P. 296   "Science Has Spoiled My Supper" by Philip Wylie. Reprinted by permission of Harold Ober Associates Incorporated. Copyright © 1954 by The Atlantic Monthly Company, Boston, Mass. Reprinted by permission.

P. 302   "I Have a Dream" by Martin Luther King, Jr. Reprinted by permission of Joan Daves. Copyright © 1963 by Martin Luther King, Jr.

P. 306   From *A Church, a School,* by Ralph McGill, Copyright © 1958, by Atlanta Newspapers, Inc. Used by permission of Abingdon Press.

P. 308   "The Tarnished Age" by TRB. Reprinted by permission of *The New Republic,* © 1974, The New Republic, Inc.

P. 311   "We Need a New Kind of Patriotism" by Ralph Nader, in *Life,* July 9, 1971. © 1971, Time-Life, Inc. Used by permission.

P. 314   From *This Is Eric Sevareid.* Copyright 1964 by Eric Sevareid. Reprinted by permission of The Harold Matson Company Inc.

P. 317   "Why Not a Commentary on Sevareid?" by Lewis S. Feuer, in *National Review,* August 15, 1975. © 1975, National Review, Inc. Used by permission.

P. 322   "What It's Like to Broadcast News" by Walter Cronkite, in *Saturday Review,* December 12, 1970. © 1970, Saturday Review/World, Inc. Used by permission.

P. 330   "It *Is* Your Business, Mr. Cronkite" by Irving E. Fang, in *Saturday Review,* January 9, 1971. © 1971, Saturday Review/World, Inc. Used by permission.

P. 333   "How *Time* Stereotyped Three U.S. Presidents" by John C. Merrill, in *Journalism Quarterly,* Autumn 1965. © 1965, Journalism Quarterly. Used by permission.

P. 343   "Are You Making Yourself Clear" by Norman Cousins, in *Saturday Review,* February 27, 1969. © 1969, Saturday Review/World, Inc. Used by permission.

P. 349   "The Language of Bureaucracy" in *The Language of America* by Henry A. Barnes. © 1969, Mrs. Henry A. Barnes. Published through the express permission to appear in *Thinking for Writing* by Mrs. Hazel Barnes. Reprint permission only allowed by express permission of Mrs. Hazel Barnes.

P. 356   "Incident at Kennebunk," from *The American Condition,* copyright © 1974 by Richard N. Goodwin. Reprinted by permission of Doubleday & Company, Inc.

P. 358   "War as a Biological Phenomenon" in *On Living in a Revolution* by Julian Huxley. Copyright, 1944 by Julian S. Huxley. By permission of Harper & Row, Publishers, Inc.

P. 366   "New River Country: Wild and Scenic" by Elizabeth Watson. Reprinted by permission from *National Parks & Conservation Magazine,* February 1975. Copyright © 1975 by National Parks and Conservation Association.

Index